INSPECTED, RATED, & APPROVED

Bed & Breakfasts ♛ Country Inns

INSPECTED, RATED, & APPROVED

Bed & Breakfasts ♛ Country Inns

Third Edition

Publisher: Sarah W. Sonke
Chief Editor: Beth Stuhlman
Cover Design: Beth Stuhlman

The American Bed & Breakfast Association
Richmond, Virginia, USA

ISBN: 0-934473-25-0

Manufactured in the United States of America
Third edition/First printing

Cover photograph is of Chalet Suzanne Country Inn and Restaurant in Lake Wales, Florida.

CONTENTS

Introduction

What's so special about bed and breakfast accommodations? Ask any B&B traveler and he or she is sure to fire back with a story drawn from personal experience.

If you ask Sue Trefry and Lori Limacher, you'll hear about their B&B trip to Montreal one summer. Soon after settling into a comfortable guest room, they were invited to come downstairs to meet an unexpected visitor, former Canadian Prime Minister Pierre Trudeau, a personal friend of their host.

Eileen Rodan, an experienced B&B hostess from New Jersey, has many happy B&B experiences to share. Imagine her surprise on Christmas Eve one year when a former guest at her B&B returned from Canada with a diamond ring and a proposal of marriage for her daughter. The wedding reception was held (where else?) but in Mrs. Rodan's B&B home overlooking the yacht harbor.

While every B&B stay might not be as dramatic as these, one thing is certain - the hospitality and unique surroundings of each B&B provide a truly memorable experience for the traveler. And because of the people-to-people contact involved, it often ends up being the highlight of a vacation.

Bed & breakfast has come a long way in North America since its humble beginnings a little over a decade ago. With an estimated 15,000 accommodations now available throughout the United States and Canada, there is a B&B for everyone's taste and budget.

The variety of accommodations can range from a lobsterman's island home off the coast of Maine to a beach house in California. From an elegant high-rise apartment in New York City to an Alaskan farm with a trout stream where the host promises, "if you catch 'em and clean 'em, I'll cook 'em for breakfast." For the adventurous, there's B&B on a tugboat. If you're a history buff, you'll enjoy the many restored antique homes, from Southern antebellum mansions to a quaint New England sea captain's house. Nature lovers might enjoy staying at a working cattle ranch out West or visiting a new cedar lodge overlooking a pure mountain river in West Virginia which is a ninety minute trip from the nearest paved road by four-wheel drive.

Definitions

The large number of bed and breakfast accommodations now available can be divided into three distinct categories: private B&B homes, guest houses and cottages, B&B inns, and country inns with restaurants. When planning your B&B stay, determine which type best suits your individuality, style, and pocketbook.

1

Introduction

B&B Homes: The "at-home-style of bed & breakfast," B&B homes are hosted by individuals who enjoy meeting other people, sharing their homes and communities, and perhaps even showing off in the kitchen with their favorite breakfast recipes. Hosts generally have jobs outside the home during the day but enjoy taking occasional guests when their schedules allow. Guests are made to feel part of the family in this people-to-people hospitality concept, which has thrived in Europe for decades. Reservations at many B&B homes are made in advance through B&B reservation agencies, and rates for two generally range from $45 to $75, depending upon location and amenities.

B&B Guest houses and cottages: Guest houses and cottages are private, separate buildings located on the property near the main house where hosts live. Breakfast is often brought to the building in a basket each morning, although guests may sometimes join hosts for breakfast in the main house. Reservations may be made directly with the guesthouse or indirectly through a B&B reservation agency.

B&B and Country Inns: B&B inns and country inns are commercial lodgings that pride themselves on providing personal attention and clean, comfortable accommodations. A wide variety of inns are available, from historic homes to contemporary mansions, each having established their own unique individuality and charm. Many inns are graced by abundant antiques and period decor. Others are particularly celebrated for fine cuisine, special weekend events, or romantic atmosphere. Rates for inns generally range from $75 to over $100, depending upon location and amenities. Reservations are usually made directly with the inn but sometimes through a B&B reservation agency.

B&B Reservation Agencies: These are businesses that arrange all of the details of a B&B stay for guests who wish to choose from a variety of accommodations but prefer to make only one phone call. Reservation agencies also develop and train B&B hosts, personally visit host homes, publicize B&B, screen guests and match guests to appropriate B&Bs, and generally handle all of the administrative details of arranging a B&B stay.

Tips in Choosing a Bed & Breakfast

The key to an enjoyable stay at a bed and breakfast is to choose one that matches your individuality, style, and pocketbook. As a potential guest, you should let your specific desires be known. Some of the points you should consider before making reservations include:

1. Location: Is the B&B location suitable for your purposes? Is parking available if you are arriving by car?
2. Purpose of your visit: If the purpose of your visit is a week-end

getaway, be sure to mention this, especially if you'd like a romantic room with a fireplace and Jacuzzi. If you are traveling on business you may want to request a quiet room with a private telephone, television, desk, and good lighting.

3. Guest rooms & baths: Do you prefer a large guest room? Do you insist upon a private bath? What decor do you prefer? Check whether the room is air-conditioned if this is important to you. If you are traveling to a scenic location check if there is a room available with a view.

4. Price: What price range do you have in mind? Would spending an additional $10 get you an upgraded room? Does the B&B accept credit cards? What is their cancellation policy?

5. Special considerations: If you are traveling with children or pets be sure to mention this on the telephone. Some bed and breakfasts do have handicapped facilities but many do not have this provision so be sure to check in advance if you have special needs. Also, be certain to discuss any special dietary needs you may have.

Once you have made reservations here are some pointers to help ensure a happy stay at a bed and breakfast:

- Call your host and give the approximate time of arrival. Get specific directions from the host that will aid you in easily finding the B&B.
- When there's an unexpected delay and you're going to be late, telephone your host and let them know in case special arrangements need to be made.
- Adhere to your host's policies regarding smoking, children, and pets.
- If you must cancel your trip contact your host immediately. Cancellation policies differ from one host to the next but if you're able to give reasonable notice, most B&Bs will return your deposit less a small service charge.
- After your visit provide feedback to your host or the reservation agency handling your accommodations. Your B&B experience reflects on the entire industry and comments and suggestions are appreciated.

American Bed & Breakfast Association

The American Bed & Breakfast Association (AB&BA) was founded in 1981 and serves as a central clearinghouse for B&B travel and trade information in North America. Objectives of the association are:

1. To encourage and support B&B travel in North America.
2. To gather and distribute reliable B&B travel information.
3. To encourage public and private sector efforts to promote B&B.
4. To unite the diverse components of the B&B industry and implement programs that support common goals.
5. To provide a forum for addressing industry-wide issues.

6. To provide services, conduct studies, disseminate information, and provide networking opportunities for the benefit of its membership.

All members of the association must meet the specific requirements of the AB&BA's Quality Assurance Program as well as agree to abide by the Member Code of Ethics.

American Bed & Breakfast Association - Code of Ethics

1. We acknowledge ethics and morality as inseparable elements of doing business and will test every decision against the highest standards of honesty, legality, fairness, impunity, and conscience.
2. We will conduct ourselves personally and collectively at all times such as to bring credit to the service and tourism industry at large.
3. We will concentrate our time, energy, and resources on the improvement of our own product and services and we will not denigrate our competition in the pursuit of our own success.
4. We will treat all guests equally regardless of race, religion, nationality, creed, or sex.
5. We will deliver standards of service and product with total consistency to every guest.
6. We will provide a safe and sanitary environment at all times for every guest and employee.
7. We will strive constantly, in words, actions, and deeds, to develop and maintain the highest level of trust, honesty and understanding among guests, clients, employees, employers and the public at large.
8. We will provide every employee at every level all of the knowledge, training, equipment, and motivation required to perform his or her own tasks according to our standards.
9. We will guarantee that every employee at every level will have the same opportunity to perform, advance, and will be evaluated against the same standard as all employees engaged in the same or similar tasks.
10. We will actively and consciously work to protect and preserve our natural environment and natural resources in all that we do.
11. We will seek a fair and honest profit.

Letters from B&B travelers are always welcome and can be sent to: AB&BA Editor, 10800 Midlothian Turnpike, Richmond, VA 23235.

The American Bed & Breakfast Association

The Association's Inspection and Rating System

The American Bed & Breakfast Association is the only organization within the bed and breakfast industry that has established national standards and a consumer rating system. Compliance with these standards is verified by an annual on-site inspection performed by trained evaluators. Every effort has been made to ensure that the ratings assigned to each bed and breakfast are fair and accurate. The ratings that appear with each bed and breakfast listed in this book are intended to give readers a true feel for the overall quality of the property, the level of hospitality, cleanliness, and how well the building and its contents are maintained. There are five principal areas which are evaluated during the on-site inspection:

1. The exterior of the building and grounds.
2. All common areas such as parlors and dining rooms.
3. Guest rooms - cleanliness, comfort, furnishings, and decor.
4. Guest bathrooms - cleanliness, safety, function, and quality of materials.
5. Hospitality, guest services, and management policies.

The basic requirements and national standards of the AB&BA insist that every bed and breakfast who is a member of the association be clean, comfortable, well-maintained, safe, serve a wholesome breakfast which is included in the overnight room rate, and offer friendly hospitality. These are the basics requirements. Each rating level above the basic is an evaluation of how the property exceeds the basic requirements in areas such as quality of furnishings and accessories, room decor, and guest amenities and services.

The basic ratings in this book are similar to grades awarded in schools throughout the United States. The rating as well as the letter grade (which sometimes show a plus or minus sign) accompany each listing within the book:

♛ - "C" - Acceptable, meets basic requirements.
♛♛ - "B" - Good, exceeds basic requirements.
♛♛♛ - "A" - Excellent, far exceeds basic requirements.
♛♛♛♛ - "AA" - Outstanding.

The ♛♛♛♛ outstanding award is the highest award given for any property during 1993. A top ♛♛♛♛♛ is available starting in 1994 to any bed and breakfast who proves to be an exceptional property over a period of at least two years and will be used to designate the top two percent of bed and breakfasts throughout the United States and Canada.

All guest comments which appear in this book have been carefully verified and affidavits signed by the guests to vouch for the authenticity of their comments are on file with the American Bed & Breakfast Association.

Sample Listing

Here is a sample description of a B&B, followed by an explanation of each specific part:

Waterman[1]
Grandma's B&B
1200 Main Street
Waterman, WI 78435
(222) 222-2222[2]

Type of B&B: B&B Inn
Rooms: 3, 2 with private bath.[3]
Rates: 1/$45; 2/$55[4]

♛♛♛ - Excellent, far exceeds basic requirements.[5]

Victorian home[6] built in 1910 is located 5 miles from downtown off Route 144.[7] Choose from three guest rooms, two with private bath.[8] Each room features individual decor, antique furnishings, and a small balcony overlooking the river. The large fireplaced parlor is a gathering place each afternoon for tea and dessert and for quiet reading or board games in the evening. Visit nearby antique and craft shops, galleries, and historic settlements. Enjoy four-season recreation nearby including fishing and boating.[9] Full breakfast includes specialties such as walnut French toast or Grandma's super-duper eggs.[10] Wedding and meetings facilities available.[11] Families welcome.[12] Wheelchair access.[13] No smoking.[14] 1/$45; 2/$55.[15] AE, MC, V.[16] Travel agent.[17]

1. City in or near where the B&B is located.
2. Name of B&B, address, and telephone number to call for reservations.
3. Number of rooms and baths.
4. Rates.
5. Overall rating of the property.
6. Architecture.
7. Location.
8. Guest rooms and baths.
9. Special features, area attractions, and recreation opportunities in the area.
10. Type of breakfast.
11. Facilities for meetings, weddings, or social functions are available.
12. Children of all ages are welcome. If a listing does not state "Families welcome," there may be restrictions on the ages of children accommodated at the B&B.
13. Some guest rooms and baths have wheelchair access.
14. Smoking is prohibited.
15. Overnight rates for a single person or two sharing the same room. All rates include breakfast.
16. Credit cards are accepted for full payment.
17. You may book reservations at this B&B through your local travel agent.

B&B Reservation Agencies and Associations

The following B&B reservation agencies and associations are members of the American Bed & Breakfast Association and will handle reservations for a great number of B&B homes, guest houses, and inns throughout the United States and Canada.

ALASKA

Alaska Private Lodgings
P.O. Box 200047
Anchorage, AK 99520-0047
(907) 258-1717
Fax (907) 258-6613

Office hours: Daily 9 a.m. - 6 p.m. in-season; off-season office hours are flexible with an answering machine for after hours.
Geographic area: Southcentral Alaska
Inspections: Annual
Deposit: A personal check covering one night's lodging must be paid in advance or a credit card guarantee can also be accepted.
Payment: AE, MC, V, cash, personal checks. There is a $5 surcharge for one night stays and a discount for cash or check payments.
5 % travel agent commission available.
Services: Despite Anchorage's 5,000 hotel rooms, 500 B&Bs rooms and 80 hostel rooms, accommodations are very tight during the summer months and advance reservations are strongly suggested. B&B accommodations range from guest rooms and suites in a variety of rural or in-town locations. Private unhosted apartments are also available with fully furnished kitchens.

ARIZONA

Mi Casa Su Casa
P.O. Box 950
Tempe, AZ 85281
(602) 990-0682 or (800) 456-0682
Fax (602) 990-3390

Office hours: Daily 8 a.m. - 8 p.m.
Geographic area: Arizona, New Mexico, Utah, and Nevada.
Inspections: Annually.
Deposit: A first night's deposit is required for stays under one week. For one-night stays, payment includes an extra $5.00 charge. For stays over seven nights, 20% of the total amount is required as a deposit.
Payment: Cash or traveler's checks only.

— Continued on next page

Guests write: *"The reservation agency was very helpful in selecting the inn considering our price range and needs. The B&B itself was a very warm, inviting place. Our room was large and well decorated in pine furniture. Our hosts greeted us with wine and cheese as we checked in during afternoon tea time."* (G. Grinis)

"We wanted to stay up for hours visiting with our lovely hosts. In the morning I was asked if we'd like to try their grapefruit. So our host went out to his tree, picked a grapefruit and we ate it. Now that was fresh! We're from the Midwest so this was very special. The smell of orange blossoms is heavenly. We trust Mi Casa Su Casa to find us a place to stay where we feel welcome and comfortable. They have never let us down." (A. Bush)

"Our hosts were absolutely the most friendly and hospitable people. We felt more like family or friends than paying guests. We were genuinely sorry to leave and have since thought about moving to Arizona. But we're not sure if it's for the weather or because of our hosts!" (E. Albrecht)

"By far the best breakfast we had in Arizona and possible one of our best ever! The bed was so divinely comfortable, soft and luxurious that only such a breakfast could have gotten us out of it." (K. Williford)

CALIFORNIA

Eye Openers Bed & Breakfast Reservations
P.O. Box 694
Altadena, CA 91001
(213) 684-4428 or (818) 797-2055
Fax (818) 798-3640

Office hours: Monday - Friday, 10 a.m. - 6 p.m.
Geographic area: Bed and breakfast homes and inns throughout the entire state of California.
Inspections: Annually.
Deposit: A $25.00 deposit is required to confirm reservations.
Payment: MC, V, personal checks, traveler's checks and cash.
Travel agent commission available.

Guests write: *"We couldn't have wanted nicer hosts or more romantic places to stay. You really did an incredible job of matching us with just the right places. Our three favorites were the Garden Room in San Diego, the Beach House in Cambria, and the fantastic Victorian with the brass bed and woodburning fireplace in San Francisco. You made a memorable time even more exciting and romantic."* (J. Gallucci)

"We particularly were pleased with the B&B accommodations that were made for us by Eye Openers B&B Reservations. Our hostess was delightful and gracious in sharing her home with us. We would like to heartily recommend them as an alternative to the standard modes of lodging." (B. Pincince)

"You certainly handled my reservation to my satisfaction and I would highly recommend your service to others." (C. Miles)

"Both of our hosts were magnificent. They not only fulfilled the basic B&B functions, they both went out of their way to provide information, supplies, services, excellent food, tickets to a concert they could not attend, and on and on. A beautiful experience!" (K. Poll)

"Arrangements were made on our behalf for a stay in San Francisco. We were delighted with our accommodations. The hosts could not have been more helpful and hospitable and we were very happy with our room in their house. We hope to return to the USA before long and will certainly be using Eye Openers B&B again." (S. de Brett)

"After spending several weeks in travel lodges there sure was no comparison to breakfast on the patio under an oak tree with an interesting hostess." (B. Wallace)

COLORADO

Bed & Breakfast Rocky Mountains
673 Grant Street
Denver, CO 80203
(303) 860-8415 or (800) 733-8415
Fax (303) 860-9054

Office hours: Weekdays: 8:30 a.m.-5:30 p.m. Saturday: 9 a.m. to 1 p.m. Closed Sunday.
Geographic area: Colorado, New Mexico, Utah
Inspections: Annually.
Deposit: A deposit equal to the first night's stay is required to confirm reservations. 50% deposit is required for more than two nights, ski areas, holidays, and special events or weekends.
Payment: AE, Diners, Discover, MC, V. Any balance owed is due in cash or traveler's check upon arrival at the host accommodation.
Services: Additional services include shuttle service from Stapleton International Airport, rental cars, ski lift tickets, mountain bike rental and tours, and special meals by Chef-on-Call.

FLORIDA

Bed & Breakfast Scenic Florida
P.O. Box 3385
Tallahassee, FL 32315-3385
(904) 386-8196

Office hours: Weekdays 9 a.m. to 5 p.m. Saturday 9 a.m. to 2 p.m. Closed Sunday.
Geographic area: North Florida (Jacksonville to Pensacola, South to Ocala, East to Fort Lauderdale).
Inspections: Annually.
Deposit: A deposit equal to one night's stay is required to confirm reservations.
Payment: MC, V, Personal Check
Services: Choose from 24 B&B hosts throughout the North Florida area.

GEORGIA

Bed & Breakfast Atlanta
1801 Piedmont Avenue, Suite 208
Atlanta, GA 30324
(404) 875-0525, 875-9672 or 800-96-PEACH
Fax (404) 875-9672

Office hours: Monday - Friday, 9-5 p.m.
Geographic area: Metropolitan Atlanta
Inspections: Annually
Deposit: A deposit equal to one night's stay is required to confirm reservations.
Payment: Personal check, AE, Diner's, Carte Blanche, MC, V.
Established in 1979, this agency covers the geographic area of metropolitan Atlanta (site for the 1996 Olympics), and selected sites around Georgia.

Guests write: *"The carriage house is a lovely, peaceful retreat. I was in Atlanta for a very busy convention, so I particularly appreciated this oasis. The neighborhood was great for walking."* (B. Steel)

"We are absolutely delighted! Great beds, lovely room, good food. But, most of all, very warm, gracious, and real hosts. We have been pampered, welcomed, and made truly comfortable. Thank you!" (L. Driver)

"We originally opted for B&B because all of Atlanta's hotels were booked. We were pleasantly surprised to find that not only was B&B cheaper but it was extremely cozy and pleasant. My wife and I plan to return for a

vacation. Our hostess was extremely gracious, helpful and a lot of fun. Overall, I have no complaints and nothing but praise for my host and this organization!" (J. Pazun)

"Our hosts were very gracious. Their home was everything as described and more. I would emphasize how very helpful the staff person was at B&B Atlanta. She not only knew the available inventory, but knew what made each home different and this helped us make a choice." (A. Farley)

"Our hosts were extremely kind to us. We didn't expect to be given rides from Marta and then the airport. We even received rides to our downtown destinations on different days when the weather was dreary and rainy." (J. Mizutani)

Quail Country Bed & Breakfast Ltd.
1104 Old Monticello Road
Thomasville, GA 31792
(912) 226-7218 or 226-6882

Office hours: Monday - Friday, 9 a.m. - 9 p.m.
Geographic area: Thomasville, Georgia.
Inspections: Annually.
Deposit: A deposit of $25 is required to confirm reservations.
Services: Accommodations can be arranged in private homes throughout the charming, historic town of Thomasville, Georgia. Activities of interest in the area include plantation tours, historic restorations, Pebble Hill Plantation Museum, walking tours, April Rose Festival and nearby hunting preserves. Thomasville is a winter resort area with excellent recreation and hunting. It's also known as the City of Roses.

HAWAII

Bed & Breakfast Honolulu (Statewide)
3242 Kaohinani Drive
Honolulu, HI 96817
(808) 595-7533 or (800) 288-4666
Fax (808) 595-2030

Office hours: Monday - Friday, 8 a.m. to 5 p.m., and Saturday, 8 a.m. to noon.
Geographic area: All islands in Hawaii.
Inspections: Annually.
Deposit: 50% deposit for stays more than 3 days. Full payment is required in advance for stays of three days or less.
Payment: Cash, traveler's check, MC, V.
Services: Car and inter-island air coupons are available at low rates.

B&B Reservation Agencies and Associations

Hawaii's Best Bed & Breakfasts
P.O. Box 563
Kamuela, HI 96743
(800) 262-9912 or (808) 885-4550
Fax (808) 885-0550

Office hours: Weekdays 9 a.m. to 5 p.m. Saturday 8 a.m. to Noon. Closed Sunday.
Geographic area: All Hawaiian islands.
Inspections: Annually.
Deposit: A deposit equal to one night's stay at each location is required to confirm reservations.
Payment: Personal checks or cash
Services: Additional services available include rental cars, and with their detailed knowledge of each property, an itinerary specifically tailored to a guest's personal travel requirements.

MARYLAND

The Traveller in Maryland
P.O. Box 2277
Annapolis, MD 21404
(410) 269-6232 or Fax (410) 263-4841

Office hours: Weekdays 9 a.m. to 5 p.m.
Geographic area: State of Maryland, specializing in Annapolis.
Inspections: Annually.
Deposit: A deposit equivalent to one nights stay is required to confirm reservations.
Payment: AE, MC, V.
Services: Reservations can be made for over 100 B&Bs in Annapolis, Baltimore, Eastern Shore, central, and western Maryland. Traveller in Maryland also represents B&Bs in the United Kingdom and Central London apartments.

MASSACHUSETTS

Bed & Breakfast Associates Bay Colony, Ltd.
P.O. Box 57166, Babson Park
Boston, MA 02157
(617) 449-5302 or (800) 347-5088

Office hours: Monday - Friday, 9:30 a.m. to 12:30 p.m. and 1:30 - 5 p.m..
Geographic area: Reservations may be made for over 170 B&B accommodations in eastern Massachusetts including greater Boston, Cambridge, the North and South Shore areas, Cape Cod, Martha's Vineyard, and Nantucket.
Inspections: Annually.
Payment: AE, MC, V, Diner, and Carte Blanche. 5% travel agency commission available on bookings of 3 nights or more.

Guests write: *"Peggy was extremely pleasant. On arrival to her brownstone, she greeted us with chilled champagne and a thorough explanation of the best places to visit in Boston. We followed every suggestion and had a fabulous time! The brownstone was lovely. Our room was quite spacious and nicely furnished. Her buffet breakfasts were great. We felt very much at home. We appreciated the thorough and professional manner in which we were treated."* (L. Weinstein)

"Our hostess was a delight. Her hospitality and breakfasts were excellent. She loves people and it shows!" (B. Love)

"Can't wait to return. Very nice hosts, beautiful room. We were extremely comfortable. Breakfasts were great and they were helpful with information about Boston. I would recommend this place highly!" (J. Sullivan)

Be Our Guest Bed & Breakfast
P.O. Box 1333
Plymouth, MA 02362
(617) 837-9867

Office hours: Daily 10 a.m. - 9 p.m.
Geographic area: Over twenty B&B accommodations are located throughout Boston, Cape Cod, Plymouth, and south of Boston.
Inspections: Annually.
Payment: AE, MC, V.

B&B Reservation Agencies and Associations

Bed & Breakfast Cape Cod
P.O. Box 341
West Hyannisport, MA 02672-0341
(508) 775-2772, Fax (508) 775-2884

Office hours: Monday - Friday 8:30 a.m. to 6 p.m. Contact by fax or leave a message on the answering machine at other times.

Geographic area: Select from 90 B&B homes, country inns, and historic homes located on Cape Cod, Nantucket, and Martha's Vineyard islands, Gloucester at Cape Ann and south of Boston at Cohasset, Scituate, and Marshfield.

Deposit: A deposit of 25% of total room rate plus a $5.00 booking charge is required to confirm reservations.

Payment: D, MC, V, AE accepted for deposit or full payment.

Guests write: *"Thanks to B&B Cape Cod for assistance in finding a lovely B&B. Hosts were gregarious, easy-going, informative, efficient, and cheerful."* (R Hage)

"Thanks to B&B Cape Cod for a fabulous recommendation. This B&B is going to be a place we shall return to. Spotlessly clean, totally engrossing ambiance with every detail accounted for." (A Vinci)

"Our B&B in Scituate Harbor was an unforgettable experience - one that I could replicate neither before nor since. The house is beautiful and wonderfully situated, the hosts congenial and they know just how much to "host" and yet give you lots of privacy. The household cats, Victorian decor, and classical music all work together. The bedrooms are beautifully decorated, the towels plentiful and of good quality. I do hope to return." (A. Tonello)

"This was a wonderful way to spend our first vacation in four years! The accommodations could not have been nicer, the food could not have been more delicious, the hosts could not have done any more to make guests feel at home." (J. McNair)

"I thank them so much for their advice and guidance in my choice of accommodations. They operate an excellent service with efficiency and expertise!" (M. Merkley)

Folkstone Bed & Breakfast Reservation Service
Darling Road
Dudley, MA 01571
(508) 943-7118 or (800) 762-2751

Office hours: Daily; messages left on the answering machine are returned promptly.
Geographic area: Select from B&B accommodations located throughout central Massachusetts and northeastern Connecticut.
Inspections: Annually.
Deposit: A deposit equal to one night's stay is required to confirm reservations.
Payment: AE, MC, V accepted for deposit or full payment.

Golden Slumber Accommodations
640 Revere Beach Boulevard
Revere, MA 08151
(617) 289-1053 or (800) 892-3231 (outside MA)

Office hours: Monday - Saturday 8 a.m. - 9 p.m.
Geographic area: Massachusetts seacoast including Boston's North and South Shores, Cape Cod and Greater Boston.
Inspections: Annually.
Deposit: One third total room rate must be paid in advance.
Payments: MC, V, traveler's checks, money orders.
Services: A wide variety of accommodations with courteous hosts are available throughout Boston, North & South Shores, and Cape Cod. Many locations welcome families with children and several have handicapped accessible accommodations. Limousine service is available to address guests' transportation needs. A complete host home directory is available for $2.00.

Panda Bed & Breakfast
446 Boston Road, Suite 305
Billerica, MA 01821-4773
(508) 262-0949 or (800) 832-9939

Office hours: Monday - Friday 8 a.m. to 6 p.m.
Geographic area: New England area
Inspections: Twice annually.
Deposit: A deposit of 25% of total charge is required.
Payment: Personal check, traveler's checks, Western Union wire.
Services: Choose from one hundred unique accommodations throughout New England. Among these are B&Bs with water views, Brownstones, and those within walking distance of historic sites or famous hospitals. Rates range from $60-$150 per night for double occupancy.

MISSISSIPPI

Lincoln, Ltd. Bed & Breakfast,
Mississippi Reservation Service
P.O. Box 3479
Meridian, MS 39303
(601) 482-5483, Fax (601) 693-7447

Office hours: Monday - Friday, 9 a.m. - 5 p.m.
Geographic area: Select from a variety of B&Bs located throughout Mississippi, Natchez to Memphis, eastern Louisiana and southwest Alabama.
Inspections: Annually.
Deposit: A deposit equal to one night's stay is required to confirm reservations.
Payment: MC, V, AE accepted for full payment.
Travel agent commission available.

MISSOURI

Ozark Mountain Country Bed & Breakfast
P.O. Box 295
Branson, MO 65616
(417) 334-4720 or (800) 695-1546

Office hours: Weekdays 1 - 9 p.m. and weekends, 1 - 5 p.m.
Geographic area: Reservations are available at over one hundred B&B homes, guest cottages, suites, and inns throughout southwest Missouri, northeastern Oklahoma, and northwest Arkansas.
Inspections: Annually.
Deposit: Reservations must be accompanied by a 50% deposit.
Payment: D, MC, V accepted.
10% travel agent commission available.

MONTANA

Bed & Breakfast Western Adventure
P.O. Box 20972
Billings, MT 59104-0972
(406) 259-7993

Office hours: May through September, weekdays 9 a.m. - 5 p.m. and Saturday 9 a.m. to 1 p.m. Winter hours are weekdays 9 a.m. - 1 p.m.
Geographic area: Montana, Wyoming, Black Hills of South Dakota, and eastern Idaho.
Inspections: Annually.
Deposit: A deposit equal to one night's stay is required to confirm reservations.
Payment: MC, V accepted for payment.
Services: 7% travel agency commission available on bookings of at least two nights.

Guests write: *"I'm a business traveler who prefers B&B to hotel/motels. All my comments come not as a vacationer but regarding a place to stay on business. I find B&Bs gearing up for people like me who like comfort and pampering. As a single, professional woman, B&Bs are the answer. There was a lovely selection of rooms to choose from. Hostess was very warm and friendly."* (T. Elliott)

"Karen is a charming hostess. She really makes you feel welcome with wonderful food. One of the nicest B&Bs we've visited!" (P. McPhee)

"The reservation process was prompt with excellent courtesy, assistance, and directions. Wonderful room and food. The town is lovely and the surroundings give you many things to do. The hostess was very helpful and friendly." (F. Thatcher)

"We always use B&Bs whenever we can and we have used B&B Western Adventure numerous times. We know we can always count on a home which has been inspected and we have always found the hosts most congenial and the accommodations most comfortable." (M. Thorndal)

B&B Reservation Agencies and Associations

NEW YORK

Abode Bed & Breakfast Ltd.
P.O. Box 20022
New York, NY 10028
(212) 472-2000

Office hours: Weekdays 9 a.m. - 5 p.m. and Saturday 11 a.m. - 2 p.m.
Geographic area: Reservations may be made for over one-hundred B&B accommodations throughout Manhattan, and Park Slope, New York. Also available are unhosted, fully equipped apartments in owner-occupied brownstones. Guests have total privacy in their own apartment and still enjoy the benefits of having hosts on hand for questions, information, advice, and whatever else they need.
Inspections: Annually.
Deposit: A deposit of approximately 25% of the stay is required to confirm reservations.
Payment: AE is accepted for deposit or full payment.
Restrictions: Minimum stay is two nights.

Guests write: *"I was greeted by a spotlessly clean facility, tastefully decorated, comfortably furnished, a cup of coffee in the waiting, and a dozen roses that lasted during my entire stay. The location was idea. My host offered us a tour - it was a nice and welcoming thing to do."* (V. LaFrance)

Bed & Breakfast & Books
35 West 92nd Street
New York, NY 10025
(212) 865-8740

Office hours: Weekdays 10 a.m. to 5 p.m.
Geographic area: Reservations can be made for over sixty B&B accommodations located throughout Manhattan - Upper West and East sides, Chelsea, Gramercy Park, Greenwich Village, and Soho.
Deposits: A deposit equal to one night's stay is required to confirm reservations.
Services: 5% travel agent commission available.

B&B Reservation Agencies and Associations

OHIO

Private Lodgings, Inc.
P.O. Box 18590
Cleveland, OH 44118
(216) 321-3213

Office hours: Weekdays 9 a.m. - noon, 3 - 5 p.m. Closed Wednesdays.
Geographic area: Reservations can be made for more than forty B&B
homes and inns located throughout the Cleveland metropolitan area.
Inspections: Annually.
Deposit: A deposit of 50% is required to confirm reservations.
Payment: Cash and traveler's checks are accepted for full payment.

PENNSYLVANIA

Bed & Breakfast Connections
P.O. Box 21
Devon, PA 19333
(215) 687-3565 or (800) 448-3619 (outside Pennsylvania)

Office hours: Monday - Saturday, 9 a.m. to 9 p.m. Phone messages left on
the answering machine on Sundays will be returned.
Geographic area: B&Bs are located in Philadelphia, Main Line suburbs,
Chestnut Hill, Germantown, Mt. Airy, Valley Forge, Brandywine Valley,
and Amish area.
Inspections: Annually.
Deposits: A deposit equal to one night's stay is required to confirm
reservations.
Payment: AE, MC, V accepted for full payment.
Services: 10% travel agency commission available.

Bed & Breakfast of Philadelphia
1530 Locust Street, Suite K
Philadelphia, PA 19102
(215) 735-1917 or (800) 220-1917

Office hours: Weekdays 9 a.m. - 5 p.m.
Geographic area: B&Bs are available throughout metropolitan
Philadelphia and the surrounding five counties.
Inspections: Annually.
Deposits: A deposit equal to one night's stay is required to confirm
reservations. On stays longer than seven days 25% of the total booking is
required.
Payment: AE, MC, V accepted for full payment.
Services: 10% travel agency commission available.

B&B Reservation Agencies and Associations

Hershey Bed & Breakfast Reservation Service
P.O. Box 208
Hershey, PA 17033
(717) 533-2928

Office hours: Weekdays 10 a.m. - 4 p.m.
Geographic area: Choose from a variety of B&Bs located throughout the south-central section of the state. Personalized service is offered in matching guests to just the right bed and breakfast whether the trip is for a family vacation, a farm experience, a long stay when transferring into the area, romantic honeymoons, or for a business retreat in a relaxing setting.
Inspections: Annually.
Deposit: A 25% deposit is required to confirm reservations.
Payment: AE, MC, V accepted for full payment.
Services: 5% travel agent commission available.

Guests write: *"When our whole family decided to get together for a vacation in Lancaster County, we knew that we wanted to stay at a B&B but we were unfamiliar with the area. I contacted Hershey B&B Reservation Service who were immediately able to recommend the perfect place. This beautiful farm turned out to be everything they promised. Their services didn't end at finding us the perfect B&B. She kept in close contact to give us helpful information and tips on things to do in the area complete with restaurant menus, easy-to-follow directions, and coupons."* (C. Schindewolf)

Rest and Repast Bed & Breakfast Reservation Service
P.O. Box 126
Pine Grove Mills, PA 16868
(814) 238-1484

Office hours: Weekdays 8:30-11:30 a.m. Closed weekends except during peak times.
Geographic area: Select from over sixty B&B homes and inns located throughout Central Pennsylvania including the Penn Station area.
Inspections: Annually.
Deposit: A $25-50 deposit per night is required to confirm reservations.
Payment: Cash only.

Guests write: *"My son loved the Penn State bedroom at our host's home. Our breakfast of fresh fruit, oven French toast, sausage, juice, and coffee was great. We felt as though we were staying with family. I was able to bring home some recipes from Pennsylvania that a lot of people in New Hampshire enjoy."* (S Kamitian)

"My B&B needs have changed dramatically in the 10 years since I left college, yet every year Rest Repast places me with the perfect host. From my every penny counts years when they saved me $70 off the cheapest hotel room to my

years when a crib and a host close to the action counted most, Rest Repast comes through with flying colors! And the food ... it seems like Center County folks just like to cook. I don't think we've ever had fewer than 3 courses for breakfast. Our hosts have always been eager to please. One woman even had guests sign the tablecloth which she later embroidered." (D. Painter)

"Our Rest and Repast hosts always prepare salt-free breakfasts for me which are exceptional. On those occasions when we were unable to obtain tickets for a football game, our host is often able to get them for us from some of her many friends. We are always made to feel at home." (B. Sacks)

"We always look forward to our visits. Our hosts are kind and gracious and never fail to make us feel wanted. They go out of their way to think of so many little things to do that make us feel we are truly with friends. No hotel could ever match their warm hospitality." (R. Savin)

"Thanks to Rest and Repast for their part in a perfect weekend... proving again that things rarely satisfy man's soulful needs the way good, caring, loving people can." (N. Clark)

SOUTH CAROLINA

Historic Charleston Bed & Breakfast
43 Legare Street
Charleston, SC 29401
(803) 722-6606, Fax (803) 853-7266

Office hours: Weekdays 9:30 a.m. - 5:30 p.m.
Geographic area: Reservations can be made for over sixty private homes and carriage houses in Charleston's Historic District as well as other cities throughout the state.
Inspections: Annually.
Deposits: A deposit equal to one night's stay is required to confirm reservations.
Payment: AE, MC, V accepted for full payment.

Guests write: "Our son had just returned to Charleston after seven months with the Navy in the Middle East. We were looking for a touch of home for Christmas Eve and Christmas Day and found it! Our hosts placed a small, decorated tree in the living room of the carriage house - a lovely touch which was greatly appreciated." (B. DeCarolis)

"I'm so glad to recommend this service. Our B&B location was very quiet and private." (B. Barnes)

"The girls and I really enjoyed our stay. Everything was so nice. The breakfasts were delicious and we loved having our own little apartment. We especially enjoyed the little garden and fountain. Charleston is truly one of my favorite cities." (A. Fuller)

VIRGINIA

Guesthouses Bed & Breakfast
P.O. Box 5737
Charlottesville, VA 22905
(804) 979-7264

Office hours: Weekdays noon to 5 p.m.
Geographic area: Select from B&Bs located throughout Charlottesville, Albemarle County, and Nelson County. The variety of B&Bs available includes distinctive private homes and guest cottages.
Inspections: Each inspected annually by Guesthouses and certified by the Virginia Health Department.
Deposits: A 25% deposit plus tax is required to confirm reservations and may be charged to AE, MC, or Visa.
Payment to hosts: Cash or personal check only.

Guests write: "The Guesthouses services were prompt and courteous." (S. Beddingfield)

"We loved our hostess and her B&B. A great find! Country charm and her warmth made for a great stay." (B. Messerly)

"We had a wonderful B&B on 1200 acres. Lovely folks! Marvelous solitude. Fabulous breakfast! I will return - recommend highly!" (B. Markesbery)

"The match between host and guest was perfect! My friend who was in a wheelchair found the house perfectly accessible, even more than her own home. She needed an escape for a few days and this was it. She went into the guest room and you should have seen her face brighten and her whole demeanor change for the better." (J. Brown)

"We have been delighted with the accommodations we've arranged through Guesthouses. We have become friends with both families with whom we've stayed and look forward to many continued years of friendship." (J. Santos)

"Guesthouses arranged our first B&B experience. Because of the warmth and hospitality shared us, I am sure it will not be my last. I would not hesitate a moment to recommend our hosts. My traveling companion, who is an experienced B&B person, agrees with me 100%." (M. Cress)

Princely Bed & Breakfast, Ltd.
819 Prince Street
Alexandria, VA 22314
(703) 683-2159

Office hours: Monday - Friday 10 a.m. - 6 p.m.
Geographic area: The agency represents bed and breakfasts in the Alexandria Old Town historic district. Accommodations are all in distinctive homes dating between 1790 and 1900.

Inspections: Annually.
Deposit: A deposit equal to one night's stay is required for reservations.
Payment: Full payment upon arrival must be by check or cash.
Cancellation policy.
Services: This area is conveniently located only 8 miles from either Washington, DC or Mount Vernon, Virginia. A new metro subway can whisk visitors into Washington, DC within 15 minutes.
Guests write: *"I was most impressed with E.J. Mansmann and the professionalism he showed. It is likely we will use his services again."* *"Thanks to Princely B&B for arranging our stay. We loved this charming cottage and the first-class hospitality. We have made a fine friendship and are thankful for the introduction. The restaurants are superb."*

CANADA, BRITISH COLUMBIA

City & Sea B&B Registry
626 Fernhill Road
Victoria, BC Canada V9A 4Y9
(604) 385-1962 or (604) 388-6669

Office hours: Daily 10 a.m. to 10 p.m.
Geographic area: Victoria and Vancouver Island
Inspections: Annual.
Deposit: A deposit equal to one night's stay is required to confirm reservations.
Payment: MC, V, Traveler's checks, personal checks.
Services: Choose from twenty B&Bs throughout Victoria or Vancouver Island. Accommodations range from Victorian homes near downtown sites to homes with mountain, city, and sea views, as well as several especially suited for families.

Town & Country Bed & Breakfast in British Columbia
Box 74542, 2803 W 4th Avenue
Vancouver, BC, Canada V6K 1K2
(604) 731-5942

Office hours: Weekdays 9 a.m. - 4 p.m. as well as some evening and weekend hours.
Geographic area: B&Bs are located throughout Vancouver, Victoria, and Vancouver Islands.
Inspections: Annually.
Deposit: A deposit equal to one night's stay is required when making reservations.
Payment: Full payment must be in cash upon arrival.
There is a $5 booking fee for reservations outside Vancouver.

CANADA, ONTARIO

Metropolitan B&B Registry of Toronto
615 Mount Pleasant Road, Suite 269
Toronto, Ontario, Canada M4S 3C5
(416) 964-2566; Fax (416) 537-0233

Office hours: Monday-Friday 8 a.m. to 8 p.m.
Geographic area: Metropolitan Toronto including Niagara Falls, Markham, and Pickering.
Inspections: Annual.
Deposit: A deposit equal to two night's stay is required to confirm reservations.
Payment: Cash, money orders, Traveler's Checks.
Services: This is a full reservation service whose B&Bs are located throughout the metropolitan Toronto area. Accommodations range from Victorian, Tudor, or Edwardian homes. Many feature fine antiques and all offer a full breakfast. Theater ticket reservations are available. 10% travel agent commission offered.

Toronto Bed & Breakfast
Box 269, 253 College Street
Toronto, Ontario, Canada M5T 1R5
(416) 588-8800, Fax (416) 964-1756

Office hours: Weekdays 9 a.m. - 7 p.m.
Geographic area: Reservations are available for more than twenty B&Bs throughout the metropolitan Toronto area.
Inspections: Annually.
Deposits: Charge card information is required for reservations or a deposit equal to one night's stay has to reach the host within seven days prior to arrival.
Services: This agency specializes in the metropolitan Toronto area but is part of a network referral system serving Niagara Falls, Kingston, and Ottawa.

Additional information about B&Bs throughout Alabama is available from Lincoln Ltd. B&B (601) 482-5483.

Forest Home

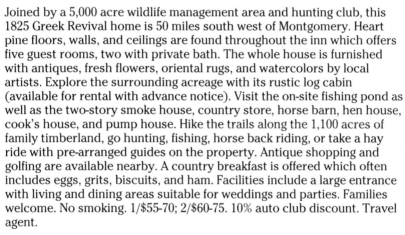

Pine Flat Plantation Bed & Breakfast
P.O. Box 33 Hwy 10 West
Forest Home, AL 36030
(205) 346-2739 or (205) 471-8024

Type of B&B: B&B Home.
Rooms: 5, 2 with private bath.
Rates: 1/$55-70; 2/$60-75.

Rating: B or ♛♛ Good, exceeds basic requirements.

Joined by a 5,000 acre wildlife management area and hunting club, this 1825 Greek Revival home is 50 miles south west of Montgomery. Heart pine floors, walls, and ceilings are found throughout the inn which offers five guest rooms, two with private bath. The whole house is furnished with antiques, fresh flowers, oriental rugs, and watercolors by local artists. Explore the surrounding acreage with its rustic log cabin (available for rental with advance notice). Visit the on-site fishing pond as well as the two-story smoke house, country store, horse barn, hen house, cook's house, and pump house. Hike the trails along the 1,100 acres of family timberland, go hunting, fishing, horse back riding, or take a hay ride with pre-arranged guides on the property. Antique shopping and golfing are available nearby. A country breakfast is offered which often includes eggs, grits, biscuits, and ham. Facilities include a large entrance with living and dining areas suitable for weddings and parties. Families welcome. No smoking. 1/$55-70; 2/$60-75. 10% auto club discount. Travel agent.

Guests write: *"This is without exception the most charming country retreat imaginable. The house itself is impeccably clean and decorated with attractive fabrics with fresh colors of yellow, blues, greens and corals. The owners retained the original style of the period while incorporating the every needed comfort of the 90s. It is a trip back in time to a life of southern ladies and gentlemen. The porches are romantic, the bathrooms large and wonderfully equipped, the breakfast grand and delicious, and the grounds are dreamy. I have travelled the world and have experienced B&Bs from London to Mississippi, and this one is more of the distinction of a country inn. Absolutely a divine get-a-way."* (S. Ashurst)

Montgomery

Red Bluff Cottage
551 Clay Street
Montgomery, AL 36104
(205) 264-0056

Type of B&B: Small inn.
Rooms: 4 with private bath.
Rates: 1/$50; 2/$55.

Rating: A or ♕♕♕ Excellent, far exceeds basic requirements.

Raised cottage style B&B is located 1 block east of I-65, exit 172, in an area known as Cottage Hill, Montgomery's oldest historic district. The four guest rooms, each with private bath, are at ground level and offer a choice of queen or twin guest beds. The light and airy common rooms are upstairs along with the large front porch with its spacious vista of the Alabama River plain and view of the Alabama State Capitol and downtown. Enjoy the harpsichord in the music room or the collection of good books. Interesting sites nearby include Montgomery's Shakespeare Festival Theater, Museum of Fine Arts, and the newly expanded zoo. Well-lit off-street parking is available. Full breakfast served. Families welcome. No smoking. 1/$50; 2/$55. Travel agent.

Guests write: *"This is our third stay at Red Bluff Cottage and it was wonderful as were two previous visits. Breakfast was great - a real treat! Very clean with charming hosts. I think the rating in your book should have been higher. The Waldo's are wonderful hosts and make our visits very enjoyable."* (M. Alvarez)

"After visiting the First White House of the Confederacy we mentioned to Anne at Red Bluff Cottage the beautiful white rose we had seen there and that we would like to purchase such a rose plant. Anne contacted the director of the foundation and was told that that particular rose was not available, however, if we would like to get some cuttings we could. We returned to Red Bluff Cottage where Anne had the proper materials to provide a start for the clippings. The hospitality provided was above and beyond even what one comes to expect as Southern hospitality. The accommodations are excellent." (A. James)

"I left my air ticket forgotten in a curious drawer in an antique dresser. How can I ever thank them for bringing the ticket to the airport? We tell our friends that Montgomery is worth a journey, if only to patronize Red Bluff Cottage." (C Donakowski)

Orange Beach

The Original Romar House Bed & Breakfast Inn
23500 Perdido Beach Boulevard
Orange Beach, AL 36561
(205) 981-6156 or (800) 48-ROMAR

Type of B&B: Seaside inn
Rooms: 6 with private bath.
Rates: 1 or 2/$79-110.

Rating: B+ or ♥♥ Good, exceeds basic requirements.

Art Deco style inn built in 1924 is located on the beach side of Highway 182, 4 miles east of Gulf Shores. Period antiques fill the six individually decorated guest rooms with private bath. Stroll along the white sandy beach to collect shells, relax in the whirlpool spa or on the deck. Enjoy the inn's two-seater bicycle for a ride down Perdido Beach Boulevard. Visit nearby golf courses, nightclubs, seafood restaurants, and local entertainment. Wine and cheese is served each afternoon in the Purple Parrot bar. A full breakfast includes "Romar House" grits, homemade pastries, biscuits, and an egg casserole. Restricted smoking. 1 or 2/$79-110. MC, V. Travel agent.

Guests write: *"Jackie is a natural who creates a truly comfortable atmosphere. A rainy period that kept us off the beach gave opportunity to examine the art deco furnishings and accents that represent the best and most interesting items from the past."* (I. Runkle)

"Each room has an original flavor and our four-poster queen-size bed with a window peeking out to an ocean view was unusually comfortable. The bathrooms are spotless and modern but retain the historic character of the inn. The wrap-around porch with deck overlooks the ocean and is unsurpassable in its tranquillity and view. And the covered patio area with cypress swing and Jacuzzi offers extra relaxation. While we knew there was much to do in the area, we never left the inn except to go to the beach." (L. Keating)

"The house is furnished with old-timey furniture and interesting bric-a-brac and is situated at the edge of the sandy border along the Gulf beach making a beach walk and a quick dip in the surf very available." (B. Stone)

"On our first morning we were sitting on the deck having a cup of coffee. It was rather chilly that morning and I had forgotten to bring a jacket. Jackie loaned me one of hers for the rest of the day. Staying there was like visiting old friends." (J. Still)

Anchorage

Arctic Loon B&B
P.O. Box 110333
Anchorage, AK 99511
(907) 345-4935

Type of B&B: B&B home.
Rooms: 3, 1 with private bath.
Rates: 1/$60-70; 2/$75-90.

Rating: A or ♛♛♛ Excellent, far exceeds basic requirements.

Contemporary Swedish Long House with bay windows is located 12 miles from the airport and situated high above the city with "million-dollar" panoramic views. Choose from three guest rooms, one with private bath, all decorated with an emphasis on light and open space. One room offers a private entrance, microwave, separate seating area, and a TV with VCR and extensive movie collection. There is a lower level recreation room for guest use with Jacuzzi, sauna, and exercise room. The second-floor music room offers a grand piano. Full breakfast includes fresh fruit, special egg dishes, and regional specialties such as smoked salmon or caribou. 1/$60-70; 2/$75-90. MC, V. 10% senior discount. Travel agent. Two night minimum.

Anchorage

The Lilac House
950 P Street
Anchorage, AK 99501
(907) 272-3553 or (907) 277-7966

Type of B&B: Small B&B Inn
Rooms: 4, 2 with private bath.
Rates: 1 or 2 /$75-$85.

Rating B+ or ♛♛ Good, exceeds basic requirements.

Designed and built to serve as a B&B, this "old Anchorage home" is found in the downtown residential district of the city. Each of the four guest rooms, two with private bath, are accessed through the private guest entrance and offer views of the mountains, Cook Inlet, or the tree-filled neighborhood. A writing desk, original art work, and comfortable chairs can be found in each room. Take a ten minute stroll to the downtown shops, restaurants, and entertainment. Explore the Coastal Trail and go biking, skiing, or walking within view of Cook Inlet. Visit the Anchorage Museum of History and Art, Portage Glacier, or the Alyeska Ski Resort, all close by. Freshly baked goods are offered every morning for a hearty continental breakfast. Families welcome. No smoking. 1 or 2/$75-85. Seasonal rates. MC, V.

— Comments continued on next page

Guests write: *"We couldn't have dreamt of a nicer place to spend our first night together as husband and wife. The patter of rain and tinkle of wind chimes were what we needed after wedding preparations."* (B. Verrier)

"The Lilac house is an oasis in the middle of an Alaskan winter. The homemade muffins and breads are amazing!" (J. and L. Benson)

"(Her) warm, friendly welcome late at night to weary travelers was a blessing. The rooms are cheery and make you feel right at home. Breakfasts are superb." (G. Kunz)

"(She) made me feel so 'at home'. This is a lovely place and all the books are a treasure! I would highly recommend the Lilac House to anyone. Cathy is an excellent hostess who went out of her way to make everyone feel welcome." (S. Leeds)

"I love the Lilac House- especially the 'Pink' room. It was an exceptional stay." (J. Slonecker)

Anchorage

Snowline Bed and Breakfast
11101 Snowline Drive
Anchorage, Alaska 99516
(907) 346-1631

Type of B&B: B&B home.
Rooms: 2, 1 with private bath.
Rates: 1 or 2/$65-110.

Rating: A- or ♛♛♛ Excellent, far exceeds basic requirements.

Alpine A-frame home is located in the quiet hillside just 20 minutes from the airport and downtown Anchorage. Two guest rooms are available, one with a king-size bed and shared bath. A second room offers over 500 square feet of living space with a magnificent view, private entrance, queen-size bed and six-person Jacuzzi. Enjoy a panoramic view of Anchorage, Cook Inlet, and Mount McKinley from the living room or sun deck. Chugach State Park, hiking trails, golf course, and the Alaska Zoo are just minutes away. Continental breakfast features homemade pastries and fresh-ground coffee. Families welcome. No smoking. 1 or 2/$65-110. MC, V. Travel agent.

Guests write: *"There was a moose on the beautiful lawn two different nights when we returned to Snowline. Dana and Ed are very pleasant and informative about the state and city. Breakfasts of homemade goodies were a delicious start for the day."* (W. Graham)

— *Comments continued on next page*

"Alaskan hospitality is alive and well at the Snowline B&B. The hosts, Ed and Dana, were friendly and informative. The inn was immaculate and comfortable. A great place to start or finish a trip to Alaska. We did both there." (S. Davison)

"Dana's homemade muffins and sourdough rolls were a wonderful taste treat. Each morning's breakfast was better than the day before. The accommodations were exquisite and had a spectacular view of Anchorage." (J. Evans)

"Very comfortable and attractive. The host's attention to detail and desire to please was evident in every aspect. Mount McKinley presented itself for our viewing pleasure. Wonderful!" (J. Price)

"Our room was enormous and charmingly and comfortably furnished - our own private Jacuzzi and sauna included!" (B. Trueheart)

"They treated me to moose, smoked salmon, homemade muffins, biscuits and lots of coffee and conversation. I took beautiful photos of sunsets and the twinkling lights of Anchorage - all from my room. Ed & Dana had lots of videos and magazines on Anchorage for me to use." (C. Wilde)

Chugiak

Peters Creek Inn
22635 Davidson Road
P.O. Box 671487
Chugiak, AK 99567
(907) 688-2776 or Fax (907) 688-2080

Type of B&B: Inn.
Rooms: 5 with private bath.
Rates: 1/$55; 2/$65.

Rating: B or ♛♛ Good exceeds basic requirements.

Located 18 miles from Anchorage, just north of Anchorage's bedroom community of Eagle River, this contemporary home provides guests with a private entrance, dining room, and living room facilities. Each of the five guest rooms with private bath have been decorated with an Alaskan theme: the Angler, the Prospector, the Musher, the Trapper, and the Sourdough. Close enough to Anchorage to enjoy the local attractions found there, the inn provides a secluded retreat in a rural setting. Nearby attractions include Eklutna Village Historical Park, Thunderbird Falls, Chugach State Park, Independence Mine State Historical Park, and the Knick Glaciers. Farm-fresh eggs and sourdough pancakes are accompanied by freshly ground coffee and fresh fruit. Small meeting facilities available. Families welcome. No smoking. 1/$55; 2/$65. MC, V.

Fairbanks

Alaska's 7 Gables Bed & Breakfast
4312 Birch Lane
P.O. Box 80488
Fairbanks, AK 99708
(907) 479-0751
Fax (907) 479-2229

Type of B&B: B&B Inn
Rooms: 10, 5 with private bath
Rates: 1/$45-75; 2/$50-85.

Rating: B or ♛♛ Good, exceeds basic requirements.

Modern Tudor home built near the river boasts a two-story sun room with floral solarium and is located one mile west of Fairbanks, between the airport and the University. Choose from ten guest rooms with cable television and phones, five with private baths. Several of the rooms are suites and four offer Jacuzzis. Relax in the garden or solarium, use one of the inn's canoes to explore the river, or borrow a bike to tour the area. Many of Alaska's unique points of interest are nearby such as the Pipeline, the Sternwheeler River boat, University of Alaska Museum, the Alaskaland Theme Park, or Santa Claus House in the North Pole. Pan for gold at the Gold Dredge #8 or visit the Musk Ox and Reindeer Farm. Gourmet full breakfasts often include homemade bran or berry muffins, egg dishes, fruit, and herbal teas. Wedding and meeting facilities. Families welcome. Restricted smoking. 1/$45-75; 2/$50-85. AE, Diners, Discover, MC, V. Seasonal rates. Travel agent.

Guests write: *"I spend only 7 days, but had very happy time. Host is very kind, even for foreigners. I'm not good at English but with his help, I am gradually getting the ability to understand English."* (T. Ojio)

"The place and the room was good. And the manager was very kind." (Y. Murai)

Fairbanks

Richards House Bed & Breakfast
1971Kingfisher Drive
Fairbanks, AK 99709
(907) 474-8448 or (907) 479-8165

Type of B&B: Private Home
Rooms: 2 with shared bath.
Rates: 1/$45; 2/$65.

Rating: B- or ♛♛ Good, exceeds basic requirements.

Nestled on a two acre lot surrounded by Aspen and Birch trees, this modern, two story house is in a quiet, residential neighborhood, just ten minutes from downtown Fairbanks. Two guest rooms, each with television, share a common entry, hallway, bath, and kitchenette. Visit nearby University of Alaska, the Pipeline, Historic gold mining fields, or Mt. McKinley at Denali National Park . The University ski/walking trail runs along the edge of the inn's property, allowing for convenient outdoor activities as well as the frequent sight of a moose grazing nearby. A continental breakfast offers a buffet-style meal which includes several fresh fruits, muffins or fresh mini-loaves, bagels with cream cheese or freshly baked breads. Families welcome. Restricted smoking. 1/$45; 2/$65. MC, V. Seasonal and long stay discounts. Travel agent.

Juneau

Pearson's Pond Luxury Inn & Travel Service
4541 Sawa Circle
Juneau, AK 99801
(907) 789-3772

Type of B&B: B&B Inn
Rooms: 3, 1 with private bath.
Rates: 1/$64-145; 2/$74-149.

Rating: A- or ♛♛♛ Excellent, far exceeds basic requirements.

With the view of the Mendenhall Glacier as a scenic backdrop, this modern cedar inn is in Alaska's capitol city, Juneau. Three guest rooms, one with private bath, are offered with private entries, queen sized beds, and VCR with stereo and tapes. Relax in the hot tub on the banks of a wilderness lily pond with its view of the glacier. Sit in front of the fire in the fireside room or in the living room. Go biking, skiing, hiking, fishing, or boating. Convenient to the river, airport, ferry, and shopping as well as to the Glacier Bay National Monument. A flexible, self-serve, breakfast is offered featuring cappuccino and fresh, home made bread. No smoking. 1/$64-145; 2/$74-149. MC, V. 10% corporate and weekly discount. Travel agent.

— *Comments continued on next page*

Guests write: *"We enjoyed the large room, the great homemade bread and the Jacuzzi. We will highly recommend it to others."* (F.Barton)

"Great hospitality. (They) have a beautiful home and I enjoyed every minute that I was there. Whether it be relaxing in the hot tub, feeding the ducks, or just sitting on the porch with a cup of coffee, the peacefulness that exudes from there is very special." (P. Coolidge)

"We arrived in the city late in the evening. Much to our disappointment, our reserved hotel room was nothing like the advertisement. Our search to find appropriate accommodations for honeymooners, we called Diane at Pearson's Pond. This contact not only salvaged our vacation, but offered us an exceptional environment for an intimate hide away. Great place!" (C. Sumrall)

"As a B&B, Pearson's Pond excels in three key areas: Location, accommodation, and hospitality." (G. Brooks)

Matanuska

Yukon Don's B&B Inn
HC 31, Box 5086
2221 Macabon Circle
Matanuska, AK 99654
(907) 376-7472

Type of B&B: Small inn.
Rooms: 5, 1 with private bath.
Rates: 1/$50; 2/$60; Suite/$80.

Rating: B+ or ♛♛ Good, exceeds basic requirements.

Historic Alaskan homestead barn with views of the Talkeetna Mountains is now an unique inn located 35 miles north of Anchorage and 4 miles south of Wasilla. Five guest rooms are available, one with private bath. All rooms are spacious, have pleasant decor, and feature a vast collection of Alaskan memorabilia. A large recreation room offers a TV with VCR, pool table and library of books and videos on Alaska. An outdoor hot tub offers magnificent mountain and water views. Arrangements can be made for guided tour groups. Continental breakfast. Families welcome. No smoking. 1/$50; 2/$60; Suite/$80. Gold dust, cash, personal checks, or traveler's checks accepted. 10% seniors and business travel discounts.

Additional information about B&Bs throughout Arizona is available from Mi Casa, Su Casa (800) 456-0682.

Bisbee

Bisbee Grand Hotel
61 Main Street, Mailing Box 825
Bisbee, AZ 85603
(602) 432-5900 or (800) 421-1909

Type of B&B: Historic hotel with restaurant.
Rooms: 11 ,7 with private baths.
Rates: 1 or 2/$50-95.

Rating: B- or ♛♛ Good, exceeds basic requirements.

Restored to an "Old West" Victorian motif, this 1908 grand hotel is located in historic downtown Bisbee, 90 miles south east of Tucson. Eleven guest rooms are filled with antiques and family heirlooms. Seven offer a private bath. Two large suites on the second floor have canopy beds and claw-foot tubs. Visit the inn's turn-of-the-century ladies parlor or spend the afternoon in the adjacent saloon. The nearby Bisbee Grand Theater is available for business meetings, Murder Mystery weekends, and sometimes is the setting for Old West melodramas. Tour the town with its antique and art shops, drive twenty minutes to explore Tombstone or Ramsey Canyon, or enjoy a tour of the Queen Mine. Bisbee Grand Special coffee, Southwestern eggs, and homemade waffles round out a full breakfast offered in the common area or balcony. Wedding and meeting facilities available. Restricted smoking. 1 or 2/$50-95. AE, MC, V. 20% Corporate discount. Travel agent.

Guests write: *"We were welcomed like family. The hospitality is unsurpassed. The antiques and time and effort in the decorating puts us into a by-gone era when we step in the door. We have especially enjoyed the Murder Mystery Weekends, playing the parts of characters and being a part of the story."*

"This place is charming, romantic, beautiful, and truly Victorian! We spent 3 anniversaries at the Bisbee Grand. The rooms are all beautifully decorated and 3 suites are breath-taking. I highly recommend this immaculately clean inn to everyone who wants an unforgettable evening, weekend, or more!" (E. Lund)

"As a business traveler, it is unique to stay in this type of lodging, but Gail and Bill have met my needs and I find myself looking forward to return trips." (J. Neff)

Phoenix

Westways "Private" Resort Inn
P.O. Box 41624
Phoenix, AZ 85080
(602) 582-3868

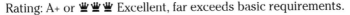

Type of B&B: Inn
Rooms: 6, each with private bath.
Rates: 1 or 2/$50-122.

Rating: A+ or ♛♛♛ Excellent, far exceeds basic requirements.

Contemporary Southwestern Mediterranean style inn has been designed as a mini "private" resort and is located in an executive estate area of Northwest Phoenix, convenient to I-17. Six individually decorated guest rooms are available, each with deluxe private bath, TV, reading area, and fine furnishings. Guests may use the satellite large-screen TV in the leisure room, as well as VCR, table games, stereo, Ping-Pong table, and a selection of books in the library. Enjoy the diving pool, fitness room, and whirlpool, or borrow ten-speed touring bikes to explore the area. Take advantage of the country club privileges including golf and tennis or just relax in the casual western comfort offered in a private atmosphere. Facilities for meetings, executive retreats, and social functions available. 2/$50-122. AE, MC, V. Senior, auto club, and business travel discounts. Travel agent.

Guests write: *"Westways is the place for stepping off the fast track! One has the feeling of exquisite seclusion here. The 'Mexican surprise' breakfast was delicious. Everything in the inn is spotlessly clean. Our hosts saw to every need with welcome refreshments, dinner reservations, turn-down service, extra towels, and information on sightseeing. First-class treatment for sure!"* (J. Yarosit)

"Just picture this...dusk deepening, fountain splashing, stars twinkling, lighted palms reflecting in the pool, a coolness descending as we star-gaze from lounge chairs in absolute silence..." (D. Grehlinger)

"Westways, and the extraordinary service by the two hosts, has created an ambiance reminiscent of days gone by, when warmth and hospitality were a way of life. An oasis of charm and total escape from stress." (J. Blanco)

"Heaven forbid you should be like all the other carbon copies. Westways is not for everyone... its for those who like their vacations to be very special." (D. Kolpin)

"It is always my concern to place my valued clients in a place that I am comfortable in knowing they will get pampered. I have visited this property many times before and have always found it clean and tidy. To me this resort could pass any white glove test." (D. Starkman)

—*Comments continued on next page*

"We have never had the opportunity to experience such hospitality in such a class act atmosphere in our many years of traveling. Our gourmet breakfast daily was more than adequate to carry us through the day until the afternoon in which creative munchies were served. M-mm-good!" (B. Kennedy)

Sedona

Casa Sedona
55 Hozoni Drive
Sedona, AZ 86336
(800)525-3756 or (602)282-2938

Type of B&B: B&B Inn.
Rooms: 11 with private bath.
Rates: 1/$85-140; 2/$95-150.

Rating: A- or ♛♛♛ Excellent, far exceeds basic requirements.

Southwest Spanish hacienda was designed by a Frank Lloyd Wright architect to blend into the surrounding desert beauty. It has outstanding views of the surrounding natural rock formations and is located 120 miles north of Phoenix; 35 miles south of Flagstaff. Each of the eleven guest rooms offer Red Rock views, terraces, private bath, spa and fireplace. Sit and watch a desert sunrise in the Sunrise Alcove or relax in the library with its fireplace and comfortable furniture. Watch television or listen to music in the Sierra Room. The area offers a variety of activities such as sightseeing, shopping, exploring local Native American ruins, jeep touring, hiking, and hot air ballooning. Take a van tour to the Grand Canyon or a scenic airplane ride to view the Red Rocks from the sky. Sedona's resorts offer live entertainment and the town is known for its artist colony and numerous galleries. A full breakfast is served in the dining room or Sunrise Room and often includes Eggs Benedict or bread pudding. Wedding and meeting facilities available. Families welcome. Wheelchair access. No smoking. 1/$85-140; 2/$95-150. MC, V. Senior and auto club discounts.

Additional information about B&Bs throughout Arkansas is available from Ozark Mountain Country B&B (800) 695-1546.

Eureka Springs

The Heartstone Inn and Cottages
35 Kings Highway
Eureka Springs, AR 72632
(501) 253-8916

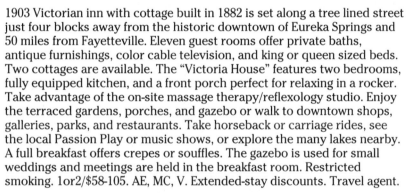

Type of B&B: B&B Inn
Rooms: 11 with private baths and two cottages.
Rates: 1 or 2/$58-105.

Rating: A- or ♛♛♛ Excellent, far exceeds basic requirements.

1903 Victorian inn with cottage built in 1882 is set along a tree lined street just four blocks away from the historic downtown of Eureka Springs and 50 miles from Fayetteville. Eleven guest rooms offer private baths, antique furnishings, color cable television, and king or queen sized beds. Two cottages are available. The "Victoria House" features two bedrooms, fully equipped kitchen, and a front porch perfect for relaxing in a rocker. Take advantage of the on-site massage therapy/reflexology studio. Enjoy the terraced gardens, porches, and gazebo or walk to downtown shops, galleries, parks, and restaurants. Take horseback or carriage rides, see the local Passion Play or music shows, or explore the many lakes nearby. A full breakfast offers crepes or souffles. The gazebo is used for small weddings and meetings are held in the breakfast room. Restricted smoking. 1or2/$58-105. AE, MC, V. Extended-stay discounts. Travel agent.

Guests write: *"One of the finest B&Bs in the state. Iris and Bill are a one-of-a-kind couple; a definite asset to the industry and to the state of Arkansas."* (K. Kraus)

"Outstanding! The best of the eight inns I have stayed at in the past year. Really top-of-the-line breakfast. Very comfortable and outstanding decor. The deck overlooking the trees and forest was beautiful. Parking was very good even though the inn was located on the historic loop. Would stay there again anytime." (D. Dryer)

"The Heartstone is still our favorite. Why? Iris and Bill-always friendly and helpful, the rooms-beautifully decorated and clean, the food-always special and delicious, convenience-on the trolley route. The Heartstone is a jewel!! From the beautifully restored rooms to the bountiful and delicious breakfasts, every detail was perfect." (S. Hembree)

Eureka Springs

Singleton House B&B
11 Singleton
Eureka Springs, AR 72632
(501) 253-9111 or (800) 833-3394

Type of B&B: Inn.
Rooms: 4, 2 with private bath.
Rates: $55-75.

Rating: C+ or Acceptable, meets basic requirements.

1890's Victorian home is now a small inn located in a residential Historic District of this unique artist's colony. Choose from four guest rooms. Two on the ground-floor level each have a private bath. Two rooms on the second floor share a bath. Each room has been simply decorated with folk art and eclectic pieces of furniture and accessories. Walk down a wooded footpath or ride the trolley to quaint shops, cafes, and galleries in town. Nearby attractions include Passion Play, Dinner Train, and Bath House. Hostess owns a B&B reservation agency and can make reservations for attractions and other accommodations throughout the area. Full breakfast. $55-75. AE, MC, V. Travel agent.

Hardy

Olde Stonehouse
511 Main Street
Hardy, AR 72542
(501) 856-2983

Type of B&B: Inn
Rooms: 5 with private bath.
Rates: 1/$50; 2/$55.

Rating: B or ♛♛ Good, exceeds basic requirements.

Historic native stone home is in an old railroad town on the Spring River. The inn is located just a block from the unique shops of Old Hardy Town and across the street from the river. Choose from five individually decorated rooms, each with private bath, queen-size bed, ceiling fan, air conditioning, and period antiques. Curl up on one of the wicker chairs or large rockers found on the two porches to enjoy a good book or to people watch. Walk to antique and gift shops in Old Hardy Town. Take an easy stroll along the river or visit nearby Mammoth Spring, Grand Gulf State Park, Cherokee Village, country music theaters and Indian cultural museum. Nearby recreation includes canoeing, horseback riding and golf. The full breakfast featuring homemade granola, strawberry butter, specialty breads, and a hot entree is served on a lace tablecloth set with Grandma's chinaware and silver. Restricted smoking. 1/$50; 2/$55. MC, V. 10% senior, business, and auto club discount. Special occasion packages and gift certificates available. Travel agent.

Guests write: *"I had a wonderful time. The home is truly lovely, everything was so clean and decorated so lovely, we truly felt at home here. The hostess really went out of her way to leave dessert and coffee for us each night and the food was delicious!"* (L. Hall)

"The breakfast served was wonderful and elegant. We had homebaked bread, German pancakes, cereal, juice, fresh fruit - best I've ever had." (J. Reagan)

"All I can say is that we've been twice and already are talking about when we are going again! They say there is no place like home but this would have to be as close as you can get." (J. Clifton)

"The history and character of the house and furnishings, the delicious food, and the beauty of the Ozarks were only surpassed by the gracious hospitality of our hosts." (S. Payne)

CALIFORNIA

Additional information about B&Bs throughout California is available from Eye Openers B&B Reservations (213) 684-4428.

Alameda

Garratt Mansion
900 Union Street
Alameda, CA 94501
(510) 521-4779

Type of B&B: Inn.
Rooms: 6, 3 with private bath.
Rates: 1/$60-100; 2/$70-120.

Rating: A- or ♛♛♛ Excellent, far exceeds basic requirements.

Victorian inn built in the Colonial Revival style was the home of a turn-of-the-century industrialist and is located just 15 miles east of San Francisco. Choose from six distinctive guest rooms, three of which offer a private bath. Enjoy the local examples of fine architecture or travel to nearby San Francisco, Berkeley, or the beach. Full breakfast specialties of the inn include treats such as "Dutch babies" which are low-fat giant popovers filled each day. All food is prepared with an accent on health using fresh herbs grown on the property and low-fat or non-fat dishes except the delicious fresh baked chocolate chip cookies served each afternoon! Wedding and meeting facilities available. Families welcome. Smoking outside only. 1/$60-100; 2/$70-120. AE, MC, V. Business traveler discount. Travel agent.

Aptos

Bayview Hotel B&B Inn
8041 Soquel Drive
Aptos, CA 95003
(408) 688-8654

Type of B&B: Country inn with restaurant.
Rooms: 7, each with private bath.
Rates: 1/$80-100; 2/$85-125.

Rating: B or ♛♛ Good, exceeds basic requirements.

Historic Victorian inn built in 1878 is a landmark building located in Aptos Village, less than a mile from the Seacliff exit off Route 1, 35 miles south of San Jose. Choose from seven guest rooms, each offering a private bath and antique furnishings. Area attractions include antique shops, fine restaurants, state beaches, redwood parks, hiking and bicycle trails, golf, and tennis. Buffet-style breakfast is served in the restaurant on the lower level and includes fresh squeezed juice, seasonal fruit, egg dish, muesli, pastries, and gourmet coffee. Restaurant on premises. No smoking. 1/$80-100; 2/$85-125. MC, V. Travel agent.

Aptos

Mangels House
570 Aptos Creek Road
P.O. Box 302
Aptos, CA 95001
(408) 688-7982

Type of B&B: Inn.
Rooms: 5 with private bath.
Rates: 1 or 2/$96-120

Rating: A- or ♛♛♛ Excellent, far exceeds basic requirements.

Four acres of orchards and woodlands near Monterey Bay's sailing and surfing is the setting for this Southern-style Colonial inn built circa 1880. Five guest rooms are available with private bath. This location is ideal as a retreat from city life and is known for the local summer music and theater festivals. Excellent restaurants can be found nearby as well as the North Monterey Bay's forests and beaches. Full breakfast and an evening sherry are offered. Restricted smoking. 1 or 2/$96-120. MC, V. Travel agent.

Guests write: *"We arrived in the rain and were right away offered tea which appeared on a teacart with little tarts fresh out of the oven - plus a most welcome decanter of Dubonnet. The beauty of the place and the warmth of the host and hostess made a cozy evening in the flooding storm."* (G. Wheeler)

"Claus Mangel's soul may grace this home but the hosts are its heart. Because of Mr. Mangel, I was able to give my wife the tranquillity of a redwood forest, but the hosts provided the lovely garden to walk through. Mr. Mangel constructed the high ceilings, redwood floor and grand fireplace, but it was the hosts who lit the hearth whenever we returned from an outing. I mentioned my wife's birthday, then magically she found three dozen roses in our room with a card signed by me. Was it my hosts or the Mangel's ghost that pulled that one off?" (C. Accardi)

Arnold

Lodge at Manuel Mill
1573 White Pines Road
Arnold, CA 95223
(209) 795-2622 or (209) 795-3935

Type of B&B: Small lodge.
Rooms: 5, each with private bath.
Rates: 1 or 2/$85-105.

Rating: A- or ♛♛♛ Excellent, far exceeds basic requirements.

Log lodge resort overlooks a 3.5 acre old mill pond and is located southwest of Sacramento in the Stanislaus National Forest, 2 miles northwest of Highway 4. The lodge is situated well off the main highway and is reached by following an old logging gravel road. Choose from five guest rooms, each with private bath, select antiques, and views of the pond. The parlor has a massive stone fireplace and an adjoining dining area. Guests enjoy gathering on the extensive outdoor decks for relaxation and breakfast. The area offers hiking, mountain biking, fishing in the stocked pond, boating and swimming. Calaveras Big Trees State Park with its giant sequoias is a short drive away as are the Columbia Historic State Park, Moaning, Mercer, and California caverns, Bear Valley skiing and ice skating. Full ranch breakfast features fresh eggs from the barnyard, and fresh home-grown fruits and vegetables. An outdoor

setting is offered for small weddings and meetings. No smoking.
1 or 2/$85-105. 10% senior discount.

Guests write: *"The natural splendor and beauty of the property was breathtaking with its towering green pines as far as the eye could see and running brook next to the lodge. Our guest room was charming with its lace curtains, wood floors and four-poster canopy bed."* (J. Horist)

Baywood Park

Baywood Bed & Breakfast Inn
1370 2nd Street
Baywood Park, CA 93402
(805) 528-8888

Type of B&B: Contemporary country inn.
Rooms: 15 with private bath.
Rates: 1 or 2/$80-140.

Rating: A or ♛♛♛ Excellent, far exceeds basic requirements.

Newly constructed contemporary inn sits on Morro Bay overlooking the coastal mountains near the San Luis Obispo area of Southern California. Fifteen guest rooms are available with individual decor and theme. Each offers a private bath, queen-size bed, sitting area, wood-burning fireplace, and kitchenette stocked with snacks and beverages. Eleven rooms offer a bay view. Visit nearby San Luis Obispo, Hearst Castle, and Montano De Oro Park. Continental breakfast and afternoon wine and cheese offered. Additional meals are available in the restaurant on the lower level. Families welcome. Wheelchair access. No smoking. 1 or 2/$80-140.

Guests write: *"Our room, the Appalachian, was beautiful. I rarely drink coffee but I have dreams of theirs and their absolutely wonderful croissants. And best of all there was no TV which "forced" us to go out and enjoy their beautiful surroundings. Everything was great, great, great!"* (B. Kudlo)

"Our unique room was decorated beautifully and was both cozy and clean. We loved the big canopy bed and ocean view. We had dinner delivered both nights so that we could eat at our table by the fireplace. I recommend it to anyone wanting a quiet romantic retreat." (S. Nuttall)

"We especially enjoyed the evening wine and cheese and room tour. Our room was just lovely and very comfortable." (L. Painter)

"All rooms are uniquely decorated. Our favorite is the Manhattan Suite with its cool mauve, gray, and white decor. A few feet out the front door is the bay and the block-long business district is filled with wonderful shops and outstanding restaurants. We can arrive on a Friday night, park our car and not drive again until Sunday when we head for home." (S. Baldwin)

Berkeley

Elmwood House
2609 College Avenue
Berkeley, CA 94704
(510) 540-5123
Fax (510) 540-5123

Type of B&B: B&B home.
Rooms: 4, 2 with private bath.
Rates: 1/$55-75; 2/$65-85.

Rating: B or Good, exceeds basic requirements.

Redwood home built in 1902 is located near the fashionable Elmwood shopping district and Berkeley campus of the University of California. Choose from four guest rooms, each with private telephone and two with a private bath. Walk to an eclectic collection of ethnic restaurants, specialty shops, and evening entertainment areas. Public transit is available right nearby to San Francisco and all Bay Area attractions and off-street parking is available for your car if you drive to the area. Enjoy nearby golf, tennis, swimming, hiking, and bicycling. Continental breakfast. Facilities for small weddings and meetings. No smoking. 1/$55-75; 2/$65-85. MC, V.

Bridgeport

The Cain House
11 Main Street
Bridgeport, CA 93517
(619) 932-7040 or (800) 433-2246.

Type of B&B: Inn
Rooms: 6 with private bath.
Rates: 1 or 2/$80-135.

Rating: A or Excellent, far exceeds basic requirements.

Historic home built in the 1930's is located off Route 182 in the Eastern Sierra Mountains near the California/Nevada border. Each of the six guest rooms with private bath has been restored and features wicker, white washed pine, oak, and other antique furnishings. The newest room offers a private entrance and large canopy bed. Enjoy complimentary wine and cheese in front of the fireplace in the parlor, relax in the hot tub, or watch the beautiful sunsets over the Eastern Sierra Mountains. Area attractions include fishing, hunting, and skiing. Yosemite, Bodie Ghost Town, and Mammoth Mountains are located nearby. A full country breakfast is offered. Families welcome. No smoking. 1 or 2/$80-135. AE, MC, V. Travel agent.

Cambria

The Blue Whale Inn
6736 Moonstone Beach Drive
Cambria, CA 93428
(805) 927-4647

Type of B&B: Inn.
Rooms: 6 with private bath.
Rates: 1 or 2/$135-165.

Rating: A+ or ♛♛♛ Excellent, far exceeds basic requirements.

Contemporary Cape Cod style inn built in 1990 is located 6 miles south of Hearst Castle, mid-way between San Francisco and Los Angeles on the Central California Coast. Each of the six guest rooms offer a private tiled bath with garden window, fireplace, canopied bed draped with French and English fabrics, as well as an armoire with hidden television, a writing desk, and an oversized dressing room. Visit with other guests in the dining, living, and library areas and enjoy the panoramic view of the ocean while having English tea. Explore the scenic Big Sur coast, nearby wineries and art galleries, and the famous Hearst Castle. A full breakfast features such specialties as gingerbread pancakes with lemon sauce and whipped cream, Blueberry crepes, Mexican quiche, Eggs Benedict, or thick French toast with sautéed apples and sour cream. No smoking. 1 or 2/$135-165. MC, V.

Guests write: *"My wife and I recently spent one of the most enjoyable weekends we have ever had at the Blue Whale Inn. The room was immaculate and the breakfast superb. We were made extremely welcome and comfortable by the owner and innkeepers. We have traveled the world and would highly recommend this inn to our friends."* (J. Whitaker)

Davenport

New Davenport B&B Inn
31 Davenport Avenue
Davenport, CA 95017
(408) 425-1818 or 426-4122

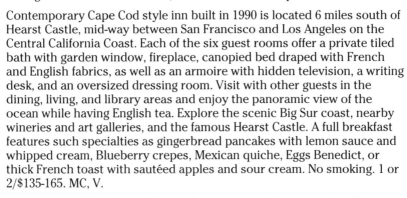

Type of B&B: Inn.
Rooms: 12, each with private bath.
Rates: 1 or 2/$60-115.

Rating: B or ♛♛ Good, exceeds basic requirements.

The New Davenport Cash Store and Restaurant is located halfway between San Francisco and Carmel on Coast Highway 1. Twelve guest rooms are available on the second floor of the main building or in the adjacent guest house. Each room offers a private bath and is furnished with antiques, ethnic treasures, collectibles, and local arts and crafts. Several rooms above the Cash Store have views of the ocean across the road. The store on the main level offers a large variety of folk art, textiles, pottery, and jewelry. Area attractions include a secluded local beach, state redwood parks for hiking and picnics, seasonal whale watching, and elephant seal tours at Nuevo State Reserve. Full breakfast. No smoking. 1 or 2/$60-115. AE, MC, V.

Eureka

Old Town Bed & Breakfast Inn
1521 Third Street
Eureka, CA 95501
(707) 445-3951 or (800) 331-5098

Type of B&B: Inn.
Rooms: 7, 5 with private bath.
Rates: 1/$60-120; 2/$75-130.

Rating: A- or ♛♛♛ Excellent, far exceeds basic requirements.

Greek Revival Italianate built in 1871 is on a quiet residential street in the heart of Eureka's Old Town, a city located on the Northern California coast, 280 miles north of San Francisco on Highway 101. Choose from seven guest rooms, five with private bath. Carlotta's Room is the inn's largest room and ideal for special occasions as it features a king-size brass bed, antiques, private bath, and a lavender and lace decor. The Maxfield Parrish room features Maxfield Parrish artwork and oak antiques. Gerri's room is quite spacious and features a collection of stuffed animals, king-size bed, and private bath with shower. The decor throughout each room combines whimsy with good fun which is evident by the Teddy Bears on each bed and rubber ducks by the bathtubs. An outdoor hot tub is surrounded by a privacy fence. Visit the nearby Redwood National Park, King Range Wilderness, and other Pacific Coast attractions. Full breakfast. No smoking. 1/$60-120; 2/$75-130. MC, V. Business traveler discount. Travel agent.

Guests write: *"Dianne helps Jeff return to his childhood with his favorite breakfast of "Green Eggs and Ham" and Leigh serves it like a character right out of Dr. Seuss. It's one of the high points of our visits."* (P. Beardsley)

"His hat. It was totally unexpected. I rang the doorbell and soon this visage wearing a tall hat appeared through the glass of the front door. It was a black hat with a broad, colored band above its brim. A tour ensued with directions for our stay. Delightful, especially the computer-produced banner hanging on our room wall wishing us a happy 20th Anniversary. After breakfast my wife

— *Comments continued on next page*

and I took our leave and, with our luggage, carried out a very special set of anniversary memories — no small part being 'the hat'." (D. Hascall)

"If anyone has ever been unhappy in a B&B and said they would never try another, try this one and your mind will be changed." (R. Wayman)

"Leigh and Diane Benson have fine-tuned B&B innkeeping to an art form. All the requisite things are here, but the inn has a personality and a sense of humor all it's own. The rest of the B&B industry should learn from these folks - they are the best." (H. Sharp)

"Our room, Carlota's Room, was charming and the brass featherbed was so comfortable. The bathroom was in keeping with the house's vintage and was fully stocked. Old Town B&B is not cheap, but it is a superb value." (M. McAuley)

"How to put it in a nutshell? We can't get over how the hominess feels like Grandma's. But there's something else - a touch of eccentricity that plays a big part in this B&B. We enjoyed everything from Vincent van Bear to the rose petals in the toilet. If Grandma ever could've cut loose, this is the way she would have lived." (N. Jackson)

"Every day the most delicious truffles would appear on the dresser. Made the whole room smell yummy! Lots of stuffed bears lounging on the bed and a huge stack of country magazines to read. The location is within walking distance to the beach and downtown restaurants. We go for the famous kinetic sculpture race and the contestants pedal by in front of the B&B." (A. Lehman)

"We drove up in our '56 T-Bird. It was raining heavily and the innkeepers were kind enough to garage our car so the leaks yet to be fixed in its restoration wouldn't destroy the interior. We've never had such first-class treatment!" (A. Richards)

"On our last visit they arranged for a guided tour of Old Town Eureka. We saw places that aren't usually available to visitors - or even locals!" (R. Simonds)

Ferndale

Shaw House
703 Main Street, P.O. Box 1125
Ferndale, CA 95536
(707) 786-9958

Type of B&B: Inn
Rooms: 6, 4 with private bath.
Rates: 1 or 2/$65-125.

Rating: A- or ♛♛♛ Excellent, far exceeds basic requirements.

Gabled Gothic inn with jutting gables, bay windows, and several balconies was built in 1854. The property is listed on the National Register of Historic Places and is situated on a one-acre landscaped lot in the village. Choose from six guest rooms, four with private bath. One large room is especially suitable for families. All feature floral wallpaper, quilted bedspreads, and fresh flowers. Relax on a secluded deck overlooking the creek or explore the beautiful gardens. Walk to village antique shops, galleries and restaurants. Area attractions include Avenue of the Giants, Pacific Ocean, Humboldt Bay, redwood forests, and wilderness hikes. Homemade continental breakfast. No smoking. 1 or 2/$65-125. AE, MC, V. Travel agent.

Ferndale

The Gingerbread Mansion Bed and Breakfast Inn
400 Berding Street
Ferndale, CA 95536
(707)786-4000 or (707)786-4006

Type of B&B: B&B Inn
Rooms: 9 with private bath.
Rates:1/$55-160; 2/$70-185.

Rating: A or ♛♛♛ Excellent, far exceeds basic requirements.

1890's Victorian Queen Anne inn is located in the State Historical Landmark Village of Ferndale. The inn is famous for its classic "gingerbread" details such as carved, gabled turrets and an elaborately landscaped English garden. All of the nine guest rooms offer a private bath and individual decor theme. Special features of some rooms include beveled and stained-glass windows, fireplaces, claw-foot tubs, and French windows. One room has a private stairway leading to a sitting room upstairs. Another room features "his" and "hers" claw-foot tubs. Guests are treated to many "little extras" such as bubble bath, bathrobes, and bedside chocolates. Enjoy the quiet privacy offered where no television or radio is present to interrupt conversation or games being played in any of the four Victorian parlors. Borrow the inn's bikes to tour the historic town. Nearby parks offer many types of recreation. Within driving distance is the ocean and redwood forest. A continental breakfast is served each morning and includes three baked items as well as fresh fruit and boiled eggs. No smoking. 1/$55-160;2/$70-185. AE, MC, V. Travel agent.

Fort Bragg

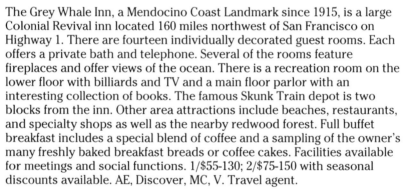

Grey Whale Inn
615 North Main Street
Fort Bragg, CA 95437
(707) 964-0640 or (800) 382-7244

Type of B&B: Inn
Rooms: 14, each with private bath.
Rates: 1/$55-130; 2/$75-150.

Rating: A- or ♛♛♛ Excellent, far exceeds basic requirements.

The Grey Whale Inn, a Mendocino Coast Landmark since 1915, is a large Colonial Revival inn located 160 miles northwest of San Francisco on Highway 1. There are fourteen individually decorated guest rooms. Each offers a private bath and telephone. Several of the rooms feature fireplaces and offer views of the ocean. There is a recreation room on the lower floor with billiards and TV and a main floor parlor with an interesting collection of books. The famous Skunk Train depot is two blocks from the inn. Other area attractions include beaches, restaurants, and specialty shops as well as the nearby redwood forest. Full buffet breakfast includes a special blend of coffee and a sampling of the owner's many freshly baked breakfast breads or coffee cakes. Facilities available for meetings and social functions. 1/$55-130; 2/$75-150 with seasonal discounts available. AE, Discover, MC, V. Travel agent.

Guests write: *"The breakfast was perfect, not too hearty - not too light for starting a full-day of business. The buffet style was relaxed and convenient since my day started very early. The staff took very clear and concise phone messages for me, even after 5:00 p.m."* (R. Middleton)

"As career people we need to bring the romance back into our marriage. Our stay at the Grey Whale Inn met our expectations and more! We departed feeling the same way when we returned from our honeymoon."
(M. Harmon)

Geyserville

Campbell Ranch Inn
1475 Canyon Road
Geyersville, CA 95441
(707)857-3476

Type of B&B: B&B Inn.
Rooms: 5 with private bath.
Rates: 1/$90-135; 2/$100-145.

Rating: A or ♛♛♛ Excellent, far exceeds basic requirements.

California-style country home is situated on a hilltop estate of 35 acres. This area of Sonoma County is famous for its vineyards and is an easy 80 mile drive north of San Francisco. Five guest rooms each offer a private bath, king-size bed, fresh flowers and fruit. Most rooms feature a balcony with views of the surrounding countryside with its gently rolling hills. The newest guest suite is in a cottage and offers a private entrance, large balcony, sitting area, and fireplace. Guests enjoy gathering in the main living room with fireplace, playing tennis on the professional court, swimming in the large swimming pool, and unwinding in the hot tub spa with a complimentary iced tea or lemonade. Hiking, horseshoes, Ping-Pong, and bicycling are available. Visit nearby wineries, Russian River, and Lake Sonoma. This is a good central location for taking day trips to the coast, Mendicino, or the Napa Valley. A full breakfast is served and homemade dessert and coffee or tea are offered each evening. Families welcome. No smoking. 1/$90-135; 2/$100-145. MC, V. Travel agent.

Groveland

The Groveland Hotel
18767 Main Street, P.O. Box 481
Groveland, CA 95321
(209) 962-4000 or (800) 273-3314
Fax (209) 962-6674

Type of B&B: Country Inn with restaurant
Rooms: 17 with private bath.
Rates: 1 or 2/$75-155.

Rating: A- or ♛♛♛ Excellent, far exceeds basic requirements.

Historic 1849 Adobe-Monterey Colonial with 1914 Queen Anne wood-frame addition is found on Groveland's historic Main Street, less than one hour from Yosemite National Park and near Sonora. The hotel has been fully restored and offers seventeen guest rooms as well as a full-service restaurant. Each guest room offers a private bath, European antique furnishings, down comforter, and decor featuring Victorian-style fabric. There are three suites with fireplace and spa tub. A small second-floor parlor with fireplace offers a spot to converse with other guests or view television. Other common areas include the restaurant, historic saloon, courtyard, and conference room. Recreation in the surrounding area includes tennis, golfing, white water rafting, fishing, and hiking. Local history is reflected in the area's antique stores as well as in the Historic Gold Country. Arrangements can be made for day-long bus tour of Yosemite. Continental breakfast includes fresh croissants, breads, and seasonal fruit. A full service restaurant offers additional gourmet meals. Wedding and meeting facilities available with a private entrance, coffee service, and audio-visual materials provided. Families welcome. Wheelchair access. No smoking. 1 or 2/$75-155. AE, MC, V. Travel agent.

Laguna Beach

Eiler's Inn
741 South Coast Highway
Laguna Beach CA 92651
(714) 494-3004

Type of B&B: Inn.
Rooms: 11, plus 1 suite, each with private bath.
Rates: 1/$80-165; 2/$85-175.

Rating: B+ or ♛♛ Good, exceeds basic requirements.

Eiler's Inn is situated near the beach in the heart of this city located less than one hour south of Los Angeles off Highway 1. The New Orleans style architecture features eleven guest rooms with private bath and individual decor. Special touches include antiques, unusual linens, fresh flowers, fruit, and candies. A large second-floor suite opens onto a spacious balcony with ocean views. Laguna Beach is famous as an art colony and has many galleries to explore. Full gourmet breakfast served each morning. Sun tea and coffee are available all day and wine and cheese each evening in the flower-scented brick courtyard with bubbling fountain. Families welcome. 1/$80-165; 2/$85-175. AE, MC, V. Travel agent.

Lotus

Golden Lotus Bed & Breakfast
PO Box 830, 1006 Lotus Road
Lotus, CA 95651-0830
(916) 621-4562

Type of B&B: B&B Inn.
Rooms: 6 with private bath.
Rates: 1/$75-90; 2/$80-95.

Rating: B or ♛♛ Good, exceeds basic requirements.

Golden Lotus B&B is just 30 miles east of Sacramento and 1 mile from Highway 49 on the South Fork of the American River between Placerville and Auburn. This two-story brick and frame pre-Victorian Cottage was built in 1857, not far from where gold was discovered in 1848. Each of the six guest rooms with private bath reflect a different theme such as the "Orient Express" with its blue and white porcelain and Chinese screens or the "Secret Garden" with its wicker/pine and lattice garden room, private entrance, and sitting room. The upstairs landing and a small library room filled with over 5,000 books are available for reading, relaxing, or playing board games. Guests enjoy walking to the river and old Indian campgrounds as well as exploring the grounds with flower and herb gardens, benches, swings, and Victorian gazing globes. Rafting, kayaking, and panning for gold are very popular activities in this area. Lotus is a small town with a Western feel and has a river rock antique-gift store, two frame buildings, and the 1855 "Red brick" restaurant which once housed a general store for gold miners. A full breakfast often includes apple sausage, Dutch pancakes, or crepes and is served in the library, on the verandah, or in the "Red Brick" which seats forty and is often used for meetings and weddings. Families welcome. 1/$75-90; 2/$80-95. Travel agent.

Guests write: " *The inn is in a lovely brick house next to a beautiful old gold rush store building which were both built during the California Gold Rush. Needless to say, as an antique lover, a history buff, and an enthusiastic gardener, I'm in heaven! Our favorite room is the Garden Room with windows on three sides. It's a great place to calm our city-frazzled nerves!"* (C. Kipp)

"The 'Secret Garden' was an excellent choice for our honeymoon. The privacy was provided in an elegant and intimate setting. The gourmet breakfasts were excellent and the hospitality of our hosts have made bed and breakfasts our choice of lodging." (A. Pierce)

"Each room is distinctive in the decor. The 'Westward Ho' room is like stepping into the days of Jesse James and offers cozy comfort. The 'Orient Express' room with the magnificent oriental screens and furnishings offer elegance and richness. Will I return to the Golden Lotus? You bet I will. I still want to stay in the 'Wish Upon' room." (L. Taylor Hartley)

Murphys

Dunbar House, 1880
P.O. Box 1375, 271 Jones Street
Murphys, CA 95247
(209) 728-2897

Type of B&B: Inn.
Rooms: 4 with private bath.
Rates: 1 or 2/$105-145.

Rating: A or ♨♨♨ Excellent, far exceeds basic requirements.

Italianate-style home built in 1880 is located southwest of Sacramento, 8 miles east of Angel's Camp on Highway 4. All four guest rooms offer a private bath and are decorated with antiques, lace, down comforters, and offer a TV/VCR with classic video collection, wood-burning stove, central air conditioning, and refrigerator stocked with a bottle of local wine. The Cedar Room is a two-room suite with a large two-person Jacuzzi. Relax on the wide porches or in front of the fire in the parlor. Calaveras Big Trees State Park nearby offers outdoor activities such as hiking, fishing, and skiing. Explore local wineries, historic towns, and caverns. Full breakfast may include house specialties such as crab cheese delight, fruit kuchen, muffins, and fresh fruit. It's served either in the fireplaced dining room or in the pleasant century-old garden. Restricted smoking. 1 or 2/$105-145. V, MC. Travel agent.

Guests write: *"The atmosphere is warm and comfortable, the breakfasts were superb. I especially enjoyed the view from our windows. My husband and I strolled the garden, sat on the swing under a tree and rocked, and read on the porch. Leisure time like we had here is very precious to us."* (L Prinvale)

"Leaving the cold and fog of the valley behind, we came into sunshine and the warmth of Dunbar House hospitality. The is the perfect place to celebrate 30 years of marriage! If you think B&B stands for bed and breakfast, then you haven't stayed at Dunbar House long enough. We know that B&B stands for Bob and Barbara." (E. Moore)

"My favorite memories will be curling up in the chair by the fire with my book as the rain poured down, the wonderful music playing in the background, and all the yummy smells coming out of the kitchen." (C. Rucker)

"Eating the gourmet breakfasts in the garden is a wonderful start to each day. Also enjoyed reading for an hour in the garden at the end of a busy day of sightseeing - so relaxing!" (P. Schuck)

"Everything from the down comforter to the large claw-foot tub filled with bubbles was thoroughly enjoyed. The food was downright delicious." (D. Anderson)

"The porch outside our room is one of my favorite parts of this inn. Sitting out there in the late afternoon with a glass of the local wine and the wonderful appetizers, reading, playing checkers, or just visiting with your spouse is such a relaxing and wonderful treat! We've stayed in more elaborate places, but not many with such a warm comfortable feeling." (P. Schaller)

Napa

Hennessey House Bed & Breakfast Inn
1727 Main Street
Napa, CA 94559
(707) 226-3774, Fax (707) 226-2975.

Type of B&B: Inn
Rooms: 10, 9 with private bath.
Rates: 1 or 2/$85-150.

Rating: A- or ♛♛♛ Excellent, far exceeds basic requirements.

Queen Anne Victorian inn is listed on the National Register of Historic Places and located in California's famous wine country, 50 miles northeast of San Francisco. Choose from ten guest rooms which offer contemporary comfort blended with 1890's style. Nine of the rooms have a private bath and several feature working fireplaces, claw-foot tubs or whirlpool baths. Relax in the parlor with its cozy seating and varied selection of books and games. A guest sauna is available on the back porch and there are rental bicycles for touring the area. Walk to the famous Napa Valley Wine Train. Other area attractions include balloon rides, mud baths, golf, tennis, and winery touring. Full breakfast includes a hot entree and is served in the dining room which features a hand-painted tin ceiling. Small wedding and meeting facilities available. Restricted smoking. 1 or 2/$85-150. MC, V. 10% senior discount. Travel agent.

Guests write: *"Breakfasts were superb in variety, quality, well-garnished, and presented and there was attention to personal preferences and dietary needs. Our room was large, well-maintained, and clean. We liked the period furnishings, skylight, fireplace, large Jacuzzi tub, tile floor, twin sinks, and fireplace. The gardens, well-lit staircases and parking areas, sauna, common room, and Heritage House added to the charm and pleasure of our stay and we appreciated the chance to use the bicycles."* (B. Dancik)

"Our room was tastefully decorated. The vanity in the bathroom was an old sideboard transformed into a vanity with two sinks. The location was perfect for visiting the wineries. The hostess was very willing to make a special breakfast dish for me which I had not informed her of until my arrival." (R. Faulkner)

Napa

La Belle Epoque
1386 Calistoga Avenue
Napa, CA 94559
(707) 257-2161

Type of B&B: Inn.
Rooms: 6 with private bath.
Rates: 1 or 2/$108-140.

Rating: A or ♛♛♛ Excellent, far exceeds basic requirements.

Queen Anne Victorian inn built in 1893 is located in the Historic District near the town center, just off Route 29. Choose from six guest rooms, each with private bath and period furnishings. The home is a fine example of Victorian architecture and features multi-gabled dormers, high-hipped roof, decorative carvings, and original stained-glass windows. The inn boasts a wine tasting room and cellar, a large dining room with piano, and a comfortable parlor where refreshments are served each afternoon. Area attractions include wine tasting, hot air ballooning, mud and mineral baths, boutiques, gourmet restaurants, and Napa Valley Wine Train. Full breakfast. No smoking. Facilities available for small meetings and social functions. Off-street parking available on the property. 1 or 2/$108-140. AE, Discover, MC, V. 10% business travel and senior discounts. Travel agent.

Guests write: *"Thank you for making our honeymoon just that bit more special. The room was great, the food marvelous, and the wine and appetizers the best yet."* (L. Buehler)

"Breakfasts were delicious and unique. The freshly ground coffee was great! The wine tasting in the evening was a nice way to unwind before dinner. Thank you for the ride to and from the Wine Train and also for loaning us your umbrella. It was the extra special care that made our stay a truly wonderful experience." (L. Bina)

Newport Beach

Portofino Beach Hotel
2306 West Oceanfront
Newport Beach, CA 92663
(714) 673-7030

Type of B&B: Inn.
Rooms: 15 with private bath.
Rates: 1 or 2/$85-235.

Rating: A+ or ♛♛♛ Excellent, far exceeds basic requirements.

Portofino Beach Hotel is on the oceanfront and boardwalk of this fashionable beach town which is located just south of Los Angeles and fifteen minutes from the Orange County Airport. Fifteen guest rooms or suites are available. Each offers telephone, TV, private bath, and individual decor featuring lovely fabrics and antiques. Several rooms include marble baths with Jacuzzis, private sun decks, and fireplaces. Beach chairs and towels are available for a day on the beach. Walk the boardwalk to visit nearby art galleries, bookstores, boutiques, and historical sites. Disneyland is a short thirty minute drive and sailing, golf, and tennis are available nearby. Continental breakfast buffet includes fresh fruit, yogurt, and croissants. Facilities are available for meetings and weddings. 1 or 2/$85-235. AE, MC, V. Travel agent.

Pacific Grove

Gosby House Inn
643 Lighthouse Ave.
Pacific Grove, CA 93950
(408) 375- 1287

Type of B&B: Large B&B Inn.
Rooms: 22, 20 with private baths.
Rates: 1 or 2/$ 85-150.

Rating: B+ or ♛♛ Good, exceeds basic requirements.

Queen Anne Victorian constructed in 1884 in located in the heart of this seaside town on the Monterey Peninsula, and only a few blocks from the ocean. Twenty-two guest rooms are available. Twenty offer a private bath and each room has been individually decorated with antique furniture, print wallpaper, and ruffled curtains. Some rooms feature a fireplace or a private entrance with a flower-filled patio. Two new suites feature fireplaces, large bathrooms with Jacuzzi tubs, and balconies. Special amenities include evening turndown, home-baked cookies, a morning paper, and terry robes. Explore the Monterey Peninsula, drive to Carmel and the 17 Mile Drive, or walk to the aquarium and several well-known restaurants. Muffins, quiches, French toast, and mueseli round out a full breakfast and afternoon tea is a daily tradition. Small wedding and meeting facilities available. Families welcome. No smoking. 1 or 2/$ 85-150. AE, MC, V. Travel agent.

Guests write: *"Our stay was wonderful. The rooms are authentically decorated with attention to detail and comfort. The staff was very congenial and accommodating. We left with the feeling we'd love to return."* (J. Morgan)

Palo Alto

Adella Villa
P.O. Box 4528
Stanford, CA 94309
(415) 321-5195, Fax (415) 325-5121

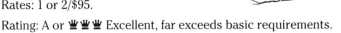

Type of B&B: Private estate.
Rooms: 3 with private bath.
Rates: 1 or 2/$95.

Rating: A or ♛ ♛ ♛ Excellent, far exceeds basic requirements.

Large Tyrolean villa on an acre estate was built in 1920 and is located 25 miles south of San Francisco near US-101 and I-280. Three guest rooms provide private baths, (one with Jacuzzi tub), remote color TV, radio, and phone. The Champagne Room with mini-kitchen has double French doors leading to the solar-heated swimming pool. Explore the estate with its surrounding trees, manicured gardens, and Japanese Koi pond or relax on the verandah while taking in the view. Area attractions include Silicon Valley, San Francisco, Stanford University, and Filoli Mansion. Full breakfast is served in the sunny breakfast room overlooking the fountain and gardens. Airport pickup available. Restricted smoking. 1 or 2/$95. AE, MC, V. 10% business travel and senior discounts. Travel agent.

Guests write: *"This was a very pleasant experience and my first stay at a B&B. It was a home away from home with breakfast served in a pleasant nook with a view of the grounds. My room was large with many personal touches — books, guides to the area, bric-a-brac, and a decanter of sherry. I had the run of the house and fresh fruit, coffee, and juice were always available."* (J. Stevens)

Red Bluff

Faulkner House
1029 Jefferson Street
Red Bluff, CA 96080
(916) 529-0520

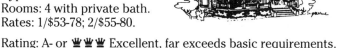

Type of B&B: Inn.
Rooms: 4 with private bath.
Rates: 1/$53-78; 2/$55-80.

Rating: A- or ♛♛♛ Excellent, far exceeds basic requirements.

Red Bluff is in Northern California about thirty miles south of Redding. Faulkner House is a Queen Anne Victorian home built in 1890 and is located one mile off I-5 near downtown. Choose from four antique-filled guest rooms with private bath. Special features of the individually decorated rooms include carved bedroom sets, wicker accessories, and a brocade fainting couch. The formal parlor or screened-in porch are great places to relax and meet other guests while enjoying afternoon refreshments. Within walking distance are restaurants, antique and specialty shops, and a historic house tour. Full breakfast includes oranges from the trees in the yard, homemade muffins, and a baked egg dish with meat. Facilities for meetings, weddings, and receptions. No smoking. 1/$53-78; 2/$55-80. Travel agent.

Redding

Palisades Paradise B&B
1200 Palisades Ave.
Redding, CA 96003
(800) 382-4649 or (916) 223-5305

Type of B&B: Private Home.
Rooms: 2 share 1½ baths.
Rates: 1/$55-70; 2/$60-70.

Rating: B or ♛♛ Good, exceeds basic requirements.

Contemporary home overlooks the Sacramento River, is surrounded by mountains, and located 160 miles north of Sacramento and 100 miles south of the Oregon border. Two guest rooms share a full and half bath. The suite offers a panoramic view of the city on the Bluffs of the Sacramento River, has a sitting area and a fifty-foot patio with spa. Both rooms offer contemporary furnishings and a few antique pieces. The fireplaced living room has a wide screen television. Guests also enjoy relaxing on the porch swing, or soaking in the garden spa. Visit nearby

Mt. Lassen Park, Shasta Lake and Caverns, or raft or water ski on the Sacramento River. Expanded continental breakfast on weekdays and full breakfast on weekends may feature the house specialty, Palisades fruit puffs. Families welcome. Restricted smoking. 1/$55-70; 2/$60-70. AE, MC, V. 10% senior or corporate discount. Travel agent.

Guests write: *"Our room was large and comfortable, the breakfasts were delicious and our innkeeper very hospitable. The real high-point of our stay was relaxing under the stars in the hot tub after a long day of hiking. The inn overlooks the twinkling lights of Redding and a river—you could see all of that from our room."* (A. Horvath)

"We had a lovely stay. The hospitality exceeds the traditional 'Southern Hospitality' which is a high compliment coming from two dyed-in-the-wool southerners." (J. Beasley and J. Scarlett)

"This was the most rewarding bed & breakfast experience in our 6 years of 'Bed & Breakfasting' from coast to coast in the USA. The breakfast of 'Palisades Fruit Puffs' was really out of this world." (H. Evans)

"The setting was outstanding and that was just the beginning of a wonderful stay. We were made to feel "at home" and really enjoyed the hot tub and delicious breakfast." (K. Erlewine)

San Diego

The Cottage
3829 Albatross Street
San Diego, CA 92103
(619) 299-1564

Type of B&B: B&B home and cottage.
Rooms: 2 with private bath.
Rates: 1 or 2/$49-75.

Rating: B+ or ♛♛ Good, exceeds basic requirements.

Redwood cottage built in 1913 is located on a cul-de-sac in the Hillcrest section of the city. The cottage can accommodate three and offers a bath, fully equipped kitchen, pump organ, wood-burning stove, and Victorian style furnishings. A guest room with private bath and separate entrance is also available in the main house. Area attractions include San Diego Zoo, Balboa Park, airport, beaches, and day trips into Mexico. Continental breakfast features freshly baked bread and seasonal fruit. Families welcome. No smoking. 1 or 2/$49-75. MC, V. Two night minimum stay. Travel agent.

Guests write: *"What a delightful cottage! The flower arrangement and garden added an elegance that was most appreciated. My favorite toy is the coffee machine. The breakfasts - they were special!"* (M. Evans)

"The cottage is a delightful hideaway located in San Diego's Hillcrest District. The proprietor has included many special touches to make each guest's visit unique. A warm fire in the pot belly stove will be on the agenda for our next visit." (J. Stradley)

"I really liked the flowers and the breakfasts, Jonathan and Harry enjoyed the pipe organ and Raya like the couch bunny and the rocks. My husband says this is our best bed and breakfast experience to date." (G. Carr)

"What a delightful way to start the day - a soft knock on the door and a nicely decorated breakfast tray with the yummiest breakfast breads one has ever tasted - muffins, croissants, fresh apple coffee cake, fresh fruit, fresh mint, fresh garden flowers, beautiful dishware, cloth napkins in rings, lace cloths lining the baskets - all served by one who cares!" (M. Oliver)

"Thanks to the Cottage for making the San Diego part of our vacation so comfortable. All the touches in the cottage and those incredible breakfasts, the suggestions of things to do - were terrific." (G. Musselman)

"A memorable four nights in San Diego at the Cottage. Remarkable for a gracious and informative hostess, fresh flowers, luxurious towels, a firm mattress, and last but not least, those decadent breakfasts." (P. Hambly)

"The Cottage has proven to be the best attraction in San Diego not to mention the best bargain! No need to go anywhere else for a sumptuous breakfast." (J. Varner)

San Diego

Heritage Park B&B Inn
2470 Heritage Park Row
San Diego, CA 92110
(619) 299-6832

Type of B&B: Inn.
Rooms: 9, 5 with private bath.
Rates: 1/$80-120; 2/$85-125.

Rating: A or ♛♛♛ Excellent, far exceeds basic requirements.

Famous Old Town in San Diego is the setting for this Queen Anne Victorian home built in 1889. It's situated in an unusual seven-acre park of historic buildings and has some outstanding architectural features. Choose from nine guest rooms, five with private bath. Each is individually decorated with oriental rugs, handmade quilts, period antiques, and Victorian wallpaper. Attractions nearby include San Diego Zoo, Mission Valley, and the San Diego Harbor cruise. Full breakfast is served daily and there is an evening social hour along with classic films available. 1/$80-120; 2/$85-125. MC, V. 10% business travel discount.

San Francisco

Albion House Inn
135 Gough Street
San Francisco, CA 94102
(415) 621-0896

Type of B&B: B&B Inn.
Rooms: 9, 7 with private bath.
Rates: 1 or 2/$75-150.

Rating: B or 👑👑 Good, exceeds basic requirements.

Edwardian brownstone built in 1906 is located in close proximity to the Performing Arts Complex and the Civic Center. Nine guest rooms are available. Seven rooms each offer a private bath, phone, and TV. The high-ceilinged living room with marble fireplace and grand piano is an inviting place to relax with a complimentary beverage. Visit the nearby Performing Arts Complex, Civic Center, opera, symphony, and ballet performances. Restaurants, shops, and art galleries are easily accessible. Homemade muffins, pancakes, and freshly squeezed orange juice are offered in the full breakfast. Small meeting facilities. 1 or 2/$75-150. A, MC, V. Travel agent.

San Francisco

Art Center B&B Suites
1902 Filbert at Laguna
San Francisco, CA 94123
(415) 567-1526 or
(800) 821-3877 for reservations
(415) 921-9023 for questions

Type of B&B: Inn.
Rooms: 5 suites with private bath.
Rates: 1 or 2/$85-115.

Rating: C+ or 👑 Acceptable, meets basic requirements.

French Colonial townhouse built circa 1857 is centrally located in the Marina District. The inn gets its name from the owners who especially cater to art lovers and who run a small private gallery and art studio on the premises. Choose from five guest suites, each with private bath and one with whirlpool bath. Each is casually furnished and includes original art work and fully equipped personal kitchen or breakfast bar. Within walking distance are Union Street shopping with boutiques, antique stores, galleries, and international restaurants. Transportation is available nearby for exploring other parts of this famous city. Fisherman's

Wharf is only a 20 minute stroll away. Prepare your own breakfast at leisure from stocked pantry. Families welcome. No smoking. 1 or 2/$85-115. AE, MC, V. Travel agent.

San Francisco

The Chateau Tivoli
1057 Steiner Street
San Francisco, CA 94115
(415) 776-5462 or (800) 228-1647

Type of B&B: Inn.
Rooms: 5 rooms and 2 suites, 5 private baths.
Rates: 1 or 2/$80-200.

Rating: A or ♛♛♛ Excellent, far exceeds basic requirements.

Victorian mansion, circa 1892, has undergone an authentic period restoration and is located in the Alamo Square Historic District. The inn's five guest rooms and two suites offer a step back into San Francisco's romantic golden age of opulence and are furnished with canopy beds, marble baths, balconies, fireplaces, stained glass, and antiques. Five rooms have a private bath. Walk to a variety of restaurants, shopping, theaters, Golden Gate Park, and Alamo Square Park. A continental breakfast is served weekdays and a full champagne breakfast is served on weekends. Meeting facilities available. Restricted smoking. 1 or 2/$80-200. AE, MC, V. Travel agent.

San Francisco

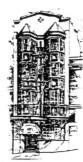

Golden Gate Hotel
775 Bush Street
San Francisco, CA 94108
(415) 392-3702 or (800) 835-1118

Type of B&B: Small urban B&B hotel
Rooms: 23 rooms, 14 have a private bath.
Rates: 1 or 2/$55-89.

Rating: B- or ♛♛ Good, exceeds basic requirements.

Narrow four-story hotel of Edwardian architecture was built in 1913 and is now a small European-style hotel located two blocks north of Union Square and two blocks down from the top of Nob Hill. Choose from twenty-three guest rooms located throughout four floors with access by elevator. There is quite a variety in room size, prices, and amenities but each offers a bay window and fresh flowers; fourteen have a private bath. The small fireplaced parlor on the main floor is where guests enjoy a continental breakfast of fresh coffee and croissants as well as afternoon tea. Walk to many of the city's famous attractions, restaurants, and shops from this location. The main cable car line stops at the corner giving easy access to Fisherman's Wharf, North Beach, and Ghirardelli Square. Families welcome. Restricted smoking. 1 or 2/$55-89. AE, MC, V. Travel agent.

Guests write: *"This has a charming, European feel and was put together with obvious loving care. Loved the tea and the cozy, top-quality breakfast. There was an interesting European-style openwork metal elevator. Best of all, knowledgeable hosts who clearly love what they do and interact graciously with a variety of guests with warmth, humor and grace."* (B. Muc.)

"Gracious atmosphere , good location, gourmet breakfasts; the hosts go out of their way to make guests feel welcome." (A. Eppy)

San Francisco

Jackson Court
2198 Jackson Street
San Francisco, CA 94115
(415) 929-7670

Type of B&B: Inn.
Rooms: 10 with private bath.
Rates: 1 or 2/$108-150.

Rating: A+ or ♛♛♛ Excellent, far exceeds basic requirements.

Jackson Court, a brownstone mansion built in 1901, is now a European-style urban inn located in the Pacific Heights area of the city. Ten individually decorated guest rooms are available. Each offers a private bath, antique furnishings, TV, and telephone. Two rooms feature fireplaces. The Garden Suite on the main floor offers a king-size bed, hand-crafted wood paneling and cabinets, an antique chandelier, and private garden patio with flower beds. Walk to many points of interest within the city or use nearby public transportation. Continental breakfast and afternoon refreshments served daily. $108-150. AE, MC, V.

San Francisco

Washington Square Inn
1660 Stockton Street
San Francisco, CA 94133
(415) 981-4220 or (800) 388-0220

Type of B&B: Urban inn.
Rooms: 15, 10 with private bath.
Rates: 1 or 2/$85-180.

Rating: B+ or ♛♛ Good, exceeds basic requirements.

Small European-style Victorian inn is located in the historic North Beach district, one block from Telegraph Hill. There are fifteen guest rooms throughout the building which offer a variety in size, decor, and amenities. Each room has a selection of English or French antiques, terry cloth robes, and down comforters. Several rooms which share baths offer an in-room sink and ten rooms or suites have private baths. The elegant parlor area features a fireplace and is an inviting setting for afternoon tea and evening hors d'oeuvres. Walk to many fine restaurants, coffee houses, and bakeries. Cannery shopping is ten minutes away. Take a cable car ride to Union Square, Financial District, or Fisherman's Wharf. Full breakfast served daily includes famous "Graffeo" coffee and fresh croissants. Families welcome. No smoking. 1 or 2/$85-180. MC, V. 10% senior and business travel discounts.

Guests write: *"I have been a guest here for five days. The staff couldn't have been more cooperative."* (A. Law)

"My mother and I thoroughly enjoyed the warm, efficient service you provided. The continental breakfast, tea hour, and the use of the terry cloth robes were quite nice." (J. Martin)

"The staff at the Washington Square Inn has consistently excellent service. During my recent visit to San Francisco, their patience and assistance helped to make my stay so much more enjoyable. Give them all big raises!" (M. Gould)

"They've restored our faith in customer service and are wonderful. The bottle of wine was perfect." (M. Patterson)

San Gregorio

Rancho San Gregorio
Route 1, Box 54
5086 La Honda Road
San Gregorio, CA 94074
(415) 747-0810

Type of B&B: B&B Inn.
Rooms: 4 with private bath.
Rates: 1 or 2/$65-125.

Rating: B+ of ♛♛ Good, exceeds basic requirements.

Early California Spanish mission-style inn is a country retreat overlooking the San Gregorio Valley and is located 45 minutes south of San Francisco. There are four guest rooms with private bath. The San Gregorio room has a private deck overlooking the garden, king-size bed, two sofa-beds, woodburning stove, refrigerator, soaking tub, and Southwest decor. There is ample common space for guest conversation and relaxation and these areas feature interesting antiques, redwood beams, and terra cotta tile floors. The ranch is situated on fifteen acres and offers badminton, volleyball, horseshoes, lawn croquet, and quiet garden corners for contemplation. Area attractions include Ano Nuevo Seal Reserve, marshland bird byways, beaches (five miles away), and state parks. Full breakfast specialties vary day to day but may include apple-filled crepes, chocolate chip muffins, Rancho soufflé or Swedish egg cake with wild blackberry sauce. Families welcome. Restricted smoking. 1 or 2/$65-125. AE, MC, V. Travel agent.

Guests write: *"We came to Rancho San Gregorio to get away and to cycle the scenic roads along the coast. Nothing can compare to bicycling along a quiet road, looking at the cows or catching glimpses of the ocean. Bud and Lee were very friendly and their breakfasts did a wonderful job of fueling these bicyclers!"* (T. Learmont)

"When our lives become especially hectic, Rancho San Gregorio is the first place that comes to mind - it has become our retreat. Each room has a different flavor and they are all so comfortable. My favorite thing is a bubble bath in an old-fashioned tub with a fire in the wood burning stove followed by a glass of wine. Absolute perfection!" (E. Swenson)

"This was a delightful couple concerned about their guests and most helpful in planning tours. There were many little home touches such as a guest refrigerator on the second floor with soft drinks, beer, wine coolers (free), VCR with large selection of movies, snacks, coffee, tea, and fruit were available in the kitchen at all times." (D. Grant)

"We have stayed in three of the four rooms and each is absolutely charming. I would have a difficult time choosing my favorite but maybe the claw-foot tub in Corte Madera would be my choice. The food is excellent. Something fresh from the garden is always part of the breakfast meal." (M. Johnson)

San Jose

The Hensley House
456 North Third Street
San Jose, CA 95112
(408) 298-3537

Type of B&B: Inn.
Rooms: 5 with private bath.
Rates: 1 or 2/$75-125.

Rating: A or 🎗🎗🎗 Excellent, far exceeds basic requirements.

Queen Anne Victorian inn built in 1884 is located downtown in the Hensley Historic District. Choose from five guest rooms, each with private bath and Victorian decor. The Judge's Chamber room features a featherbed, refrigerator, sitting area, and plush bathroom with whirlpool tub. Relax in the large living room with beamed ceiling, six-foot fireplace, and built-in leaded glass cabinets. Special services for business travelers include fax, personal computer, answering service, access to law library, and conference facilities. Full breakfast. Families welcome. Facilities available for meetings and social functions. 1 or 2/$75-125. AE, MC, V. 10% auto club, business travel, and senior discount.

Guests write: *"Our meeting was a success thanks to the peaceful surroundings, the delightful lunch, and the level of service provided. We especially enjoyed the opportunity to play the piano and burst into song occasionally. I look forward to holding future off-site meetings at the Hensley House."* (L. Crane)

"The whirlpool tub was a luxurious romantic treat in the Judge's Chamber room. After staying at the Hensley House, my husband and I are planning to purchase a featherbed as our bed was one of the most comfortable beds we have ever slept in." (J. Stroh)

"The accommodations are lovely, the breakfasts tasty, the historical environment gracious. The innkeepers did a wonderful thing in giving me an economy rate while I worked in San Jose for two weeks." (K. Maxson)

"The breakfast was served beautifully on lovely English china and the variety of food each day was excellent. The accouterments in the room showed that a great deal of thought had been given to the comfort of the traveler. We were also pleased with the wine selection for the afternoon

— Comments continued on next page

wine and hors d'ouevres. The decor of the house was truly Victorian style including the attire of the innkeeper." (S. Civiletti)

"Another nice thing about the Hensley House stay was the snapshot they took at the end of your stay and mailed to you. It's such a nice remembrance of a very nice visit with them." (L. Maddox)

"We stay at a B&B somewhere in the U.S. for our annual meeting. The service at Hensley House exceeded everything we had experienced before. Not only did she give us wonderful hints on what to see and how to get there, but the way she treated us while in the house was beyond the normal requirements." (R. Ames)

San Luis Obispo

Garden Street Inn
1212 Garden Street
San Luis Obispo, CA 93401
(805) 545-9802

Type of B&B: B&B Inn.
Rooms: 13 with private bath.
Rates: 1 or 2/$90-120; Suites/$140-160.

Rating: A or ♛♛♛ Excellent, far exceeds basic requirements.

Built in 1887, this Victorian Italianate/Queen Anne inn has been recently restored and is located four hours south of San Francisco off Highway 101. Choose from nine guest rooms and four suites. Each offers a private bath, king or queen-size bed, armoire, attractive wall coverings, rich fabrics, and antiques. Enjoy the Victorian decor in the McCafery Morning room with its original stained glass windows or sit on one of the outside decks with a good book from the Goldtree Library room. Walk to the 1772 Mission and historic downtown or drive to nearby Hearst Castle, Pismo Beach, Morro Bay, and Cambria. Outdoor activities nearby include tennis, golf, horseback riding, and hiking. A homemade full breakfast includes specialty breads and can be served in the guest room by request. Facilities for small weddings and meetings available. Wheelchair access. Restricted smoking. 1 or 2/$90-120; Suites/$140-160. AE, MC, V. Travel agent.

Santa Barbara

Blue Quail Inn and Cottages
1908 Bath Street
Santa Barbara, CA 93101
(805) 687-2300 or
(800) 549-1622 (in California)
(800) 676-1622 (USA)

Type of B&B: Inn and cottages
Rooms: 9 with private bath.
Rates: 1 or 2/$74-165.

Rating: B+ or ♛♛ Good, exceeds basic requirements.

California bungalow and adjacent cottages are conveniently located near beaches and downtown shopping. Choose from nine guest rooms throughout the main house or cottages. Each has unique decor and features a sitting area, fireplace, antique pieces, colorful accessories and private bath. Walk three blocks to Cottage Hospital and Sansum Clinic. Stroll or borrow bicycles for a ride to the beach, distinctive shops, art galleries, and historic sites. Full breakfast. No smoking. 1 or 2/$74-165. AE, MC, V. Travel agent. Closed Christmas Eve and Christmas Day.

Guests write: *"The charm of the cottages, the brick walkways, and perfectly beautiful gardens, home-baked goodies, friendly faces, all serve to captivate. The warmth just oozes all over the place."* (G. Sugarman)

"The cozy Mockingbird room was perfect for our 5th anniversary! The old-fashioned tub and bed full of soft pillows really lends itself to a night of romance. The wine, hot cider, and special treats in the evening are a nice touch. Riding bikes all around Santa Barbara was fun." (M. Van Ness)

"What fun answering our door to be greeted with smiling faces, balloons, and champagne in recognition of our 1st anniversary. What a thoughtful and personal gesture." (D. LeBarron)

"We loved the balloons, the champagne, soap, the blue hearts that hold the curtains, the bikes, the dogs, the delicious food, the charming staff, and most of all the adorable books - we couldn't put them down." (A. East)

Santa Barbara

The Cheshire Cat Inn
36 West Valerio Street
Santa Barbara, CA 93101
(805) 569-1610 Fax (805) 682-1876

Type of B&B: B&B Inn.
Rooms: 14 with private baths.
Rates: 1 or 2/$79-249.

Rating: A or ♛♛♛ Excellent, far exceeds basic requirements.

The Cheshire Cat Inn, located near the downtown area, is comprised of two adjacent Victorian Queen Anne-style homes that have been fully restored. The inn's name and guest room decor come from characters in "Alice in Wonderland". Each of the fourteen rooms is whimsically decorated with Laura Ashley wallpapers and fabrics and features English antiques and a sitting area. Some rooms offer a fireplace, patio, or spa. Common rooms feature high ceilings and quiet nooks for reading and relaxing. The sitting room has a wood burning fireplace and an old oak settee. Relax on the brick patio or in the spa nestled into a gazebo to insure privacy. Borrow one of the complimentary bicycles provided to explore the town and nearby beach. Area attractions include museums, golfing, tennis, shopping, horseback riding, hiking, and the old Santa Barbara Mission. Full breakfast features homemade coffee cakes, granola, and fresh, imported coffee. No smoking. 1 or 2/$79-249. MC, V. Travel agent.

Santa Barbara/Summerland

Inn on Summer Hill
2520 Lillie Avenue
Summerland, CA 93067
(805) 969-9998 or (800) 845-5566

Type of B&B: Inn.
Rooms: 16 with private bath.
Rates: 1 or 2/$145-260.

Rating: AA+ or ♛♛♛♛ Outstanding.

New England-style inn in a quiet seaside village is surrounded by rolling foothills and located 2 miles south of Santa Barbara, 90 miles north of Los Angeles. Choose from sixteen exceptionally well-furnished guest rooms. Each features a private bath, canopy bed, gas fireplace, down comforter, antiques, original art, and ocean view. The decor in each room is outstanding with rich fabrics, lovely wall coverings, and unique accessories. The large armoire in each room hides a TV/VCR and guest refrigerator stocked with beverages. The whimsical garden features English country benches, bird houses, and observation deck with spa. Full breakfast and evening refreshments served daily. No smoking. Facilities available for small meetings and social functions. 1 or 2/$145-260. AE, MC, V. 10% business travel and senior discounts offered midweek.

Guests write: *"Every room has a wonderful balcony overlooking the ocean across the road. As soon as we saw the fireplace, Jacuzzi tub, down quilt on canopy bed, pine ceiling, beautiful wallpaper and window coverings, fresh flowers (even in the bathroom) — we knew that we were in an exceptional place! The room also has complimentary tea, coffee, cocoa, and mineral water. The quiche and bread pudding with banana sauce were fantastic and the chocolate chip cookies were out of this world! I looked in several rooms and each was just beautiful."* (J. Harold)

"Goldilocks should be so lucky! Inn on Summer Hill is just right the first time. Wonderful room with great treats." (J. Kleiss)

"I will never be able to stay anywhere else without being disappointed. I have never had such a wonderful stay. I was made to feel like their most important guest." (G. Altshuler)

"Possibly the best stay I've ever had anywhere! What wonderful rooms and great staff. I love the no-surcharge phones and the way the staff bent over backwards to accommodate our schedule." (V. McDermott)

"The decor was really magnificent and the setting superb." (B. Reichel)

"We really enjoyed our stay. Everything was perfect from the decor to the sweets at turn-down time." (W. Chang)

"We loved the classical music, Jacuzzi, robes, spa, hair dryer, down comforter, fireplace, food, and newspaper in the morning." (C. Bocian)

"We cannot say enough for the overall effect of the inn. It was beautiful, clean, and charming. The attention to detail was incredible and not overlooked by us. We loved the canopy bed, Jacuzzi tub, fireplace, balcony and view, outside spa, beautiful grounds, and service was more than excellent. The stereo speakers were nice, too, as were fresh flowers everywhere." (G. Olsen)

Santa Barbara

Simpson House Inn
121 East Arrellaga
Santa Barbara, CA 93101
(805) 963-7067 or (800) 676-1280.

Type of B&B: Inn.
Rooms: 10 with private bath.
Rates: 2/$76-185.

Rating: A+ or ♛♛♛ Excellent, far exceeds basic requirements.

Victorian inn built in 1874 is secluded on an acre of gardens within the city. Choose from ten guest rooms with private bath each featuring antiques, lace, Oriental rugs, goose-down comforters, fresh flowers, claw-foot tub and private deck. A newly renovated carriage house on the property offers well-designed guest suites with private entrances and spacious quarters. Enjoy a relaxing stroll through the extensive gardens with curving paths, mature oaks, magnolias, and pittosporums. Walk to restaurants, theaters, downtown shops, and museums. Among area attractions are swimming, boating, and bicycling. Full breakfast featuring homemade breads and house specialties is served overlooking the gardens. Afternoon tea, wine and hors d'oeuvres served daily. No smoking. 2/$76-185. AE, Discover, MC, V. Travel agent.

Guests write: *"We especially enjoyed our breakfast on the sunroom deck. The scones were light and airy and homemade lemon curd! It was then a joy to lie out on our teak sun lounges to digest and read, to look out over the mountains and beautiful gardens below. There was no need to go anywhere."* (P. Young-Wolff)

"We felt so rested and pampered by the elegant furnishings, romantic gardens and sumptuous food - especially by Gillean's hospitality. The artful hors d'ouevres brought to our room on a silver tray were a wonderful treat." (B. Kendall)

"Staying here is like coming home to the English country house which haunts my dreams. Nestled behind tall Eugenia hedges, surrounded by lawns and gardens, the house itself soothes and comforts world-weary travelers. Sumptuous breakfasts on the balcony with a view of the mountains, wine and cheese in the late afternoon, pleasant chats with the staff - these are memories to savor." (P. Dickson)

"I can always count on a peaceful stay in elegant surroundings here. The special feeling indoors comes from the furniture, bedding, china and flowers. The outdoor decks and patios help you enjoy the carefully nurtured flowers and greenery. I leave with uplifted spirits." (G. Palace)

Santa Cruz

Babbling Brook Inn
1025 Laurel Street
Santa Cruz CA 95060
(408) 427-2437 or (800) 866-1131
FAX: (408) 427-2457

Type of B&B: Inn.
Rooms: 12 with private bath.
Rates: 1 or 2/$85-135.

Rating: A+ or ♛♛♛ Excellent, far exceeds basic requirements.

The Babbling Brook Inn is located 90 miles south of San Francisco and was built on the foundation of a former 1795 tannery and grist mill. It's name comes from the extensive gardens, brook, waterwheel, and waterfalls which surround the inn. Twelve guest rooms with private bath are available. Each is unique in size, amenities, and decor but some special features include French country decor, antiques, fireplaces, skylights, color cable TV, private phone, whirlpool baths, private outside entrances and decks. The Degas Room features a unique bed used by a local repertory group in their production of Shakespeare's "Romeo and Juliet". The inn is within walking distance of the beach, wharf, boardwalk, shopping, and tour of historic homes. Full country breakfast includes fresh-baked croissants. Wine and cheese are offered in the evening along with Mrs. King's special cookies. No smoking. 1 or 2/$85-135. AE, MC, V. 10% auto club and business travel discounts. Travel agent.

Guests write: *"We loved the gardens and the Honeymoon suite. The bath tub is great and big enough for two."* (J. Sczepanski)

"We stayed in the Renoir room until the last minute enjoying the view and music of the waterfall." (I. Lusebrink)

"The Countess room was spacious, charming, and lovely. The Talouse Lautrec room on the 2nd night was beautiful. Breakfast here was delicious and staff are so generous and attentive, yet unobtrusive - fantastic!" (S. Nachenberg)

"Our room was the Farmer's Garden room - very quaint and so nice we didn't want to be away from it too much." (G. Metzler)

"We're real homebodies because nothing is usually as comfortable but Babbling Brook is every bit as comfortable plus being enchanting." (C. Unruh)

"Time apart from work and worries, distanced too from a world that hurries. Breakfast treats, cookies, and goodies of the kind that bring one thoughts of a gentler time. An experience of total pleasure. Lucky us with the memories to treasure." (M. Osborne)

— *Comments continued on next page*

"This is the place where not only dreams are made of but already existing dreams come true. We of course had the Honeymoon Suite and although well-traveled, never had we seen such beauty and warmth incorporated into a room for lovers." (L. Lewis)

Santa Monica

Channel Road Inn
219 West Channel Road
Santa Monica, CA 90402
(310) 459-1920
Fax (310) 454-9920

Type of B&B: Inn.
Rooms: 14 with private bath.
Rates: 1 or 2/$95-195.

Rating: A+ or ♛♛♛ Excellent, far exceeds basic requirements.

Channel Road Inn is a large Colonial Revival home built in 1910 and located 2 miles north of I-10 in the Los Angeles metropolitan area. This building is the oldest residence in the surrounding vicinity and is convenient to cultural attractions as well as the beach. Fourteen guest rooms with large private baths are available. Each has distinctive period decor and furnishings but all offer an ocean or garden view, fresh cut flowers, and home-baked cookies. Bicycles are available for the oceanside bike paths and horseback riding as well as tennis are nearby. Area attractions include Getty Museum, pier, beaches, and Will Rogers Park. Full breakfast served in the mint-green and pink breakfast room features fresh California fruits and baked egg dishes. Complimentary refreshments are offered each evening. No smoking. Families welcome. 1 or 2/$95-195. MC, V. 10% business travel discount. Travel agent.

Guests write: *"The comfort and warmth provided by the staff are wonderful for someone who's homesick. They patiently answer all my questions, serve a fabulous breakfast, give great directions for driving, and stop to chat when I'm feeling lonely. I'll be coming back here as long as my business keeps bringing me to Los Angeles."* (S. Rosenberg)

"The inn is beautifully decorated in a Victorian manner - lots of wicker furniture and chintz covers. It is all new furniture - not old and musty. Our bedroom was very special and the bed had a wonderful pink and white hand-made quilt and there was an adjoining bathroom." (J. Kennedy)

"It's the little touches that make the Channel Road Inn a special hideaway. The Battenburg lace, the ocean view, the blooming hillside, waking to the smell of fresh coffee, and blueberry coffeecake, and your own key to the front door. I enjoyed reading the thoughts of past guests in the diaries in each room - especially Room #6 - the Honeymoon suite!" (D. Riley)

Seal Beach

Seal Beach Inn and Gardens
212 5th Street
Seal Beach, CA 90740
(310) 493-2416
Fax (310) 493-2416

Type of B&B: Country inn.
Rooms: 23 rooms or suites with private bath.
Rates: 1 or 2/$118-185.

Rating: A- or ♛♛♛ Excellent, far exceeds basic requirements.

Seal Beach Inn and Gardens is located in a seaside village south of Los Angeles and is a complex of French/Mediterranean architecture with a lush garden setting. There are twenty-three distinctive guest rooms or suites. Each offers a private bath and several have full kitchens. Walk one block to the beach or pier. Interesting sites and activities in the area include gondola rides, candlelight dining, seaside strolls, harbor cruises, specialty shops, Disneyland, and Knott's Berry Farm. Hearty buffet breakfast. Facilities available for small meetings. 1 or 2/$118-185. AE, MC, V. 10% senior, auto club, and business travel discounts. Travel agent.

Guests write: *"The gardens are impressive; a dazzling collection of natural beauty. Staying in the villa is like visiting someone's home rather than staying at a hotel. Room rates and service are excellent with regard to level of service and staff responsiveness."* (D. Ishikawa)

"We love the Old World charm with a fantastic breakfast and its nearness to the beach is a great addition to the other attractions." (L. Simons)

"Management and personnel are extremely courteous and helpful. Some rooms are small but very clean. Breakfasts are excellent, location great. All in all a wonderful B&B modestly priced." (J. Harrison)

"This is our 10th visit here. Our compliments on the improvements that have been made since our last stay and the beautiful way that breakfast is being presented now." (R. Wilcox)

"I stay at the Seal Beach Inn on business five times a year. The place is fantastic. Everything is in apple pie order. I would recommend the Inn to anyone. The location is superb, the food is great, and the staff is wonderful." (S. Sunderland)

Sonoma

The Hidden Oak
214 East Napa St.
Sonoma, CA 95476
(707) 996-9863

Type of B&B: B&B Inn.
Rooms: 3 with private bath.
Rates: 1/$95; 2/$95-130.

Rating: A or ♛♛♛ Excellent, far exceeds basic requirements.

The Hidden Oak is located 45 minutes north of San Francisco and is a restored 1913 California Craftsman Bungalow with a brown shingled exterior and high gabled roof. Three guest rooms each offer a private bath and antique or wicker furniture. Browse through the library, sit by the fire in the reading room, borrow the inn's bicycles to explore the nearby wineries, or tour the Mission or the historic Plaza, just a block and a half away. Restaurants, art galleries, concerts, and plays are all a part of the surrounding area. Full breakfast is offered and dietary restrictions are taken into consideration. No smoking. 1/$95; 2/$95-130. AE.

Sonoma

Sonoma Hotel
110 West Spain Street
Sonoma, CA 95476
(707) 996-2996

Type of B&B: Historic hotel with restaurant.
Rooms: 17, 5 with private bath.
Rates: 1 or 2/$62-105.

Rating: B- or ♛♛ Good, exceeds basic requirements.

Historic hotel situated on the city's tree-lined plaza has been completely restored by the present owners who have worked hard at retaining the historic atmosphere of the building. There are seventeen individually decorated guest rooms with pleasant decor, antiques, and brass and iron appointments. Several rooms offer private baths with deep claw-foot tubs and herbal bubble bath. Most rooms on the third floor share two large "his" and "hers" baths at the end of the hall. Nearby attractions include wineries, hot air balloon rides, art galleries, shops, and historic landmarks. Continental buffet breakfast is served in the lobby and often includes fresh-baked pastries. Dining available on the premises. Families welcome. 1 or 2/$62-105. AE, MC, V.

Tahoe City

Chaney House
PO Box 7852, 4725 West Lake Blvd.
Tahoe City, CA 96145
(916) 525-7333

Type of B&B: B&B inn.
Rooms: 4, 2 with private baths.
Rates: 1 or 2/$95-110.

Rating: B or ♛♛ Good, exceeds basic requirements.

Old European-style stone home with gothic arches was built in the 1920s and is nestled among native pine trees along the shore of Lake Tahoe, 5 miles south of Tahoe City and 60 miles west of Reno. Four guest rooms are available three in the main house with the main level guest room having a private bath. The large master bedroom on the second floor has a private half bath and shares a shower with another room on this floor. A private entrance, alcove with futon couch, separate bedroom, and full kitchen is offered in the apartment over the garage. Guests enjoy gathering in front of the massive stone fireplace that reaches to the top of a cathedral ceiling. Just across the road is a private beach and pier. Rent a paddle boat or bicycle to explore the area. There's an abundance of recreation in the area including golfing, hiking, rafting, boating, and skiing. A full breakfast is served in the dining room or on the patio overlooking the lake and often features quiche, blackberry French toast, or egg stratas. Afternoon refreshments are offered in front of the fireplace. Restricted smoking. 1 or 2/$95-110.

Guests write: *"Besides Chaney House being warm and comfortable, we found our host to be extremely hospitable. We enjoyed wine and cheese with them after skiing, and there was always a really superb breakfast waiting for us each morning."* (D. Thompson)

"We enjoyed our stay at the Chaney House. Our hosts, Gary and Lori were warm and friendly. We spent a romantic weekend in front of their big stone fireplace, watching the snow fall." (C. Penney)

Yosemite – See Arnold, Bridgeport, Murphys, and Groveland.

Additional information about B&Bs throughout California is available from B&B Rocky Mountains (800) 733-8415

Breckenridge

Cotten House Bed & Breakfast
102 South French Street, P.O. Box 387
Breckenridge, CO 80424
(303)453-5509

Type of B&B: B&B Inn
Rooms: 3, 1 with private bath.
Rates: 1 or 2/$40-90 (Seasonal).

Rating: B or ♛♛ Good, exceeds basic requirements.

Breckenridge is a major recreation area located 90 miles west of Denver. Cotten House B&B is an 1886 Victorian home on the National Historic Register that is situated in the town's historic district which dates back over one hundred and thirty years ago. Each of the three guest rooms at the Cotten House feature fresh flowers and special decor themes. The Victorian room offers a turn-of-the-century bed and dresser in a romantic setting. The Room with the View offers views of the slopes, two twin beds, Southwestern American furnishings, and native art. The Colorado Room has a private bath, large four-poster with down bedding and Mining Era decor theme. Enjoy afternoon refreshments in the common room which has a TV/VCR and stereo. A free shuttle bus travels to nearby shopping, restaurants, music festivals, and Main Street nightlife. There's a local recreation center, historical tours of the area, and an abundance of recreation including skiing, snowmobiling, biking, hiking, fishing, and boating. Full breakfast often features crepes, omelets, or French toast, as well as hot breads, fruit, and yogurt. Wedding facilities available and being situated between two churches makes housing the family and helping with arrangements easy. Honeymoon and wedding packages. Families welcome. No smoking. Seasonal rates. 1 or 2/$40-90.

Guests write: *"We enjoyed so much the friendly hospitality of Cotten House that have returned for another week. Both Peter and Georgette make us feel at home and we commend them for their outstanding breakfasts and spotless accommodations."* (H. Baers, M.D.)

Crested Butte

Alpine Lace Bed & Breakfast
726 Maroon
Crested Butte, CO 81224
(303) 349-9857

Type of B&B: Small inn.
Rooms: 4, 2 with private bath.
Rates: 1 or 2/$60-95.

Rating: B+ or ♛♛ Good, exceeds basic requirements.

Swiss chalet-style inn is surrounded by mountain and valley views and is situated in the National Historic District near Highway 135. Four guest rooms are available. Special features include balconies with garden or valley views. The two guest rooms with private baths are slightly larger and have extra amenities. A spacious sunroom on the main floor offers a Jacuzzi tub, guest refrigerator, wine glasses, and towels. The main living room has a large stone fireplace and interesting collection of books on Colorado. A mud room offers secure and accessible storage for skis, bicycles, and hiking equipment. This is a year-round recreation area which offers skiing, ice fishing, snow shoeing, sleigh rides, biking, and horseback riding. Walk to unique shops and restaurants in the village area. Full gourmet breakfast served and beverages are available throughout the day. Facilities available for small social functions. No smoking. 1 or 2/$60-95. MC, V.

Guests write: *"Spending Christmas alone is a bummer unless you're at the Alpine Lace in which case it becomes a memorable high. The genuine warmth here quickly took off the chill for this flatlander. The food was excellent and will be missed immediately when I wake up in Florida upon my return. Also, if Ward can teach me to ski, he can teach anybody anything."* (R. Booth)

"Alpine Lace is our home away from home. The luxurious towels, the flowers on the table, Loree's warmth and friendship, Ward's efficiency and attention to detail, the hot tub soothing our tired muscles, the wonderful atmosphere of town - these are the things that made our trip a wonderful memory." (S. Sabo)

"We loved our week here and lost all track of time. A really great spot! The shuttle bus to the slopes made life effortless. Every breakfast was better than the one the day before." (D. Killen)

Denver

Castle Marne B&B
1572 Race Street
Denver, CO 80237
(303) 331-0621 or (800) 92-MARNE

Type of B&B: Inn.
Rooms: 9 rooms or suites with private bath.
Rates: 1/$70-155; 2/$80-155.

Rating: A+ or ♛♛♛ Excellent, far exceeds basic requirements.

Historic Victorian mansion built in 1889 is now a luxury urban inn located near the intersection of Routes 40 and 287, 20 blocks east of downtown. Nine guest rooms or suites are available, each with period antiques, family heirlooms, and private bath. The spacious guest suites feature Jacuzzi bath tubs. The original character of the mansion is still evident in its hand-rubbed woods, circular stained-glass peacock window, and ornate fireplaces. Business travelers will appreciate the quiet office setup in the lower level with desk and office equipment ready for use. Full breakfast and afternoon tea served daily. Candlelight dinners are available on Friday and Saturday evenings by advance reservation. Facilities available for small meetings. No smoking. 1/$70-155; 2/$80-155. AE, MC, V. 5% auto club, business travel, and senior discounts. Travel agent.

Denver

Queen Anne Inn
2147 Tremont Place
Denver, CO 80205
(303) 296-6666
Fax (303) 296-2151

Type of B&B: Inn.
Rooms: 14 with private bath.
Rates: 1/$54-99; 2/$64-109

Rating: A or ♛♛♛ Excellent, far exceeds basic requirements.

Two large Queen Anne Victorian homes facing a quiet city park offer the atmosphere and ambiance of Denver's Historic District, yet are located only four blocks from the center of downtown. There are fourteen guest rooms with private bath. Each has a unique decor, fresh flowers, classical music intercom system, period lighting, air conditioning, and telephone. The Aspen Room's unusual architectural features are enhanced by an original mural of aspen trees and this central theme is carried out with unique wood lighting fixtures. Four new suites have been recently added which feature spacious rooms, upscale furnishings, and Jacuzzi tubs. The Capitol, 16th Street Pedestrian Mall, specialty shops, galleries, and restaurants within walking distance. Horse-drawn carriages are available for special occasions. Continental breakfast and evening refreshments served daily. Off-street parking is available on-site. 1/$54-99; 2/$64-109. No smoking. AE, Discover, Diners, MC, V. 10% auto club and business travel discount. Travel agent.

Denver/Arvada

The Tree House
6650 Simms Street
Arvada, CO 80004
(303) 431-6352

Type of B&B: Inn.
Rooms: 5, each with private bath.
Rates: 1 or 2/$49-$79.

Rating: A- or ♕♕♕ Excellent, far exceeds basic requirements.

Chalet style inn is set far back from the road on ten wooded acres and is located only 25 minutes West of Denver's Stapleton Airport near the Ward exit off I-70. Each of the five guest rooms offers a private bath and is furnished with brass bed, handmade quilts, and interesting antiques. Four rooms feature a wood-burning fireplace. Several balconies provide a quiet spot for taking in the wooded views. Enjoy a leisurely walk through the forest that surrounds the inn. A large parlor offers a fireplace and comfortable oak and leather furniture. Area attractions include the Rocky Mountains, Denver Mint, Denver Zoo, and Coors Brewery. Full breakfast includes special homemade cinnamon rolls, omelets, and fresh fruit. Families welcome. No smoking. 1 or 2/$49-79. MC. V. Business traveler discount. Travel agent.

Guests write: *"Beautifully decorated and comfortable interior and wooded surroundings. The crowning touch was the gourmet breakfast. As a host of breakfast eaters who feel the day should begin with a good meal, we were all delighted with Amanda's wonderful cooking."* (N. Arnold)

Leadville

The Apple Blossom Inn Victorian Bed & Breakfast
120 West Fourth Street
Leadville, CO 80461
(719) 486-2141 or (800) 982-9279

Type of B&B: Small B&B Inn.
Rooms: 5, 3 with private bath.
Rates: 1/$45; 2/$75.

Rating: B or ♛♛ Good, exceeds basic requirements.

The Apple Blossom Inn is named for a famous antique stained-glass work displayed in a front window of the house. Built in 1879, this small Victorian home is in downtown Leadville, 110 miles from Denver. Five guest rooms are available. Three of the rooms offer a private bath and all have been decorated with Victorian accents and antiques and feature carved woodwork, beveled mirrors, and maple and mahogany floors. Two living rooms are available for relaxing, playing the piano, or reading one of the many books on the library shelves. Area attractions include scenic train rides, skiing, hiking, fishing, white water rafting, snowmobiling, and horseback riding. Full breakfast may feature specialties such as Italian potatoes, home baked breads and muffins, and Chili Relleno casserole. Small meeting and wedding facilities. Families welcome. Restricted smoking. 1/$45; 2/$75. MC, V. 10% senior and corporate discount. Travel agent.

Guests write: *"Some of the huge plusses are: the fireplace with unlimited wood supply in our room, Maggie's cooking-varied and excellent. Her roasted potatoes, yeast breads, and frittatas are superb as are the "to die for" brownies. Overall decor and warmth of the inn coupled with Maggie's welcoming hospitality make it a place I always hate to leave."* (L. Carter)

"We stayed with Maggie this season for ski trips. After reserving the least expensive room we were pleasantly surprised when she gave us her best room which was more expensive since no one booked that room. We felt that this was a wonderful business practice. It's not often a person runs into a person who takes so much pride in her business and who remembers that the customer is important." (A. Evans)

"A 5 star performance for quiet, friendly hospitality, cozy atmosphere, in a scenic wonderland. Could be called "The Awesome Blossom Inn".
(J. Seavey)

Leadville

Delaware Hotel
700 Harrison Ave
Leadville, CO 80461
(719)486-1418 or (800) 748-2004

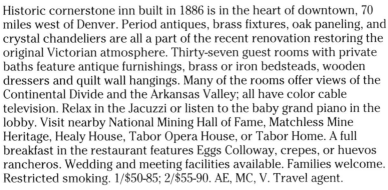

Type of B&B: Historic hotel with restaurant
Rooms: 37 with private bath.
Rates: 1/$50-85; 2/$55-90.

Rating: B- or ♛♛ Good, exceeds basic requirements.

Historic cornerstone inn built in 1886 is in the heart of downtown, 70 miles west of Denver. Period antiques, brass fixtures, oak paneling, and crystal chandeliers are all a part of the recent renovation restoring the original Victorian atmosphere. Thirty-seven guest rooms with private baths feature antique furnishings, brass or iron bedsteads, wooden dressers and quilt wall hangings. Many of the rooms offer views of the Continental Divide and the Arkansas Valley; all have color cable television. Relax in the Jacuzzi or listen to the baby grand piano in the lobby. Visit nearby National Mining Hall of Fame, Matchless Mine Heritage, Healy House, Tabor Opera House, or Tabor Home. A full breakfast in the restaurant features Eggs Colloway, crepes, or huevos rancheros. Wedding and meeting facilities available. Families welcome. Restricted smoking. 1/$50-85; 2/$55-90. AE, MC, V. Travel agent.

Guests write: *"We loved the renovation. The Victorian flair and the decor was very well done. The breakfasts were also wonderful with very generous portions!"* (T. Young)

"The Historic Delaware Hotel has an excellent atmosphere for capturing the spirit of Colorado. It has a traditional western motif. In the city of Leadville, it stands as a renovation example for renewing the entire city." (H. Cleary)

"Comfortable, restored with the look and feel of the past, with a few modern additions for comfort. Bathrooms were added to the rooms. A hot tub was added to the lobby for the benefit of the many skiers that flock to the hotel." (K. Cope)

"The room was very pleasantly furnished with very big windows." (M. Cirrito)

Redstone

Cleveholm Manor
0058 Redstone Boulevard
Redstone, CO 81623
(303) 963-3463

Type of B&B: Large mansion.
Rooms: 16, 8 with private bath.
Rates: 1 or 2/$80-175.

Rating: A- or ♛♛♛ Excellent, far exceeds basic requirements.

English Manor-style mansion built originally for a wealthy mining baron at the turn-of-the-century sits overlooking the Crystal River and red mountain cliffs and is located south of Glenwood Springs, 200 miles west of Denver, and 45 miles northwest of Aspen. Sixteen guest rooms are available which offer a variety in price, decor and amenities. Eight rooms have private baths. Several small rooms which share baths offer fresh, updated decor. Other choices include the suites with period furnishings and decor, private baths, and fireplaces. The main floor has an impressive entry, parlor, and dining rooms whose features include elegant woodwork, stone and marble fireplaces, inlaid floors, gold leaf ceilings, and Persian rugs. The lower level offers a small lounge and bar, television room, and billiards room. Outdoor recreation available nearby includes high country skiing, hiking, bicycling, horseback riding, and fishing. Continental buffet breakfast. Groups up to 100 can be easily accommodated. Families welcome. Restricted smoking. 1 or 2/$80-175. AE, Discover, MC, V. Senior and off-season discounts. Travel agent.

Steamboat Springs

The Country Inn at Steamboat Llama Ranch
46915 County Road 129
Steamboat Springs, CO 80487
(303) 879-5767

Type of B&B: B&B Inn.
Rooms: 3 with private bath; 1 suite; 1 cabin.
Rates: 1 or 2/$65-165.

Rating: A- or ♛♛♛ Excellent, far exceeds basic requirements.

A four wheel drive vehicle is recommended in winter months to reach this renovated, circa 1912 ranch found 157 miles west of Denver and 8 and 1/2 miles north of Steamboat Springs. Three guest rooms with private baths, one suite, and a cabin are available for guests. The cabin offers a private entrance, complete kitchen, and fireplace. Three new rooms and a large suite have recently been added to the main house and offer private decks. A separate building offers two floors for guests to meet and relax and it features an entertainment center, library, and refreshment center. There is also a small shop located in the registration barn which specializes in llama gift items. Watch the llamas graze in the fields from one of the private decks, or enjoy area sports such as snowmobiling, hot air ballooning, hiking, and downhill skiing. Continental Plus breakfast. Small wedding and family reunion facilities available. No smoking. 1 or 2/$65-165. Some minimum stays required. Seasonal rates. Large group discounts. MC, V. Travel agent.

Telluride

Alpine Inn Bed & Breakfast
440 West Colorado Ave.
P.O. Box 2398
Telluride, CO 81435
(303) 728-6282

Type of B&B: B&B Inn.
Rooms: 9, 5 with private bath.
Rates: 1 or 2/$50-170.

Rating: B+ or ♛♛ Good, exceeds basic requirements.

Restored Victorian built in 1907 is located on the main street of this historic town which is secluded in the San Juan Mountains, 330 miles southwest of Denver; 67 miles south of Montrose. Each of the nine guest rooms has been individually decorated with antiques and Victorian accents. Five rooms offer a private bath. The sunroom, where breakfast is served, offers panoramic views of the mountains as does the hot tub room where guests relax after a day of hiking, skiing, or cycling. Main Street offers interesting shopping and a good variety of restaurants. Area attractions include the Telluride Ski Resort, Bridal Veil Falls, Hot Air Balloon Rally, and several choices of music and film festivals. Fresh fruit accompanies a full breakfast. No smoking. 1 or 2/$50-170. AE, MC, V. Travel agent.

Guests write: *"I found the Alpine Inn a thoroughly delightful place to stay. The hospitality is in the tradition of the Southwest. The accommodations are very immaculate and comfortable. The added extras of a hearty breakfast and beverages after skiing made it a truly desirable place to stay."* (L. Longo)

"Cozy, different rooms are very inviting — like going to Grandma's house. The sunroom that looks out on the mountain is very nice." (J. Knopinski)

"The inn was clean, neat, and beautifully decorated? The hosts stories of the town were interesting and amusing." (L. Gouthro)

Telluride

San Sophia
330 West Pacific Avenue
Telluride, CO 81435
(800) 537-4781

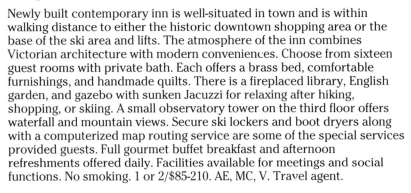

Type of B&B: Inn.
Rooms: 16 with private bath.
Rates: 1 or 2/$85-210.

Rating: A+ or ♛♛♛ Excellent, far exceeds basic requirements.

Newly built contemporary inn is well-situated in town and is within walking distance to either the historic downtown shopping area or the base of the ski area and lifts. The atmosphere of the inn combines Victorian architecture with modern conveniences. Choose from sixteen guest rooms with private bath. Each offers a brass bed, comfortable furnishings, and handmade quilts. There is a fireplaced library, English garden, and gazebo with sunken Jacuzzi for relaxing after hiking, shopping, or skiing. A small observatory tower on the third floor offers waterfall and mountain views. Secure ski lockers and boot dryers along with a computerized map routing service are some of the special services provided guests. Full gourmet buffet breakfast and afternoon refreshments offered daily. Facilities available for meetings and social functions. No smoking. 1 or 2/$85-210. AE, MC, V. Travel agent.

CONNECTICUT

Additional information on B&Bs in Connecticut is available from Folkstone B&B Reservation Service (800) 762-2751.

Mystic

Adams House
382 Cow Hill Road
Mystic, CT 06355
(203) 572-9551

Type of B&B: B&B home.
Rooms: 6 rooms and 1 cottage, all with private bath.
Rates: 1 or 2/$65-135; Suite/$135.

Rating: B+ or ♛♛ Good, exceeds basic requirements.

Historic home built in 1790 is located in a quiet residential setting near Mystic Seaport and Aquarium. Choose from six guest rooms in the main house with private baths; two feature fireplaces. The guest cottage offers complete privacy and is a perfect getaway for honeymooners and anniversary couples. The historic atmosphere of the home has been retained with original fireplaces and wide plank wood floors. Interesting area attractions include USS Nautilus Museum, US Coast Guard Academy, submarine base, and sailing. Continental breakfast includes fresh fruit, juice, homebaked breads and jams. No smoking. 1 or 2/$65-135; Suite/$135. MC, V.

New London

Queen Anne Inn
265 Williams Street
New London, CT 06320
(800) 347-8818 or (203) 447-2600

Type of B&B: Inn.
Rooms: 10, 8 with private bath.
Rates: 1/$73-150; 2/$78-155.

Rating: A or ♛♛♛ Excellent, far exceeds basic requirements.

Victorian inn built in 1903 is located off I-95 in a shoreline resort area. Choose from ten guest rooms, eight with private bath. Each room offers antique furnishings, air conditioning, and unique decor. Several rooms feature working fireplaces. A private cable TV and telephone are available in certain rooms upon request. The home's original beauty has been retained and is showcased in its carved alcove, fireplaced foyer, stained-glass windows, and main staircase circular landing. Transportation by bus, train, and ferry is within walking distance. Area attractions include Mystic Seaport and Aquarium, US Coast Guard Academy, Nautilus Submarine Memorial, and Block Island. Full gourmet breakfast and afternoon tea served daily. Facilities for meetings and social functions available. 1/$73-150; 2/$78-155. AE, Discover, Diners, MC, V. Seasonal senior, auto club, and business travel discounts available.

Guests write: *"Ray's gourmet full breakfasts and teas are both deliciously prepared and graciously served. Our room with brass bed and fireplace was warm and elegant. We were delightfully surprised to return to our room and find champagne chilled and ready to toast our second wedding anniversary. Their note thanking us for celebrating with them really touched us.."*
(B. Veronesi)

New Milford

Homestead Inn
5 Elm Street
New Milford, CT 06776
(203) 354-4080

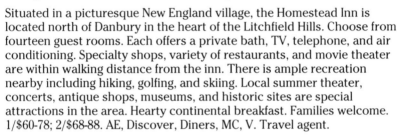

Type of B&B: Inn.
Rooms: 14 with private bath.
Rates: 1/$60-78; 2/$68-88.

Rating: B or ♛♛ Good, exceeds basic requirements.

Situated in a picturesque New England village, the Homestead Inn is located north of Danbury in the heart of the Litchfield Hills. Choose from fourteen guest rooms. Each offers a private bath, TV, telephone, and air conditioning. Specialty shops, variety of restaurants, and movie theater are within walking distance from the inn. There is ample recreation nearby including hiking, golfing, and skiing. Local summer theater, concerts, antique shops, museums, and historic sites are special attractions in the area. Hearty continental breakfast. Families welcome. 1/$60-78; 2/$68-88. AE, Discover, Diners, MC, V. Travel agent.

Guests write: *"Clean, moderately priced, central location to a great area. The owners are friendly but not intrusive. Breakfasts were shared with other couples who were fun to meet. Surprisingly, several couples were married folk from the same area who enjoy a weekend there occasionally to get away from the kids."* (S. Brannock)

"Exceptional hosts. The inn is beautiful and spotless. Nice thick fluffy towels and great water pressure. Candy in the room for our Valentine's Day stay and a bountiful continental breakfast." (D. Schlicher)

"Hosts couldn't have been nicer. They made me feel at home and had suggestions for places to see and have dinner. The continental breakfast was delicious and nicely served." (V. Shindell)

Norfolk

Manor House
P.O. Box 447, Maple Avenue
Norfolk, CT 06058
(203) 542-5690

Type of B&B: Inn
Rooms: 9 with private bath.
Rates: 1 or 2/$90-160.

Rating: A or ♛♛♛ Excellent, far exceeds basic requirements.

The Manor House was built as a Victorian home in 1898 and is set on five acres within the village and located just off Route 44. Choose from nine guest rooms with private bath. Each room differs in size and decor but special features include fireplaces, private balconies, and antique furnishings. Area attractions nearby include Yale Summer School of Music and Art, Tanglewood, Music Mountain, Lime Rock Park, and several theaters and vineyards. Enjoy the area's variety of activities such as skiing, hiking, bicycling, horseback riding, golfing, and water sports. Full breakfast features homemade breads. Facilities available for meetings and social functions. Restricted smoking. 1 or 2/$90-160. AE, MC, V. Travel agent.

Guests write: *"The guest rooms, house, grounds, and general ambiance are absolutely exquisite. The breakfasts served in the beautifully appointed dining room are fabulous. However the Manor's outstanding asset is its proprietors - whether it be directing you to the nearest music festival, suggesting the best antique shops in the area, providing guidance on restaurants, offering you seeds from their lush garden, or donating that warm bowl of popcorn to munch in front of the fireplace."* (A. Phillips)

"Thanks to two wonderful hosts for making us feel as if we're visiting friends in the country. The beautiful home weaves a special magic for all times of the day." (E. Charipper)

"The combination of the warm manner, the fireplace roaring, and the CD player loaded with Schutz, Debussy, George Winston, and John Coltrane was magic! It made for a great, relaxing eighth anniversary celebration." (J. Donner)

"We were so impressed on our first visit we've made it a tradition to go back the same time every year; and have done so for the last five years as well as other visits throughout the year. We look to the Manor House as a sanctuary away from our hectic day-to-day lives and the hosts have always made us feel welcome, at home, and relaxed." (B. McKane)

"We are booked there for our fourth Christmas there. When the moon is full, we make it a romantic weekend with a sleigh ride when there's snow or a carriage for two when there is no snow. The horses and carriages are ready at a nearby stable." (B. Tyler)

Ridgefield

West Lane Inn
22 West Lane
Ridgefield, CT 06877
(203) 438-7323

Type of B&B: Inn.
Rooms: 20 with private bath.
Rates: 1/$90-115; 2/$120-165.

Rating: A+ or ♛♛♛ Excellent, far exceeds basic requirements.

Victorian inn built in 1848 is set at the end of a broad lawn, surrounded by majestic maples, and located one hour north of New York City and three hours southwest of Boston. Choose from twenty individually decorated rooms, each with private bath, temperature control, and color television. Several rooms feature working fireplaces. There are ample common areas for guest relaxation in front of a fireplace or with a good book. Take long walks on the wooded trails or visit nearby historic sites, museums, art galleries, and antique stores. Area recreation includes swimming, sailing, bowling, skating, and skiing. Continental breakfast is included in the rates but a full breakfast is available. Families welcome. Wheelchair access. 1/$90-115; 2/$120-165. AE, MC, V.

WASHINGTON, DC
(See Silver Spring, Burtonsville, and Olney, MD)

Additional information on B&Bs throughout Florida is available from B&B Scenic Florida (904) 386-8196.

Amelia Island

Elizabeth Point Lodge
98 South Fletcher Street
Amelia Island, FL 32034
(904) 277-4851

Type of B&B: Inn.
Rooms: 20 with private bath.
Rates: 1/$75-105; 2/$85-115.

Rating: A or ♛♛♛ Excellent, far exceeds basic requirements.

New oceanfront Nantucket-style inn built in a turn-of-the-century manner is found just off Route A1A, 25 miles north of Jacksonville, and fifteen miles off I-95. Twenty guest rooms, each with private bath, have been carefully decorated to emphasize a maritime theme and include oversized tubs and fresh flowers. Enjoy a glass of lemonade and a homemade snack on the main floor's wrap-around porch or visit the deserted beaches nearby. Special children's activities are regularly scheduled and assistance is given in arranging special tours and outings with sailing, fishing charters, golfing, biking, and horseback riding nearby. A full breakfast is served in the oceanfront sunroom and includes special egg dishes and fresh baked goods. Meeting and reception facilities available. Families welcome. Wheelchair access. 1/$75-105; 2/$85-115. AE, MC, V. Senior and auto club discounts. Travel agent.

Amelia Island

Florida House Inn
20 and 22 South Third Street
Amelia Island, FL 32034
(904) 261-3300 or (800) 258-3301

Type of B&B: Inn with restaurant.
Rooms: 12 with private bath.
Rates: 1 or 2/$55-120.

Rating: B+ or ♛♛ Good, exceeds basic requirements.

In continuous operation since 1857, this Greek Revival country inn with restaurant is located 35 miles north of Jacksonville off I-95. All twelve guest rooms boast private baths, air-conditioning, country oak and pine antiques, and handmade quilts. Some rooms offer fireplaces and whirlpool tubs. Guests are invited to enjoy swimming, golfing, tennis, and antiquing nearby as well as explore twenty miles of beaches, a Civil War fort, Cumberland Island, Big and Little Talbot Island, and state parks. Full country breakfast. Wheelchair access. Restricted smoking. 1 or 2/$55-120. AE, MC, V. 10% senior, business travel, and auto club discounts. Travel agent.

Daytona Beach

Live Oak Inn and Restaurant
448 South Beach Street
Daytona Beach, FL 32114
(904) 252-4667

Type of B&B: Country inn with restaurant.
Rooms: 16, each with private bath.
Rates: 1/$50-175; 2/$55-180.

Rating: A- or ♛♛♛ Excellent, far exceeds basic requirements.

Restored Victorian home is listed on the National Register of Historic Places and offers views of the Halifax Harbor Marina from its location one hour north of Orlando off Interstates 4 and 95. Choose from sixteen guest rooms with private bath which offer a variety of size, decor, period furnishings, and amenities. Each room's decor theme depicts people or events which helped shape Florida's history and each offers views of Halifax Harbor or the inn's historical garden. Several rooms feature a Jacuzzi or Victorian soaking tub. Nearby attractions include Jackie Robinson Memorial Stadium and Park, St. Augustine, Cape Kennedy Space Center, and Orlando attractions. Explore area beaches, art galleries, museums, and historic sites. Continental plus breakfast is served in the restaurant and includes fresh fruit and orange juice, muffins, cheese, and pate or sausage. Facilities available for meetings and weddings. Families welcome. Wheelchair access. Restricted smoking. 1/$50-175; 2/$55-180. AE, MC, V. Travel agent.

Holmes Beach

Harrington House B&B
5626 Gulf Drive
Holmes Beach, FL 34217
(813) 778-5444

Type of B&B: Inn.
Rooms: 7 with private bath.
Rates: 1 or 2/$59-149

Rating: A or ♛♛♛ Excellent, far exceeds basic requirements.

Unspoiled Anna Maria Island is located south of Tampa on the Gulf. Harrington House sits directly on the beach and offers casual elegance throughout its seven guest rooms. Each room is unique in size, decor, and amenities but all have private baths and air conditioning. Special features include French doors leading out to private balconies with views of the Gulf of Mexico. Moonlight strolls on the beach are a favorite activity here but guests also enjoy gathering around the swimming pool and the high ceilinged living room with fireplace and large collection of interesting books. Disney World is a two hour drive but nearby sites include Ringling Mansion and Museum, Selby Gardens, and Bishop's Planetarium. Full breakfast. No smoking. $59-149. MC, V. Travel agent.

Guests write: *"What can we say to describe our trip here? The welcome was warm and inviting. We loved the room - so cozy and super clean. Breakfast was delicious. We just had a great time. And our only sorrow was it wasn't long enough."* (D. Yeager)

"Our room was lovely and I most appreciated the attention to detail - iced tea on the porch, mints on the dresser, refrigerator in the room, and the little basket with shampoo, etc. in the bath. Those are the things that make it special. Breakfasts were delightful." (K. Goss)

"The setting was wonderful. We want the Sunset Room when we return. Friendliness of staff and guests was like home. Food was wonderful. I appreciated the little touches - decor, accessories, colors, warmth." (C. Cavanagh)

"These folks treat their guests like kings and queens. The service is second to none. The atmosphere is very unique and enjoyable. They create a warm and friendly environment for all." (D. Traudt)

"The room, the ambiance, the staff, breakfasts, the view, the beach - all too nice for words." (T. Ennis)

"Our visit was so much more than expected. The charm and personality of the Inn is equal to the wonderful people we met both working here and visiting. We intend to become regulars." (B. Pruette)

Key West

Heron House
512 Simonton Street
Key West, FL 33040
(305) 294-9227

Type of B&B: B&B Guesthouse.
Rooms: 18 with private bath.
Rates:1/$55-125; 2/$105-195.

Rating: B+ or ♛♛ Good, exceeds basic requirements.

Heron House is a historic property built in 1856. It is centrally located near all major tourism attractions in Key West yet located on a quiet residential street off Route 1. There are eighteen guest rooms with private bath available. Each is unique in size, decor, and amenities. Several luxury rooms feature large mirrored walls and unusual wood decorative artwork as well as marble baths. The rooms are located in two buildings that surround a pleasant swimming pool and patio with lush foliage, large pots of tropical plants, and orchids. Nearby attractions include Hemingway House, Mel Fischer's Treasure Museum, snorkeling cruises, tennis, golf, fishing, and hiking. Continental breakfast includes waffles or French toast, bagels and muffins. Wheelchair access. 1/$55-125; 2/$105-195. AE, MC, V. Travel agent.

Key West

La Mer Hotel
506 South Street
Key West, FL 33040
(800)354-4455 or (305) 296-5611

Type of B&B: Inn that's part of a hotel complex.
Rooms:11 with private baths.
Rates:1/$104; 2/$240.

Rating: A or ♛♛♛ Excellent, far exceeds basic requirements.

Located directly on the Atlantic Ocean, this Victorian "Conch" house is surrounded by tropical foliage and palm trees in the heart of Old Town Key West. Each of the newly renovated guest rooms, eleven in all, feature private bath, cable television, air conditioning, in-room safe, and private phone. Most rooms, decorated with a contemporary theme, offer private patios or balconies overlooking the ocean or tropical surroundings. Relax at one of the three pools, a Jacuzzi, or the sunning pier. Bike and moped rentals are available for exploring the area. Visit the only coral reef in the country, take a sunset cruise, scuba dive or snorkel, or take advantage of the ample shopping, historic attractions, and nightlife found in the resort area. Extensive continental breakfast is served and daily newspaper delivery is complimentary. 1/$104; 2/$240. AE, MC, V. Travel agent.

Guests write: "The thoughtfulness of the managers, Matt & Carrie Babich and all their supporting staff is exceptional and greatly appreciated. The sun brightly shining, the blue sky and water, with the waves washing against the shore, and a sand beach are at your door. The decor is electric- soft pastels, wicker furniture with just the right feeling of casual living and relaxing." (B. Isabel)

"My wife and I find La Mer to be perfectly located. It's at the quiet end of Duval Street with a pool and beach on the Atlantic, a sunning pier from which we can enjoy a drink for Key West's legendary sunsets. Elegant verandah for watching the parade of character's pass on South Street. The rooms are well-appointed and quiet (recently renovated) and breakfasts are generous and varied." (A. Wimett)

Key West

The Watson House
525 Simonton Street
Key West, FL 33040
(305) 294-6712 or (800) 621-9405

Type of B&B: Guesthouse
Rooms: 3 suites with private bath.
Rates: 1 or 2/$95-360.

Rating: A+ or ♛ ♛ ♛ Excellent, far exceeds basic requirements.

Bahamian-style guest house built in 1860 has been fully restored and expanded and is located in the heart of the Historic District. Choose from two guest accommodations in the main house or the Cabana, which is a four-room private apartment. Each is individually furnished and features hardwood floors, paddle fans, wicker and rattan furnishings, floral patterns and textures, private bath, telephone, color cable TV, fully equipped kitchen, and air-conditioning. Private decks overlook a tropical garden setting enhanced by a waterfall, large spa, and heated swimming pool. Walk to many fine restaurants, live theater, Hemingway House, boating, deep sea fishing, Conch tour trains, and the nightlife of Duval Street. Continental breakfast basket is brought to each suite. 1 or 2/$95-360. AE, MC, V. Travel agent.

Lake Wales

Chalet Suzanne Country Inn & Restaurant
3800 Chalet Suzanne Drive
Lake Wales, FL 33853
(813) 676-6011 or (800) 433-6011

Type of B&B: Country inn with restaurant.
Rooms: 30 with private bath.
Rates: 1 or 2/$105-185.

Rating: A or ♛♛♛ Excellent, far exceeds basic requirements.

Chalet Suzanne is an unusual private estate that is a family-owned and operated European-style inn with restaurant. The inn is listed on the National Register of Historic Places and located in central Florida off US-27. Choose from thirty individually decorated guest rooms with private bath. There is a variety in the size, decor, and amenities of the rooms but each features air conditioning, telephone, and TV. The complex includes a ceramic studio, antique shop, and historic chapel. There are extensive grounds which include a swimming pool and secret garden area where special guests have been invited to sign tiles which are fired in the ceramic studio and used to create a garden wall. Area attractions include Bok Tower Gardens, Cypress Gardens, Disney World, Epcot Center, Sea World, and Busch Gardens. Full breakfast is included in the room rate. Lunch and candlelight dinner available at additional charge. Families welcome. Facilities for meetings and social functions. Guests can fly in as there is a private landing strip on the property. 1 or 2/$105-185. AE, MC, V. 10% business travel discount. Travel agent.

Guests write: *"Our stay at Chalet Suzanne was exceptional (as usual). It's amazing how we can make Lake Wales on our way to everywhere we go in Florida. From the warm welcome greeting on arrival to the excellent service at dinner, to the morning smiles from staffers and the come again waves as we left, we were made to feel this is our Southern home. Although we brought our children, we purposely fed them early so we could enjoy our candlelight romantic dinner alone. The presentation of each course was superb. The melody of flavors and textures and color makes our memories of dinner here linger long after we've left."* (D. Thorsen)

"We think the Chalet Suzanne is fabulous. Since we have flown in 475 times for breakfast, it must be great! The food is superb and the hospitality of the Hinshaws and their staff is simply marvelous." (E. Bowman)

"The Chalet is really out of this world in all respects. The atmosphere, the food, the furniture, the rooms, the classical music, the extremely friendly employees. I was so happy to get to know Mrs. Vita Hinshaw personally and I really was overwhelmed by her warmth, her style, her spirit, her charm, her personality - so I'm sure this is one reason for the aura here. Vita means Life - so there has to be a lot of real life here at this magnificent place." (D. Buck)

Miami

Miami River Inn
118 SW South River Drive
Miami, FL 33130
(305) 325-0045

Type of B&B: Inn.
Rooms: 40, 38 with private bath.
Rates: 1 or 2/$70-110.

Rating: B or ♛♛ Good, exceeds basic requirements.

Four restored Victorian clapboard buildings built between 1906 and 1914 comprise this inn which is located in downtown Miami's Riverview Historic District. There are forty guest rooms available, each with color cable TV and central air conditioning. Thirty-eight rooms offer a private bath. Each room is individually appointed with themes ranging from white wicker to others featuring ornately carved gothic headboards and elaborately swagged drapes. The grounds feature tropical plantings, a swimming pool, spa, and croquet lawn. The inn is a ten minute walk from the heart of downtown, Flagler Street shopping, great restaurants, and cultural centers. Facilities available for meetings and conferences. Continental breakfast. 1 or 2/$70-110. Travel agent.

Orlando

The Courtyard at Lake Lucerne
211 North Lucerne Circle East
Orlando, FL 32801
(407) 648-5188

Type of B&B: B&B Inn.
Rooms: 22 with private bath.
Rates: 1 or 2/$65-150.

Rating: B+ or ♛♛ Good, exceeds basic requirements.

Comprised of three historic buildings, built in 1883, 1916, and 1947 successively, this B&B inn is located in the heart of Downtown Orlando. Choose from twenty-two guest rooms with private bath. Six rooms with Victorian decor are located in the Norment-Parry Inn. Twelve rooms with Art Deco-style suites are in the Wellborn building. Three suites in the Antebellum style are found in the I.W. Phillips House. Explore the private garden, turn-of-the-century English fountain, and wide verandah porches. A burled oak grand piano graces the large reception hall. Just a few blocks away is downtown Orlando with its many attractions including Church Street and the Arena. Disney World and Sea World are only minutes away. Continental breakfast. Wedding and meeting facilities available. Families welcome. Restricted smoking. 1 or 2/$65-150. AE, MC, V. Senior, corporate, and auto club discounts. Travel agent.

Orlando

Perri House Bed & Breakfast Inn
10417 State Road 535
Orlando, FL 32836
(407) 876-4830 or (800) 780-4830

Type of B&B: B&B inn.
Rooms: 4, each with private bath.
Rates: 1/$50-60; 2/$65-75.

Rating: A- or ♛♛♛ Excellent, far exceeds basic requirements.

Nestled in "Disney's back yard," this 5,400 square foot home is located 3.6 miles north of exit 27 off I-4 on State Road 535 North. Four guest rooms are available, each individually furnished with contemporary decor theme, air conditioning, private bath, private entrance, and brass queen-size bed or four-poster king-size bed. There is a Jacuzzi as well as swimming pool on the property for guest use. Historic downtown Orlando is twenty minutes away by car and Disney World, Sea World, Universal Studios, and Pleasure Island are also nearby. Visit fine area restaurants, golf courses, shopping areas, and water parks. Continental breakfast features fresh fruit, giant muffins, danish, and cereals. Families welcome. Restricted smoking. 1/$50-60; 2/$65-75. AE, MC, V. Family and senior discounts. Travel agent.

Guests write: *"The Perrettis run a wonderful B&B. In addition to charmingly furnished rooms and lovely surroundings, they are extremely warm, friendly, and helpful. They repeatedly asked us if we had any special needs and met each and every one. Breakfast was a potpourri feast of fresh fruit, cereals, juices, and always a special muffin or cake. The house was immaculate. The breakfast area overlooked the yard and pool. There are many birds and the Perrettis are encouraging guests to donate bird feeders as they intend to start a bird sanctuary."* (F. Leoussis)

"The house is modern and each individually decorated room has its own entrance and private bath. At night, you can sit in the Jacuzzi by the pool and sip a glass of wine. I particularly liked the fact that Perri House combines the best elements of a first-class hotel (it's completely private and you can come and go as you please) with the hominess and hospitality you expect in a B&B." (K. Monaghan)

"We were delighted with the convenient location, the quiet, relaxing surroundings, and especially the graciousness of our hosts. The accommodations were clean and homey, and the breakfasts were overwhelming." (H. Flynn)

"After spending five days at the Perri House we decided to spend our last 3 days at a Disney Hotel. While it was very nice, the additional expense wasn't worth it because we never had time to enjoy the resort amenities." (T. Pappas)

Orlando/Maitland

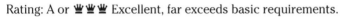

Thurston House
851 Lake Avenue
Maitland, FL 32751
(407) 539-1911

Type of B&B: B&B Inn.
Rooms: 4 with private bath.
Rates: 1 or 2/$70-80.

Rating: A or ♛♛♛ Excellent, far exceeds basic requirements.

Boasting a cross gable roof and three screened-in porches, this circa 1885 Queen Anne Victorian is situated in a rural lakefront setting, but is just 5 miles from downtown Orlando. All four newly restored guest rooms have a private bath and feature period decor. Each room is named after one of the four families that have occupied the house over the last one-hundred years. Common rooms include a front and back parlor as well as wrap-around porch. The grounds offer gardens, acres of fruit trees, and lakefront view. Visit nearby museums, restaurants, state parks, beaches, and Disney attractions. An expanded continental breakfast and afternoon snack are offered daily. No smoking. 1 or 2/$70-80. AE, MC, V. Corporate discount. Travel agent.

Orange Park

Club Continental Suites
2143 Astor Street
Orange Park, FL 32073
(904) 264-6070

Type of B&B: Large B&B Inn.
Rooms: 22 with private bath.
Rates:1/$60; 2/$135.

Rating: A- or ♛♛♛ Excellent, far exceeds basic requirements.

Italian Renaissance inn with classic Mediterranean red tile roof, multiple arches, and wrought iron is 12 miles south of downtown Jacksonville. Built in 1923 as the Palmolive Family estate, it is surrounded by giant live oaks and native palms. All of the twenty-two guest rooms, including several two-rooms suites, are individually decorated and have oversized private baths. Several rooms offer special features such as a fireplace, Jacuzzi, and view of the St. Johns River. A third floor tower apartment has a full kitchen and large balcony. Stroll the manicured courtyard or relax by one of the two full-sized pools. Play tennis on one of the inn's seven courts or take the path to the river where a Pre-Civil War cottage is now a local gathering place featuring entertainment (Thursday through

Saturday). St. Augustine and First Coast Beaches are thirty-five minutes away and Orlando attractions are two hours south. Continental breakfast. The riverfront view and spacious grounds are an ideal setting for weddings and meetings, accommodating up to 250 people. Families welcome. Wheelchair access. 1/$60; 2/$135. AE, MC, V. Travel agent.

Palm Beach

Palm Beach Historic Inn
365 South County Road
Palm Beach, FL 33480
(407) 832-4009

Type of B&B: B&B Inn.
Rooms: 9 with private bath; four suites.
Rates: 1 or 2/$60-210 (seasonal).

Rating: A- or ♛♛♛ Excellent, far exceeds basic requirements.

Restored Mediterranean-style inn built in 1923 is situated in the heart of Palm Beach, 1 block from the beach. Each of the nine guest rooms feature individual decor, private bath, air conditioning, telephone, and cable television. Four suites are also available. Walk to the beach or to Worth Avenue; enjoy water sports as well as cruises, golfing, tennis, Jai-Alai, shopping, galleries, theater, and shopping. Cultural events and performing arts as well as museums and concerts are nearby. Continental breakfast features fresh Florida fruits and baked goods served in the guest room. Families welcome. Restricted smoking. 1 or 2/$60-210. AE, MC, V. Travel agent.

Sanibel

Sanibel's Song of the Sea
863 East Gulf Drive
Sanibel Island, FL 33957
(813) 472-2220 or (800)231-1045

Type of B&B: B&B Inn.
Rooms: 30 with private baths.
Rates: 1 or 2/$124-263.

Rating: A or ♛♛♛ Excellent, far exceeds basic requirements.

Surrounded by tropical foliage and flowering plants, this recently renovated, European-style seaside inn is located on the Gulf of Mexico, 10 miles west of Fort Myers. Thirty guest rooms offer private baths as well as Mediterranean tile floors, Country French furnishings, fresh flowers, ceiling fans, fully equipped kitchens, and screened terraces. Relax in the whirlpool, borrow a book to read from the lending library, or borrow a bicycle to explore the island bike paths. Recreation here includes golf, fishing, sailing, tennis, and shelling on the miles of private beaches that Sanibel Island is famous for. Expanded continental breakfast is offered with a complimentary newspaper each morning and guests are encouraged to take their breakfast out onto to the terrace. Weddings on the beach. Families welcome. 1 or 2/$124-263. AE, MC, V. Travel agent.

St. Petersburg

Mansion House
105 5th Avenue Northeast
St. Petersburg, FL 33701
(813)821-9391
Fax (813) 821-9754

Type of B&B: B&B Inn.
Rooms: 6 with private bath.
Rates: 1/$50-55; 2/$55-60.

Rating: B or ♛♛ Good, exceeds basic requirements.

English-style inn built at the turn-of-the-century is within the St. Petersburg city limits, just 2 minutes off of Highway 375. Each of the six guest rooms with private bath has been decorated with a English Country theme. The Carriage room boasts a beamed ceiling and four-poster bed. Relax on the indoor porch with its peach and green cane furniture and white and teal tiled floor or on the outdoor screened porch which sits under a large oak tree. The formal lounge has a variety of reading material, big chairs for relaxing, and a piano. Take a short walk to Straub Park where open air concerts and festivals are held or to the pier, where live music, fishing, and boating are available. Take a thirty minute drive to Busch Gardens or visit nearby Sunken Gardens, Museum of fine Arts, Dali museum, and the Pat Buckley Moss Gallery. A full English breakfast is offered in two dining rooms which serve specialties such as Welsh cakes, sausage, bacon, eggs, and fried tomatoes. Wedding and meeting facilities available. Families welcome. No smoking. 1/$50-55; 2/$55-60. MC,V. Travel agent.

Guests write: *"This B&B has a special charm not often found in the United States. Alan and Suzanne welcomed us into their newly restored home and made us feel like a part of the family."* (T. Kurzweg)

"Better than home for two retired guests. Cheery-light living and reading rooms- clean, comfortable- nicely decorated bedroom- very well located for a walking visit of St. Petersburg Bay Front. Excellent breakfasts." (B. Harmon)

— *Comments continued on next page*

"Meticulously clean, friendly, personal attention. Privacy was respected." (T. McEachern)

"What a wonderfully pleasant surprise to find such a fresh and clean, large older home remodeled to perfection and operated by a young, friendly Welsh couple. Allan's a great English breakfast cook- even to the Welsh cake he prepares along with a full breakfast to your order." (D. Lapworth)

GEORGIA

Additional information on B&Bs throughout Georgia is available from B&B Atlanta at (800) 96-PEACH and Quail Country B&B at (912) 226-7218.

Atlanta

Oakwood House
951 Edgewood Avenue, NE
Atlanta, GA 30307
(404)521-9320 or (404)688-6034

Type of B&B: B&B Inn.
Rooms: 4 with private bath.
Rates: 1/$60-80; 2/$65-85.

Rating: B or ♛♛ Good, exceeds basic requirements.

Turn-of-the-century Craftsman post-Victorian style inn still shows off its original woodwork and is located in the historic neighborhood of Inman Park, near downtown and midtown Atlanta. The four guest rooms with private bath have been furnished to compliment the style of the early part of this century but have been recently remodeled to include modern fixtures and telephones. Relax on the front porch, the backyard decks, or under the shady oak tree, for which the inn was named. Take a short walk to Little 5 Points, Atlanta's "Off Broadway", or "Soho". Visit nearby Underground Atlanta as well as downtown, World Congress Center, the zoo, Cyclorama, World of Coke, the Martin Luther King Jr. Grave and National Park, as well as many wholesale marts, universities, and stadiums. Health oriented continental breakfast includes home baked goods and fresh fruit. Wedding and meeting facilities available in the historic "Trolley Barn" found immediately next door to the inn. Families welcome. No smoking. 1/$60-80; 2/$65-85. MC, V. 10% auto and extended stay discounts. Travel agent.

Guests write: *"We stayed in the master suite and it was nicely appointed and very spacious. The high ceilings and large rooms give the whole house an airy feel."* (A. Bowden)

"Quiet; great breakfasts. Lovely." (B.J. Smith)

"I recently had the enjoyment of staying at the Oakwood House. A very convincing recommendation from a friend led me to plan the stay. The immaculate upkeep, warm atmosphere, and even more so, the genuine hospitality of both Judy and Robert, made my several days in Atlanta a pleasurable experience." (C. Smith)

"Love the style, fresh flowers, good breakfast! Comfy home away from home" (D. Hall)

Blairsville

Souther Country Inn
2592 Collins Lane
Blairsville, GA 30512
(706)379-1603

Type of B&B: B&B Inn.
Rooms: 9 with private bath.
Rates:1/$75; 2/$85.

Rating: A or ♛♛♛ Excellent, far exceeds basic requirements.

Set in a rural area and built in the style of an English country manor, this 1992 inn is located 112 miles north of Atlanta. Choose from nine guest rooms, each with private bath. Enjoy the area's many outdoor activities such as white-water rafting, hiking on the Appalachian Trail, fishing, swimming, boating, and golfing. Antique shopping as well as seasonal fairs and festivals round out vacation plans here. Full breakfast. Wedding and meeting facilities available. Wheelchair access. No smoking. 1/$75; 2/$85. AE, MC, V. Travel agent.

Dahlonega

Mountain Top Lodge at Dahlonega
Route 7, Box 150
Dahlonega, GA 30533
(706) 864-5257

Type of B&B: Inn.
Rooms: 13 rooms or suites with private bath.
Rates: 1/$45-105; 2/$65-125.

Rating: A or ♛♛♛ Excellent, far exceeds basic requirements.

Mountain Top Lodge is a secluded rural retreat located 60 miles north of Atlanta. Choose from thirteen guest rooms or suites with private bath.

Each is unique in size, decor, and amenities but all are furnished with mountain crafts and antiques. Suites feature sitting rooms and private decks. Two deluxe rooms have gas fireplaces and whirlpool tubs. Enjoy the great room with cathedral ceiling, wood stove, card room loft and library, as well as the large, heated outdoor spa. The inn is surrounded by towering trees and pleasant pastoral scenery. Area attractions include Gold Museum, Amicalola Falls, tennis, fishing, hiking, canoeing, bicycling, and horseback riding. Full breakfast. Facilities available for meetings and social functions. Four bedrooms on lower level have wheelchair access. No smoking. 1/$45-105; 2/$65-125. AE, MC, V.

Savannah

Ballastone Inn and Townhouse
14 East Oglethorpe Avenue
Savannah, GA 31401
(912) 236-1484 or (800) 822-4553

Type of B&B: Large inn.
Rooms: 22 with private bath.
Rates: 1/$95; 2/$175.

Rating: A+ or ♕ ♕ ♕ Excellent, far exceeds basic requirements.

Built in 1838, this restored four-story Federal and Victorian mansion is situated in the center of Savannah's historic district. All of the twenty-four guest rooms feature a private bath, color TV, air conditioning, period antiques, and decor that reflects Savannah's rich past. Visit the area's two historic districts, museum houses, riverfront attractions, historic forts, and the nearby beach. A continental plus breakfast offers specialties such as Southern-style muffins and fruit compote, and is served in guest rooms, the courtyard, or the downstairs parlor. Wheelchair access. 1/$95; 2/$175. AE, MC, V. 10% senior and business discount. Travel agent.

Savannah

Eliza Thompson House
5 West Jones Street
Savannah, GA 31401
(912) 236-3620 or (800) 348-9378

Type of B&B: Inn.
Rooms: 24 with private bath.
Rates: 1/$68-98; 2/$88-108.

Rating: B+ or ♛♛ Good, exceeds basic requirements.

The Eliza Thompson House is a Federal home built in 1847 and located in the heart of Savannah's Historic District. Choose from twenty-four guest rooms, each with private bath, heart pine floors, period furnishings, telephone, and color TV. A relaxing parlor is offered as well as an inviting landscaped courtyard with fountains. Area attractions within walking distance include museums, Forsyth Park, and River Street shopping. Continental breakfast includes croissants, muffins, and danish. Afternoon wine and cheese and evening sherry offered. Families welcome. 1/$68-98; 2/$88-108. 10% senior and auto club discounts.

HAWAII

Additional information on B&Bs in Hawaii is available from B&B Honolulu (Statewide) (800) 288-4666 or Hawaii's Best B&B (800) 262-9912.

Hilo, Island of Hawaii

Hale Kai-Bjornen
111 Honolii Pali
Hilo, HI 96720
(808) 935-6330

Type of B&B: B&B home.
Rooms: 4 with private bath; guest cottage.
Rates: $75-98.

Rating: A+ or ♛♛♛ Excellent, far exceeds basic requirements.

Modern home of Scandinavian and Japanese design sits on a bluff facing the ocean and is located 2 miles from downtown Hilo. Choose from four guest rooms (2 kings and 2 queens) with private bath, cable TV, ocean view, and easy access to the bar room, pool, Jacuzzi, patio, and lanais. The guest cottage offers a living room, kitchenette, bedroom with queen-size bed, private bath, cable TV, and faces the ocean. Explore the entire island from this location including nearby Rainbow Falls, Botanical Gardens, Akaka Falls, the volcanos, Waipio Valley, and cities of Hilo and Kona. Full breakfast features dishes such as macadamia nut waffles, Portuguese sausage, fruit platters, and Kona coffee. Restricted smoking. Rates $75-98. Three day minimum for the main house and five day minimum reservation for the guest cottage.

Guests write: *"We found our Blue Hawaii as we sipped champagne in Evonne's Jacuzzi and watched the tangerine sunrise on the Pacific Ocean through her swaying coconut and papaya trees. A real second Honeymoon!"* (P. Butler)

"We enjoyed a view of Hilo Harbor that is beautiful and can be seen from the room, pool, or Jacuzzi. The breakfast was as good as I've eaten with island fruits and breads, and macadamia nut waffles, Portuguese sausage and Norwegian eggs. The best thing was the friendliness of the hosts who can tell you all the do's and don'ts of the island." (D. McHugh)

"We didn't want to leave! The hosts shared their collections and personal travel experiences with us. Such an interesting and warm couple! They directed us to delicious restaurants for dinner and served delicious full course breakfasts. They treated us as family and kings." (J. Glass)

"The fresh tropical flowers in each room were beautiful. Our room was spotless. I wish I could close my eyes and still hear the sound of the surf like I could from our patio. Loved the Jacuzzi under the stars after a long day of sightseeing." (D. Talbot)

"Our room was very well done with interesting things about to make you feel close to the host and hostess. We had a view overlooking the bay. Paul directed us to very special places I am sure a tour guide would overlook. He is a native and knew where to send us. The breakfast was always gourmet. Flowers were everywhere and fresh daily." (H. Hagen)

"While the accommodations could easily be termed spectacular, the real attractions are Paul and Evonne. Their warmth and style gave us a sense of family. We especially like their style in bringing guests together. In fact, we established an ongoing friendship with another visiting couple." (D. Hergenrether)

"We had a glass of wine with Evonne and Paul on the deck and watched a Princess cruise ship head out of the harbor and steam past. Kona coffee and macadamia-nut waffles started our day." (C. Hailey)

Kamuela, Island of Hawaii

Waimea Gardens Cottage
PO Box 563
Kamuela, HI 96743
(800)262-9912 or (808) 885-4550

Type of B&B: Private cottage.
Rooms: 2 with private bath.
Rates: 1 or 2/$90-95.

Rating: A- or ♕♕♕ Excellent, far exceeds basic requirements.

Country cottage on 1.5 acres is located two miles west of the ranch town of Waimea, 8 miles from the beach, and 45 miles from Kailua-Kona. Each cottage offers two guest rooms that feature a private bath, hardwood floors, wainscoting, antique furnishings, and French doors. Sit by the fireplace in the Waimea Wing, explore the Parker Ranch and the island's white sand beaches. Guests gather their own eggs and prepare their own breakfast with provisions provided, including homemade bread. Hosts live on the premises in the main house. Families welcome. Wheelchair access. No smoking. 1 or 2/$90-95.

Volcano, Island of Hawaii

Chalet Kilauea at Volcano
P.O. Box 998
Volcano, HI 96785
(808) 967-7786 or (800) 937-7786

Type of B&B: Inn.
Rooms: 4 with shared or private bath.
Rates: 1 or 2/$75-95

Rating: B+ or ♕♕ Good, exceeds basic requirements.

Hawaiian chalet has a lush tropical setting outside the village of Volcano. Choose from three guest rooms in the main house which are decorated with Oriental, African, or Victorian themes. The two-level Treehouse suite is adjacent to the main building and offers complete privacy with a bedroom upstairs, a sitting area on the lower level, and private bath. A large parlor with fireplace offers ample comfortable seating among an interesting collection of crafts from around the world. The grounds are spacious and include a hot tub. Volcano National Park is nearby where visitors enjoy hiking, golfing, biking, swimming, birdwatching, and lava viewing. A full two-course gourmet breakfast boasts international and local dishes as well as Kona coffee. Families welcome. Restricted smoking. 1 or 2/$75-95. MC, V. Travel agent.

— *Comments continued on next page*

Guests write: *"Chalet Kilawea is a most unique B&B that is beautifully decorated and serves delicious breakfasts. The hosts are gracious well-traveled couple who have considered all needs. I especially liked the Tree House Suite."* (H. Haan)

Volcano, Island of Hawaii

Kilauea Lodge
P.O. Box 116
Volcano, HI 96785
(808) 967-7366

Type of B&B: Lodge.
Rooms: 12 with private bath.
Rates: 1 or 2/$85-105

Rating: A or ♛♛♛ Excellent, far exceeds basic requirements.

This 1930's Midwest style lodge is located near Volcano National Park on the Hilo side of the island. Twelve guest rooms all have private bath and six feature fireplaces for the cool mountain evenings. Relax in front of the unique "friendship" fireplace or enjoy the inn's restaurant. Nearby attractions and activities include Volcano National Park, Kilauea Volcano, Botanical Gardens, hiking, golfing, and bird watching. Full breakfast frequently features specials such as pancakes and French toast. Families welcome. Wheelchair access. 1 or 2/$85-105. MC, V.

Guests write: *"Excellent food, hospitality, accommodations in a beautiful surrounding. Would recommend this lodge to anyone and everyone. Can't think of any way in which improvement could be made. Lodge staff also have an excellent first-aid kit available for minor injuries, falls, and scrapes on the lava flows."* (E. Murray)

"Life doesn't get any better than this. We have been home for three months and still feel the same way about the Kilauea Lodge." (F. Harman)

"I almost didn't want to say anything nice about this place because I would like to keep this charming B&B to ourselves. Philip kept wanting to hike around the Volcano while I wanted to return to our cozy room and sip a cocktail by our own fireplace. The staff couldn't have been more courteous, the food was consistently excellent." (A. Rauenhorst)

"Our cottage was beautifully maintained and wonderfully cozy. The staff was exceptionally polite and helpful, and our meals at the lodge were delicious and reasonably priced. Our stay at the lodge will certainly be one of our favorite Honeymoon memories." (J. Lowe)

Kapaa, Island of Kauai

Kay Barker's B&B
P.O. Box 740
Kapaa, Kauai, HI 96746
(808) 822-3073 or (800) 835-4845

Type of B&B: B&B home and private cottage.
Rooms: 4 with private bath.
Rates: 1/$30-60; 2/$40-70.

Rating: B or ♛♛ Good, exceeds basic requirements.

Kay Barker's B&B is a ranch home set on the slopes of Sleeping Giant Mountain in a quiet residential area. There are four guest rooms in the main house, each with a private bath. A separate cottage offers complete privacy along with a king-size bed, living room, private lanai, and kitchenette. Guests relax and gather together on the lanai or in the living room of the main house which has a comfortable TV viewing area and extensive library. Beach supplies such as boogie boards, ice chests, towels, and beach mats are available as well as a washer and dryer. Popular attractions in the area include Wailua River and the Fern Grotto. Area recreation includes snorkeling, tennis, and hiking. Full breakfast often includes fresh fruit, banana nut muffins, macadamia nut hotcakes, or quiche. Families welcome. 1/$30-60; 2/$40-70. MC, V. Travel agent.

Guests write: *"Excellent B&B! The room was very spacious and clean and the house was very comfortable. The breakfasts were delicious and I looked forward to them every day. I paid the least at this B&B and got the best B&B."* (G. Young)

Poipu, Island of Kauai

Gloria's Spouting Horn B&B
4464 Lawai Beach Road
Poipu, Kauai, HI 96756
(808) 742-6995

Type of B&B: B&B home.
Rooms: 3 with private bath.
Rates: 1 or 2/$100-125.

Unrated as construction work not completed at press time.

Gloria's Spouting Horn B&B is located on the ocean at Spouting Horn which offers a marvelous secluded beach and famous ocean vistas. Guest accommodations have been completely rebuilt in 1993 and offer a private bath and entrance as well as phone, wet bar, TV/VCR, queen-bed, and oceanfront deck or patio. A hammock is strategically located near the water for those who've dreamed of sleeping under a coconut palm tree on the beach. Whales have been spotted from the private decks off the guest rooms. Popular attractions in the area include Spouting Horn, Waimea Canyon, Hanalei Bay, and Poipu Beach as well as golfing, tennis, and horseback riding. The area offers a good selection of galleries, shops, and restaurants. Tropical continental breakfast features Gloria's own fresh homemade pastries and fresh island fruits and juices. No smoking. 1 or 2/$100-125. MC, V.

Haiku, Island of Maui

Haikuleana Bed & Breakfast Plantation Style
555 Haiku Road
Haiku, Maui, HI 96708-8974
(808) 575- 2890

Type of B&B: Private Home.
Rooms: 3 with private bath.
Rates: 1/$65; 2/$80.

Rating: A- or ♛ ♛ ♛ Excellent, far exceeds basic requirements.

Original 12 foot ceilings and Hawaiian architecture mark this 19th century Plantation-style home situated among pineapple fields and pine trees 12 miles east of Kahului and the airport. Choose from three guest rooms with private bath. Each has been filled with period pieces and antiques. Explore the secluded park-like grounds with natural tropical foliage or relax in the comfortable living room or on the front porch. Stroll the scenic country roads and visit the nearby village of Haiku, one of the original settlements on Maui. Beaches are nearby offering surfing, windsurfing, swimming, and hiking. Waterfalls with fresh water pools and the Hana and Haleakala Craters are other Maui attractions. Tropical fruits, jams, home-made Hawaiian pastries, and breads are part of the morning continental breakfast. No smoking. 1/$65; 2/$80. MC, V. 10% senior and extended-stay family discounts. Travel agent.

Information on additional B&Bs in Idaho is available from B&B Western Adventure (406) 259-7993.

Sun Valley

Idaho Country Inn
134 Latigo Lane
Sun Valley, ID 83340
(208) 726-1019

Type of B&B: Large inn.
Rooms: 10 with private bath.
Rates: 1 or 2/$95-145.

Rating: AA or ♛♛♛♛ Outstanding.

Contemporary mountain-style inn built of logs and river rock is located high on a hill with panoramic mountain views. Choose from ten guest rooms which offer a private bath, remote control, color TV, refrigerator, and special themes ranging from the "Wagon Days" room to the "Wildflower" room. Many of the pieces of furniture and artwork are created by the host who is also an accomplished fishing guide. Six rooms have air conditioning. There are two parlors with fireplaces, a well-stocked library including books on Idaho, 24 hour beverage service, and well-organized information center. A specially-designed Jacuzzi in the back yard offers views of surrounding mountain peaks. This is a major year-round recreation center offering skiing, ice skating, sleigh rides, trout fishing, and golfing. Generous "Idaho-style" full breakfast. Meeting facilities available. Families welcome. No smoking. 1 or 2/$95-145. AE, MC. V. Travel agent.

Evanston

The Margarita European Inn
1566 Oak Avenue
Evanston, IL 60201
(708) 869-2273 or (708) 869-2283

Type of B&B: Urban inn with restaurant.
Rooms: 34, 17 with private bath.
Rates: 1/$40-80; 2/$45-90.

Rating: B or Good, exceeds basic requirements.

Originally a woman's private club, this Georgian mansion north of Chicago has been reopened as an inn with an Italian restaurant on the main level. Choose from thirty-four guest rooms, half with newly decorated private baths. Relax in the spacious parlor which features a molded fireplace and floor-to-ceiling arched windows. A paneled library and party rooms are also available. Explore Evanston's fine restaurants, art galleries, theater companies, cultural arts center, specialty shops and five universities. Nearby Lake Michigan offers sand beaches, historic walking paths, and biking trails that begin at Northwestern University and lead to downtown Chicago. Continental breakfast includes muffins, pastries, and fresh fruit. Lunch and dinner are available in the restaurant. Facilities for weddings and meetings available. 1/$40-80; 2/$45-90. Travel agent.

Galena

The Goldmoor
9001 Sand Hill Road
Galena, IL 61036
(815) 777-3925 or (800) 255-3925

Type of B&B: Guesthouse.
Rooms: 6 with private bath.
Rates: 2/$95-225.

Rating: A+ or Excellent, far exceeds basic requirements.

Grand estate in the country offers quiet seclusion and views of the mighty Mississippi River. Six guest rooms with private bath are available. Two special honeymoon suites each feature an extra large room with sitting area, Jacuzzi, fireplace, and entertainment system with stereo. An atrium spa and sauna are located on the main level of the inn and there are several private decks and patios along with extensive landscaped grounds. Romantic getaway, honeymoon and anniversary packages available. Area attractions include twenty-five antique shops, General Grant's home, and Chestnut Mountain Resort Ski Lodge. Full breakfast includes homemade jams and jellies and fresh baked rolls as well as house specialties. 2/$95-225. AE, Discover, MC, V. Travel agent.

Rockford

Victoria's B&B Inn
201 North 6th Street
Rockford, IL 61107
(815) 963-3232

Type of B&B: Inn.
Rooms: 4 with private bath.
Rates: 1 or 2/$69-169.

Rating: A or ♛ ♛ ♛ Excellent, far exceeds basic requirements.

Victoria's B&B Inn was built at the turn-of-the-century and is centrally located in the city which is 90 miles west of Chicago off I-90. There are four guest suites with private bath. Each has been decorated with antiques, rich wallpaper and fabrics, and offers a TV and Jacuzzi. The Victorian parlor on the main floor has been the setting for several weddings and it features unusually detailed wallpaper which in itself is a work of art. Popular attractions in the area include Burpee Museum, Tinker Cottage, riverboat rides, and Victorian Village's seventy shops and restaurants. Continental breakfast. Facilities for meetings, receptions and weddings. 1 or 2/$69-169. Weekday special rates and corporate rates as low as $39 per night. MC, V.

Wheaton

The Wheaton Inn
301 West Roosevelt Road
Wheaton, IL 60187
(708) 690-2600 or (708) 690-2623

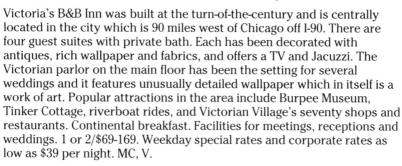

Type of B&B: Large inn.
Rooms: 16 with private bath.
Rates: 1 or 2/$99-195.

Rating: A- or ♛ ♛ ♛ Excellent, far exceeds basic requirements.

Built in 1987 in a design to reflect Colonial Williamsburg, this urban inn is located 25 miles west of Chicago. Several of the sixteen rooms feature a Jacuzzi tub or gas fireplace. All offer a private bath with European towel warmers and amenities. There are several common rooms including a living room with fireplace, breakfast atrium room with French doors leading onto the patio, and lower-level conference rooms. Explore the historic town of Wheaton or nearby Geneva for shopping and unique restaurants. Nearby attractions include Morton Arboretum, Cantigny War Museum, McCormick Mansion, Wheaton Water Park, or the Billy Graham Center found on the Wheaton College campus. A full breakfast and afternoon refreshments are offered daily. Two meeting rooms available for family reunions, weddings, and business functions. Families welcome. Wheelchair access. 1 or 2/$99-195. AE, MC, V. 10% senior, business and auto club discounts. Travel agent.

INDIANA

Columbus

Columbus Inn
445 5th Street
Columbus, IN 47201
(812) 378-4289
Fax (812) 378-4289

Type of B&B: Large inn.
Rooms: 34 with private bath.
Rates: 1/$80-90; 2/$95-275.

Rating: A or ♛♛♛ Excellent, far exceeds basic requirements.

Columbus Inn, noted for its Romanesque architecture, is listed on the National Register of Historic Places. Originally built as City Hall, the inn has been completely restored and rivals other examples of fine architecture throughout this city. Thirty-four individually decorated guest rooms are available, each with private bath. The Sparrell Suite is reached by a grand staircase and its main floor serves as an impressive parlor or meeting area with a two-story ceiling, antique furnishings and fine fabrics and upholstered pieces. Columbus is known as the "architectural showplace of America," with more than fifty buildings providing a concentrated and outstanding collection of contemporary architecture. Full breakfast. Facilities for meetings and social gatherings. 1/$80-90; 2/$95-275. AE, Discover, Diners, Carte Blanche, MC, V. Business travel discount. Travel agent.

Evansville - See Newburgh.

Hagerstown

Teetor House
300 West Main Street
Hagerstown, IN 47346
(317) 489-4422 or (800) 824-4319

Type of B&B: Inn
Rooms: 4 with private bath.
Rates: 1/$70-85; 2/$75-90.

Rating: A or ♛♛♛ Excellent, far exceeds basic requirements.

Imposing private mansion built in 1936 is situated on a ten acre wooded estate in a small town just 5 miles north of Route 70 in the east/central part of the state. There are four large air-conditioned guest rooms with twin or king sized beds and private bath. Explore this historic home which features carved cherry paneling in the foyer and living room, Steinway concert piano, and in-house museum; or just sit and relax on the pleasant screened-in porch. Popular attractions in the area include fine restaurants, unusual shops, the world's largest antique mall, tennis, golf, and historic tours. Full breakfast. Families welcome. Facilities available for meetings and social functions. Restricted smoking. 1/$70-85; 2/$75-90.

Guests write: *"Jack did a fine job both describing the house and telling about one of the great minds of the 20th Century. Hosts were very cordial with prompt attention. Good breakfast was well served. The screened-in porch was especially nice in the evenings."* (C. Tucker-Ladd)

"Exceeded our expectations. The Warmoth's add warmth and a unique perspective." (P. Healey)

"The tour was a highlight that impelled us to bring guests for the weekend on our second visit. The house is an expression of the genius and character of Ralph Teetor. The hosts, through their devotion to the house and to the guests, properly memorialize that genius." (H. Hensold)

"We appreciated all the extra touches. The omelet was superb! The tour was fascinating and inspiring. I'd rather stay at a bed and breakfast than any hotel if others are as nice as the Teetor House." (K. Hudson)

"The butler's necktie and coat at breakfast gave the meal an extra bit of class. The pecan rolls were just like mom makes. Jack gave us a wonderful tour and spend an extraordinary amount of time with us."
(C. Staudenheimer)

Middlebury

Patchwork Quilt Country Inn
11748 County Road #2
Middlebury, IN 46540
(219) 825-2417

Type of B&B: Inn.
Rooms: 9, 6 with private bath.
Rates: 1/$43; 2/$53-95.

Rating: B+ or ♛♛ Good, exceeds basic requirements.

Historic farmhouse in the heart of the Northern Indiana Amish Country is now a country inn and restaurant located on County Road #2, 1 mile west of SR-13. Choose from nine guest rooms, six with private bath, and each decorated with handmade quilts and distinctive folk art. The most interesting attractions in the area include Amish settlement, Shipshewana flea market, antique auction, Midwest Museum of Art, quilt shops, and Amish back road tours which can be arranged from the inn. Full country breakfast includes fresh eggs, farm-grown fruits, and home baked goods. No smoking. 1/$43; 2/$53-95. MC, V.

Middlebury

Varns Guest House, Inc.
205 South Main Street
Middlebury, IN 46540
(219) 825-9666

Type of B&B: Guesthouse.
Rooms: 5 with private bath.
Rates: 1/$60; 2/$65.

Rating: A- or ♛♛♛ Excellent, far exceeds basic requirements.

Varn's Guest House is a modest turn-of-the-century home built in 1898 and located on a tree-lined street in the heart of town. This area is known as Amish country and it is located 5 miles south of the Indiana Toll Road's Middlebury exit. Choose from five guest rooms. They offer a variety of size, decor, and amenities, but each has a private bath, air conditioning, comfortable furnishings, and has been named after relatives and childhood memories. A wrap-around porch is a popular place to watch the activities in this small town but in cold weather guests enjoy gathering around the parlor's brick fireplace. Popular attractions nearby include the giant Shipshewana flea market, Amish communities, and a selection of interesting shops and restaurants with good home-cooked food. Continental plus breakfast includes homemade pastries. No smoking. 1/$60; 2/$65. MC, V.

Guests write: *"Varn's Guest House is a jewel. After more than 200 B&Bs and inns it takes a lot to impress us! Ask for the China Rose Room. It is exquisite."* (K. Wellage)

Newburgh

Phelps Mansion Inn Bed & Breakfast
208 State Street
Newburgh, IN 47630
(812) 853-7766 or (812) 853-3706

Type of B&B: Small inn.
Rooms: 4 with private bath.
Rates: 1/$50-65; 2/$55-70.

Rating: A or ♛♛♛ Excellent, far exceeds basic requirements.

Georgian-style manor home built in the 1850's is located approximately 2 miles east of I-164, exit 5, 10 miles east of downtown Evansville. All four guest rooms have private bath, individual climate control, and cable TV. Two guest rooms have fireplaces and the other two have kitchenettes. There is ample common area for guest relaxation on the main level which features 12 foot ceilings, living room with two fireplaces and Oriental carpets, and the library with fireplace and "Safari" decor highlighting the host's interesting collection of African art. In the main hall is found an eight foot carved antique door frame from Madurai, India. Two ninety foot porches span the back of the inn and have comfortable seating for rocking, reading, or relaxing. Walk to the Ohio River nearby or historic downtown area with an old country store, tea room, restaurants, antique and craft shops. Interesting sites in this area include the utopian community of New Harmony, Angel's Mound State Park, Evansville Museum, and Ellis Park thoroughbred race track. Continental breakfast. Restricted smoking. 1/$50-65; 2/$55-70. AE, Discover, MC, V.

Warsaw

White Hill Manor
2513 East Center Street
Warsaw, IN 46580
(219) 269-6933

Type of B&B: Inn.
Rooms: 8 with private bath.
Rates: 1/$68-105; 2/$75-112.

Rating: A or ♛♛♛ Excellent, far exceeds basic requirements.

Imposing English Tudor stone mansion is now an inn conveniently
located on spacious grounds off Route 30, 40 miles west of Fort Wayne.
There are eight guest rooms available. Each has a private bath, quality
furnishings, and lovely fabric bedspreads and drapes. Special features of
some rooms include four-poster beds, antique claw-foot tub, spa bath, or
king-sized brass bed. This is a popular area for lake recreation, Amish
settlements, and Shipshewana markets. Guests enjoy local theater and
fine dining which are available nearby. Full European breakfast and
afternoon tea are included. Facilities available for small weddings and
conferences. Restricted smoking. 1/$68-105; 2/$75-112. AE, MC, V.

IOWA

Amana Colonies/Homestead

Die Heimat Country Inn
Amana Colonies
Homestead, IA 52236
(319) 622-3937

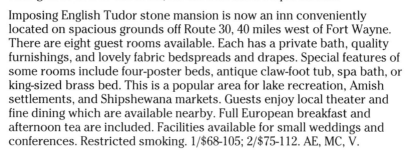

Type of B&B: Inn.
Rooms: 19 with private bath.
Rates: 2/$36-63.

Rating: B or ♛♛ Good, exceeds basic requirements.

Historic inn is conveniently situated on Main Street at the junction of US-
151 and SR-6. There are a total of nineteen guest rooms available. While
there is a wide variety to the size of the rooms, each has a private bath,
television, quilt, and traditional Amana furniture. Relax on the shaded
lawn in the Amana wooden glider or visit nearby "family-style"
restaurants, Colony wineries, antique stores and unique craft shops. Take
a tour of the colonies and discover the seven historic villages that make

up the Amana Colonies which were founded by settlers in 1844. Full breakfast features Amana pastries. Facilities for small groups. 2/$36-63. D, MC, V.

Dubuque

The Hancock House
1105 Grove Terrace
Dubuque, IA 52001
(319) 557-8989

Type of B&B: Inn.
Rooms: 9 with private bath.
Rates: 1 or 2/$75-150.

Rating: A or ♛♛♛ Excellent, far exceeds basic requirements.

Imposing Queen Anne Victorian mansion is set on the bluffs of this historic town and is located at the intersections of Routes 151, 61, 52, and 20 in the Northeast corner of the state. Nine individually decorated guest rooms are available, each with private bath (two with whirlpool tub). Enjoy a spectacular view of the Mississippi River from this location. Nearby Dubuque offers restored Victorian mansions serving as museums, art galleries, and antique and specialty shops. Don't miss taking a riverboat ride on the Mississippi River. The area's mountains offer hiking, biking, and skiing. Full breakfast. Families welcome. No smoking. 1 or 2/$75-150. AE, Discover, MC, V. Travel agent.

Fort Madison

Kingsley Inn
707 Avenue H
Fort Madison, IA 52627
(319) 372-7074

Type of B&B: Historic hotel.
Rooms: 14 with private bath.
Rates: 1 or 2/$65-105.

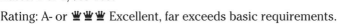

Rating: A- or ♛♛♛ Excellent, far exceeds basic requirements.

Century-old Victorian hotel is located in a Mississippi River town one-hundred miles south of Davenport. Fourteen guest rooms with private bath offer individual decor and Victorian antiques. Several rooms have a whirlpool tub or a view of the river. Within walking distance are antique and specialty shops, galleries, and the historic Victorian residential area

— Comments continued on next page

where the Sheaffer Pen Company is headquartered. Take a historic tour on the "Little Red Train". Visit nearby Old Fort Madison, Mississippi River, Lee City Historical Museum, Mormon Settlement, or the villages of Van Buren, Lock, and Dam at Keokuk. A continental plus breakfast includes granola, home made pastries, and Kingsley Inn coffee. Wedding and meeting facilities available. Wheelchair access. No smoking. 1 or 2/$65-105. AE, MC, V. 10% senior, corporate, or auto club discounts. Travel agent.

Guests write: *"We have enjoyed the hospitality, service, and the beauty of this luxury inn. This is the type of quality that hopefully one day will become the standard in America. 'The Dream Facility'! We look forward to returning. "* (T. Evans)

"We love this place! The elegant surroundings and pampering by the staff are very much appreciated. In our hectic lives we have little time for such pleasures." (D. Johnson)

"This was the perfect get-away. The room was very romantic. The staff was very hospitable." (B. Gerst)

"Valentines Day to Wedding Day. What a way to end a perfect day and begin a new life. Elegance doesn't begin to express the aura of the Kingsley." (J. Dieckmann)

Maquoketa

Squiers Manor Bed & Breakfast
418 West Pleasant
Maquoketa, IA 52060
(319) 652-6961

Type of B&B: B&B Inn.
Rooms: 6 with private bath.
Rates: 1 or 2/$70-140.

Rating: A- or ♛♛♛ Excellent, far exceeds basic requirements.

Queen Anne brick mansion built in 1882 is located 30 miles south of Dubuque and 40 miles north of Davenport. The inn retains it's original features including the butternut and walnut staircase, three fireplaces, and American Victorian antiques. Six guest rooms are named for Squiers family members and former residents of the mansion. Each has a private bath with single or double whirlpool tub, telephone, color TV, and queen-size antique bed. The downstairs guest room is often used for special occasions such as honeymoons and anniversaries and is available as a suite with adjoining private parlor. Walk to the library, churches, restaurants, and movie theater. Take a short drive to the Quad Cities, Cedar Rapids, Iowa City, Clinton, and Galena, Illinois. Explore the

Maquoketa Caves State Park. A full breakfast might include seafood quiche or Eggs Katrina and is accompanied with fresh fruit and home made breads. A candlelight evening dessert is served nightly in the parlor or in the Victorian dining room. Families welcome. Restricted smoking. 1 or 2/$70-140. MC, V. Seasonal corporate discount.

Guests write: *"The home was wonderfully decorated with pieces that fit the era of the house. It was a well-planned mixture of the old and the new. Nice extras included a box of chocolates, dessert at night, and coffee delivered in the morning. The breakfast served was a banquet of huge portions and gourmet flavors. We didn't eat for the rest of the day. "* (P. Ochrlein)

"Virl and Kathy make my business trip seem like a mini-vacation. Their hospitality, scrumptious breakfasts and beautifully decorated manor always makes me feel like someone special. I'm sure that other guests would agree." (S. Henderson)

"Squiers Manor is the best of the best in uniqueness and elegance. Service is delivered to perfection from the rooms that look like you're the first to ever stay in them with the little 'Thank you for staying with us' on the nightstand or pillow, to the evening desserts and morning feeding extravaganzas accompanied by the charming host. The conversation and warmth shared at the breakfast table not only encourages you to kick your shoes off and relax but also reminds you to do this again soon!" (D. Day)

KANSAS

Wichita

Inn at the Park
3751 East Douglas
Wichita, KS 67218
(316) 652-0500 or (800) 258-1951

Type of B&B: Inn.
Rooms: 10 rooms and 2 suites, all with private bath.
Rates: 1/$75-125; 2/$85-135.

Rating: AA or ♛♛♛♛ Outstanding.

The Inn at the Park is a mansion built in 1910 that has been completely renovated. In 1989 the entire inn was professionally decorated by a number of well known area designers for use as a Designer's Showcase. There are ten guest rooms with private bath in the mansion and their

— *Comments continued on next page*

decor ranges from French Country to Oriental, from Neoclassical to Art Nouveau. A carriage house on the grounds offers two private suites. Amenities include fireplaces, private courtyard, hot tub, cable TV, VCR, and phone. Continental breakfast features fruits, pastries, and often includes quiche or chili rellenos. Special services for business travelers include a conference room, secretarial services, and fax machine. Families welcome. 1/$75-125; 2/$85-135. AE, MC, V. 10% senior, auto club, and business travel discounts. Travel agent.

Guests write: *"They are doing a fine job of providing people with a quality place to spend a night or a Honeymoon. I think that next year we will spend our anniversary at the Inn at the Park."* (T. Chamberlain)

Wichita

Max Paul, An Inn
3910 East Kellogg
Wichita, KS 67218
(316) 689-8101

Type of B&B: Inn and cottages.
Rooms: 14 rooms or suites with private bath.
Rates: 1/$55-95; 2/$80-125.

Rating: B or ♛♛ Good, exceeds basic requirements.

Max Paul is an inn which is comprised of three English Tudor cottages located just west of the intersection of Highways 135 and 54. There are a total of fourteen guest rooms. While the rooms vary in size, decor, and amenities, each offers a private bath, cable TV, European antiques, and a featherbed. Large executive suites feature vaulted ceilings, fireplaces, skylights, and private balconies. There is a spa and exercise room on the premises but guests are also encouraged to walk to the nearby public park for tennis, jogging paths, and children's pool. Airport, downtown shopping centers, and major corporate headquarters are nearby. Continental breakfast. Facilities for business meetings or social functions. 1/$55-95; 2/$80-125. AE, Discover, MC, V.

Lexington/Versailles

Sills Inn
270 Montgomery Avenue
Versailles, KY 40383
(606) 873-4478 or (800) 526-9801

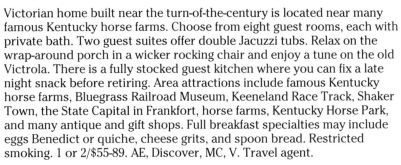

Type of B&B: Inn.
Rooms: 8 with private bath.
Rates: 2/$55-89.

Rating: A or ♛♛♛ Excellent, far exceeds basic requirements.

Victorian home built near the turn-of-the-century is located near many famous Kentucky horse farms. Choose from eight guest rooms, each with private bath. Two guest suites offer double Jacuzzi tubs. Relax on the wrap-around porch in a wicker rocking chair and enjoy a tune on the old Victrola. There is a fully stocked guest kitchen where you can fix a late night snack before retiring. Area attractions include famous Kentucky horse farms, Bluegrass Railroad Museum, Keeneland Race Track, Shaker Town, the State Capital in Frankfort, horse farms, Kentucky Horse Park, and many antique and gift shops. Full breakfast specialties may include eggs Benedict or quiche, cheese grits, and spoon bread. Restricted smoking. 1 or 2/$55-89. AE, Discover, MC, V. Travel agent.

LOUISIANA

Additional information on B&Bs in this state is available from B&B Inc. (800) 729-4640 or Lincoln Ltd. B&B (601) 482-5483.

New Orleans

Bed and Breakfast As You Like It
3500 Upperline Street
New Orleans, LA 70125
(504)821-7716

Type of B&B: Private home.
Rooms: 2 with private bath.
Rates: 1/$60; 2/$80.

Rating: B or ♛♛ Good, exceeds basic requirements.

Turn-of-the-century, Mediterranean-style home is in the University area near Tulane and Loyola, just 6 miles from the heart of New Orleans and the French Quarter. Two guest rooms feature hand-made, tufted headboards on the beds, American antiques, and artifacts collected by the host. Enjoy welcome drinks and hors d'oeuvres in the living room or relax on the garden deck. The sitting room has French doors that lead out to the courtyard. Tipitina's Jazz and some of the city's best restaurants are within one mile, as is the Garden District, St. Charles Avenue Trolley, Audubon Park and Zoo, and the Mississippi River. The hostess will prepare individualized packets detailing area attractions. Wake up to Cafe Du Monde coffee or tea set outside the door. Continental breakfast includes New Orleans croissants, breads, or muffins accompanied by fresh fruit and served on Blue Willow china. No smoking. 1/$60; 2/$80. Suite/$100. Special events rates. Travel agent.

Guests write: *"A most enjoyable stay in a lovely home. The hospitality was the highlight of our short visit."* (J. Wheeler)

"Now we know the meaning of Southern hospitality. We enjoyed our stay and appreciated her making it so comfortable for us." (E. Ulrich)

New Orleans

La Maison Marigny
Bourbon Street near Esplanade
Mail to: Box 52257
New Orleans, LA 70152-2257
(800) 729-4640 or (504) 488-4640

Type of B&B: Private Home.
Rooms: 3 with private bath.
Rates: 1 or 2/$81-126.

Rating: A or ♛♛♛ Excellent, far exceeds basic requirements.

Restored Victorian is located at the edge of the French Quarter in the heart of New Orleans. Three guest rooms with private bath are tastefully decorated with a blend of antiques and rich fabrics that soothe the senses after a long day of seeing sights in the city. A small sitting room with TV on the lower floor overlooks the traditional New Orleans walled garden and courtyard. Stroll to Jackson Square with its street performers and artists, famous restaurants and Bourbon Street. Sit at an open air cafe by the river. Visit the many galleries, jazz clubs, and antique shops, or take a Mississippi Riverboat ride. A riverfront streetcar or minibus is available for trips to convention centers and the Riverwalk Mall. Continental plus breakfast includes a variety of fresh fruit. Families welcome. Restricted smoking. 1 or 2/$81-126. Travel agent.

Guests write: *"I fell in love with New Orleans and with this wonderful and warm home. Why leave the house when you've got those wonderful scones in the morning and Frank's PB&J sandwiches in the evening!"* (D. Blakney)

"We suggest that guests use Jeremy and her knowledge of the area to the hilt. Her observations are rational, reasonable and down to earth. Fortunate are those of us whose paths cross hers!" (E. Schubert)

"For our first stay in a B&B, she certainly has shown us how it should be done. Such a warm, generous accommodating person! We're glad she gave up the law stuff to open up this very quaint, very comfortable, very homey Maison Marigny. We'll be back." (K. Parker)

"Her expert knowledge of New Orleans helped me to fully enjoy this most sensuous of cities - its sights, its sounds, its smells, and most importantly of all, its people. Her hospitality, attention to detail, and patience knew no bounds." (N. Kent)

New Orleans

Lafitte Guest House
1003 Bourbon Street
New Orleans, LA 70116
(504) 581-2678 or (800) 331-7971

Type of B&B: Inn.
Rooms: 14 with private bath.
Rates: 1 or 2/$69-155.

Rating: A or ♛♛♛ Excellent, far exceeds basic requirements.

Lafitte Guest house is an historic mansion with French architectural influence which is conveniently located in the heart of the French Quarter of the city. Choose from fourteen guest rooms which offer a variety in size, decor, and amenities but each has a selection of period furnishings, rich fabrics and appointments, and a private bath. Several rooms have private balconies with views of the city skyline and French Quarter and these rooms are especially popular during Mardis Gras. Walk to an abundance of world famous restaurants, renowned nightclubs, specialty shops, museums, and colorful Creole and Spanish cottages. Continental breakfast features fresh pastries. 1 or 2/$69-155. AE, MC, V. Travel agent.

Bar Harbor

Breakwater-1904
45 Hancock Street
Bar Harbor, ME 04609
(207) 288-2313

Type of B&B: Inn.
Rooms: 6 with private bath.
Rates: 1 or 2/$120-295.

Rating: AA or ♛♛♛♛ Outstanding.

Turn-of-the-century English Tudor estate is located on Bar Harbor's historic shore path which overlooks Frenchman Bay and the Porcupine Islands. Recently restored and listed on the National Register of Historic Places, the inn offers six guest rooms. Each is spacious and elegantly furnished with private bath, fireplace, queen-sized bed, and ocean front views. There are ample common areas for guest relaxation including the front verandah, formal parlor, and billiard room. Explore nearby Acadia National Park and surrounding areas by hiking, biking, kayaking, canoeing, and beach combing. A full breakfast is served in the formal dining room overlooking the ocean. Specialties of the house include raspberry almond French toast, eggs Benedict, or apple crepes with homemade sausage. No smoking. 1 or 2/$120-295 with off-season discounts. AE, MC, V. Travel agent.

Bar Harbor

Manor House Inn
106 West Street
Bar Harbor, ME 04609
(800) 437-0088 or (207) 288-3759

Type of B&B: Inn.
Rooms: 14 with private bath.
Rates: 1 or 2/$60-150.

Rating: A or ♛♛♛ Excellent, far exceeds basic requirements.

Three story Victorian mansion set on a landscaped acre is situated on an historic, tree-lined street in the West Street National Historic District. The Manor House complex consists of the summer mansion, original chauffeur's cottage, and two guests cottages. There are fourteen guest accommodations throughout the complex. Each has individual Victorian wall coverings, original maple floor, period antiques and accessories, and a private bath. Some rooms offer working fireplaces and a garden view. Walk to Bar Harbor's shops, restaurants, whale watching events, schooner rides, and Bar Island. Explore Acadia National Park. A full breakfast is served and specialty of the house includes baked stuffed blueberry French toast. Restricted smoking. 1 or 2/$60-150. AE, MC, V.

Bar Harbor

The Tides
119 West Street
Bar Harbor, ME 04609
(207) 288-4968

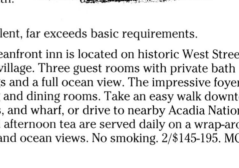

Type of B&B: Inn.
Rooms: 3 with private bath.
Rates: 2/$145-195.

Rating: A or ♛♛♛ Excellent, far exceeds basic requirements.

Classic Greek Revival oceanfront inn is located on historic West Street, just off of Route 3 in the village. Three guest rooms with private bath feature period furnishings and a full ocean view. The impressive foyer leads into gracious living and dining rooms. Take an easy walk downtown to the shops, restaurants, and wharf, or drive to nearby Acadia National Park. A full breakfast and afternoon tea are served daily on a wrap-around verandah with fireplace and ocean views. No smoking. 2/$145-195. MC, V. Travel agent.

Bath

The Inn at Bath
969 Washington Street
Bath, ME 04530
(207) 443-4294

Type of B&B: Inn.
Rooms: 5 with private bath.
Rates: 1or 2/$55-90

Rating: A- or ♛♛♛ Excellent, far exceeds basic requirements.

Early 19th-Century Greek Revival inn is situated a half mile off of Route 1 in the heart of Maine's mid-coast region. Five guest rooms offer either single, double, queen, or king-size beds and a variety of amenities including sitting areas, fireplaces, and water views. All rooms have a private bath. Relax in the twin parlors with marble fireplaces and overstuffed sofas. Bath is known as the city of ships and offers historic tours and the Maine Maritime Museum. A short drive away are the white sand beaches of Popham Beach and Reid State Park as well as active lobster harbors and

Orr's and Bailey Islands. Nearby Boothbay Harbor, Freeport, Brunswick, and Camden offer shopping, dining, and cultural activities. A full breakfast may include eggs, bacon, muffins, and fresh fruit. Wedding and meeting facilities available. Restricted smoking. 1 or 2/$55-90. AE, MC, V. Corporate discount. Travel agent.

Belfast

Frost House
6 Northport Avenue
Belfast, ME 04915
(207) 338-4159

Type of B&B: Inn.
Rooms: 3 with private bath.
Rates: 1/$50-70; 2/$60-80.

Rating: A- or ♛♛♛ Excellent, far exceeds basic requirements.

Victorian turn-of-the-century home is less than a mile off Route 1 on a 1.2 acre lot with gardens. Choose from three guest rooms with private bath which are decorated with period antiques and offer views of the water. The harbor is just blocks away with bay cruises, live theater, concerts, shopping, and dining. Bar Harbor is an hour drive and Camden can be reached in 20 minutes by car. Blueberry pancakes, Amaretto French toast, Belgian waffles, and fresh muffins are some of the full breakfast specialties. No smoking. 1/$50-70; 2/$60-80. Travel agent.

Boothbay Harbor

Atlantic Ark Inn
64 Atlantic Avenue
Boothbay Harbor, ME 04538
(207) 633-5690

Type of B&B: Inn.
Rooms: 5 with private bath.
Rates: 1 or 2/$55-85.

Rating: B+ or ♛♛ Good, exceeds basic requirements.

Small, intimate Victorian inn built in 1875 is found across the harbor on the east side of the village, 11 miles from Route 1. Five guest rooms with private bath are available. Each has been decorated with period antiques, fresh flowers, mahogany poster beds with firm mattresses, and Oriental rugs. Several rooms offer private balconies with harbor views. A separate guest cottage on the property is also available. The front porch is a good spot to view the sunset each evening. Crossing the small foot bridge at the edge of the property leads to the Inner Harbor shops, galleries, and fine restaurants. Full breakfast is served on fine linen and china and features specialties such as English scones, old-fashioned biscuits, cinnamon popovers, and sweet baked goods such as apricot nut bread or strawberry muffins. No smoking. 1 or 2/$55-85. AE, MC, V.

Guests write: *"Waking up in a four-poster bed with the sun shining in through lace curtains is one of our most lasting memories. We truly enjoyed the beautiful front porch where we could watch the fishing boats in the harbor with our morning coffee or evening cordials. We happened upon the Atlantic Ark the first weekend they opened, and have been back every summer since."* (M. Sternberg)

"It is especially clean, well-managed, and comfortable. The hosts are able to get your day started on the right course by serving a unique and delicious breakfast. Its charm is evident throughout." (H. Craig)

"As we arrived we were greeted and escorted past beautiful petunias to a private chalet overlooking views of a pond to the side and the harbor in front. Tall glasses of iced-tea adorned with fresh mint from the garden were over-shadowed only by the specially prepared muffins, fresh fruit, and full breakfast served at a private table overlooking the veranda." (M. Caporaso)

Camden

Blue Harbor House
67 Elm Street
Camden, ME 04843
(207) 236-3196 or (800) 248-3196
Fax (207) 236-6523

Type of B&B: Inn.
Rooms: 10 with private bath.
Rates: 1/$75-125.

Rating: A- or ♛♛♛ Excellent, far exceeds basic requirements.

Classic New England Cape Cod inn built prior to 1835 is 85 miles north of Portland on Route 1. Choose from ten guest rooms with private bath. Each room features country antiques, hand-fashioned quilts, and stenciled walls. Several rooms also offer whirlpool tubs, air-conditioning, and TV/VCR with movies. This village is the home of the Windjammer Fleet which offers day sails. Popular activities nearby include hiking, skiing, biking, concerts, theater, art, and craft shops. Full breakfast is served on the sun porch overlooking the Camden Hills. Country suppers, picnic lunches, and gourmet dinners are available with advance notice as well as an authentic Down East Maine lobster bake on the lawn. Indoor sun porch accommodates small meetings and weddings. Restricted smoking. 1/$75-125. AE, MC, V. 10% auto club discount. Travel agent.

Camden

Hartstone Inn
41 Elm Street
Camden, ME 04843
(207) 236-4259

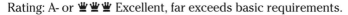

Type of B&B: Inn.
Rooms: 8 rooms and carriage house with private baths.
Rates: 1/$60-85; 2/$75-90.

Rating: A- or ♛♛♛ Excellent, far exceeds basic requirements.

Intimate Victorian inn is located in the heart of the village, a stones throw from the harbor. There are eight guest rooms with comfortable antiques and private baths. Two have fireplaces. There is also a parlor with fireplace and a library with a variety of good books and cable TV. Two efficiency apartments are in the carriage house and available at weekly rates. Shops, galleries, and restaurants are only steps away from the front door. Skiing, golf, swimming, sailing, or kayaking are all nearby. Full breakfast. Candlelight dinners and picnic lunches available by advance reservation. 1/$60-85, 2/$75-90.

Camden

Hawthorne Inn
9 High Street
Camden, ME 04843
(207) 236-8842

Type of B&B: Inn.
Rooms: 10 with private bath.
Rates: 1/$60-135; 2/$65-140.

Rating: A+ or ♛♛♛ Excellent, far exceeds basic requirements.

Victorian mansion with turrets and a circular drive was built in 1894 and is located near exit 22 off Route 95. Ten individually decorated guest rooms with private bath are available. Several feature views of the Camden Hills or harbor. The main foyer is graced with a three-story staircase and original stained-glass windows. An adjoining carriage house offers townhouse apartments and studio rooms with kitchen and private deck. Concerts and plays take place at the amphitheater just past the back yard. Within walking distance are restaurants, galleries, and specialty shops that line the harbor. Area attractions include Mount Battie and Camden State Park which offer hiking, climbing, skiing, and boating. Full breakfast and afternoon tea served daily. Wedding and meeting facilities available. Families welcome. No smoking in the main house or carriage house. 1/$60-135; 2/$65-140; Apartment:$140-225. MC, V. Travel agent.

Maine

Camden

Maine Stay Inn
22 High Street
Camden, ME 04843
(207) 236-9636

Type of B&B: Inn.
Rooms: 8, 4 with private bath.
Rates: 1 or 2/$65-100

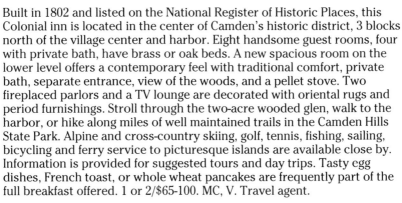

Rating: A or ♥♥♥ Excellent, far exceeds basic requirements.

Built in 1802 and listed on the National Register of Historic Places, this Colonial inn is located in the center of Camden's historic district, 3 blocks north of the village center and harbor. Eight handsome guest rooms, four with private bath, have brass or oak beds. A new spacious room on the lower level offers a contemporary feel with traditional comfort, private bath, separate entrance, view of the woods, and a pellet stove. Two fireplaced parlors and a TV lounge are decorated with oriental rugs and period furnishings. Stroll through the two-acre wooded glen, walk to the harbor, or hike along miles of well maintained trails in the Camden Hills State Park. Alpine and cross-country skiing, golf, tennis, fishing, sailing, bicycling and ferry service to picturesque islands are available close by. Information is provided for suggested tours and day trips. Tasty egg dishes, French toast, or whole wheat pancakes are frequently part of the full breakfast offered. 1 or 2/$65-100. MC, V. Travel agent.

Guests write: *"The innkeepers couldn't be more gracious. Even after the first visit, you feel like family. I've stayed with them on several occasions. Breakfasts are delicious! I especially appreciate their knowledge of the area offering ideas for daily trips and local eateries if you are undecided on what to do or where to go. Definitely a high quality inn! I've referred many to the Camden Main Stay Inn."* (D. West)

Freeport

181 Main Street B&B
181 Main Street
Freeport, ME 04032
(207) 865-1226

Type of B&B: Inn.
Rooms: 7 with private bath.
Rates: 1/$65-75; 2/$75-95.

Rating: A or ♥♥♥ Excellent, far exceeds basic requirements.

Cape Cod-style inn built in 1840 is located on US-1 near I-95. Seven guest rooms are available. Each offers a private bath, queen or double bed, handmade quilt, antique furnishings, Oriental rugs, and artwork. Two common rooms on the main floor offer areas for conversing, playing board games, or watching TV. The swimming pool with deck is a popular gathering place during warm weather and there are several Adirondack chairs strategically placed around the lawn for rest and relaxation. Freeport center outlet shops and L.L. Bean are within walking distance from the inn. Bowdoin College, Maine coast, Portland, or Brunswick are a short drive away. Full breakfast includes homemade breads. No smoking. 1/$65-75; 2/$75-95. MC, V.

Freeport

Kendall Tavern Bed & Breakfast
213 Main Street
Freeport, ME 04032
(207) 865-1338

Type of B&B: B&B inn.
Rooms: 7 with private bath.
Rates: 1/$80; 2/$100-110.

Rating: A or ♛♛♛ Excellent, far exceeds basic requirements.

1850s farmhouse accented with Victorian trim has been completely restored and is situated on three acres at the north end of the village. Choose from seven guest rooms with private bath. While there is a variety in the size, decor, and amenities of the rooms, each is comfortably furnished and freshly decorated. Two parlors with fireplaces grace the main floor and breakfast is served in a pleasant dining room with small tables. Popular activities in the area include shopping at local outlets and L.L. Bean's retail stores. Full breakfast specialties include homemade muffins, coffee cakes, pancakes, and waffles. No smoking. 1/$80; 2/$100-110. MC, V.

Freeport

Porter's Landing Bed & Breakfast
70 South Street
Freeport, ME 04032
(207) 865-4488

Type of B&B: Inn.
Rooms: 3 with private bath.
Rates: 1/$65-80; 2/$75-90.

Rating: A or ♛♛♛ Excellent, far exceeds basic requirements.

Carriage house built in 1870 is located in Freeport's quiet Maritime district, one mile from town and L.L. Bean's retail store. Three guest rooms on the second floor offer a private bath and feature handmade quilts and fresh cut flowers. Also upstairs is a quiet loft for reading. On the main floor is a parlor with Count Rumford fireplace and comfortable window seats with views of the flower gardens. Walk along Main Street and explore more than 100 factory outlet stores. Visit nearby Wolf Neck or Winslow Parks and enjoy biking, sailing, fishing, cross-country skiing, or hiking along the edge of the ocean. A hearty breakfast features fresh fruits, homemade breads and muffins, and specialties such as Belgian waffles with spiced apples and wild Maine blueberry pancakes. No smoking. 1/$65-80; 2/$75-90. MC. V. Travel agent.

Guests write: *"We enjoyed a small but very lovely room with private bath. The common area was warm and attractive with lots of information available on the Freeport area."* (T. Lane)

"I had intended to come up for the cross-country skiing but my husband was deployed in the Persian Gulf. You can be sure upon his return we'll be up for a weekend. After all, he's an L.L. Bean addict and I can't think of a more peaceful and romantic haven to spend time with a long-lost spouse. I can't say enough about Porter's Landing. Upon our arrival, Peter, who had been washing windows, greeted me by name and welcomed me. He ushered us in and Barbara took over and cooled our parched throats with fresh iced tea in the sitting room. The decor was beautiful but comfortable. Our hosts offered us their knowledge about the area and acted on our behalf when making reservations for us locally." (M. Smith)

"The most memorable part of my trip to Maine was my stay at Porter's Landing. Barbara and Peter made us feel welcome the moment we arrived and went out of their way to accommodate us. Their hospitality is second to none." (J. Dodgson)

Fryeburg

Admiral Peary House
9 Elm Street
Fryeburg, ME 04037
(800) 237-8080 or (207) 935-3365

Type of B&B: Inn.
Rooms: 4 with private baths.
Rates: 1/$65-100; 2/$70-108.

Rating: A+ or ♛♛♛ Excellent, far exceeds basic requirements.

Once the home of the famous American explorer, this historic Victorian home is now an inn and is located 50 miles west of Portland. Choose from four guest rooms with private bath, sitting area, dressing table, air conditioning, and individually controlled heat. Some rooms feature mountain views, king-sized brass beds, or slanted roof lines that create interesting nooks and crannies. Soak in the outdoor spa, play tennis on the inn's clay court, read a book from the library in the guest living room, play pool in the Billiard room, or relax on the large screened-in porch where afternoon tea is offered daily. Area attractions include the White Mountains National Forest, Saco River Canoeing, Fryeburg Fair, alpine and Nordic skiing, and outlet shopping. A full breakfast offers such specialties as Maine blueberry pancakes, Belgium waffles, or Admiral Peary breakfast pie, served with home-made muffins and breads. Wedding and meeting facilities available. No smoking. 1/$65-100; 2/$70-108. MC, V. Travel agent.

Guests write: *"I consider the Admiral Peary House to be the quintessential B&B. The Inn is scrupulously clean and most attractive. Wonderful breakfasts are served in a light, airy kitchen-sitting area. The Greenbergs are a fun host and hostess. I would recommend this inn to all of my friends."* (J. Bliss)

Kennebunk Beach

Sundial Inn
P.O. Box 1147
48 Beach Avenue
Kennebunk, ME 04043
(207) 967-3850
Fax (207) 967-4719

Type of B&B: Inn.
Rooms: 34 with private bath.
Rates: 1 or 2/$65-150.

Rating: A+ or ♛♛♛ Excellent, far exceeds basic requirements.

Large oceanfront inn offers a quiet setting with beach access. There are thirty-four guest rooms with private bath, cable TV, air conditioning, and turn-of-the-century antique furnishings. Several luxury rooms offer ocean views and whirlpool baths. An attractive living room furnished with Oriental rugs and chintz-covered chairs and sofa offers a pleasant area for conversing or just enjoying the ocean breezes. Popular attractions in the area include shopping at the local art galleries, gift and outlet shops, whale-watching, deep-sea fishing, and hiking at the nearby wildlife refuge and estuary. Continental breakfast features homemade muffins. Wheelchair access. 1 or 2/$65-150. AE, MC, V.

Kennebunkport/Cape Porpoise

Inn at Harbor Head
R.R. 2, Box 1180, Pier Road
Kennebunkport, ME 04046
(207) 967-5564

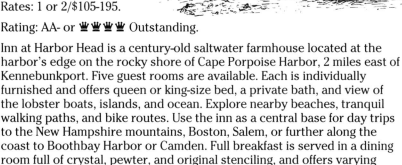

Type of B&B: Inn.
Rooms: 5 with private bath.
Rates: 1 or 2/$105-195.

Rating: AA- or ♛♛♛♛ Outstanding.

Inn at Harbor Head is a century-old saltwater farmhouse located at the harbor's edge on the rocky shore of Cape Porpoise Harbor, 2 miles east of Kennebunkport. Five guest rooms are available. Each is individually furnished and offers queen or king-size bed, a private bath, and view of the lobster boats, islands, and ocean. Explore nearby beaches, tranquil walking paths, and bike routes. Use the inn as a central base for day trips to the New Hampshire mountains, Boston, Salem, or further along the coast to Boothbay Harbor or Camden. Full breakfast is served in a dining room full of crystal, pewter, and original stenciling, and offers varying specialties such as stuffed French toast, eggs Florentine, or homemade roast beef hash with poached eggs and salsa. No smoking. 1 or 2/$105-195. MC, V. Travel agent.

Guests write: *"The Greenery room is wonderfully tranquil and comforting with its walls wrapped in windows and the bed sinking under all those pillows. Joan and David's gourmet breakfasts have turned us into morning people."* (M. Costa)

"Joan is the epitome of a bed and breakfast hostess reaching that rare balance of attention to every detail while maintaining a warm, cozy, friendly, inviting haven for her guests. My soul is restored from the classical guitar, the crystal, silver, starched linens, hammock, and my own bird singing to me from outside the window." (D. Beto)

"The Harbor Suite with its beautiful murals and view is by far the best room in which we've ever stayed and we've been all over the world." (E. Volk)

"The Summer Suite was romantic, done in exquisite taste, the view divine. The breakfasts were more than delicious and they were presented as a work of art." (A. Ferraro)

"The chocolate covered French toast made my daughter Barbra's day." (F. Johnson)

"Joan and David are the quintessential innkeepers who make you feel at home yet pampered without being fussed over." (D. McKillop)

Kennebunkport

Inn on South Street
PO Box 478A
Kennebunkport, ME 04046
(207) 967-5151

Type of B&B: Inn.
Rooms: 3 rooms and 1 suite,
all with private bath.
Rates: 1/$85-165; 2/$95-185.

Rating: A+ or ♛♛♛ Excellent, far exceeds basic requirements.

Inn on South Street is an early nineteenth-century Greek Revival home situated on a quiet side street 5 miles from I-95 at exit 3. There are four guest rooms. Each offers a private bath, individual decor, fresh flowers, period antique furnishings, brass bed, and a working fireplace. One room is actually a large suite of three rooms with fireplace and Jacuzzi. Walk down tree-lined streets to restaurants, shops, and the beach or drive to nearby golf courses as well as fishing, boating, and hiking areas. Full gourmet breakfast features homemade family specialties such as over-sized German pancakes, herbed cheese soufflè, or a light breakfast flan with blueberry sauce. Afternoon refreshments served daily. No smoking. 1/$85-165; 2/$95-185. MC, V.

Guests write: *"Breakfast is in the tree tops in the 2nd floor kitchen with a view of the Kennebunk River. Featured on the menu were homemade breads and jams, colorful and tasty combinations of fresh fruits and egg dishes served on blue and white china. Elegant, yet unpretentious."*
(J. Chalmers)

"This inn should be used as an example of how to run an inn properly. All the comforts such as clean, well-appointed rooms were provided but somehow the whole was greater than the sum of its parts. Jack and Eva were delightful hosts not just innkeepers. You felt extremely comfortable yet there was still a degree of elegance that comes only with knowledge and experience. This gives you the feeling of living in Maine, not just being a tourist." (E. DuBose)

Kennebunkport

Kennebunkport Inn
P.O. Box 111, Dock Square
Kennebunkport, ME 04046
(207) 967-2621

Type of B&B: Inn with restaurant.
Rooms: 34 with private bath.
Rates: 1 or 2/$54-165.

Rating: A- or ♛♛♛ Excellent, far exceeds basic requirements.

Large sea captain's home situated along the Kennebunk River was built in 1899 and is now an inn with restaurant. There are thirty-four guest rooms available. Each offers a private bath, color TV, and period furnishings. The restaurant lounge with fireplace and swimming pool with patio are popular spots for relaxation in the evening. Antique shops, boutiques, and restaurants are within walking distance from the inn. Local theaters, horseback riding, golf, and fine beaches are within a short drive. Full breakfast is included in the overnight rates. The restaurant serves candlelight dinners. Families welcome. Meeting facilities available. 1 or 2/$54-165. AE, MC, V. 10% senior and business travel discounts. Travel agent.

Kennebunkport

Kilburn House
P.O. Box 1309, Chestnut Street
Kennebunkport, ME 04046
(207) 967-4762

Type of B&B: Guesthouse
Rooms: 5 rooms or suites, 3 with private bath.
Rates: 2/$45-75.

Rating: B or ♛♛ Good, exceeds basic requirements.

Small Victorian home built in 1890 is situated on a quiet side street one block from the village center. The four guest rooms offer twin or double beds; three have a private bath. A third floor suite offers complete privacy, two bedrooms, separate living room, and private bath. Specialty shops and restaurants are within easy walking distance from the inn. Beaches, nightly entertainment, and the L.L. Bean retail store are a short drive away. Full breakfast. No smoking. 2/$45-75. AE, MC, V.

Kennebunkport

Kylemere House 1818
P.O. Box 1333, 6 South Street
Kennebunkport, ME 04046
(207) 967-2780

Type of B&B: Inn.
Rooms: 4 with private bath.
Rates: 1/$70-95; 2/$90-125.

Rating: A+ or ♛♛♛ Excellent, far exceeds basic requirements.

Historic Federal inn is located on a quiet street a few minutes walk to shops, beaches, and restaurants. Choose from four guest rooms with private bath. All are furnished with period antiques and soft colors that enhance the ambiance and true New England decor of this seaport inn. Guests enjoy afternoon refreshments in the sitting room or on the porch overlooking the gardens. The inn is a short walk from the ocean and Dock Square. Nearby sights include beaches, Trolley Museum, Monastery, Maritime Museum, and Portland Museum of Art. A variety of outdoor sporting activities available. Full gourmet breakfast. No smoking. 1/$70-95; 2/$90-125. AE, Discover, MC, V.

Guests write: *"I forgot my dress shoes and asked her where there was a shoe store close by. She asked what size and brought me several pairs to pick from. At the same time there was a couple staying who were getting married and he forgot his tie. Not to worry. Mary showed him her husband's for him to choose from."* (K. Dubois)

"Breakfasts were superb and unique. Having cocktails for us before our special dinner was a delightful surprise." (G. Spieth)

"Breakfasts were served in their formal dining room which looks out onto the professionally landscaped gardens. The table place settings are different every day on a five day cycle but not to be outdone by the elegant breakfasts with a variety of juices, warmed exotic fruit cocktails, and our favorite puffed pastry filled with eggs, cheese and bacon. During our 2nd visit Maine was in the direct path of Hurricane Bob. We had restaurant reservations but all commercial establishments were boarded up and closed. We were not to be denied though as the hosts very graciously made dinner for all guests and even popped a bottle of champagne in honor of our daughter's 21st birthday. We were very touched." (C. Jonke)

"This place is like finding a four-leaf clover in a clover patch! If everyone had any idea what a gem of a find this place is, there'd never be any rooms left for us." (D. Hallersey)

Kennebunkport

Maine Stay Inn and Cottages
P.O. Box 500-A, 34 Maine Street
Kennebunkport, ME 04046
(207) 967-2117 or (800) 950-211

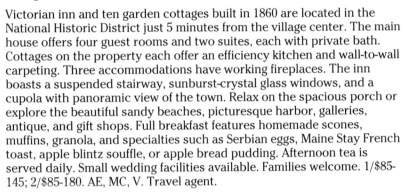

Type of B&B: Inn with cottages.
Rooms: 17 rooms or cottages, each with private bath.
Rates: 1/$85-145; 2/$85-180.

Rating: A or ♛♛♛ Excellent, far exceeds basic requirements.

Victorian inn and ten garden cottages built in 1860 are located in the National Historic District just 5 minutes from the village center. The main house offers four guest rooms and two suites, each with private bath. Cottages on the property each offer an efficiency kitchen and wall-to-wall carpeting. Three accommodations have working fireplaces. The inn boasts a suspended stairway, sunburst-crystal glass windows, and a cupola with panoramic view of the town. Relax on the spacious porch or explore the beautiful sandy beaches, picturesque harbor, galleries, antique, and gift shops. Full breakfast features homemade scones, muffins, granola, and specialties such as Serbian eggs, Maine Stay French toast, apple blintz souffle, or apple bread pudding. Afternoon tea is served daily. Small wedding facilities available. Families welcome. 1/$85-145; 2/$85-180. AE, MC, V. Travel agent.

Guests write: *"The bungalow efficiencies at the back of the main building are excellent for a family, particularly if one needs to be able to provide food to children at 3 a.m. because of the time change (from Europe) without annoying other guests. As a vegetarian, I also found the healthy breakfasts a far cry from the usual animal-fats-with-everything level of American cuisine."* (S. Yarnold)

"Even the towels are wonderful - so nice and thick and a pretty color." (M. Newman)

"They know how to make their guests feel comfortable. The accommodations and the pleasant atmosphere provided made us feel right at home." (D. Goegelman)

"The bottle of wine was such a nice gesture. The food, fireplace, and advice on activities in the area were all excellent. We enjoyed the backyard area for reading." (N. Johnson)

"On our 2nd Anniversary we were introduced to another couple at the inn. The four of us have become fast friends and see each other often. Carol and Lindsay have always been helpful in making reservations for evenings out, picnics, and other places of interest." (J. Ellison-Taylor)

Portland

Andrews Lodging Bed & Breakfast
417 Auburn Street
Portland, ME 04103
(207)797-9157 or Fax (207)797-9040

Type of B&B: Inn.
Rooms: 6, 1 with private bath.
Rates: 1/$45-60; 2/$50-65; Suite/$130-155.

Rating: B+ or ♛♛ Good, exceeds basic requirements.

Circa 1740s Colonial house situated on 1.5 acres is surrounded by country gardens and located five miles from the center of Portland on the outskirts of the city. There are a total of six guest rooms and one offers a private bath. Each room has been decorated with antiques and traditional furnishings and features a unique decor theme. The Golf room has antique golf pictures while the Victorian Room offers 1860 furniture including a signed Miller lamp. The Oriental room has wicker furniture and Oriental bird prints while the Shaker suite offers the timeless simplicity of Shaker furniture and also has a whirlpool tub. The Amish room has pencil post beds and folk quilts. A guest kitchen provides a sitting area with cable television and laundry facilities and there's a comfortable living room with fireplace. Explore the gardens, sit on the deck, or relax on the brick patio. Downtown Portland, a short drive away, offers the Historic Old Port, museums, restaurants, and the waterfront. Within a day trip by car are the L.L. Bean and the Freeport Factory outlets and nearby ocean activities. Continental breakfast is served in the formal dining room on silver and crystal and often features hot oatmeal with Maine syrup, fresh muffins and sweet breads, as well as fresh fruits grown in the summer garden. Wedding facilities available. Families welcome. No smoking. 1/$45-60; 2/$50-65; Suite/$130-155. AE, MC, V. 10% senior discount.

Portland

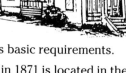

West End Inn
146 Pine Street
Portland, ME 04102
(207) 772-1377

Type of B&B: Inn.
Rooms: 4 with private bath.
Rates: 1/$70-80; 2/$80-90.

Rating: B+ or ♛♛ Good, exceeds basic requirements.

Brick Victorian townhouse built in 1871 is located in the Western Promenade Historic District where there are many fine Victorian homes.

Four guest rooms are offered, each with private bath. Take an easy walk to nearby downtown and area attractions such as the Portland Museum of Art, Old Port Exchange, Cumberland County Civic Center, Performing Arts Center, and many fine restaurants. Catch the International Ferry to Nova Scotia nearby. Full breakfast features homemade muffins and a special entree of the day. No smoking. 1/$70-80; 2/$80-90. AE, MC, V.

Searsport

Thurston House B&B
P.O. Box 686, 8 Elm Street
Searsport, ME 04974
(207) 548-2213

Type of B&B: Inn.
Rooms: 4, 2 with private bath.
Rates: 1/$40; 2/$45-60.

Rating: B or ♛♛ Good, exceeds basic requirements.

Colonial home built in 1831 is located on a quiet side street of the village opposite Penobscot Marine Museum and just off US-1. Four guest rooms are available with pleasant decor and selected antique furnishings. Two rooms offer a private bath. Walk to local restaurants, galleries, specialty shops, and beach park. Popular local attractions include state parks and forts, ocean cruises, and day trips to Blue Hill, Castine, Bar Harbor, and Camden. Indulge in a "forget-about-lunch" full breakfast. No smoking. 1/$40; 2/$45-60. 10% senior, military, and veteran discounts. Travel agent.

Spruce Head

Craignair Inn
Clark Island Road
Spruce Head, ME 04859
(207) 594-7644

Type of B&B: Inn with restaurant.
Rooms: 22, 8 with private bath.
Rates: Shared bath: $40-65; Private bath: $72-87

Rating: B+ or ♛♛ Good, exceeds basic requirements.

Waterfront country inn is surrounded by natural beauty and located 8 miles from Route 1 in Thomaston. There are twenty-two guest rooms in the main house or annex. Each is furnished with homemade quilts, hooked rugs, and colorful wallpaper; eight offer a private bath.

— Comments continued on next page

A comfortable porch overlooks the water and there are attractive gardens whose paths lead to the coastline's tidal pools, clam flats, meadows, and offshore islands. Within a short drive are Rockland, Camden, antique shops, art galleries, museums, tennis, golf, sailing, and festivals. Full breakfast. There's a restaurant on the premises as well as facilities for meetings and social functions. Families welcome. Shared bath/$40-65; Private bath/$72-87. AE, MC, V. Open March through November.

Guests write: *"The hospitality shown led to a lasting friendship. Terry, upon my 1st visit, invited me to go antiquing with her and gave me the use of her car for my independent excursions. If I missed meals, I was made to feel welcome to take my meals with her family."* (B. Sajdak)

"The setting is beautiful and not crowded - right on the ocean. The food and service was excellent and moderately priced. The innkeepers have always made our stays fun." (J. Dacey)

Sullivan Harbor

Island View Inn
HCR 32, Box 24
Sullivan Harbor, ME 04664
(207) 422-3031

Type of B&B: Country inn with restaurant.
Rooms: 7, 5 with private bath.
Rates: 1 or 2/$40-70.

Rating: A or ♛♛♛ Excellent, far exceeds basic requirements.

Quiet waterfront property was built as a turn-of-the-century summer cottage and is located just off Route 1, fifteen minutes from Ellsworth and thirty minutes from Bar Harbor. Seven guest rooms feature original furniture and detailed restoration work; five offer a private bath. The spacious common room on the main floor has a fireplace and pleasant water views. Right outside the back door is a private beach and picturesque views of Frenchman's Bay and the mountains of Mt. Desert Island. Sailing excursions on an 18-foot Rhodes sailboat are available by advance reservations. Full breakfast often features a selection of eggs, pancakes, French toast, breakfast meats, and English muffins. Facilities for small weddings and meetings. Restricted smoking. 2/$40-70. MC, V. Open Memorial Day through mid-October.

Tenants Harbor

The East Wind Inn
PO Box 149
Tenants Harbor, ME 04860
(800) 241-VIEW or (207) 372-6366

Type of B&B: Country Inn with restaurant.
Rooms: 26, 12 with private bath.
Rates: 1/$48; 2/$74-130.

Rating: B or ♛♛ Good, exceeds basic requirements.

East Wind Inn built in 1920 was fully restored in 1974 and sits at harbor's edge offering views of the ocean. It is located nine miles from Thomaston and thirteen miles outside of Rockland in the heart of mid-coast Maine. A total of twenty-six guest rooms are available. The Meeting House offers one full apartment, two suites, and seven rooms with private bath. The inn has fourteen guest rooms with shared bath, one suite and a room with private bath. The inn's lobby is a place to relax, watch television, read, or play the baby grand piano. Additional common areas in the Meeting House include a living room with television, books, and magazines. Take a bike ride to explore the peninsula. Walk to the beach and explore the tidal pools or board a ferry to Monhegan, Vinalhaven, or North Haven Island. Sail from the inn's dock aboard the Friendship Sloop Surprise. Visit nearby museums, antique shops, lighthouses, or just relax watching the harbor activity from the large porch. Continental breakfast features blueberry muffins. A full breakfast and dinner are available at extra charge in the dining room. Meeting facilities include a conference room with up-to-date audio visual equipment. Families welcome. 1/$48; 2/$74-130. AE, MC, V. Extended-stay discounts.

Wiscasset

The Squire Tarbox Inn
RR2 Box 620
Wiscasset, ME 04578
(207) 882-7693

Type of B&B: Country inn with restaurant.
Rooms: 11 with private bath.
Rates: 1/$55-75; 2/$70-140.

Rating: A or ♛♛♛ Excellent, far exceeds basic requirements.

The original board floors, timbers, and wainscoting of this 1763 farmhouse are still visible today in what is known as the Squire Tarbox

Inn. The inn is found on Westport Island 8.5 miles off Route 1 between Wiscasset and Bath. Choose from eleven guest rooms, each with private bath. There are four rooms in the main house which feature fireplaces. The connected carriage barn houses seven more rooms with exposed beams and country decor. Relax in front of the fireplace with a book from the inn's bookshelves, play a game in the barn after dinner, take a walk down to the saltwater marsh, or sun on the open deck overlooking the woods. The innkeepers raise floppy-eared, friendly Nubian dairy goats and process natural cheeses from their own dairy and cheese samples are offered by the fire before dinner. The inn is in the country, away from tourist centers but near many Maine coast attractions such as beaches, harbors, antique and craft shops, museums, and lobster shacks. A full breakfast for B&B guests offers granola, fresh fruit, quiche, and a choice of five cakes and breads. Dinner is available at an additional charge. Restricted smoking. 1/$55-75; 2/$70-140. AE, MC, V. Travel agent.

Guests write: *"Being a tour operator, I have stayed at many B&Bs. The Squire Tarbox Inn is a very special place. We had a lovely, although short, visit. The animals are delightful, the marsh is peaceful, the food is healthy and delicious. I have already highly recommended the inn to some of our Maine guests for the 1993 season."* (D. Mann)

"Never stayed at a nicer place. The best food I've ever tasted! And the best atmosphere!" (L. Smith)

"We thoroughly enjoyed the stay, the room, the goats, and especially the food! Everyone was friendly and gracious. We continue to relate our wonderful experience at the Squire Tarbox to our friends." (J. Miller)

"We along with another couple, were on a two-week vacation in New England where we stayed exclusively in B&Bs. Squire Tarbox was our very favorite — the food, cordiality, atmosphere, and our spotless room were super." (R. Graydon)

Additional information on B&Bs in Maryland is available from the
following: The Traveller in Maryland (410) 269-6232.

Annapolis

The Charles Inn
74 Charles Street
Annapolis, MD 21401
(410) 268-1451

Type of B&B: Inn.
Rooms: 4, 2 with private baths.
Rates: 1/$50-95; 2/$69-149.

Rating: B or ♛♛ Good, exceeds basic requirements.

Civil War era home in the heart of the Annapolis Historic District is
located 30 minutes from either Washington D.C. or Baltimore, MD.
Choose from four guest rooms, two with private bath. Each room offers a
down feather comforter and antique furnishings. Stroll the narrow streets
lined with historic homes, shops, galleries, and antique stores. Explore
the waterfront with taverns and restaurants or visit the United States
Naval Academy. A full breakfast which features fresh fruit crepes,
pancakes, or waffles is served on crystal and china set on Battenburg lace
tablecloths. Small wedding facilities available. Families welcome.
Restricted smoking. 1/$50-95; 2/$69-149. AE, MC, V. 10% senior discount.
Travel agent.

Annapolis

William Page Inn
8 Martin Street
Annapolis, MD 21401
(410) 626-1506 or (800) 364-4160

Type of B&B: Inn.
Rooms: 5, 3 with private bath.
Rates: 1 or 2/$65-140.

Rating: A or ♛♛♛ Excellent, far exceeds basic requirements.

Victorian turn-of-the-century home is on a quiet street in the Historic
district near the Naval Academy. Choose from five guest rooms, three
with private bath. Each room features a queen-size bed, sitting area, and
air conditioning. One large suite offers a private whirlpool tub. Antiques
and period reproductions, chandeliers, and original artwork enhance the
inn's elegance. Walk to historic William Paca House and Gardens, a

variety of fine restaurants, shops, and the city dock. Off-street parking is available. Full breakfast is served on a side board and banquet table in the parlor and may include homemade Belgian waffles, Colonial eggs, or a sausage casserole. Facilities for small meetings and social functions. No smoking. 1 or 2/$65-140. AE, MC, V. Travel agent.

Berlin

Merry Sherwood Plantation
8909 Worcester Highway
Berlin, MD 21811
(410) 641-2112

Type of B&B: Inn.
Rooms: 8, 6 with private bath.
Rates: 2/$95-150.

Rating: A+ or ♛♛♛ Excellent, far exceeds basic requirements.

Victorian mansion with over 8,500 square feet was completed in 1859 and built for lavish parties — the perfect home for accommodating discerning guests. It sits on over eighteen acres and is located on Maryland's Eastern Shore, 130 miles east of Baltimore and 140 miles East of Washington, D.C. Choose from eight guest rooms, six with private marble bath. Each room has authentic period antiques and lovely architectural details such as large scaled baseboard, loblolly pine flooring, nine fireplaces, window moldings, and floor to ceiling "peer" mirrors. The first floor has a formal ballroom, grand entrance hall with four-story mahogany stair railing, a sitting parlor, rosewood dining room, library, sun parlor, and wrap-around verandah. Explore the surrounding grounds that are still landscaped in a typical 19th-century style, sit in the outdoor Victorian patio setting, or stroll the walking path. Visit nearby beaches and the National Wildlife Reserve. Activities in the area include swimming, fishing, boating, tennis, hunting, and antiquing. A full breakfast offers puffed apple pancakes, tomato rarebit, "Bubble and Squeak", as well as home-made muffins, jams, and jellies. Wedding, retreat, and meeting facilities available. No smoking. 2/$95-150. MC, V. Travel agent.

Burtonsville

Upstream at Water's Gift
3604 Dustin Road
P.O. Box 240
Burtonsville, MD 20866
(301) 421-9562 or 421-9163

Type of B&B: Guesthouse.
Rooms: 2 with private bath.
Rates: 1 or 2/$80-100

Rating: A+ or ♛♛♛ Excellent, far exceeds basic requirements.

Country home situated on a fifty-three acre Colonial horse farm is surrounded by several thousand acres of secluded woods and located halfway between Baltimore and Washington, D.C. The guesthouse offers two rooms, each with air conditioning and a private bath. The great room features a large fireplace, cathedral ceilings and unusual antique pine paneling. An expansive glass wall provides a spectacular view of the rolling landscape and horse pastures. Enjoy the many outdoor activities available such as hiking and mountain biking. Full gourmet breakfast. Facilities available for meetings, weddings and social functions. Restricted smoking. 1 or 2/$80-100. Travel agent.

Hagerstown

Beaver Creek House B&B
20432 Beaver Creek Road
Hagerstown, MD 21740
(301) 797-4764

Type of B&B: Inn.
Rooms: 5, 3 with private bath.
Rates: 1/$55-75; 2/$65-85.

Rating: A- or ♛♛♛ Excellent, far exceeds basic requirements.

Beaver Creek House is a restored farmhouse built at the turn-of-the-century and located 4 miles east of Hagerstown in historic Beaver Creek. Five guest rooms are available with air conditioning, antique furnishings, and family memorabilia. A honeymoon suite is available for special occasions. A common room on the main floor offers an area for watching TV or reading. Explore the country garden and attractive courtyard with fountain. Popular local attractions include antique shops, Civil War battlefields, Appalachian Trail hiking, skiing, golf, and trout fishing. Full breakfast features homemade muffins, biscuits, and rolls, as well as a hearty serving of eggs, sausage, and pancakes. Afternoon tea is served in the parlor. No smoking. 1/$55-75; 2/$65-85.

Guests write; *"Don and Shirley are perfect hosts. And Don makes the best breakfasts! I wanted to move in. Very helpful with points of interest and history. There were wonderful snacks. This is a lovely home with very comfortable beds. I can't say enough!"* (H. McCrae)

Olney

The Thoroughbred Bed & Breakfast
16410 Batchellors Forest Road
Olney, MD 20832
(301) 774-7649 or 774-7571

Type of B&B: Country estate.
Rooms: 13, 7 with private bath.
Rate: 1 or 2/$65-125.

Rating: B+ or ♛♛ Good, exceeds basic requirements.

Country estate situated on 175 acres is located 12 miles from Washington, D.C. on a site where champion race horses have been bred and raised for years. The main house has five guest rooms, three with private bath. The farm house annex has four rooms, each with shared baths and a newly built cottage offers four guest rooms with private bath, fireplace, and double whirlpool tub. Popular activities here include swimming in the pool, relaxing in the hot tub, and playing billiards. Full breakfast offered with egg dishes, waffles or pancakes, and homemade muffins. 1 or 2/$65-125. MC, V. Travel agent.

Guests write: *"We thoroughly enjoyed our stay including the marvelous food, conversation (especially golf and horses), and the lovely surroundings."* (S. Pierce)

"My husband wants to return to play the golf course. The quiet serenity of this beautiful B&B was wonderful as was the hospitality of our hostess and her gourmet culinary skills." (H. VanSant)

"Thoroughbreds cross the fields, time to relax around the pool, complete comfort in our room, and memorable mornings enjoying breakfast made this an exceptional experience." (A. Miller)

Oxford

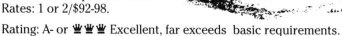

1876 House
110 North Morris Street
Oxford, MD 21654-0658
(410) 226-5496

Type of B&B: Inn.
Rooms: 3 with private bath.
Rates: 1 or 2/$92-98.

Rating: A- or ♛♛♛ Excellent, far exceeds basic requirements.

Historic Victorian home built in 1876 is 11 miles south of Easton on Route 333. There are two guest rooms, each with private bath. Two rooms offer queen-sized beds and the two room suite offers a double bed and sitting/dressing area which can accommodate a third person. The home is furnished in Queen Anne decor and Oriental rugs with ten-foot ceilings and wide-plank pine floors. Walk to village boutiques, fine restaurants, and antique shops. Recreation available in the area includes swimming, golf, tennis, bicycling, fishing, boating, and hunting. Continental breakfast served in formal dining room usually includes English muffins, croissants, fruit-filled turnovers, and fresh-brewed coffee and tea. 1 or 2/$92-98. Off-season and extended-stay discounts available.

St. Michaels

Kemp House Inn
412 Talbot St. Box 638
St. Michaels, MD 21663
(410) 745-2243

Type of B&B: Inn.
Rooms: 8, 6 with private bath.
Rates: 1 or 2/$65-105.

Rating: C or ♛ Acceptable, meets basic requirements.

Three story brick Georgian dates back to 1805 and is located in historic Waterman's village on the Eastern Shore of the Chesapeake Bay just 40 miles southeast of Baltimore and 100 miles south of Philadelphia. Six of the eight rooms feature a private bath, period furnishings, candlelight, quilt patchwork, four-poster rope bed, quilted down pillows, and old fashioned nightshirts. Four rooms have working fireplaces with the original mantels. A separate cottage is available which features a cathedral ceiling, full bath, and private patio. Relax on the front porch in a rocking chair. The Maritime Museum, shops, antique stores, restaurants, and the harbor are all nearby. Go biking, golfing, sailing, or play tennis. Continental breakfast includes pastry, cheese, and fruit. Families welcome. 1 or 2/$65-105. MC, V. Senior discount. Travel agent.

Guests write: *"From the flannel nightshirts to the working fireplace, we enjoy the Kemp House Inn for its simple early 19th-century flavor. The innkeepers have installed modern conveniences throughout the inn such as a sink in each room and easy shower access without spoiling that 19th-century appeal. The inn has adequate parking and is a short walk from St. Michaels shops and restaurants. You want an extra muffin or directions for an afternoon tour? All you need do is ask. The guests we've encountered are always quiet and courteous. The Kemp House Inn is the best per dollar value we've found for country living away from home."* (C. Houston)

St. Michaels

Parsonage Inn
210 North Talbot Street
St. Michaels, MD 21663
(800) 394-5519

Type of B&B: Inn.
Rooms: 8 with private bath.
Rates: 1 or 2/$72-114.

Rating: A or ♛♛♛ Excellent, far exceeds basic requirements.

Brick Victorian home built in 1883 is situated in the heart of this small coastal village on Maryland's Eastern Shore. Choose from eight guest rooms with king or queen-size bed, private bath, ceiling fans, Queen Anne-style furnishings, and Laura Ashley linens. Three rooms have working fireplaces. Popular gathering spots include the library with collection of good books, upstairs deck for sunbathing, and quiet parlor with fireplace. Bicycles are available for exploring the village. Walk to great seafood restaurants, antique and gift shops, the historic harbor, and Maritime Museum. Full breakfast. Families welcome. Restricted smoking. 1 or 2/$72-114 + 8% tax. MC, V.

Salisbury

White Oak Inn
804 Spring Hill Road
Salisbury, MD 21801
(410) 742-4887

Type of B&B: Inn.
Rooms: 4 with shared bath.
Rates:1/$55-60; 2/$60-65.

Rating: B- or ♛♛ Good, exceeds basic requirements.

Colonial home nestled among white oaks, pines, and red oaks, is situated on four acres one mile west of Salisbury, the largest city on the Eastern Shore of Maryland. Four guest rooms with king, queen, or twin-sized beds share two baths. The central open staircase in the foyer, as well as the wainscoting and crown moldings are all features typical to this authentic Colonial period. Relax on the large glass-enclosed porch or sit by the pond to enjoy local wildlife and landscaped grounds. Area attractions include the Ward Museum of Wildfowl Art, Pemberton Hall, Ocean City, Crisfield, and the islands of Assateague and Chincoteague. A continental breakfast includes fresh fruits, home-made muffins, and breads served on the porch. Wedding and meeting facilities available. No smoking. 1/$55-60; 2/$60-65. MC, V. Senior discount. Travel agent.

Silver Spring

Varborg
2620 Briggs Chaney Road
Silver Spring, MD 20905
(301) 384-2842

Type of B&B: B&B home.
Rooms: 3 with shared bath.
Rates: 1/$30; 2/$50.

Rating: C or ♛ Acceptable, meets basic requirements.

Colonial home in a residential area just west of Route 29 offers a convenient location midway between Baltimore and Washington D.C., yet with lovely views of the countryside. Three comfortable guest rooms share a bath. Guests use Varborg as a convenient base for day trips by car or subway to Gettysburg, Baltimore, Annapolis, or Washington, D.C. Tennis, swimming, and hiking are available nearby. Continental breakfast. No smoking. 1/$30; 2/$50.

— Comments continued on next page

Guests write: *"They are excellent hosts and I enjoyed my stay when I came for collaborative work with the Applied Physics Lab and Johns Hopkins University. I have used their home for a number of years. They are nice people looking to the comfort and happiness of their guests. The place is nice and quiet and well-kept."* (D. Venkatesan)

"Their welcome and the freedom of their house beats hotels anytime - as do their rates! The perfect antidote to lonely business trips." (M. Pinnock)

"I feel that the highlight of my stays are the interesting and stimulating discussions we have on a large variety of subjects. Any slack time goes by quickly with Pat and Bob." (A. Kelln)

"Bob and Pat have a broad knowledge of D.C. and Baltimore and are able to provide excellent detailed maps and directions. Their home is conveniently located between the two areas. Their knowledge of fine restaurants was a plus. They helped us find interesting ones that a tourist would not find without help. These are very special people." (A. Vieweg)

"The room was large and clean and Bob and Pat even invited me to dinner. They made their lovely home available for my use (not just my room). The area is rural, even though close to Washington, D.C. Perhaps the best of all is that the cost is about a third of the cost of a typical hotel room." (J.D. Menietti)

Snow Hill

River House Inn
201 East Market Street
Snow Hill, MD 21863
(410) 632-2722

Type of B&B: Inn.
Rooms: 8 with private bath.
Rates: 1 or 2/$65-99.

Rating: A or ♛♛♛ Excellent, far exceeds basic requirements.

Historic river-front Victorian country home built in 1860 is situated on two acres of rolling lawn on Maryland's Eastern Shore about fifteen miles southwest of Ocean City on Route 394. Eight guest rooms are available. Each of five rooms in the main house has a private bath and air conditioning and several feature a marble fireplace and porch. A newly renovated house built in 1835 provides three additional rooms. There are several common areas throughout the inn including two spacious parlors, living room, and elegant dining room, each with fireplace. Porches with ceiling fans overlook the back lawn, gardens and the river front. Popular activities in the area include walking the village's picturesque streets and exploring the Pocomoke River which offers canoeing and fishing. Assateague and Chincoteague are nearby as are Ocean City beaches. Guests have their choice of full breakfast from a variety of entrees and afternoon refreshments are served daily. Box lunches and dinners can be prepared by advance arrangement. Small wedding and meeting facilities available. Restricted smoking. 1 or 2/$65-99. V, MC. 5% family, senior, and auto club discount. Travel agent.

Guests write: *"We had a lovely time here. Everything was perfect including their attention to our two-year-old."* (D. Pankratz)

"Our host family was very hospitable. The breakfasts were delicious. The house and grounds are lovely and well-kept. We were within walking distance of canoe rentals and enjoyed canoeing on the Pocomoke River. They provided us with a pass to enjoy Assateague Island and the ocean beaches there. We look forward to a return visit." (J. Nieberding)

"We gathered our closest friends together for a wedding on their property and it was beautiful! They took care of so many details and made each of our guests feel at home. I cannot think of another inn at which such an event could be carried out with such ease." (J. Christodoulou)

"What makes the River House Inn so special, besides its lovely decor, large comfortable rooms, and quiet location, is the Knudsen's. They love people and running their inn. Their rare enthusiasm for life makes their inn a pearl indeed." (S. Jones)

Solomons Island

Davis House
PO Box 759
Solomons, MD 20688
(410) 326-4811

Type of B&B: Inn.
Rooms: 7, 5 with private bath.
Rates: 1 or 2/$75-125.

Rating: B or ♛♛ Good, exceeds basic requirements.

Turn-of-the-century Victorian inn commands a frontal view of the harbor and is located 60 miles southeast of Washington, DC on Maryland's Eastern Shore. Seven guest rooms, five with private bath, have been restored and feature air conditioning and queen-size beds. Four offer a harbor view as does a studio apartment covering the third floor. Relax in the living room or library, both of which open to the verandah. Explore the surrounding grounds, enjoy the view, and go boating, fishing, hiking, golfing, or antiquing nearby. Calvert Cliffs and St. Mary's City are a short drive. Full breakfast offers such specialties as eggs Benedict, crab deviled eggs, or country hash. Restricted smoking. 1 or 2/$75-125. MC, V.

Guests write: *"The Davis House is our favorite escape place in that it is comfortable but still creates a special atmosphere. Breakfast is spectacular! Runa and her personal touch make Davis House unique!"* (L. Smith)

"I would recommend Davis House to anyone. It's everything a B&B should be." (E. Fitzsimmons)

MASSACHUSETTS

Additional information on B&Bs throughout this state is available through the following:
B&B Associates Bay Colony (800) 347-5088
Be Our Guest B&B (617) 837-9867
B&B Cape Cod (508) 775-2772
Folkstone B&B Reservation Service (800) 762-2751
Golden Slumber Accommodations (800) 892-3231
Panda B&B (800) 832-9939

Amherst

Allen House Victorian Inn
599 Main Street
Amherst, MA 01002
(413) 253-5000

Type of B&B: Inn.
Rooms: 5 with private bath.
Rates: 1/45-85; 2/$55-95.

Rating: A or ♕♕♕ Excellent, far exceeds basic requirements.

Constructed in 1886 in the Victorian Queen Anne "stick style", this historic inn sits on three acres and is found in a small college town, 20 miles north of Springfield. Eastlake-style furnishings, "Aesthetic Movement" decor, period art, and art-wall coverings fill the five guest rooms, each of which has a private bath. Visit the five-college area, Historic Deerfield, and Old Sturbridge Village. Walk to nearby Emily Dickinson House, Amherst College, and the University of Massachusetts as well as fine galleries, museums, theaters, concerts, shops, and restaurants. Stuffed French toast, eggs Benedict, Swedish pancakes, and eggs Southwest are some of the special dishes offered at the full breakfast. Restricted smoking. 1/$45-85; 2/$55-95.

Guests write: *"The Allen House is an oasis in the New England area. The hosts are warm, convivial people. I never knew that authentic Victorian furniture could be so comfortable. The hearty breakfasts and personal attention to my wife and I have made us come back frequently."* (G. Garrow)

"It was a wintry day when I arrived for a weekend. My bones were stiff from the cold until I walked into the Allen House. My room was cozy with a down mattress and comforter. The bath was immaculate. The decorating of the room was in true "livable" Victorian style. My breakfast of oatmeal was laced with sweet maple syrup. It's just great!" (E.L. Roif)

"This was our first experience with B&B and it was just great. We were there for four days and found the owners very friendly and knowledgeable about their Victorian house and furniture. The breakfasts were excellent, particularly the Swedish pancakes. We had a very comfortable queen-size bed." (R. Schloerb)

"I have traveled around the world and have never encountered an inn, hotel, or motel equal to the Allen House in Amherst where we stayed during my recent visit to Amherst College for my 50th reunion. There is plenty of parking and the area is quiet. As the brochure indicates, it is extremely close to the cultural life of Amherst and the beauty of the surrounding countryside. These are overnight accommodations at their best." (S. Hess)

Attleboro

The Colonel Blackinton Inn
203 North Main Street
Attleboro, MA 02703
(508) 222-6022

Type of B&B: Inn.
Rooms: 16, 11 with private bath.
Rates: 1/$42-68; 2/$52-72.

Rating: B or ♛♛ Good, exceeds basic requirements.

Colonial Blackinton Inn is a Greek Revival structure built in 1850 and located just south of I-95, exit 5. Sixteen guest rooms are available and eleven have a private bath. The rooms have simple yet comfortable furnishings and pleasant decor. Two guest parlors are on the main floor with a fireplace, TV viewing area, and sunny porch. The turret offers a view of the river nearby. Recreation in the area includes golf, tennis, and fishing. Full breakfast is served in the two dining rooms on the main floor. This is also the setting for a formal tea in the afternoon that is open to the public. A remodeled carriage house on the grounds is available for social functions. Wheelchair access. 1/$42-68; 2/$52-72. AE, MC, V. 10% business travel discount.

— Comments continued on next page

Guests write: *"In the past 3 or 4 years my job has me staying in hotels and inns four nights a week and I must say that this fine B&B is the best. The warmth and friendliness made me feel quite at home except more pampered. From the peach pancakes to the Victorian sitting room, this B&B rates a top shelf rating. The large common room with comfy couches and fireplace is right out of a magazine."* (J. Walsh)

Barre

The Jenkins House Bed & Breakfast Inn
RT. 122, Barre Common
Barre, MA 01005
(508) 355-6444 or Fax (508)355-6449

Type of B&B: Inn.
Rooms: 5, 3 with private bath.
Rates: 1/$50-90; 2/$60-100.

Rating: B+ or ♕♕ Good, exceeds basic requirements.

1834 Victorian is due north of Barre Common on scenic Route 122. Five guest rooms offer a mix of antiques from several different periods and three of the rooms have a private bath. Special features in the guest rooms include a sleigh bed, fireplace, semi-private balcony overlooking North Park on the Common, and a queen-sized canopy bed surrounded by three walls of cafe windows. Relax in front of one of the four fireplaces, sit on the wrap-around porch, rent a bicycle to explore the area, or take a walk on the common. It's just a short drive to Sturbridge Village and State Parks, Wachusett Mountain, Quabbin Reservoir, and Cooks Canyon Audubon Society. Take in the view from the breakfast room while enjoying a full breakfast which features oat scones, various muffins, pancakes, or French toast. 1/$50-90; 2/$60-100. MC, V. Senior and corporate discount. Travel agent.

Guests write: *"I've stayed at Jenkins on three separate occasions and have found the accommodations very pleasant. Breakfasts are delightful, especially the baked items. Hosts are friendly but not obtrusive."* (W. Hosley)

Boston

Newbury Guest House
261 Newbury Street
Boston, MA 02116
(617) 437-7666

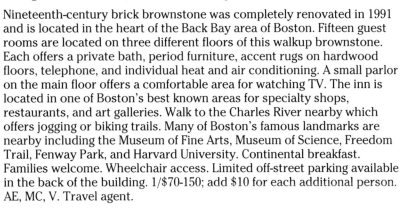

Type of B&B: Urban inn.
Rooms: 15 with private bath.
Rates: 1 or 2/$70-150.

Rating: B or ♕♕ Good, exceeds basic requirements.

Nineteenth-century brick brownstone was completely renovated in 1991 and is located in the heart of the Back Bay area of Boston. Fifteen guest rooms are located on three different floors of this walkup brownstone. Each offers a private bath, period furniture, accent rugs on hardwood floors, telephone, and individual heat and air conditioning. A small parlor on the main floor offers a comfortable area for watching TV. The inn is located in one of Boston's best known areas for specialty shops, restaurants, and art galleries. Walk to the Charles River nearby which offers jogging or biking trails. Many of Boston's famous landmarks are nearby including the Museum of Fine Arts, Museum of Science, Freedom Trail, Fenway Park, and Harvard University. Continental breakfast. Families welcome. Wheelchair access. Limited off-street parking available in the back of the building. 1/$70-150; add $10 for each additional person. AE, MC, V. Travel agent.

Cambridge

Cambridge House B&B
2218 Massachusetts Avenue
Cambridge, MA 02140
(617) 491-6300 or (800) 232-9989

Type of B&B: Inn.
Rooms: 17, 9 with private bath.
Rates: 1/$59-119; 2/$79-149.

Rating: A or ♕♕♕ Excellent, far exceeds basic requirements.

Historic Colonial Revival home built in 1892 is located near Harvard Square and only three minutes from the subway to downtown Boston. Choose from seventeen guest rooms, nine with private bath. The inn has undergone extensive renovation during 1993 and several new private baths have been installed. One spacious room on the second floor offers a full private bath, working fireplace, telephone, color TV, and elegant furnishings.There are two parlors on the main floor. Both feature fireplaces, comfortable upholstered furnishings, and rich drapery fabric. This location is near all major colleges and hospitals and is easily accessible to Routes 2 and 93 or Mass-Turnpike. Full breakfast and evening refreshments are served in the parlors. No smoking. 1/$59-119; 2/$79-149. AE, MC, V. Travel agent.

Chatham, Cape Cod

The Old Harbor Inn
22 Old Harbor Road
Chatham, MA 02633
(508) 945-4434 or (800) 942-4434

Type of B&B: Inn.
Rooms: 7 with private bath.
Rates: 1/$85-145; 2/$95-155.

Rating: A or ♛♛♛ Excellent, far exceeds basic requirements.

Classic Colonial Cape Cod-style inn built in the early 1930's is situated in a residential area one block from the village center of Chatham which is located on the elbow of Cape Cod. The inn was carefully restored in 1986 and offers six guest rooms with private bath. Each has individual English country decor accented with designer linens and antique and wicker furnishings. Choose from king, queen or twin beds. A fireplaced living room offers a quiet spot to read, relax, play the baby grand piano, or converse. Walk to the nearby beaches, gift and antique shops, art galleries, outdoor concerts, museums, wildlife sanctuary, restaurants, golf, tennis, and boating. Continental buffet breakfast includes home-baked muffins and scones, fresh fruit, yogurt and granola, juices, gourmet coffee and tea and is served in the sun room or on the outside deck overlooking flower gardens. 1/$85-145; 2/$95-155. AE, MC, V.

Cohasset

The Inn At Actor's Row
90 Howard Gleason Road
Cohasset, MA 02025
(617) 383-9200

Type of B&B: Inn.
Rooms: 5 with private bath.
Rates: 1 or 2/$100-135.

Rating: A+ or ♛♛♛ Excellent, far exceeds basic requirements.

Inn at Actor's Row overlooks Cohasset Harbor and is located 19 miles south of Boston. This rambling Colonial Cape dates back to 1840 when the first section was built. Three of the five guest rooms have fireplaces and feature harbor views, two other rooms have balconies overlooking the gardens and pool. Each room offers a private bath. There is an abundance of common areas throughout the inn including an exercise room and fireplaced living room. The swimming pool, Jacuzzi, and tennis court are surrounded by large lawns, flowering trees, and gardens. Borrow a bike and explore the surrounding area with its panoramic views and rocky coastline.The verandah offers views of lobster boats in the harbor. Attractions nearby include a scenic ferry trip to Boston, Plimoth Plantation and the South Shore Music Circus. Cohasset is a small village with unique shops and restaurants. Continental breakfast. No smoking. 1 or 2/$100-135. Travel agent.

Guests write: *"I have traveled every other week for the past year staying at B&Bs wherever I can. Actor's Row is #1 on my list. From accommodations, to the owners, to the small town setting, to the local restaurants — they just don't come any better. I only wish that my travels took me to that area more often."* (C. Bryant)

"Their guests are trusted like visiting friends or family. Kind and thoughtful gestures are evident everywhere from flying the Canadian flag in our honor, to a kind note left with a bottle of wine, assorted cheeses and crackers in our room to celebrate our return visit. The Tibbets possess a rare and wonderful charm. This spirit is infectious and expansive. It is present in the good natured humor around the breakfast table, and in the comings and goings of guests. As for the charming rooms, the spectacular views, the well groomed tennis courts, the various, and many charms of Cohasset, the porch at sunset, the gentle breeze of the Atlantic, and the quiet sound of halyards slapping masts in the harbor well...As the late Brother Simon at nearby Glastonbury Abbey was fond of saying, 'Tis the little things that make the big difference.' The Tibbets understand the profound wisdom of this simple maxim." (J. Fox)

Concord

Hawthorne Inn
462 Lexington Road
Concord, MA 01742
(508) 369-5610

Type of B&B: Inn.
Rooms: 7 with private bath.
Rates: 1/$75-110; 2/$110-150.

Rating: B+ or ♥ ♥ Good, exceeds basic requirements.

Ralph Waldo Emerson, the Alcotts, and Nathaniel Hawthorne once owned the land this 1870 Colonial inn sits on. Choose from seven guest rooms, each with private bath and individual decor. Each room features a selection of antique furnishings, handmade quilts, and wood floors graced with Oriental and rag rugs. Popular attractions in this area steeped in history include Wayside, Walden Pond, Great Meadows Wildlife Sanctuary. Many guests have enjoyed canoeing and quiet picnics in the area. Continental breakfast. Families welcome. No smoking. 1/$75-110; 2/$110-150. Travel agent.

Guests write: *"I'm happy to report that the law of diminishing returns has spared Marilyn and Gregory Burch's charming Hawthorne Inn. I returned recently and the place (and therefore I) was undiminished. The nurturing and enriching ambiance of the inn with its books, art, distinctive beds, masterful quilts, location, location, location, and appetizing aromas nudges me into planning yet another stay."* (D. Dasch)

Dennis, Cape Cod

Isaiah Hall B&B Inn
152 Whig Street
Dennis, MA 02638
(508) 385-9928 or (800) 736-0160

Type of B&B: Inn.
Rooms: 11, 10 with private bath.
Rates: 1/$46-88; 2/$52-98

Rating: A or ♛♛♛ Excellent, far exceeds basic requirements.

Isaiah Hall is a Greek Revival farmhouse built in 1857 and located 10 miles north of Hyannis. There are eleven guest rooms in the main inn or the adjacent restored barn. Ten offer a private bath. Each room features fine antiques, Oriental rugs, and handmade quilts. There are several common rooms offering private areas for reading, playing board games, or conversing with other guests. Within walking distance can be found the Museum of Fine Arts, Playhouse, and cinema. Bicycle trails and golf courses are nearby. Continental plus breakfast. Resident cat. Limited wheelchair access. Restricted smoking. 1/$46-88; 2/$52-98. AE, MC, V. Travel agent. Open April 2 through October 17.

Guests write: *"Marie Brophy is the most delightful and personable innkeeper we have encountered in our travels. She makes Isaiah Hall the friendly, unpretentious, and comfortable home to travelers that it is."* (J. Meuse)

"Our first visit to Cape Cod was much enhanced by our stay at the Isaiah Hall B&B Inn. The hospitality was excellent, the comfort and decor in our rooms and the house in general reflected the true "New England" style we had hoped to find." (M. Kunle)

"Breakfasts are always fun at the Isaiah Hall Inn - good food, especially the cranberry muffins, and good conversation with Marie and the other guests. Marie's good spirits and enthusiasm are very much what makes the inn a special place to stay. The inn is lovely with common rooms that are warm and inviting. The guest rooms are spacious and always immaculate. Our favorite room is #10, overlooking the flower gardens in the back of the house." (L. Garavalia)

"We have never experienced anything but clean rooms with everything in working order. Every room we have stayed in has had good lighting for reading at night and windows to open to savor the Cape breezes. We have stayed in both the main house and the attached renovated barn. We've had a hard time deciding which we enjoy the most, but have over time found we like the barn. Furnishings are country casual with a mix of antiques. The innkeepers are there when you need them but don't force themselves upon you." (T. Stapleton)

"The historic house is homey, beautiful and furnished with authentic antiques. However, the one thing that makes Isaiah Hall Inn different from any other inn we have visited and brings us back year after year is the warm hospitality of the host and hostess. They make their guests feel at home. The comforts, cleanliness, and amenities we pay for but this sincere interest and caring is priceless." (A. Coveney)

Dennisport, Cape Cod

Rose Petal B&B
152 Sea Street
P.O. Box 974
Dennisport, MA 02639
(508) 398-8470

Type of B&B: Inn.
Rooms: 4 with shared baths.
Rates: 1 or 2/$40-55.

Rating: B+ or ♛♛ Good, exceeds basic requirements.

Quaint New England-style farmhouse built in 1872 is located 7 miles east of Hyannis on Cape Cod. There are four second-floor guest rooms with shared baths. A pleasant parlor on the main floor offers a piano, selection of reading material, and comfortable area for watching TV. Warm-water beaches of Nantucket Sound are nearby as are several antique shops, theaters, museums, and restaurants. Recreation available in the area includes golf, fishing, boating, and bicycle trails. The ferries to Nantucket and Martha's Vineyard are a short drive away. Full breakfast includes home-baked goods. Families welcome. Restricted smoking. 1 or 2/$40-55.

— *Comments continued on next page*

Guests write: *"This home is lovely. We found the accommodations tastefully decorated , meticulously clean, and very comfortable. Breakfast was always a treat. A hearty breakfast that gave us a great start to the day."* (D. Ewing)

"Genuine friendliness but non-intrusive - a tough balance to strike and done with graciousness and topped with some of the most delicate buttery pastry we've ever had." (K. McLeod)

"Perfect. Every detail was appreciated. Breakfast was tasty and the right way to start our day. The map and guides Gayle gave us were extremely useful. We also like having the bathrobes and fan. Everything was very comfortable and homey." (B. Polk)

"We were made to feel at home almost immediately. Nothing was missing: comfortable bed, nice bath, conveniences. Breakfast was a welcome day's beginning — ample and tastefully done." (J. Bulkley)

"They were extremely helpful in pointing us in the right direction and making suggestions. Always a smile and friendly conversations each morning. The accommodations were very charming and like Old New England. The rooms and bathrooms were immaculate. Breakfast was delicious. They really won my husband over with the Eggs Benedict. He is sure to return just for that." (L. Grimm)

East Orleans, Cape Cod

Ship's Knees Inn
186 Beach Road, P.O. Box 756
East Orleans, MA 02643
(508) 255-1312

Type of B&B: Inn.
Rooms: 22 rooms, 8 with private bath; also an efficiency and 2 cottages.
Rates: 1 or 2/$45-100.

Rating: B+ or ♛♛ Good, exceeds basic requirements.

160-year-old sea captain's home has been restored and is located a short walk from Cape Cod's Nauset Beach. Twenty-two guest rooms are available, eight with private bath. All rooms offer a selection of antique furnishings and several have ocean views, beamed ceilings, quilts, and old four-poster beds. Two housekeeping cottages on the water are available for weekly rentals and off-season on a daily basis. The landscaped grounds feature a tennis court and swimming pool with golf and horseback riding available nearby. Continental breakfast offers muffins, baked breads, and jams. 1 or 2/$45-100. Open year round. Travel agent.

East Sandwich, Cape Cod

Wingscorton Farm Inn
11 Wing Boulevard
East Sandwich, MA 02537
(508) 888-0534

Type of B&B: Inn.
Rooms: 7 with private bath.
Rates: 1/$95; 2/$115-150.

Rating: C or 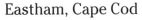 Acceptable, meets basic requirements.

Colonial landmark built in 1758 is situated on seven landscaped acres off Route 6A on Cape Cod. Seven guest rooms each offer a private bath, working fireplace, and restored antique furnishings. An historic carriage house on the property features completely modern decor and amenities with fireplace, full kitchen, private sun deck, and brick patio. There is a private ocean beach within a short walk and other area attractions include golf, whale watching, antique shops, and outdoor recreation. Full breakfast includes eggs, breakfast meats, and vegetables from the inn's own livestock and gardens. Resident dogs and cats in the main inn. Families welcome. 1/$95; 2/$115-150. AE, MC, V. Travel agent.

Eastham, Cape Cod

Over Look Inn
3085 County Road
P.O. Box 771
Eastham, MA 02642
(800) 356-1121 or (508) 255-1886

Type of B&B: Inn.
Rooms: 10 with private bath.
Rates: 1 or 2/$75-125

Rating: B or ♛♛ Good, exceeds basic requirements.

Overlook Inn is a Victorian mansion built in 1869 and located across from Cape Cod National Seashore in the heart of Eastham's historic district. Ten guest rooms offer a private bath, brass bed, antique and wicker furniture, and lace curtains. There are several common areas which include a Victorian parlor, Hemingway room with billiard table, and library with good selection of books. Popular attractions in the area include beaches, nature trails, historic homes, Audubon wildlife sanctuary, bicycle paths, specialty shops, galleries, and restaurants. Scottish hospitality and a full breakfast are offered daily as well as afternoon tea. Facilities available for small meetings. Restricted smoking. 1 or 2/$75-125. AE, Discover, MC, V. Travel agent.

Eastham, Cape Cod

The Whalewalk Inn
220 Bridge Road
Eastham, MA 02642-3374
(508)255-0617 or Fax (508)240-3374

Type of B&B: Inn.
Rooms: 12 with private bath.
Rates: 1 or 2/$75-150.

Rating: A or ♛♛♛ Excellent, far exceeds basic requirements.

Originally an 1830s whale master's home, this restored, "outer cape" area inn is 90 miles from either Boston or Providence. Choose from twelve guest rooms with private bath that are housed in the main inn, or suites found in the restored barn, the Salt Box, and the guest house. Each room has been decorated in pastel colors with a mix of antiques, painted furniture, and brass and wooden beds. Accessories include comforters, extra pillows, decorator bed skirts, and fresh flowers. Visit with other guests in the living room with fireplace and antiques, relax on the patio surrounded by the garden, or explore the nearby forty miles of sandy beaches and nature trails. Attractions nearby include Cape Cod National Seashore, Audubon Wildlife Sanctuary, fishing, sailing, antiquing, whale watching, and golfing. Grand Marnier French toast, cranberry/blueberry pancakes, or apple raisin crepes are some of the specialties offered for a full breakfast. Hors d'oeuvres are served each evening. Restricted smoking. 1 or 2/$75-150. Travel agent.

Edgartown (see Martha's Vineyard)

Essex

George Fuller House
148 Main Street
Essex, MA 01929
(508) 768-7766

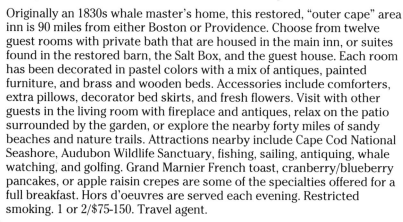

Type of B&B: Inn.
Rooms: 6 with private bath.
Rates: 1 or 2/$70-100.

Rating: A or ♛♛♛ Excellent, far exceeds basic requirements.

George Fuller House was built in 1830 and is located 30 miles north of Boston on Cape Ann. There are six guest rooms. and each offers a private bath, television, telephone, country decor, antique furnishings, braided

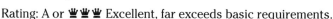

rugs, comfortable rockers, and a brass or canopy bed. Three rooms have working fireplaces. The inn's original architectural features have been retained and include folding Indian shutters, fireplaces, Colonial paneling and woodwork. There are over fifty antique shops to visit in Essex as well as the Shipbuilding Museum. The inn offers a mid-week sailing package on board a thirty-foot cruising sailboat. Full breakfast may include Grand Marnier French toast or Belgian waffles. 1 or 2/$70-100. AE, MC, V. Travel agent.

Guests write: *"My husband and I have stayed at many B&Bs all over New England and in the Midwest. The George Fuller House is our favorite! It's a wonderful location overlooking the salt marshes and within walking distance of great restaurants and antique shops. The decor is warm, relaxing, and very tasteful"* (N. McRay)

"The owners have lovingly restored an old New England house with Oriental rugs, beautiful art work, colonial antiques, rooms with four-poster beds, fireplaces, and their warmth pervades the whole thing. Cindy is a par-excellence cook and our breakfast was served on Lenox china." (L. McKinley)

"The hospitality was extraordinary and the accommodations superb! The availability of the telephone, TV, and individual control of heating and air conditioning in our room was very much to our liking." (M. Cominsky)

"Cindy and Bob were friendly and helpful hosts. The room had everything - private bath, a phone, a fireplace, TV. We had the best breakfast ever. The food was 4-star. We had pears in cream, Belgian waffles with yogurt and orange sauce, apple strudel, coffee, juice, and seconds on anything we wanted. After this I'm afraid other B&Bs might be a let down!" (J. Saggerer)

"The Andrew Suite we relished is The Best. From the canopy bed to the blazing fireplace, we couldn't have dreamt of a nicer inn. The breakfast is without equal in our experience. If George Fuller was awarded only three crowns, what does a four or five crown inn have that they don't? I would like to visit one of them because I think it would be hard to beat our favorite." (J. Donaher)

"I travel 50% of the time throughout the Eastern U.S. As a business traveler I try to stay in B&Bs whenever I can. The George Fuller House has provided the best stay I have had anywhere. What really makes a noticeable difference at places to stay are the innkeepers. All three mornings I had to leave by 6:30 a.m. for meetings. Each morning I woke to a full gourmet breakfast at 6:00 a.m.!" (Rosenwinkel)

"Only minutes after our late morning arrival we were sitting on the porch deep in good conversation with another guest over hot coffee and a delicious cranberry coffee cake just out of Cindy's oven." (T. Cromwell)

Falmouth, Cape Cod

Peacock's "Inn on the Sound"
313 Grand Ave., PO Box 201
Falmouth, MA 02541
(508) 457-9666

Type of B&B: Inn.
Rooms: 10 with private bath.
Rates: 1/$50-85; 2/$65-125.

Rating: B or ♛♛ Good, exceeds basic requirements.

1880s Victorian with multiple additions is situated across the street from the ocean in a quiet residential area of Falmouth which is located 75 miles south of Boston and 85 miles east of Providence. Ten newly renovated guest rooms each offer a private bath and are decorated in a country style. Most offer ocean views. Relax on the front porch or beside the large stone fireplace in the common room with its view of the ocean. Read a book in the library or sip hot cider during the cooler months. Attractions in the area include miles of beaches, whale watching, local historic sites, museums, and live band concerts and theater. Full breakfast specialties include banana-stuffed French toast with blueberry compote, raspberry poached pears, or Belgium waffles with fruit. No smoking. 1/$50-85; 2/$65-125. AE, MC, V. Travel agent.

Guests write: *"The bed was very comfortable, view outstanding, and warm hospitality. Also, heavenly gourmet breakfasts."* (H. Cook)

"The Peacocks know their community extremely well and know instantly what to recommend for activities, entertaining, or dining." (K. Coll)

"They made our honeymoon extra special! The hospitality was out of this world! The rooms are homey and beautiful. I can't forget to mention the breakfasts were outstanding!" (C. Underwood)

"Bud gave us a computerized map of what roads to take, the amount of time on each stretch of highway, and our time of arrival. This was a very kind gesture. We're planning on going to the Peacock Inn for our 3rd straight year." (K. Cashatt)

Falmouth, Cape Cod

Village Green Inn
40 West Main Street
Falmouth, MA 02540
(508) 548-5621

Type of B&B: Inn.
Rooms: 5 with private bath.
Rates: 1/$65-100; 2/$75-110

Rating: A or ♕♕♕ Excellent, far exceeds basic requirements.

The Village Green Inn is a combination Victorian/Colonial structure built in 1804 and located on the village green, 15 miles south of Cape Cod Canal. Four guest rooms and one suite each offer a private bath and working fireplace. A lovely parlor offers a comfortabe setting where guests relax and converse during tea-time. Popular area attractions include beaches, museums, plantations, and Woods Hole Oceanographic Institute and Aquarium. Walk to village specialty shops and a variety of restaurants. Full breakfast includes homemade specialties such as blueberry-almond bread or nutmeg muffins. No smoking. 1/$65-100; 2/$75-110.

Great Barrington

Windflower Inn
SR 65, Box 25, Route 23
Great Barrington, MA 01230
(413) 528-2720

Type of B&B: Country inn.
Rooms: 13 with private bath.
Rates: 2/$160-200 (MAP)

Rating: A- or ♕♕♕ Excellent, far exceeds basic requirements.

Built in 1862, this Colonial country inn is located in the Berkshire Hills area. All thirteen guest rooms are individually furnished and offer a private bath. Several have working fireplaces. Two living rooms on the main floor offer several areas for conversing, playing board games or the piano, or curling up with a good book. Area attractions include Tanglewood, Jacobs Pillow, Berkshire Theater, museums, and antique shops. Recreation nearby includes skiing and hiking. Rates include a full breakfast and dinner featuring seasonal berries, herbs, and vegetables from the garden. Small meeting facilities available. Families welcome. Limited wheelchair access. Restricted smoking. 2/$160-200 MAP (includes full breakfast and dinner).

Harwichport, Cape Cod

Dunscroft By-The-Sea B&B Inn & Cottage
24 Pilgrim Road
Harwichport, MA 02646
(800) 432-4345 or (508) 432-0810

Type of B&B: Inn and cottage.
Rooms: 9 with private bath.
Rates: 1/$75-120; 2/$85-150.

Rating: B or ♕♕ Good, exceeds basic requirements.

Gambrel roofed Colonial inn was built in 1920 and is located on Cape Cod. Nine guest rooms with private bath are available. Each has a romantic decor with unusual quality linens. A fireplaced living room is a popular gathering spot for guests and there is an extensive library with an interesting selection of books. Walk to the nearby mile-long private beach. Popular attractions in the area include Plymouth Rock, Plymouth Plantation, National Seashore, Kennedy Memorial, sand dunes, nature trails, fishing, and sailing. Full breakfast includes fresh-ground coffee and homemade breads. Facilities for small meetings available. Restricted smoking. 1/$70-120; 2/$85-150. AE, MC, V. Travel agent.

Hyannis, Cape Cod

Sea Breeze Inn by the Beach
397 Sea Street
Hyannis, MA 02601
(508) 771-7213, or 771-2549

Type of B&B: Inn.
Rooms: 14 with private bath.
Rates: 1 or 2/$45-85.

Rating: B or ♕♕ Good, exceeds basic requirements.

Historic Victorian inn is in a secluded setting a short walk from the Sea Street Beach. Fourteen guest rooms each offer a private bath, TV, radio, and air conditioning. Several feature ocean views. Popular area attractions include the Kennedy family Compound, summer theater, nightclubs, whale watching, boating, golfing, and shopping at local galleries and specialty shops. The dock for ferry boats to Nantucket and Martha's Vineyard is nearby. Expanded continental breakfast. 1 or 2/$45-85. AE, MC, V.

Martha's Vineyard/Edgartown

Colonial Inn of Martha's Vineyard
P.O. Box 68, 38 North Water Street
Edgartown, MA 02539
(508) 627-4711

Type of B&B: Inn.
Rooms: 42 with private bath.
Rates: 1/$75-170; 2/$85-170.

Rating: B+ or ♛♛ Good, exceeds basic requirements.

Large Colonial inn built in 1911 is located in the historic district of downtown Edgartown and overlooks the harbor. The forty-two guest rooms are light and airy and offer private bath, cable TV, telephone, and air-conditioning. On the premises are two restaurants, eight shops, and a beauty salon. Walk to a historical village, variety of restaurants, unique shops, swimming, boating, fishing, windsurfing, and museums. Continental breakfast is served with fresh baked muffins. Facilities for small meetings available. Families welcome. Wheelchair access. 1/$75-170; 2/$85-170. AE, MC, V. Travel agent.

Guests write: *"The rooms were beautifully decorated with white pine furniture and plush carpeting. The rooms were modern but maintained that feeling of a stately sea captains home, just perfect for the island!"* (R. Lewis)

"With four children ages 1-8, a vacation trip can easily turn into an adventure, sometimes a nightmare. The staff at the Colonial Inn made our stay a real treat. Our room had a beautiful view of the harbor, the location is downtown, the breakfast muffins and fresh fruit eaten on wicker porch furniture on the deck was right out of travel brochure accounts. In fact, the Colonial Inn was everything it claimed to be. It's 'Bid Deals for Big Wheels' rate (super discount with bike rentals included) saved us money on the room and bike transport on the ferry." (J. Rok)

Martha's Vineyard/Edgartown

The Governor Bradford Inn of Edgartown
128 Main Street
Edgartown, MA 02539-0239

Type of B&B: Inn.
Rooms: 16 with private bath.
Rates: 1 or 2/$60-195

Rating: A or ♛♛♛ Excellent, far exceeds basic requirements.

Restored Gothic Revival inn is located on the main road into Edgartown near the village center. The sixteen guest rooms all have a private bath, ceiling fan, and king sized brass or four-poster beds. Relax with other guests in the comfortable wicker room with bar, curl up with a book in the library in front of the fireplace, or share a complimentary sherry at the day's end with other guests in the parlor. There's a large meeting room on the lower level with TV and movies. Enjoy historic Edgartown's attractions including sunning, swimming, fishing, and sightseeing. Shops, galleries, restaurants, and beaches are all nearby. Full breakfast specialties include Belgium waffles, omelets, pancakes, or frittatas. Wedding and meeting facilities available. Wheelchair access. Restricted smoking. 1 or 2/$60-195. AE, MC, V. Travel agent.

Martha's Vineyard, Oak Bluffs

Dockside Inn
Box 1206, Circuit Ave. Extension
Oak Bluffs, MA 02557
(508) 627-3337

Type of B&B: Inn
Rooms: 20 with private bath.
Rates: 1 or 2/$75-220

Rating: B+ or ♛♛ Good, exceeds basic requirements.

Two-story inn with colorful paint and flower baskets on the porch is across from the ferry dock in Oak Bluffs and an easy walk to the village center. Choose from twenty guest rooms. Each offers a private bath, queen-size bed, color cable TV, and air conditioning. Several rooms offer private porches and water views. There is a small yard with a grill for guest's use. Walk to village specialty shops, restaurants and the beach. The inn's lobby is where a continental breakfast buffet is served each morning. Families welcome. Restricted smoking. 1 or 2/$75-220. AE, MC V.

Martha's Vineyard, Oak Bluffs

Martha's Vineyard Racquet Club
31 New York Avenue
Oak Bluffs, MA 02557
(508) 693-6249

Type of B&B: Private club with
accommodations for non-members
Rooms: 6 with private bath
Rates: 1 or 2/$75-150.

Rating: C+ or ♛ Acceptable, meets basic requirements.

Newly built Colonial inn is situated on the main road a mile from the village center. Six second-floor guest rooms with private bath are available for non-members of the racquet club. Each room offers a queen-size bed, TV and telephone. On the main level is the lobby and registration area along with several comfortable seating groups and a billiard table. A lower level houses the "jazz club" which is open most weekends during the season and serves late night chicken and waffles. Tennis court and miniature golf available on the premises. Nearby attractions include beaches, shops, galleries, and restaurants. Families welcome. 1 or 2/$75-150. AE, MC, V. 10% auto club discount. Travel agent.

Martha's Vineyard, Oak Bluffs

Oak House
Seaview Avenue, P.O. Box 299-BB
Oak Bluffs, MA 02557
(508) 693-4187

Type of B&B: Inn.
Rooms: 10 rooms or suites with private bath.
Rates: 1 or 2/$110-220.

Rating: A- or ♛♛♛ Excellent, far exceeds basic requirements.

Quintessential Victorian Cape Cod inn across the street from the beach offers ten guest rooms or suites, each featuring private bath and Victorian furnishings. Most rooms also have private balconies and water views. This Victorian seaside resort includes miles of bicycle paths and beaches. Walk to Oak Bluffs landing and the village from the inn. Continental breakfast includes fresh baked breads. Facilities available for small meetings and social functions. 1 or 2/$110-220 with off-season discounts. Discover, MC, V. Open mid-May through mid-October.

Martha's Vineyard, Vineyard Haven

The Hanover House
P.O. Box 2107
10 Edgartown Road
Vineyard Haven, MA 02568
(508) 693-1066

Type of B&B: Inn.
Rooms: 15 with private bath.
Rates: 1 or 2/$50-158.

Rating: B+ or ♛♛ Good, exceeds basic requirements.

Walk to the ferry from this renovated inn built in 1930. Fifteen guest rooms each offer a private bath, cable TV, and individually controlled air conditioning and heating. Many rooms have sun decks and housekeeping units are available with full kitchens. The village of Vineyard Haven offers quaint shops and restaurants. Shuttle buses are convenient to take guests to Oak Bluffs and Edgartown. Nearby beaches provide swimming, sailing, fishing, and windsurfing. Fresh baked muffins round out a hearty continental breakfast served on an enclosed sun porch. Families welcome. 1 or 2/$50-158. AE, MC, V. Travel agent.

Nantucket
The Four Chimneys
38 Orange Street
Nantucket, MA 02554
(508) 228-1912

Type of B&B: Inn.
Rooms: 10 with private bath.
Rate: 2/$125-225.

Rating: A or ♛♛♛ Excellent, far exceeds basic requirements.

Greek Revival sea captain's home built in 1835 is a short walk from cobblestoned Main Street. Choose from ten guest rooms with private baths that have been authentically restored and furnished with period antiques, oriental rugs, and canopy beds. A suite on the third floor features pine and country furnishings and a harbor view. Many of the area attractions are a short walk away including shops, art galleries, golf, windsurfing, fishing, tennis, fine restaurants, and beaches. Continental breakfast can be served in guest rooms or on the porch furnished in white wicker. A large double parlor with twin fireplaces easily accommodates weddings. Resident dog. 2/$125-225.

Nantucket

Ten Lyon Street Inn
10 Lyon Street
Nantucket, MA 02554
(508) 228-5040

Type of B&B: Inn.
Rooms: 7 with private bath.
Rates: 2/$65-150.

Rating: A or ♛♛♛ Excellent, far exceeds basic requirements.

Colonial inn built in 1849 has been completely renovated and is located in the center of town on a quiet side street near the harbor. Choose from seven guest rooms with double or queen-size beds and private bath. Each room offers quality antique furnishings, linens, down comforters and pillows, and interesting prints. Walk to historic sites, beaches, water sports such as sailing and windsurfing, fine restaurants, or rent bicycles to tour the island. Continental breakfast. 1 or 2/$65-150. MC, V.

Nantucket

Centerboard Guest House
8 Chester Street
Nantucket, MA 02554
(508) 228-9696

Type of B&B: Inn.
Rooms: 6 with private bath.
Rates: 1 or 2/$85-245 (Seasonal).

Rating: A or ♛♛♛ Excellent, far exceeds basic requirements.

1890s Victorian home renovated in 1986 is located on the edge of the Historic district just a few blocks from the village center. Guests are accommodated in five second-floor guest rooms which each offer a private bath, a queen or double-size bed, telephone, refrigerator, and color television. A large suite on the main level offers a Jacuzzi and extra amenities. Spend a snowy winter afternoon in front of the fire or sit in a sunny window seat on a summer's day. Walk the cobblestone streets to the nearby village center where shops, antiques stores, museums, galleries, and restaurants can be found. Rent mopeds or bikes to explore beaches and conservation lands. Continental breakfast includes homemade muffins and granola, locally baked goods and fresh fruit salad. 1 or 2/$85-245 (Seasonal). AE, MC, V. Travel agent.

Nantucket

Eighteen Gardner Street Inn
18 Gardner Street
Nantucket, MA 02554
(508)228-1155 or (800) 435- 1450

Type of B&B: Inn.
Rooms: 17, 15 with private baths.
Rates: 1 or 2/$95-185.

Rating: B or ♛♛ Good, exceeds basic requirements.

Restored Colonial Nantucket inn built in 1835 is in the historic residential district; 90 miles south of Boston on the island of Nantucket. The seventeen guest rooms, fifteen with private bath, have been decorated with antiques and period reproductions including canopied or four-poster beds. Some have working fireplaces and color television. Borrow one of the inn's bikes for an easy ride to one of the many beaches. Go golfing, sailing, or fishing, play tennis, or explore the nearby shops and museums. A full breakfast is offered in the dining room. Wedding and meeting facilities available. Families welcome. No smoking. 1 or 2/$95-185. AE, MC, V. Travel agent.

Oak Bluffs (See Martha's Vineyard)

Princeton

Harrington Farm
178 Westminster Road
Princeton, MA 01541
(508) 464-5600

Type of B&B: Country inn with restaurant.
Rooms: 5, 2 with private bath.
Rates: 1 or 2/$68-100.

Rating: B or ♛♛ Good, exceeds basic requirements.

Historic Colonial farmhouse is now a country inn located north of Worcester off Route 2 near the western slope of Wachusett Mountain ski area. Choose from five guest rooms which feature original antique farm furniture and Colonial period stenciling. Two rooms offer a private bath and three rooms share three hall baths. A small parlor on the second floor offers board games, and VCR movies as well as an intimate restaurant. Popular activities here include a quiet walk around the farm, bicycling, hiking, skiing, and exploring an Audubon Society reservation nearby. Full breakfast. A four-star restaurant is on the main level and dinner is served Wednesday through Sunday by reservation. No smoking. Facilities available for small weddings or group meetings. 1 or 2/$68-100. MC, V.

Rockport

Yankee Clipper Inn
96 Granite Street
Rockport, MA 01966
(508) 546-3407 or 546-3408

Type of B&B: Country Inn with restaurant.
Rooms: 27 with private bath.
Rates: 1/$60-175; 2/$98-204.

Rating: A+ or ♛ ♛ ♛ Excellent, far exceeds basic requirements.

Impressive oceanfront Victorian mansion is located 45 minutes north of
Boston near the northeast end of Route 128. There are twenty-seven
guest rooms in the mansion or two smaller inns on adjacent properties.
Each room differs in size, decor, and amenities but special features found
in some rooms include ocean views, canopy beds, glass-enclosed
porches, and 19th-Century furnishings. The landscaped grounds invite
exploration and feature a heated salt water swimming pool and paths that
end at the rocky water's edge. Two of the three buildings offers a parlor
with television lounge. The mansion's living room features floor to ceiling
bookcases and original wall murals. Full breakfast. Candlelight dinner
available at the restaurant. The lower level offers an attractive function
room with large windows. Families welcome. Restricted smoking. 1/$69-
175; 2/$98-204. AE, MC, V. Travel agent.

Rockport

Ralph Waldo Emerson Inn
1 Cathedral Ave., P.O. Box 2369
Rockport, MA 01966
(508) 546-6321 or Fax (508) 546-7043

Type of B&B: Country inn with restaurant.
Rooms: 36 with private bath.
Rates: 1/$57-124; 2/$86-137.

Rating: B or ♛ ♛ Good, exceeds basic requirements.

Imposing Greek Revival inn overlooking the rocky coastline was built in
1840 and is located 40 miles northeast of Boston. The inn has been
renovated several times and now blends modern amenities with the
atmosphere of an earlier era. Choose from thirty-six guest rooms with
telephone, private bath, and a choice of single, twin, or double bed. Relax
on the old-fashioned verandah with ocean view or several common areas
inside the inn. Nearby attractions include Hammond Castle, Rocky Neck,
and Halibut State Park. Stroll along the shady streets, visit art galleries

and shops, go boating, fishing, sightseeing, or whale watching. A full breakfast features such specialties as strawberry pancakes and a variety of omelets. Wedding and small meeting facilities available. Families welcome. Wheelchair access. 1/$ 57-124; 2/$86-137. MC, V. Tour and business meeting discount.

Sandwich, Cape Cod

Bay Beach B&B
1-3 Bay Beach Lane
Sandwich, MA 02563
(508) 888-8813

Type of B&B: Inn.
Rooms: 3 suites with private bath.
Rates: 1 or 2/$100-175.

Rating: AA or ♛♛♛♛ Outstanding.

New oceanfront contemporary inn overlooks a private beach and Cape Cod Bay. Choose from three spacious guest suites, each with ocean view, private balcony, contemporary wicker furnishings, and ceiling fan. The Honeymoon suite features a whirlpool bath and each room offers a private bath, cable color TV, phone, refrigerator, and air-conditioning. There are several common rooms for guest relaxation and an exercise bike for work-outs. Visit nearby museums, historic sites, and fine restaurants within walking distance. Full breakfast. No smoking. 1 or 2/$100-175. Travel agent.

Sandwich, Cape Cod

Captain Ezra Nye House
152 Main Street
Sandwich, MA 02563
(800) 388-2278 or (508) 888-6142

Type of B&B: Inn.
Rooms: 7, 5 with private bath.
Rates: 1 or 2/$55-85.

Rating: B+ or ♛♛ Good, exceeds basic requirements.

Historic clapboard Federal-style home is located in the heart of Sandwich near Route 6, exit 2. Seven guest rooms have hand-stenciled walls, original artwork, and furnishings collected from around the world including Oriental rugs, spindle beds, sleigh beds, and claw-foot tubs. Five of the rooms offer a private bath. A small den houses a fine library of books and comfortable seating for watching TV. Area attractions include Sandwich Glass Museum, beaches, Heritage Plantation, Thornton Burgess Museum, Doll Museum, Shawme Lake, and Hoxie House, the oldest house on Cape Cod. Full breakfast. No smoking. 1 or 2/$55-85. AE, MC, V. Travel agent.

"I can't say enough for their warm hospitality during my first B&B experience. It is fascinating to reflect upon the historical beauty of the Nye house and I felt as if I were living in another era!" (A. Gilson)

Stockbridge/South Lee

Merrell Tavern Inn
Route 102, Main Street
South Lee, MA 01260
(800) 243-1794 or (413) 243-1794

Type of B&B: Inn.
Rooms: 9 with private bath.
Rates: 1/$65-115; 2/$75-145.

Rating: A+ or ♛♛♛ Excellent, far exceeds basic requirements.

Historic Federal home built in 1800 as a stagecoach inn and listed on the National Register of Historic Places, is in a small village 3 miles from exit 2 on I-90. Nine guest rooms are available, each with private bath, antique furnishings, and period decor. Some feature fireplaces and all have lovely canopy beds. Relax in the parlor, sit by the fire in the tavern room, or stroll on the grounds which extend to the banks of the Housatonic River. The gardens feature the original stone walls of the inn's barns and livery stables. Area attractions include Norman Rockwell Museum, Tanglewood Music Festival, golf, tennis, fishing, hiking, and skiing. A choice of full breakfast is offered from a menu. Families welcome. Restricted smoking. 1/$65-115; 2/$75-145. MC, V.

Guests write: *"The peace of a riverbank at the bottom of the garden where you can recline for hours in a gazebo is guaranteed to dispel every care. Inside the house, the antiques are tastefully used as furnishings which makes the inn a home and not a museum. They are thoughtful innkeepers, ready to give any advise or assistance requested but never imposing themselves. It is a pleasure to chat with such cultured hosts and have the benefit of their gentle but richly informed enthusiasm for history and the arts."* (L McRedmond)

"Over a span of ten years my wife and I have enjoyed the warm hospitality and gracious accommodations afforded by the Merrell Tavern Inn. The rooms are meticulously attended to. Their bright, warm period atmosphere is made all the more pleasant by the unobtrusive and thoughtful attentiveness of our hosts." (D. Scheufele)

— *Comments continued on next page*

Each day you have choices and you can sit at your own private table where you can choose to talk to your neighbors or have a quiet time for yourself. The price was excellent!" (B. Huff)

"We chose room #10 which had a bath tub and was beautifully decorated with antiques and checked fabrics. We were given a crib for our baby at no extra charge. The breakfast was substantial with a good choice. We chose pancakes with maple syrup and sausages and scrambled eggs and sausage. Delicious!" (C. Harvey)

"The Merrell Tavern Inn is a rare find. Not only is it a very comfortable late 18th-Century timepiece but it is also the source of very generous and gracious hospitality. The innkeepers serve tea and freshly-baked cake at 5 p.m. We felt very much at home." (W. Nicholls)

Sturbridge

Colonel Ebenezer Crafts Inn
Fiske Hill
Sturbridge, MA 01566
(508) 347-3313

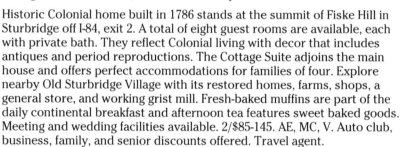

Type of B&B: Inn.
Rooms: 8 with private bath.
Rates: 2/$85-145.

Rating: B+ or ♛♛ Good, exceeds basic requirements.

Historic Colonial home built in 1786 stands at the summit of Fiske Hill in Sturbridge off I-84, exit 2. A total of eight guest rooms are available, each with private bath. They reflect Colonial living with decor that includes antiques and period reproductions. The Cottage Suite adjoins the main house and offers perfect accommodations for families of four. Explore nearby Old Sturbridge Village with its restored homes, farms, shops, a general store, and working grist mill. Fresh-baked muffins are part of the daily continental breakfast and afternoon tea features sweet baked goods. Meeting and wedding facilities available. 2/$85-145. AE, MC, V. Auto club, business, family, and senior discounts offered. Travel agent.

Vineyard Haven (See Martha's Vineyard)

West Yarmouth, Cape Cod

The Manor House
57 Maine Avenue
West Yarmouth, MA 02673
(508) 771-9211

Type of B&B: Inn.
Rooms: 6 with private bath.
Rates: 1 or 2/$56-65.

Rating: B- or ♛♛ Good, exceeds basic requirements.

Built in the 1920's, this Dutch Colonial home has views of Lewis Bay and is located 3 miles from exit 7 off Route 6. Choose from six guest rooms with private bath and pleasant decor. A small sitting room serves as the breakfast area and offers comfortable seating while viewing TV. Within walking distance of the inn are beaches, a boat launch area, antique shops, and restaurants. The island ferries to Nantucket and Martha's Vineyard are a short drive away. Continental breakfast features homemade muffins. Facilities available for small meetings and social functions. 1 or 2/$56-65. MC. V.

Yarmouthport, Cape Cod

The Colonial House Inn
Route 6A, 277 Main Street
Yarmouthport, MA 02675
(508) 362-4348 or (800) 999-3416

Type of B&B: Inn with restaurant.
Rooms: 21 with private bath.
Rate: 1/$45-80; 2/$60-95.

Rating: B or ♛♛ Good, exceeds basic requirements.

Victorian inn with restaurant was originally constructed in the 18th-Century and is located less than two miles from Route 6, midway between exits 7 and 8. Each of the twenty-one guest rooms is air-conditioned, offers a private bath, is decorated with antiques, and has its own view of the grounds and surrounding historic homes. An indoor heated swimming pool is on the premises. Local area attractions include nature trails, antique shops, beaches, and theaters. Continental breakfast. Meeting facilities are available for up to 150 people. Families welcome. Wheel chair access. 1/$45-80; 2/$60-95. Rates include breakfast and dinner. AE, MC, V. 10% auto club, business travel, family, and senior discounts. Travel agent.

Guests write: *"We had the two most beautiful rooms one could ask for. Ours had a canopy bed and complete bathroom with claw-foot tub. My parent's had a fireplace ready to use. We will never forget the warm reception."* (M. de Prada)

Yarmouthport

Wedgewood Inn
83 Main Street
Yarmouthport, MA 02675
(508) 362-5157 or 362-9178

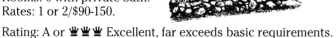

Type of B&B: Inn.
Rooms: 6 with private bath.
Rates: 1 or 2/$90-150.

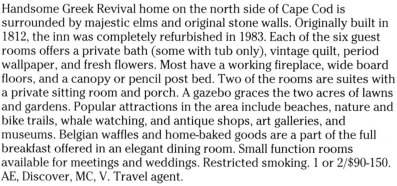

Rating: A or ♛♛♛ Excellent, far exceeds basic requirements.

Handsome Greek Revival home on the north side of Cape Cod is surrounded by majestic elms and original stone walls. Originally built in 1812, the inn was completely refurbished in 1983. Each of the six guest rooms offers a private bath (some with tub only), vintage quilt, period wallpaper, and fresh flowers. Most have a working fireplace, wide board floors, and a canopy or pencil post bed. Two of the rooms are suites with a private sitting room and porch. A gazebo graces the two acres of lawns and gardens. Popular attractions in the area include beaches, nature and bike trails, whale watching, and antique shops, art galleries, and museums. Belgian waffles and home-baked goods are a part of the full breakfast offered in an elegant dining room. Small function rooms available for meetings and weddings. Restricted smoking. 1 or 2/$90-150. AE, Discover, MC, V. Travel agent.

MICHIGAN

Battle Creek/Augusta

The Lodge at Yarrow
10499 North 48th Street
Augusta, MI 49012-9500
(616) 731-2090 Fax (616) 731-2091

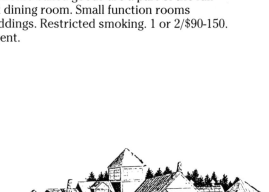

Type of B&B: Small resort lodge
Rooms: 8 with private bath.
Rates: 1/$109; 2/$125.

Rating: A or ♛♛♛ Excellent, far exceeds basic requirements.

The Lodge at Yarrow is a unique retreat and conference center situated on 350 acres just outside Battle Creek. Three secluded cottages house eight guest accommodations. Each cottage offers a queen-size bed, private entrance, sitting porch, TV, and private bath. The main lodge, a short walk from each cottage, overlooks the Potawatomi Valley and was designed to emulate an American Gothic farmhouse. Here is where guests gather to converse and dine. The grounds offer biking, birdwatching, canoeing, cross-country skiing, fishing, horseback riding, hiking, and a 50-foot Alpine Tower used by groups to help teach self-confidence and group problem solving. A continental breakfast is included in the overnight rate although a full breakfast, lunch, and dinner are available for an additional charge. No smoking. Wheelchair access. 1/$109; 2/$125. AE, V, MC. Travel agent.

Fennville

Hidden Pond Bed & Breakfast
5975 128th Avenue
Fennville, MI 49408
(616) 561-2491

Type of B&B: B&B home.
Rooms: 2 with private bath.
Rates: 2/$64-110.

Rating: A- or ♛ ♛ ♛ Excellent, far exceeds basic requirements.

Hidden Pond combines modern amenities with a secluded rural atmosphere on twenty-eight acres of private, wooded grounds, 40 miles southwest of Grand Rapids. Two guest rooms are available, each with private bath. There is a large common room with comfortable seating for conversing with other guests, playing board games, or reading. Bird watching and hiking on the property have proven popular with guests and golf, tennis, skiing, hiking, bicycling, and water sports are nearby. Full breakfast is served on an enclosed porch overlooking a wildlife pond. 2/$64-110.

Saugatuck

Sherwood Forest Bed & Breakfast
PO Box 315, 938 Center St.
Saugatuck, MI 49453
(616) 857-1246

Type of B&B: Inn.
Rooms: 5 with private bath.
Rates: 1 or 2/$70-130

Rating: B or ♛ ♛ Good, exceeds basic requirements.

Victorian-style home built in the 1890s boasts a wrap-around porch and is located near the village center, 40 minutes south of Grand Rapids. Five newly renovated guest rooms are named for their color scheme and each has a private bath, queen size bed, and traditional furnishings. The Black and White room on the second floor is spacious and offers an oversized Jacuzzi tub. Original features of the home have been preserved and are visible in the hardwood floors, oak trim, and leaded glass windows. Relax on the patio or take a dip in the heated swimming pool. The surrounding forests are perfect for hiking or cross country skiing in winter. The Douglas Public Beach is within walking distance and Saugatuck Oval Beach is just minutes away. The area's white sandy beaches are the perfect place for strolling, swimming, or watching sunsets. Visit art galleries, restaurants, public golf courses, state parks, summer theater, and boat charter tours. Continental plus breakfast may feature such specialties as lemon-yogurt bread, blueberry muffins, and fresh fruit salad. Wedding and small meeting facilities available. No smoking. 1 or 2/$70-130. A separate cottage adjacent to the inn is also available. MC, V. Travel agent.

Guests write: *"Our family of four (including two children) really love Sherwood Forest. We found the meticulously decorated and remodeled guest rooms very pretty, quiet, and restful. Our children particularly liked the swimming pool in its wooded setting and the one-block walk to a great Lake Michigan beach."* (N. McGarrity)

"My fiancé wanted to take me away for a long weekend after being gone for four months and the Sherwood Forest couldn't have been a better choice. Keith and Susan were the best hosts! They were extremely helpful with making dinner reservations, recommendations, and things to do besides being fun people to get to know." (K Watt)

"The pool is wonderful in summer and nearby cross country skiing in the winter provides effortless recreation. Our innkeepers, Sue & Keith, were very friendly and hospitable. The interior decor is very lovely and inviting, right down to the hand knit booties in the closet. We always have a great time!" (C. Winters)

"Keith and Susan were extremely friendly and made us feel as if their home was our home. Conversations over breakfast were as delicious as the food. In a town full of quaint establishments and charm, Sherwood Forest fits in handsomely. Worth going out of your way for in order to spend a night. " (M. Kubik)

"The accommodations were attractive, comfortable, quiet, cozy, and very clean. Our host served a wonderful breakfast each morning. Our short walks to the beach on Lake Michigan, our swim in their heated pool, and our tandem bike ride into town certainly added to our stay." (D. Greenfield)

Union Pier

Pine Garth Inn
15790 Lakeshore Road
Union Pier, MI 49129
(616) 469-1642

Type of B&B: Inn.
Rooms: 7 with private bath
plus five housekeeping cottages.
Rates: 1 or 2/$70-130; cottages/$140-225.

Rating: A+ or ♛♛♛ Excellent, far exceeds basic requirements.

Restored summer estate and nearby cottages overlook Lake Michigan and are located 90 miles from Chicago. Each of the inn's seven guest rooms feature antique furnishings, whirlpool tub, fireplaces, and a lake view. Five country cottages, each with two bedrooms offer a complete bath, private deck and hot tub, fully equipped kitchen, TV with VCR, and wood-burning fireplace. The inn has a private beach, beautiful lake views, and a pleasant Great Room with fireplace where breakfast is served and guests gather for evening refreshments. Full breakfast is included in the rates for the guest rooms in the main inn only. Families are welcome in the cottages. Restricted smoking. 1 or 2/$70-130; Cottages/$140-225. AE, MC, V. Business travel discount. Travel agent.

MINNESOTA

Duluth

Barnum House Bed & Breakfast
2211 East Third Street
Duluth, MN 55812
(800) 879-5437 or (218) 724-5434

Type of B&B: Inn.
Rooms: Five with private bath.
Rates: 1 or 2/$100-125.

Rating: A or ♛♛♛ Excellent, far exceeds basic requirements.

Overlooking a rugged ravine, this 1910 three-story brick mansion is found at the end of a residential street lined with tall maples, pines, and birch trees in the historic district of Duluth. Five guest rooms are available. Each offers a private bath and antiques reflecting three centuries of decor. Some special features of different rooms include working fireplaces, large picture window with views, or a verandah overlooking the ravine and brook. Morning coffee is served on china and silver and delivered to each guest room. The 8,000 square foot home features a grand staircase with a fireplace tucked underneath as well as a 1,000 square-foot glass-enclosed verandah with fireplace and view of the lawn and wooded ravine. Visit nearby Lake Superior, Canal Park, and the Tourist center. Watch 1,000 foot long freighters arrive from all over the world. There is an abundance of four-season recreation including swimming, boating, and skiing. Full breakfast is served in the dining area and often includes such specialties as hash brown quiche, stuffed French toast, or ham and cheese soufflé. No smoking. 1 or 2/$ 100-125. MC, V. 10 % senior, corporate, and auto club discounts. Travel agent.

Guests write: *"The Barnum House has provided us a wonderfully peaceful haven for the past three days to both celebrate our 20th wedding anniversary and to explore Duluth. From our start in the morning with a newspaper in front of a cheery, lit fireplace followed by a breakfast garnished with molded butter in shapes of cherubs and birds, real flowers tucked into the napkin ring — it was all we had hoped for."* (N. Crary)

"It is easy to say that this is one of the finest B&Bs. They've achieved something I would call comfortable elegance. They've combined the finest antiques with all the comforts of home. That leather couch is hard to leave — especially when you're gazing at a beautiful fire. I also appreciate the immaculate cleanliness of the home as well as the gracious hospitality of our host and hostess. Breakfast was delicious also." (S. Miller)

"Best features: immaculately clean, beautiful decor with fabulous antiques everywhere, delicious gourmet breakfast, and an in-town yet quiet location with beautiful stream and ravine adjacent to the house. Gourmet coffee is brought to you before breakfast and everything is served with exquisite china and silver service!" (D. Voegeli)

Independence

The House of Hoyt
626 North Delaware
Independence, MO 64050
(816) 461-7226

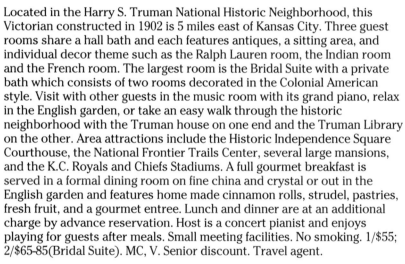

Type of B&B: B&B home.
Rooms: 4, 1 with private bath.
Rates: 1/$55; 2/$65-85.

Rating: B or ♛♛ Good, exceeds basic requirements.

Located in the Harry S. Truman National Historic Neighborhood, this Victorian constructed in 1902 is 5 miles east of Kansas City. Three guest rooms share a hall bath and each features antiques, a sitting area, and individual decor theme such as the Ralph Lauren room, the Indian room and the French room. The largest room is the Bridal Suite with a private bath which consists of two rooms decorated in the Colonial American style. Visit with other guests in the music room with its grand piano, relax in the English garden, or take an easy walk through the historic neighborhood with the Truman house on one end and the Truman Library on the other. Area attractions include the Historic Independence Square Courthouse, the National Frontier Trails Center, several large mansions, and the K.C. Royals and Chiefs Stadiums. A full gourmet breakfast is served in a formal dining room on fine china and crystal or out in the English garden and features home made cinnamon rolls, strudel, pastries, fresh fruit, and a gourmet entree. Lunch and dinner are at an additional charge by advance reservation. Host is a concert pianist and enjoys playing for guests after meals. Small meeting facilities. No smoking. 1/$55; 2/$65-85(Bridal Suite). MC, V. Senior discount. Travel agent.

Guests write: " *We so enjoyed our stay on our wedding night. We cannot imagine a more romantic evening. From the beautiful Honeymoon Suite adorned with floral arrangements to the delicious food and peaceful atmosphere, all was what we had hoped for and more. We will never forget waking the next day to the wonderful breakfast aromas wafting up the stairs, nor will we forget the virtuoso piano performance we witnessed later that morning. In short, our stay was perfect.* " (D. Hemphill)

Springfield

Walnut Street Inn
900 East Walnut
Springfield, MO 65806
(800) 593-6346 or (417)864-6346

Type of B&B: Inn.
Rooms: 11 with private bath.
Rates: 1 or 2/$65-120.

Rating: A or ♛♛♛ Excellent, far exceeds basic requirements.

Turn-of-the-century Victorian urban inn with hand-painted Corinthian columns, wide verandah with porch swing, and beveled-glass front door is listed as a National Historic Site and is located in the heart of the city. Each of the eleven guest rooms has individual decor, a private bath, in-room telephone, writing desk, chairs for reading, and Turkish bathrobes. Some suites offer a Jacuzzi, fireplace, or claw foot tub. Relax in one of the soft chairs by the fireplace, play games, watch television, or read books in the sitting room with its leaded, lace covered windows. The back deck is shaded by large sycamores and the front porch offers wicker rockers and a porch swing. Regional specialties are featured at the full breakfast which can be eaten in the dining room, on the deck, or as a romantic breakfast-in-bed. Visit nearby Southwest Missouri State, Bass Pro Shops, performing art centers, theater, restaurants, antique shops, boutiques, art museums, and Wilson Creek National Battlefield. Wedding and meeting facilities available. Families welcome. Wheelchair access. No smoking. 1 or 2/$65-120. AE, MC, V. Senior and corporate discounts. Travel agent.

Guests write: *"This is an excellent place to stay for the money. There was plenty of room, we were very comfortable and enjoyed the good breakfast, cheerful hosts, and excellent parking. What a reasonable rate for everything you get!"* (D. Dryer)

Additional information on B&Bs throughout this state is available from B&B Western Adventure (406) 259-7993.

Columbia Falls

Bad Rock Country Bed & Breakfast
480 Bad Rock Drive
Columbia Falls, MT 59912
(800) 422-3666

Type of B&B: Inn.
Rooms: 3 with private bath.
Rates: 1/$75-85; 2/$85-95.

Rating: A- or ♛♛♛ Excellent, far exceeds basic requirements.

Experience the Montana country lifestyle in this ranch-style farmhouse located in a farming valley 11 miles east of Kalispell and 125 miles north of Missoula. All of the guest rooms feature a private bath, antique furniture, and queen sized beds. Three living rooms offer guests a place to relax, read, sit by the fireplace, or watch satellite television. Explore the surrounding pastures and lawns or sit in the hot tub half hidden by trees. Winter recreation nearby includes downhill or cross county skiing, snow mobiling, dog sledding, and ice skating. Glacier National Park is fifteen miles south and offers breathtaking views. Flathead Valley and Flathead Lake offer fishing, hiking, rafting, horseback riding, and swimming. Museums, art galleries, antique shops, casinos, and antique stores are all found in the nearby towns of Kalispell, Whitefish, Bigfork, and Columbia Falls. "Sundance" eggs, Montana potato pie, and huckleberry muffins are some of the unusual, Montana-style specialties offered at a full breakfast. No smoking. 1/$75-85; 2/$85-95. AE, MC, V. Travel agent.

Columbia Falls

Turn in the River Inn
51 Penney Lane
Columbia Falls, MT 59912
(800)892-2474 or (406)257-0724

Type of B&B: Inn.
Rooms: 3 with private bath.
Rates: 1 or 2/$75-85.

Rating: A- or ♛♛♛ Excellent, far exceeds basic requirements.

Nestled on the banks of the Whitefish River between farmland and forest, this contemporary Craftsman Farmhouse is 7 miles north of Kalispell and

5 miles south of Whitefish. All of the three guest rooms, with names such as Alaska, Connecticut, and Colorado, have a private bath, queen or king-sized bed, and decor that reflects the hosts' personalities, travels, and interests. Relax by the massive stone fireplace in the Great Room, in the television lounge, or play piano in the music room. There is a hot tub on the backyard deck which has pastoral scenery. Afternoon hors d'oeuvres and complimentary beverages or a "proper English tea" is offered daily. Visit Glacier National Park, Big Mountain Winter/Summer Resort, Bigfork Summer Theatre, or let the hosts arrange adventure reservations, tee-times, or theater tickets. Skiing, canoeing, swimming, white-water rafting, boating, fishing, and hiking are nearby. Waffles with fresh fruit, seasonal produce locally grown, and home-baked goods are a part of a full breakfast. Special dietary requests are met. Small wedding facilities available. Families welcome. Wheelchair access. Restricted smoking. 1 or 2/$75-85. MC, V. 10% senior and auto discounts. Travel agent.

Guests write: *" An incredible haven. Everything from tea mid-afternoon to hot-tubbing under the stars late at night, was perfect. The open hospitality makes it all that more special. A true Western Montana gem. A must-stay for visitors to the Whitefish/Glacier National Park region of the Flathead Valley!"* (H. Johnson)

"The many personal touches were greatly appreciated. It made our honeymoon night a special one. Seeing the Northern Lights and sitting out on the beautiful balcony all added to our very romantic evening. Our breakfast was delicious, just like Mom used to make (even better, but don't tell Mom)." (L. Gibbard)

"The early coffee, lovely flowers everywhere and the hospitality will never be forgotten. How dull our waffles seem!" (E. Jepson)

"I sat in a beautiful room, sipping coffee and listening to the wonderful sounds of nature. This (inn) is a slice of heaven." (P.Reifil)

"A swim in the river, the deer in the meadow, the stars by hot tub, the coffee at the door, the waffles with peaches, the wildflowers everywhere!...What could be better?" (K. True)

Helena

Upcountry Inn
2245 Head Lane
Helena, MT 59601
(406) 442-1909

Type of B&B: Country inn with restaurant.
Rooms: 8, 1 with private bath.
Rates: 1/$50; 2/$60.

Rating: B+ or ♛♛ Good, exceeds basic requirements.

Upcountry Inn is located 2 miles west of Helena off US-12. Quilts, stencils, iron beds, and wicker chairs fill the eight guest rooms and add to the inn's home-style hospitality. One room offers a private bath. The dining hall and great room are decorated country-estate style with wood, wool, and leather. Area attractions include Spring Meadow Lake State Recreation Area, historic Helena, Green Meadow Golf Course, and the Archie Bray Pottery Studio. Enjoy a full breakfast by the fire. Afternoon tea and dining in the Red Fox Restaurant are available by advance reservation. Facilities for weddings and meetings available. Families welcome. Wheelchair access. No smoking. 1/$50; 2/$60. MC.

Three Forks

Sacajawea Inn
5 North Main Street
Three Forks, MT 59752
(406) 285-6934

Type of B&B: Historic hotel with restaurant.
Rooms: 33 with private bath.
Rates: 1/$45-55; 2/$55-85.

Rating: A- or ♛♛♛ Excellent, far exceeds basic requirements.

Guests have enjoyed the Sacajawea Inn since William Howard Taft was president! This mid-19th-Century Western lodge has been in operation as an inn since 1910 when it was built to serve the travelers on the Milwaukee Railroad and it's located 50 miles east of Butte and 28 miles west of Bozeman off I-90. The inn was totally renovated in 1992 and offers thirty-three guest rooms with private bath. The large lobby with polished wood beams, high ceilings, and original light fixtures serves as a gathering place for summer guests and outdoorsmen visiting Yellowstone National Park. A large front verandah offers comfortable rocking chairs. Popular attractions in the area include Yellowstone Park, Gallatin Valley, Lewis and Clark Caverns, Madison Buffalo Jump State Monument, Three Forks Museum, and Museum of the Rockies. Area recreation includes hunting, fishing, skiing, horseback riding, biking, and hiking. Continental breakfast includes home-baked pastries. Small meeting facilities are available in the restaurant's dining room. Families welcome. No smoking. 1/$45-55; 2/$55-85. AE, MC, V. 10% senior, business, and auto club member discount. Travel agent.

NEVADA

Additional information on B&Bs in this state is available from Mi Casa Su Casa (800) 456-0682.

NEW HAMPSHIRE

Bartlett

Country Inn at Bartlett
P.O. Box 327, Route 302
Bartlett, NH 03812
(603) 374-2353

Type of B&B: Country inn.
Rooms: 17 with shared or private bath.
Rates: 1/$42-48; 2/$64-96.

Rating: B- or ♛♛ Good, exceeds basic requirements.

Historic Victorian Inn built in 1885 is located in the White Mountain region of the state. Set in a tall stand of pines and surrounded by National Forest, this inn is a quiet haven for hikers, skiers, and all who love to be outdoors. Choose from seventeen guest rooms, six in the main inn, or eleven guest rooms in the cottages with some offering private bath. Relax on the front porch in one of the rockers or by the fire in the large living room. Cross-country skiing and an outdoor hot tub are available. This household of active hikers offers hiking tips to guests. Full country breakfast. Restricted smoking. 1/$42-48; 2/$64-96. AE, Discover, MC, V. Travel agent.

Guests write: *"This inn is the kind of place I could move to. Honest people, environmentally minded community, no lines at the post office, infinite opportunities for outdoor activities. These are the type of things which make life enjoyable and exciting and the inn provided for me a wonderful place to experience this community."* (J. Hoffman)

"We had a charming room on the first floor with a working fireplace whose ample supply of wood was replenished at our request. Breakfast was served

in courses beginning with fresh fruit, plenty of fresh hot coffee, followed by delicious home-baked lemon poppy seed muffins and a full cooked-to-order breakfast." (W. McGrath)

"We very much appreciated being able to return post-hill climb for a hot tub and pre-journey snack." (C. Muskat)

"We just enjoyed our 7th stay at the country inn. It's always delightful, especially the people and food." (P. Curda)

Concord/Hopkinton

Windyledge Bed & Breakfast
Hatfield Road, RFD #3
Hopkinton, NH 03229
(603) 746-4054

Type of B&B: B&B home.
Rooms: 3, 1 with private bath.
Rates: 1/$45-65; 2/$55-75.

Rating: A or ♛♛♛ Excellent, far exceeds basic requirements.

Colonial home overlooks the White Mountains and is located eleven miles west of Concord off Route 202/9. Three guest rooms are available, one with private bath. Special features of the rooms include pencil-post bed, hand-stenciled walls, hand-made antique furnishings, and Oriental rugs. The sitting room has a fireplace, piano, and comfortable seating for viewing TV. Popular spots for relaxation include the deck and swimming pool. Area attractions include antique shops, New England College, St. Paul's School, country fairs, concerts, boating, fishing, golfing, skiing, canoeing, and biking. Rooms for small functions available. Families welcome. Full gourmet breakfast features house specialties such as apricot glazed French toast, sour cream souffle, and honey and spice blueberry pancakes. No smoking. 1/$45-65; 2/$55-75. MC, V. Senior, family, business, and auto club discounts. Travel agent.

Guests write: *"When my husband announced that he had found a place for us to stay outside of Concord for only fifty-five dollars per night for the two of us, plus breakfast, I was understandably leery. How nice could this place be? Happily my fears were groundless. The Windyledge B&B would have been a bargain and a treat at twice the price. We were served breakfasts that were simply wonderful ranging from fruit-filled pancakes to vegetable frittatas. The Vogts have set up a wonderful, cozy family room which not only has a video library of immense proportions but also comes with a nice fire in the winter and glass of wine. A truly memorable stay."* (K. Berky)

— *Comments continued on next page*

"Windyledge was a cinch to find and what a haven on a blustery, frigid night! The warmth of their welcome was only equal to the warmth and charm of the home - super. Also, those blueberry-spice pancakes are destined for fame." (R. Willcox)

"After a five-hour drive and our arrival at Windyledge, Dick and Susan greeted us with warmth and friendliness and most importantly a much needed cold beer to unwind and relax. Our stay was like a visit with friends." (E. Botz)

"Susan thought of every detail to make our room beautiful and cozy from the white eyelet bedding on the four-poster bed to the fresh flowers on the antique dressing table." (B. Whyte)

Franconia

The Franconia Inn
Easton Valley Road
Franconia, NH 03580
(603) 823-5542 or (800) 473-5299

Type of B&B: Country inn with restaurant.
Rooms: 34, 4 with shared bath.
Rates: 1/$60-80; 2/$75-95.

Rating: B+ or ♛♛ Good, exceeds basic requirements.

Traditional New England white clapboard structure is situated on 107 acres and located in the northwestern side of the state off I-93 near Littleton. There are thirty-four guest rooms, most with private bath. Ten rooms have an extra bed for a third guest. Two suites are especially suited for families. The Honeymoon suite includes a Jacuzzi tub and queen-size bed. An oak-paneled library and large living room offer beautiful views of the mountains. Two porches offer comfortable seating and views of the surrounding countryside. The Rathskeller Lounge on the lower level has a hot tub and game room with movies available. Year-round recreation includes riding, tennis, swimming, trout fishing, hiking, skiing, and sledding. Area attractions include the Robert Frost home, Franconia State Park, and Maple Sugar Museum. Full breakfast served. Dinner is available at the restaurant at an additional cost. Facilities for weddings and functions available. Families welcome. 1/$60-80; 2/$75-95. AE, MC, V. Travel agent.

Guests write: *"We can suggest nothing to improve. Everything and everyone was very nice and pleasant."* (R. Stavnitsky)

"This year we are going to stay in the same room on the 1st floor next to the library. This place has fantastic food, plenty to do and the people are just great." (A. Greenberg)

"Our return stay (the 3rd or 4th time) was just as enjoyable as the previous visits. It is heartwarming to return and recognize members of the staff and have them recognize you - acknowledging your previous visits! It is like a homecoming of sorts and certainly increased our desire to continue our treks to Franconia Inn." (J. Wright)

Gorham

Gorham House Inn
55 Main Street
P.O. Box 267
Gorham, NH 03581
(603) 466-2271

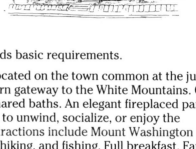

Type of B&B: Inn.
Rooms: 4 with shared bath.
Rates: 1/$41; 2/$60

Rating: B- or Good, exceeds basic requirements.

Victorian inn built in 1891 is located on the town common at the junction of Routes 2 and 16, the northern gateway to the White Mountains. Choose from four guest rooms with shared baths. An elegant fireplaced parlor offers a relaxing area in which to unwind, socialize, or enjoy the entertainment center. Area attractions include Mount Washington auto road and train, ski areas, golf, hiking, and fishing. Full breakfast. Families welcome. 1/$41; 2/$60.

Hampton

Inn at Elmwood Corners
252 Winnacunnet Road
Hampton, NH 03842
(603) 929-0443 or (800) 253-5691

Type of B&B: Inn.
Rooms: 7, 2 with private bath.
Rates: 1/$40-55; 2/$50-85.

Rating: B+ or ♛♛ Good, exceeds basic requirements.

Colonial home built in 1870 by a sea captain has retained much of its original charm and is located near the ocean, 3.5 miles east of I-95, exit 2. Choose from seven guest rooms including two studio apartments with private bath, air conditioning, and kitchenette. Each room is decorated with a theme in mind and features hand-quilted bedspreads, wall hangings, and varied collections of baskets, dolls, needlework, or antique teddy bears. Area attractions include Hampton Beach, playhouse, whale watching, bicycling, factory outlets, skiing, tennis, fishing, and hiking. Full breakfast may feature home-made sausage, poached trout, or eggs Benedict. Families welcome. Restricted smoking. 1/$40-55; 2/$50-85. MC, V.

Hampton

The Victoria Inn
430 High Street
Hampton, NH 03842
(603) 929-1437

Type of B&B: Inn.
Rooms: 6, 3 with private bath.
Rates: 1/$55-70; 2/$65-90

Rating: A- or Excellent, far exceeds basic requirements.

Elegant Victorian home recently renovated was originally built as a carriage house and is located on the coast, 20 minutes south of Portsmouth near I-95, exit 2. Six guest rooms are available, three with private bath. Area attractions include Hampton Beach, Seabrook Race Track, and the White Mountains. Boston is a forty-five minute drive. Full breakfast is included in the rates with dinner available by advance reservation. Facilities available for weddings, reunions, and functions. No smoking. 1/$55-70; 2/$65-90. MC, V. Travel agent.

Jackson

Inn at Jackson
P.O. Box H
Jackson, NH 03846
(603) 383-4321 or (800) 289-8600

Type of B&B: Inn.
Rooms: 9 with private bath.
Rate: 1/$44-86; 2/$61-86.

Rating: B+ or ♛♛ Good, exceeds basic requirements.

Victorian inn built in 1902 is located near the village's covered bridge on Route 16A in the White Mountain National Forest. Choose from nine guest rooms, each with private bath. Enjoy panoramic views of the village or Presidential Mountain Range. Among area attractions are cross-country skiing from the inn's front door, outlet shops, and hiking. Full breakfast is served in the fireside dining room or on the glassed-in porch. Families welcome. 1/$44-86; 2/$61-86. AE, Discover, MC, V. 10% service charge is added on to the bill. Travel agent.

Jackson

Nestlenook Farm on the River
P.O. Box Q
Jackson, NH 03846
(603) 383-9443

Type of B&B: Inn.
Rooms: 7 rooms or suites with private bath.
Rates: 1 or 2/$125-295

Rating: AA or ♛♛♛♛ Outstanding.

Riverfront estate on 65 acres was built in 1780 and is reached through a covered bridge which sets the scene for escaping into a Victorian past. The inn is located 3 hours north of Boston off Route 16. Choose from seven guest rooms or suites, each with private bath and oversized Jacuzzi, fine antique furnishings, and original paintings. Special features of the inn include horse-drawn Austrian sleigh rides, ice skating, cross-country skiing on groomed trails, heated pool, gazebo, and a gingerbread chapel. Full family-style breakfast. No smoking. 1 or 2/$125-295.

Guests write: *"The atmosphere and decor are something out of a magazine. The rooms and outside grounds were great. This place will be highly recommended."* (P. Fritz)

"It was our 36th Wedding Anniversary and what a wonderful place to celebrate here at Nestlenook. This place takes you into Fantasyland. My husband and I have only one regret. The fact that we have to leave this beautiful setting." (F. Rattigan)

"A step into the past with eyes to the future. What a wonderful place to reflect on the blessings of the past and the expectations for the future." (B. Kokko)

Manchester/Jaffrey

Benjamin Prescott Inn
Route 124 East
Jaffrey, NH 03452
(603) 532-6637

Type of B&B: Inn.
Rooms: 9 with private bath.
Rates: 1/$55-75; 2/$60-130.

Rating: A- or ♛♛♛ Excellent, far exceeds basic requirements.

Stately Greek Revival inn built in 1853 is located in the Monadnock region, 2.3 miles from Jaffrey on Route 124 East. Each of the nine guest rooms with private bath is named for a member of the Prescott family. Panoramic views, comfortable country furnishings, and antiques are an integral part of the inn. This is a convenient location near golf, tennis, fishing, boating, skiing, swimming, hiking, bicycling, winter sleigh rides, and theatrical productions. Full breakfast. Restricted smoking. 1/$55-75; 2/$60-130. AE, MC, V. Travel agent.

Manchester/Wilton Center

Stepping Stones Bed & Breakfast
Bennington Battle Trail
Wilton Center, NH 03086
(603) 654-9048

Type of B&B: Private Home.
Rooms: 3, 1 with private bath.
Rates: 1/$35; 2/$45-50.

Rating: B or ♛♛ Good, exceeds basic requirements.

Built as an addition to a pre-Revolutionary period structure, this 19th century Greek Revival home is found 60 miles north of Boston and 20 miles west of Nashua. Guests are accommodated in three guest rooms that have been decorated in the Shaker style with natural fibers and soft colors. Each room has hand-woven throws, down pillows and puffs, fresh flowers and feature windows overlooking the countryside. One room offers a private bath. Guests gather in the solar breakfast room with plants, pottery, and views of the garden. The comfortable parlor offers books, games, television, and stereo. There is a sheltered porch and secluded lawn area within the extensive garden for quiet contemplation. Take a country walk to a waterfall, antique mill, or around the reservoir. Visit local antique markets, summer theaters, and chamber music. The back roads in the area offer excellent bicycling and hikers regularly explore the nearby Wapack Trail. Home baking and local fresh fruit are a part of the full breakfast served. Small, private garden wedding facilities available. Families welcome. Restricted smoking. 1/$35; 2/$45-50. Travel agent.

Guests write: *"A visit to Ann Carlsmith's house is like being Ann's own guest, rather than staying at a B&B. She is such a warm and welcoming person that you feel immediately at home. Her gourmet breakfasts are worth the visit, and lively and spirited conversations usually follow. Stepping Stones is beautifully decorated and surrounded by a garden that is delightful in any season."* (J. Patterson)

"After my many visits here's what makes this special: Ann Carlsmith, the quiet, woodsy setting replete with paths, fields, babbling brooks, and a

sumptuous breakfast in a floridly green atrium. This makes this haven not merely an extremely welcoming place, but actually, for me, a state of mind." (C. Cobert)

Manchester/Hampstead

Stillmeadow Bed & Breakfast at Hampstead
P.O. Box 565
545 Main Street
Hampstead, NH 03841
(603) 329-8381

Type of B&B: Inn.
Rooms: 4 with private bath.
Rate: 1/$50; 2/$60-90.

Rating: A or ♛♛♛ Excellent, far exceeds basic requirements.

1850 Greek Renaissance Colonial home is located on Main Street (Route 121) near the junction of Route 111. Four guest rooms or suites are available, each with private bath. A large suite offers queen-size bed and sitting room with trundle bed. Another suite is ideal for families with crib, changing table, and stairs leading to a playroom - all child-proof. Children will also enjoy the fenced-in play yard. The home is adjacent to the Hampstead Croquet Association's twin grass courts. Other area attractions include the Robert Frost Farm, America's Stonehenge, Rockingham Park Race Track, and Kingston State Park. This location is convenient to Manchester, NH and is less than an hour from Boston. Expanded continental breakfast. Small meeting facilities available. Families welcome. No smoking. 1/$50; 2/$60-90. AE.

Guests write: *"Our stay at the Stillmeadow was the only peaceful and pleasant time in our lengthy moving-in process. We can wholeheartedly recommend their hospitality to future visitors."* (P. Broadwater)

"You can't go too many places where someone would even loan you their own makeup. They sure helped me get off to a good start. They've done such a lovely job here that we felt right at home." R. Snyder)

"They played a part in our big reunion weekend and smaller clan gathering. It had been four years since we had all been together. All week long one or another of us would say how we have to get together at a place like Stillmeadow more often. It was perfect." (D. Rozeboom)

North Conway

Buttonwood Inn
P.O. Box 1817, Mt. Surprise Road
North Conway, NH 03860
(603) 356-2625
or 1-800-258-2625 (U.S. and Canada)

Type of B&B: Inn.
Rooms: 9, 3 with private bath.
Rates: 1/$40-55; 2/$50-100.

Rating: A- or ♛♛♛ Excellent, far exceeds basic requirements.

New England Cape Cod inn is situated in a quiet, secluded mountain setting two miles north of North Conway. Nine guest rooms are furnished with antiques and three offer a private bath. A comfortable ski lounge or TV room is popular with guests after a busy day of skiing or hiking and there is an outdoor swimming pool. This area offers year-round recreation including cross-country skiing out the back door on groomed trails. Full breakfast. Resident dog and cat. 1/$40-55; 2/$50-100. AE, MC, V. Travel agent.

North Conway

Cranmore Mountain Lodge
Kearsarge Road
P.O. Box 1194
North Conway, NH 03860
(603) 356-2044 or (800) 356-3596

Type of B&B: Inn.
Rooms: 16 with private bath.
Rates: 1 or 2/$59-99.

Rating: A- or ♛♛♛ Excellent, far exceeds basic requirements.

New England farmhouse inn built in 1865 is located in Mt. Washington Valley, less than 2 miles northeast of town off Route 16. The lodge has sixteen guest rooms, each with private bath. Stay in either the main house or the renovated barn which has spacious rooms ideal for families and groups with private bath, cable TV, and fireplaced recreation room. Abundant area recreation includes hiking, bicycling, rock climbing, kayaking, cross-country and downhill skiing, golf, and fishing. Enjoy the on-site swimming pool, Jacuzzi, tennis, volleyball, tobogganing, ice skating, and the farm animals on the property. Full breakfast. Families welcome. 1 or 2/$59-99. AE, Discover, MC, V. 10% auto club discount.

North Conway/Intervale

Old Field House
P.O. Box 1, Route 16A
Intervale, NH 03845
(603) 356-5478

Type of B&B: Motor inn.
Rooms: 17 with private bath.
Rates: 1 or 2/$59-109.

Rating: A- or ♛♛♛ Excellent, far exceeds basic requirements.

Colonial-style motor inn with a stone facade is located 3 miles north of
North Conway on Route 16A. Choose from seventeen guest rooms, each
with private bath, air conditioning, phone, and TV. Sit in front of the
fireplace in the living room, relax with a book, or listen to soothing music.
On the premises are clay tennis courts, an outdoor heated swimming pool,
Jacuzzi, shuffleboard, and cross-country skiing. Area attractions include
alpine ski resorts, hiking, mountaineering, fishing, canoeing, and factory
outlets. Continental breakfast. Families welcome. No smoking. 1 or 2/$59-
109. AE, MC, V. 10% auto club and business travel discounts. Travel agent.

North Conway

Victorian Harvest Inn
Locust Lane
North Conway, NH 03860
(603) 356-3548

Type of B&B: Inn.
Rooms: 6, 4 with private bath.
Rates: 1/$55; 2/$55-85

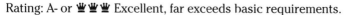

Rating: A or ♛♛♛ Excellent, far exceeds basic requirements.

Restored multi-gabled Victorian inn is found one-half mile south of North
Conway off Route 16 tucked away on a quiet side street. Each of the six
guest rooms, four with private bath, have ample sitting room, air-
conditioning, and antique furnishings. Swim in the Victorian decorated
pool, relax on the enclosed porch or large deck, play the new piano in the
library-sitting room. Four-season recreation nearby includes downhill and
cross-country skiing, ice skating, kayaking, canoeing, hiking, swimming,
and viewing the magnificent autumn leaves. Full country breakfast.
Facilities available for social functions. No smoking. 1/$55; 2/$55-85. AE,
MC, V. Travel agent.

Guests write: *"We have stayed at this inn enough times to try all the rooms
and each one has been so wonderfully comfortable. The innkeepers are*

— *Comments continued on next page*

exceptional. We feel so at home and wake up to the wonderful aromas of a great breakfast." (E. LaVena)

"I am a fairly private person and avoided B&Bs for that reason. A friend finally talked me into joining her at the Victorian Harvest for some cross-country skiing. I had a wonderful time and was extremely comfortable. I experienced a true interest in my well-being and comfort with a deep respect for my privacy. This takes real sensitivity on the part of the innkeepers." (L. Howard)

"We enjoyed our previous stay here so much that we returned for a week with our family. We've had a wonderful week — great food, beautiful and comfortable accommodations with warm, thoughtful and caring hosts. If all B&Bs were like this the hotel/motel business would be in trouble." (D. Wills)

"Since I discovered the Victorian Harvest Inn in the Autumn of 1988, I have had the pleasure of staying there nine times. It's elegant yet comfortable, and the atmosphere is always warm and welcoming. The innkeepers, Bob and Linda, have a flair for making people feel special. The breakfasts were exceptional. They are quite talented in the kitchen" (V. Hagstrom)

North Woodstock

Wilderness Inn Bed & Breakfast
Rtes. 3 & 112
North Woodstock, NH 03262
(603) 745-3890

Type of B&B: Inn.
Rooms: 7, 5 with private bath.
Rates: 1/$30-75; 2/$40-85.

Rating: B or ♥♥ Good, exceeds basic requirements.

1912 Craftsman cottage in the White Mountains overlooks Lost River and the south ridge of Loon Mountain and is 120 miles north of Boston. Each of the seven guest rooms offers a view of the river, mountains, or garden and five of the rooms have a private bath. Enjoy a winter's evening sitting in front of a fire with a cup of hot mulled cider, swim in the swimming hole in the summer, or leaf watch in the fall. Visit the nearby White Mountain National Forest, Franconia Notch State Park, Loon Mountain, or Cannon Mountain. Full breakfast specialties include crepes with home-made applesauce or cranberry walnut pancakes. Breakfast is served on the front porch or is available on a tray for breakfast in bed. Wedding and meeting facilities available. Families welcome. Restricted smoking. 1/$30-75; 2/$40-85. AE, MC, V. Travel agent.

"There aren't enough superlatives to do justice to the Wilderness Inn. This large, well-kept house is comfortably and functionally furnished, the common rooms inviting, the bedrooms cozy, and the grounds peaceful. They make every guest feel as if you're being pampered in your own home."
(K. Reagan)

North Woodstock

Woodstock Inn
80 Main Street
North Woodstock, NH 03262
(603) 745-3951 or (800) 321-3985

Type of B&B: Country inn with two restaurants.
Rooms: 17, 11 with private bath.
Rates: 1 or 2/$45-135

Rating: A or ♛♛♛ Excellent, far exceeds basic requirements.

Century old Victorian inn is nestled in the middle of the White Mountains. Seventeen guest rooms are available in the main house or the inn; eleven offer a private bath. All rooms feature air conditioning, color TV, and telephone, with some offering Jacuzzis, a separate sitting area, or porch overlooking the Pemigewasset River. There is an outdoor Jacuzzi for guest use. The Cascade swimming area is a short walk from the inn and additional recreation nearby includes hiking and skiing. Popular attractions in the area include Old Man of the Mountain, Kancamagus Highway, Lost River, Fantasy Farm, Mount Washington Cog Railway, the Whales Tale Water Slide. Full breakfast is served in the glass-enclosed porch. Lunch and dinner are available in the area's original train station that is attached to the back of the inn. Facilities available for large functions. Families welcome. 1/$45-135. AE, MC, V.

Wentworth

Hilltop Acres
East Side and Buffalo Road
Wentworth, NH 03282
(603) 764-5896 or (718) 261-2919

Type of B&B: Inn.
Rooms: 4 with private bath
and two cottages.
Rates: 1 or 2/$65-80

Rating: B- or ♛♛ Good, exceeds basic requirements.

Colonial inn and cottages built in 1806 are located at the foot of the White Mountains, approximately 20 minutes from I-93, exit 26. There are four guest rooms with private bath and double brass or twin beds in the main inn. Each has scenic views, plants, a selection of books, and a ceiling fan. Two housekeeping cottages especially suited for families are available May through mid-November and include full kitchen unit, separate bedroom, fireplace, and screened-in porch. A pine-paneled recreation room offers games, a large collection of books, and cable TV. Wentworth has three swimming holes, several hiking trails, and fishing streams. Area attractions include Polar Caves, Ruggles Mine, Lost River, and Franconia Notch. Continental breakfast includes an assortment of muffins, pastries, and breads. Families welcome. Room/$65; Cottage/$80. MC, V. Travel agent.

Guests write: *"Hilltop Acres is at once a great amalgam of old-fashioned decor, style and elegance with truly modern, luxurious facilities, conveniences, and services. In all the cozy bedrooms there are big, comfortable old-fashioned brass rail beds. On the walls are pictures and maps tracing New England tradition and history. Upbeat friendliness and wonderful services provided by Ms. Kauk, the proprietress, complement the great setting."* (L. Warshaw)

"For those of us enmeshed in the 9-5 syndrome, my recent stay at Hilltop has become a memorable experience. It was a reminder that the simple things in life oftentimes are the most wonderful. The inn isn't ritzy but rather luxuriates comfort in a simple way - comfy bed, cozy fireplace, wonderful breakfast room which basks in the morning sunlight. Our discovery of a brook meandering through the woods behind the inn was a delightful surprise and added to the serenity of our visit which was much too brief. We look forward to another refreshing dip in the local swimming hole - another unexpected treat. I didn't know those types of places still existed." (R. Doukas)

"They've done a splendid job of decorating with a modest Victorian touch that allows a visitor to enjoy the uniqueness of the accommodations while feeling completely at home. The downstairs paneled living room was thoughtfully designed for easy mingling and it succeeds wonderfully. After a long country walk, the jazz concert on the lawn made our stay even more memorable." (R. Jorgensen)

Bay Head

Conover's Bay Head Inn
646 Main Avenue
Bay Head, NJ 08742
(908) 892-4664

Type of B&B: Inn.
Rooms: 12 with private bath.
Rates: 1/$65-130; 2/$70-165.

Rating: A or ♛♛♛ Excellent, far exceeds basic requirements.

Shingle-style inn built in 1905 as a summer cottage is located in a small town at the seashore. Choose from twelve guest rooms, each offering private bath, air conditioning, and featuring dramatic color-coordinated decor including matching spreads and ruffled pillows. Enjoy the views of the ocean, bay, and marina from one of the expansive porches or large windows. Area attractions include ocean and bay recreation, quaint shops, golf, tennis, fishing, and hiking. Full breakfast includes fresh-baked goods and is served in the dining room, front porch, or on the manicured front lawn. No smoking. 1/$65-130; 2/$70-165. AE, MC, V. 10% business travel discount.

Cape May

Carroll Villa B&B Hotel
19 Jackson Street
Cape May, NJ 08204
(609) 884-9619

Type of B&B: Historic hotel with restaurant.
Rooms: 21 with private bath.
Rates: 1 or 2/$55-120.

Rating: B+ or ♛♛ Good, exceeds basic requirements.

Historic Victorian hotel built in 1881 is a half block from the beach in the center of the town's Historic District. Twenty-one guest rooms are available,. Each has a private bath and is individually decorated with antique furnishings, Victorian period wallpaper, lace curtains, and overhead fans. Some rooms offer air-conditioning. Common areas include a wicker-filled living room, garden terrace, and cupola with panoramic views. Walk to the Victorian Mall, lighthouse, bird sanctuaries, and picturesque village shops. Full breakfast. Families welcome. Facilities available for social functions and meetings. 2/$55-120. MC, V.

— Comments continued on next page

Guests write: *"One morning my husband and I slept in and realized that we both couldn't make it in time for the continental breakfast. As I was pregnant I told my husband I didn't want to rush and would get something later but he should go ahead. He returned with breakfast in hand. The people at Carroll Villa had packed an entire continental breakfast for two for our room. Needless to say, we look forward to returning."* (G. Richad)

"Room #12 was delightful. Here's why. The room was immaculate and airy with noiseless ceiling fan. There were two large windows for circulation and a third window had an air conditioner. There was a queen-size bed with attractive bed covering and antique furniture. The bathroom was large. The people at the desk were nice. There was a pleasant seating area on each floor with live hanging plants and Victorian sofa, and the continental breakfast was delicious with fresh-squeezed orange juice." (J. Migliorato)

"We very much enjoyed our stay. the accommodations were comfortable and charming. The staff was very friendly and helpful. Breakfast and dinner were delicious. Everything we experienced was positive." (S. Bevenour)

Cape May

Columns by the Sea
1513 Beach Drive
Cape May, NJ 08204
(609) 884-2228

Type of B&B: Inn.
Rooms: 11 with private bath.
Rates: 1/$100-165; 2/$110-175.

Rating: A+ or ♛ ♛ ♛ Excellent, far exceeds basic requirements.

Oceanfront Italianate Colonial Revival mansion was built in 1905. There are eleven guest rooms, each with private bath, Victorian furnishings and collectibles, hardwood floors, and Oriental rugs. There are several common areas including a first floor wicker TV room, and third floor library. A large front porch has ocean views and wicker furnishings and a sheltered hot tub. Bicycles are available to explore the historic village with its interesting shops and sites. Popular attractions in the area include Cold Spring Village, fishing, boating, swimming, antique shopping, and bird watching. Hosts speak German. Full gourmet breakfast and complimentary afternoon tea served daily. No smoking. 1/$100-165; 2/$110-175

Cape May

Mason Cottage
625 Columbia Avenue
Cape May, NJ 08204
(609) 884-3358

Type of B&B: Inn.
Rooms: 9 with private bath.
Rates: 1 or 2/$85-165.

Rating: A or ♥♥♥ Excellent, far exceeds basic requirements.

Victorian seaside home with lofty ceilings, sweeping verandah, and full length windows was built in 1871 and is located two hours from Philadelphia at the end of the Garden State Parkway. Choose from five elegant guest rooms and four suites, all with antique furnishings. Several rooms and all suites are air conditioned. Three suites offer whirlpool baths. The verandah offers an ocean view. Popular attractions in the area include Lewes Ferry, village shopping, golf, tennis, fishing, boating, swimming, hiking, and bicycling. Full breakfast. 2/$85-165. MC, V. 5% senior discount.

Guests write: *"We have been going to the Mason Cottage every June since 1985. Being one block from the ocean and a couple of blocks from some of the best restaurants make this one of our favorite places. Dave and Joan and the staff always go out of the way to make our stay comfortable and they always have suggestions for something different to do."* (E. Ross)

"When our daughter was married in Cape May the summer of 1991, we reserved the Mason Cottage for ourselves, family, and friends. The Mason's gracious hospitality is unsurpassed! In the midst of all the wedding preparations, the Mason Cottage was a haven to which we could return, rock on the porch, feel the ocean breezes, enjoy the aroma of flowers and be pampered. Being from the Midwest, we especially enjoyed the location near the ocean and in the center of the Victorian district. One of our favorite activities was strolling the lanes of the Victorian homes in the neighborhood during the day and night." (J. Colson)

Cape May

Queen Victoria
102 Ocean Street
Cape May, NJ 08204
(609) 884-8702

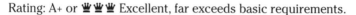

Type of B&B: Inn.
Rooms: 24 with private or shared bath.
Rate: 1 or 2/$55-225.

Rating: A+ or ♛♛♛ Excellent, far exceeds basic requirements.

Three restored Victorian seaside villas comprise the Queen Victoria which is located one block from the ocean in the center of the Historic District. There are twenty-four guest rooms which feature hand-made quilts, ceiling fans, and private or shared baths. Each room offers individual decor and several have fireplaces, whirlpool tubs, and air conditioning. Use the inn's bicycles to tour historic sites, antique shops, and the town center. Area attractions include restaurants, specialty shops, tennis, fishing, boating, swimming, and biking. Hosts speak English and French. Full breakfast. Facilities available for small weddings and meetings. 1 or 2/$55-225. MC, V.

Guests write: *"Our room was beautifully decorated in period Victorian and spotlessly clean. The room and bath were large with modern conveniences (refrigerator and firm mattress). There were lots of complimentary toiletries and chocolates on the pillows at night. In the common rooms were complimentary sherry, candies, popcorn, selection of soft drinks, tea, and coffee."* (F. Harris)

"Our room was bright, cheery, airy, and very comfortable and clean. The bath had a Jacuzzi and came with bath crystals, shower cap, shampoo, and conditioner. At night your bed is turned down, you are given fresh towels, and a large piece of chocolate is placed on each pillow. Hospitality is outstanding. With all the pampering and little extras, the Wells make you feel as if you are their only guest." (S. Hartman)

"The atmosphere at the Queen Victoria was perfect and very relaxing. Each room is named after an English royal and decorated accordingly. The whirlpools are a wonderful touch. The inn is located in the center of it all in Cape May and gives access to all the activities. " (M. Silva)

" Our suite oozed charm. We had a sitting room which stepped into a bedroom which took us back to the Victorian days. We have stayed in many B&Bs and this Queen Victoria has topped them all. This was our first Christmas in thirty-nine years away from our children and family. Joan and Dane and all of their guests made Christmas 1991 one to remember and we would do it again." (N. Martin)

"The first thing we noticed was that the grass and walks were extremely well-manicured. We liked the location within walking distance to so many things and the ocean. I could not believe it when they emptied the wastebaskets twice a day and turned down the bed with chocolates on each pillow. We could get really spoiled at the Queen Victoria." (R. Mylod)

"We particularly appreciated the restaurant information they provided including menus, food critic's reports, and guest's comments." (R. McGuinnes)

"We were very impressed with the booklet of information they provided for each guest. One other extra they provided that we really enjoyed was the free use of their bicycles for touring the city. Theirs was the 7th B&B we have reviewed but while we enjoyed all of them, the Queen Victoria had the most to offer and left us with the most pleasant memories of hospitality." (K. Sasdelli)

"The atmosphere was very hospitable, comfortable and very inviting. All staff members were courteous and friendly. At breakfast each morning, one of the owners or staff joined the guests for breakfast (while serving and attending to any special needs) and offered pleasant conversation, points of interest, and ideas of things to do. The breakfasts were absolutely wonderful. Plenty to eat and delicious!" (M. Rohrer)

Chatham

Parrot Mill Inn
47 Main Street
Chatham, NJ 07928
(201) 635-7722

Type of B&B: Inn.
Rooms: 11 with private bath.
Rates: 1 or 2/$95.

Rating: B or ♛♛ Good, exceeds basic requirements.

Large Gambrel-roofed home built around 1780, is located three miles from Route 78. Choose from eleven guest rooms, each with private bath. Relax before the fireplace in the keeping room. Area attractions include New York City, museums, shopping, hiking, and bicycling. Continental breakfast. Families welcome. 1 or 2/$95. AE, MC, V.

Guests write: *"The Parrot Mill Inn was a home away from home for five weeks during our relocation from South Carolina. Our stay was a vacation as Betsy and her staff were so warm, friendly, and helpful. The room was delightful and her breakfasts most enjoyable. Thanks to them our move has been much easier than we would have thought possible."* (L. Spieth)

Hacketstown/Hope

The Inn at Millrace Pond
Route 519
Hope, NJ 07844
(908) 459-4884

Type of B&B: Country Inn with restaurant.
Rooms: 17 with private bath.
Rates: 1or 2/$80-$130.

Rating: A or ♛♛♛ Excellent, far exceeds basic requirements.

Restored Colonial inn situated on 23 acres along Beaver Brook is comprised of the Millrace House, the Grist Mill, and Wheelwright's Cottage and is located approximately 65 miles west of New York City. Antique furnishings, wide board flooring, Oriental rugs, and period furnishings accent the Colonial decor found in each of the seventeen guest rooms with private bath. Explore the 1760s Grist Mill which is now a restaurant that features a millrace chamber, open staircase, and massive stone wall. Area attractions include The Delaware Water Gap National Recreation area, Waterloo Village, music festivals, craft shows, winery tours, and antique shopping. Bike along country roads, hike, golf, play tennis on the premises, or go canoeing on the nearby Delaware River. A hearty continental breakfast offers homemade pastries and fresh fruit. Small wedding and meeting facilities available. Families welcome. 1 or 2/$80-$130. AE, MC, V. Senior, corporate, and auto club discounts offered Sunday through Thursday. Travel agent.

Spring Lake

Sea Crest By the Sea
19 Tuttle Avenue
Spring Lake, NJ 07762
(908) 449-9031

Type of B&B: Inn.
Rooms: 12 with private bath.
Rates: 1 or 2 $84-147.

Rating: A+ or ♛♛♛ Excellent, far exceeds basic requirements.

Thirty-five room Victorian mansion is situated a half block from the ocean and located 5 miles east of the Garden State Parkway at exit 98. Choose from twelve individually decorated guest rooms, each with private bath. Two rooms offer a fireplace. Play croquet in the yard or borrow a bicycle to explore the town with its charming Victorian homes, lovely beaches, restaurants, antique shops, and boutiques. Golf, tennis, sailing, Garden

State Art Center, and Monmouth race tracks are also nearby. Extended continental breakfast features scones, fruit tarts, carrot cake, and home-baked bread. Restricted smoking. 1 or 2 $84-147. MC, V.

NEW MEXICO

Additional information on B&Bs in this state is available from Mi Casa Su Casa (800) 456-0682 or B&B Rocky Mountains (800) 733-8415.

Albuquerque

Casas de Suenos Old Town Bed & Breakfast Inn
310 Rio Grande Boulevard S.W.
Albuquerque, NM 87104
(505) 247-4560 or (800) CHAT W/US

Type of B&B: Large inn complex.
Rooms: 12 with private bath.
Rates: 1/$66-125; 2/$66-250.

Rating: B+ or ♛♛ Good, exceeds basic requirements.

Casas de Suenos is a Southwestern garden compound built in 1930 with a main house and small "casitas" or cottages. Originally built as an artist's colony, the inn is located one block from Old Town shops and restaurants. Entrance to the inn is beneath a contemporary structure added recently by world famous architect, Bart Prince. Each of the twelve guest rooms offers a private bath and eclectic blend of Southwestern decor and furnishings with European antiques, American Indian rugs, thick down comforters, and original art. There are two large common rooms as well as several patios and secluded garden areas. From the inn it's a short walk to museums, galleries, restaurants, nature park, and historic sites. Popular attractions include wineries, the world's longest aerial tram, ancient ruins, and archaeological sites. Full breakfast includes a hot entree and home-baked goods. Function rooms are available. Restricted smoking. Wheelchair access. 1/$66-125; 2/$66-250. AE, MC, V. Travel agent.

Guests write: *"The casitas are so comfortable and complete, with sitting room and garden, that we consider Casa de Suenos our home in New Mexico. Each suite we visit becomes our favorite. La Miradora for the elegance with its Chinese silk rug and antique furniture or the Taos suite with its built-in adobe headboard and pueblo-like atmosphere. The birdsongs in the garden and the gas lamps at night make this a magical world of its own."* (J. Cassidy)

Corrales

Corrales Inn Bed & Breakfast
58 Perea Road
Corrales, NM 87048
(505) 897-4422

Type of B&B: Inn.
Rooms: 6 with private bath.
Rates: 1/$55-65; 2/$65-75.

Rating: A- or ♛♛♛ Excellent, far exceeds basic requirements.

Newly built Territorial adobe-style inn is located in a quaint village about thirty minutes north of Albuquerque. There are six guest rooms. Each offers a private bath, individual temperature control, dressing area, and decor themes such as Oriental, Hot Air Balloons, Victorian, and Southwestern. A large common room features comfortable seating and a library which houses 2,000 books. There is a small, secluded courtyard with hot tub, fountain, and shade trees. There are a number of small restaurants in the village as well as interesting shops with handmade crafts and original art. The nearby Bosque Trail is a popular nine-mile hiking trail along the Rio Grande. Full breakfast. Rooms for small functions or seminars available. Families welcome. Wheelchair access. Restricted smoking. 1/$55-65; 2/$65-75. MC, V.

Guests write: *"Nestled off the main street of Corrales away from the city bustle, the warm hospitality and planning of the owners and the tastefully, peaceful rooms created a stay of true Southwest pleasure. There is easy access to areas of interest to visitors and a peak experience at breakfast!"* (L. Dunne)

"I enjoyed the hot tub on the cool moonlit night - it was so relaxing. It was truly a gift to have the good fortune to stay at this B&B." (G. Yee)

Los Ojos

Casa de Martinez
P.O. Box 96
Los Ojos, NM 87551
(505) 588-7858

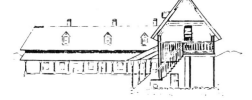

Type of B&B: Inn.
Rooms: 7, 3 with private bath.
Rates: 2/$65-85.

Rating: A- or ♛♛♛ Excellent, far exceeds basic requirements.

Historic Spanish adobe inn built in 1861 has been in the same family for several generations and is located in a rural area 13 miles south of Chama on old US-84 in the small community of Los Brazos. Choose from seven guest rooms decorated with antique furniture and local crafts; three offer a private bath. One large first-floor guest suite offers a private bath and fireplace. The inn is hosted by the great-granddaughter of early settlers in the area and has views towards the famous Brazos waterfall named El Chorro. Popular attractions in the area include fishing, hunting, cross-country skiing, and train rides over the Rocky Mountains. Full breakfast is served. Families welcome. The newest addition to the inn is a small conference room and gift shop. Wheelchair access. No smoking. 2/$65-85. 10% senior discount. Travel agent. Open February through October.

Guests write: "Clorinda's special breakfast meals are worth the drive to Casa de Martinez. She and her husband are both interesting to talk to as well as informative about the area." (D. Crone)

"We enjoy the romantic atmosphere on our annual winter get-away." (J. Ghahate)

"This is a great and pleasant place with wonderful hospitality." (B. Cherin)

"I enjoyed my stay very much since it was such a warm and cozy atmosphere. I will be back." (S. Gonzales)

"I had a very comfortable room and outstanding breakfasts. Clorinda and Medardo treated us like family. Casa de Martinez was a delightful place to stay and I would recommend it to anyone." (J. Rundquist)

"Love this place and their great cook! Gracias. Nos vemos el año que entra." (R. Johnson)

Santa Fe

Inn on the Alameda
303 East Alameda
Santa Fe, NM 87501
(800) 289-2122

Type of B&B: Urban inn.
Rooms: 47 with private bath.
Rates: 1/$145-320; 2/$155-330.

Rating: A+ or ♕♕♕ Excellent, far exceeds basic requirements.

Large adobe and Spanish-Colonial inn is located 5 miles north of I-25, exit 289 in downtown. The inn has forty-seven guest rooms, each with private bath, fireplace, TV, and phone. Relax in the ground floor main lounge with fireplace, seating, and cocktail service. Area attractions include Southwest Center for the Arts, Native American and Spanish cultural sites, desert wilderness, tennis, fishing, hiking, and skiing. Hearty gourmet continental breakfast is served in the "country kitchen" with a choice of pastries, cheeses, and seasonal fruits. Families welcome. Wheelchair access. 1/$145-320; 2/$155-330. AE, MC. V. 10% senior, auto club, business travel, and family discounts. Travel agent.

Santa Fe

Pueblo Bonito Bed & Breakfast Inn
138 West Manhattan
Santa Fe, NM 87501
(505) 984-8001

Type of B&B: Urban inn.
Rooms: 15 with private bath.
Rates: 1/$65-115; 2/$75-125.

Rating: B or ♕♕ Good, exceeds basic requirements.

Historic adobe estate is located in downtown Santa Fe, three blocks south of the Plaza. Choose from fifteen guest rooms, each with private bath, unique corner fireplace, and foot-thick adobe walls and window sills. While there is a variety of size, decor, and amenities throughout the rooms, each has been furnished with native antiques, Indian rugs, sand paintings, and works of local artists. Area attractions include historic downtown sites, museums, Indian pueblos, and specialty shops. Continental "create your own" breakfast buffet offers a variety of fresh fruits, Danish, muffins, and croissants. 1/$65-115; 2/$75-125. MC, V. Travel agent.

Taos

Casa Europa Inn and Gallery
157 Upper Ranchitos Road
Taos, NM 87571
(505) 758-9798

Type of B&B: Inn.
Rooms: 6 with private bath.
Rates: 1/$60-100; 2/$80-110.

Rating: A or ♛♛♛ Excellent, far exceeds basic requirements.

Historic Southwestern adobe has been completely restored with modern European finishing and has a rural setting outside the city. There are six guest rooms that vary in size, decor, and amenities but all have a selection of interesting antiques and a private bath. Several offer a fireplace or wood stove and full-size Jacuzzi. There are several common areas throughout the inn offering quiet places for reading, conversing with other guests, or viewing the traditional or contemporary crafts and paintings of native American artists. A quiet courtyard offers a Swedish sauna and hot tub. A ski area is nearby as are Indian pueblos and white-water rafting. Full breakfast and afternoon refreshments served daily. Families welcome. Restricted smoking. 1/$60-100; 2/$80-110. MC, V.

Additional information on B&Bs in this state is available from Abode B&B (212) 472-2000 or Bed & Breakfast & Books (212) 865-8740

Albany/Dolgeville

Adrianna's Bed & Breakfast
44 Stewart Street
Dolgeville, NY 13329
(315) 429-3249

Type of B&B: B&B home.
Rooms: 3 share 2 baths.
Rates: 1/$45; 2/$55-58.

Rating: B+ or ♛♛ Good, exceeds basic requirements.

Modern raised ranch home is located 6 miles north of exit 29-A off I-90 on the New York Thruway. There are three air conditioned guest rooms that share two baths and have been decorated with comfort in mind. A living room on the main floor offers a fireplace, TV, and comfortable seating. Relax in the swimming pool or visit the local golf course. Nearby attractions include Saratoga Raceway and Performing Arts Center, Herkimer Diamond Mines, Herkimer Home, Daniel Green Slipper Outlet, Erie Canal in Little Falls, and the Lyndon Lyon Greenhouses which specialize in violets. Full traditional breakfast served. Families welcome. Restricted smoking. Resident cat. 1/$45; 2/$55-58.

Guests write: *"The accommodations are very comfortable and spacious. Adrianna serves a terrific breakfast and is an informed and hospitable hostess."* (G. Romanic)

"Our trip to Dolgeville was for my Dad's funeral. The funeral director suggested Adrianna's. She didn't know us from Adam but she made us feel like her home was ours and we almost felt like family when we left. The decor was very tastefully done throughout. The food was wonderful and the setting and service just beautiful. In each of the bedrooms was a tastefully selected library that made me want to stay for a month to read, read, read." (B. Luft)

"At no place we have been - motels, hotels, B&Bs - have we received hospitality, cordiality and accommodations akin to Adrianna's B&B. Hers is tops on our list." (F. Belford)

"Our brief stay was more than a wonderful night's rest followed by a delectable breakfast, it was an experience in friendship. Never before have we met a stranger who immediately by her friendliness and warmth, was transformed into a charming friend." (G. McCloskey)

— *Comments continued on next page*

"This is our favorite stop-over when we drive East. It's like a friend's house and we always look forward to an elegant breakfast before we drive on." (M. Pendergast)

"This was my best night's sleep in weeks. Adrianna is a wonderfully talented hostess." (B. Campbell)

Barneveld

Sugarbush Bed & Breakfast
RR 1, Box 227, Old Poland Road
Barneveld, NY 13304
(315) 896-6860 or (800) 582-5845

Type of B&B: Inn.
Rooms: 5, 2 with private bath.
Rates: 1/$40; 2/$55-80.

Rating: B+ or ♛♛ Good exceeds basic requirements.

Historic Colonial home is nestled among old maple trees and located twelve miles north of Utica off Route 12. There are five guest rooms on the first or second floor; two offer a private bath. The rooms differ greatly in size and amenities, but all have a pleasant decor, comfortable chairs, and fresh flowers. A large guest suite on the first floor offers a private bath, bedroom and sitting room. There are several common rooms including a living room with comfortable seating, fireplace, and views of the countryside. Area attractions include Adirondack Park with skiing and water sports. Full breakfast includes eggs, bacon, and waffles topped with New York state maple syrup. Afternoon refreshments are offered and additional meals are available upon request. Families welcome. Restricted smoking. 1/$40; 2/$55; Suite/$80. MC, V. Senior, family, business, and auto club discounts. Travel agent.

Canandaigua

The Acorn Inn
4580 Bristol Balley Road, Bristol Center
Canandaigua, NY 14424
(716) 229-2834 or (716) 747-6483

Type of B&B: Inn
Rooms: 3 with private bath.
Rates: 1 or 2/$75-125.

Rating: A+ or ♕♕♕ Excellent, far exceeds basic requirements.

1795 Federal Stagecoach inn was renovated in 1989 to reflect 18th-Century style and is located eight miles west of Canandaigua, 30 miles south of Rochester. Choose from three air-conditioned guest rooms with private bath and sitting area. Each room has been furnished with antiques, canopy bed, and luxury linens. There is nightly turn-down service with chocolates and ice water provided. Afternoon tea is served in front of the large colonial fireplace outfitted with antique crane and hanging iron pots. There are extensive private gardens perfect for a quiet stroll. Area attractions include Canandaigua Lake, Sonneneberg Gardens, Bristol Harbor Golf Club, Bristol Mountain skiing, Finger Lakes Performing Arts Center, and the Cumming Nature Center. Acorn apple bread pudding, artichoke fritatta, or filled French toast are frequent specialties offered at a full breakfast. Wheelchair access. No smoking. Resident dog. 1 or 2/$75-125. MC, V. Senior and auto club discount. Travel agent.

Canandaigua

Morgan-Samuels Inn
2920 Smith Road
Canandaigua, NY 14424
(716) 394-9232

Type of B&B: Inn.
Rooms: 6 with private bath.
Rates: 1/$60; 2/$79-195

Rating: A or ♕♕♕ Excellent, far exceeds basic requirements.

Stone mansion built in 1810 sits at the top of a hill in the rural setting in the Finger Lakes area of west-central New York. Six guest rooms are available and each has distinctive decor and air conditioning. The Morgan Suite offers a wood-burning fireplace and Jacuzzi. The Victorian Room also has a Jacuzzi and the Farmer's Daughter's room offers a fireplace. There are several common rooms throughout the inn as well as a pleasant patio overlooking the countryside. The property has forty-six acres of fields and woods to explore as well as a tennis court. Popular attractions in the area include lake recreation, wagon rides, skiing, wineries, antique shops, and outdoor theaters as well as Sonnenberg Gardens, Bristol Mountain, Granger Homestead, and the Radio Museum. Full gourmet breakfast is served by candlelight and an afternoon tea is offered daily. Dinner is available by advance reservation. No smoking. 1/$60; 2/$79-195. MC, V. 10% business discount. Travel agent.

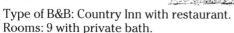

Cazenovia

The Brewster Inn
6 Ledyard Ave., P.O. Box 507
Cazenovia, NY 13035
(315) 655-9232

Type of B&B: Country Inn with restaurant.
Rooms: 9 with private bath.
Rates: 1 or 2/$60-195.

Rating: A or ♛♛♛ Excellent, far exceeds basic requirements.

1890 Victorian mansion situated on Cazenovia Lake is 20 miles southeast of Syracuse and features an interior finished entirely of hardwood. Guests are accommodated in nine antique-filled guest rooms with private bath. Several rooms offer a Jacuzzi and others feature a queen-size canopy bed or sun porch. The adjacent shoreline and grounds offer swimming and boating. Within walking distance is the village of Cazenovia with its historic homes and Lorenzo, the 18th century estate of the founder of the village. Take day trips to Cooperstown, Chittenango Falls State Park, and to the Finger Lakes/Wine country. A continental breakfast is offered. Wedding and meeting facilities available. Families welcome. 1 or 2/$60-195. MC, V. Travel agent.

Guests write: *"Outstanding building and grounds. Spacious, beautifully restored and decorated rooms. Homey feeling with fireplaces and friendly staff. Excellent value with reasonable prices. A wonderful, relaxed feeling. The nicest inn that I've stayed in.* (D. Goverts and P. Kanz)

"Our room was spacious and yet very warm and cozy but the staff is what would make us come back. We were snowed in for the storm of '93 and they were bending over backwards to make it as pleasant as could be under the situation. You will also never go wrong with any meal you order. It was fabulous." (D. Greene)

"The Brewster Inn in beautiful Cazenovia is the ideal place. It is truly a winter wonderland. Every member of the staff at Brewster Inn is most friendly and helpful!" (M. Barreras)

Cooperstown

Angelholm
14 Elm Street, Box 705
Cooperstown, NY 13326
(607) 547-2483
Fax: (607) 547-2309

Type of B&B: B&B home.
Rooms: 4 with shared or private bath.
Rates: 1 or 2/$70-90.

Rating: A+ or ♛♛♛ Excellent, far exceeds basic requirements.

Located on a quiet side street in the heart of Cooperstown, this historic Colonial house built in 1815, is just a four-minute walk from Main Street and the Baseball Hall of Fame. There are four guest rooms with private or shared bath and each offers a collection of antique furniture, period wallpaper, fine linens, and accessories. Afternoon tea is served daily in the fireplaced living room or on a comfortable side porch that overlooks the garden. Cooperstown is located 25 miles south of I-90 in central New York and is known for its historic homes, parks, museums, and shops. Area attractions include Baseball Hall of Fame, Farmer's Museum, Fenimore House Museum, and outdoor recreation. Full breakfast is served in the formal dining room. Off-street parking. 1 or 2/$70-90. MC. V.

Guests write: *"Janet and Fred make their guests feel like they are visiting old and dear friends. The breakfasts are outstanding. The hosts enjoy answering questions about Cooperstown and the surrounding area. Oh, and don't forget to get Janet's house tour. We are quite glad that we chose Angelholm."* (J. Sloan)

Cooperstown

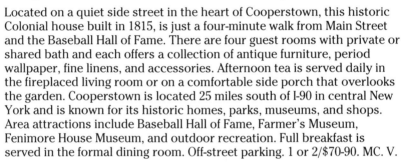

The Inn at Cooperstown
16 Chestnut Street - A
Cooperstown, NY 13326
(607) 547-5756

Type of B&B: Historic hotel.
Rooms: 17 with private bath.
Rates: 1/$68-78; 2/$78-88.

Rating: B or ♛♛ Good, exceeds basic requirements.

Built in 1874 as the annex to the Hotel Fenimore, this Second Empire inn is situated in Cooperstown's Historic District. The Inn was designed by Henry Hardenberg, noted architect of the Dakota Apartments and the Plaza Hotel in New York City and has received acclaim for the fine preservation work of the building. Seventeen guest rooms are available on the second or third floor of the inn. Each has a private bath and comfortable reading chair. Relax in a rocking chair on the veranda or in front of the fireplace in the parlor. Walk to the many nearby shops and restaurants. Area attractions include Baseball Hall of Fame and Museum, Fenimore House Museum, The Farmers' Museum, Glimmerglass Opera House, golf, tennis, and fishing. Continental breakfast. Wheelchair access. 1/$68-78; 2/$78-88. AE, MC, V. Travel agent.

Corning

Rosewood Inn
134 East First Street
Corning, NY 14830
(607) 962-3253

Type of B&B: Inn.
Rooms: 7 with private bath.
Rates: 1/$73-89; 2/$83-115.

Rating: B+ or ♛♛ Good, exceeds basic requirements.

English Tudor-style home built in 1855 and restored in 1980 to reflect a Victorian splendor, is one block south of Route 17 as it goes through the city. Each of the seven rooms are named for famous individuals and offer pleasant decor combining fine antiques, wallpapers, and draperies. All rooms have a private bath and are air conditioned. A sitting room furnished with antique Cooper rockers invites conversation and television viewing. Local attractions include the Corning Glass Center and Rockwell Museum as well as the restored Market Street. Full breakfast is served in a candlelit Victorian dining room. Families welcome. No smoking. 1/$73-89; 2/$83-115. AE, Diners, Discover, MC, V.

Croton on Hudson

Alexander Hamilton House
49 Van Wyck Street
Croton on Hudson, NY 10520
(914) 271-6737

Type of B&B: Inn.
Rooms: 9, 3 with private bath.
Rates: 1/$50-60; 2/$60-250.

Rating: A or ♛♛♛ Excellent, far exceeds basic requirements.

Historic Victorian home built in 1889 is located four blocks east of Route 9 and offers sweeping views of the valley and river below. Choose from nine individually decorated and air conditioned guest rooms, three with private bath. The Aaron Burr suite features a private bath, queen-size bed, and fireplaced sitting room with sofa-bed. A separate apartment offers private entrance, bath, and full kitchen. The newly opened Penthouse Bridal Chamber features king bed, skylights, private bath with Jacuzzi, and fireplace. Guests are invited to use the in-ground swimming pool and outdoor patio with gas grill. Area attractions include Van Cortlandt Manor, Teatown Reservation, West Point, and easy train access to New York City sights. Full breakfast. Families welcome. No smoking. 1/$50-60; 2/$60-85; Suite/$125; Bridal Chamber/$250. AE, MC, V. Travel agent.

Elizabethtown

Stony Water Bed & Breakfast
R.R. 1, Box 69
Elizabethtown, NY 12932
(518) 873-9125

Type of B&B: Private home.
Rooms: 4 with private bath.
Rates: 1/$55; 2/$65-75.

Rating: A- or ♛♛♛ Excellent, far exceeds basic requirements.

Federal Colonial house built around 1870 is situated on 87 acres of fields and woodlands and located 30 minutes from Lake Placid, midway between Albany and Montreal. The four guest rooms offer views of the surrounding countryside, antique furnishings, and a private bath. One room features French doors that open onto the swimming pool and woodlands. Enjoy afternoon tea or sit by the fireplace in the library, bicycle or hike along scenic country roads, play the baby grand piano in the parlor, swim in the pool, or relax in the hammock. Adirondack High

Peaks, Lake Champlain, and the Lake Placid Olympic Center are an easy drive away. Area attractions include the John Brown Farm and many Revolutionary War sites. A full breakfast entree is accompanied by home-made breads, muffins, and fresh fruit. Small meeting facilities available. Families welcome. Wheelchair access. No smoking. 1/$55; 2/$65-75. MC, V.

Guests write: *"The spirit of the house has been warmed by the hosts who prepared us for our hike and made us look forward to coming out of the woods (something that we usually do reluctantly)."* (A. Stidfole)

"In all seasons the drive up the road to the beautiful B&B expands the heart and readies us for a great trip. We love the warmth and comfort of the hearth and library, the delicious, wholesome food, the relaxed innkeepers who impose no rules (not even as to the time of breakfast), and the special Adirondack setting." (N. Gershon and B. Fried)

"The 'loft' above the garage overlooking the hills & meadow is superb — what serenity." (M. Meade)

"The lovely room, the fresh flowers, the good food, the cozy fire, and the warm hospitality made my stay so delightful." (M. E. Cornell)

Hammondsport

The Blushing Rose Bed & Breakfast Inn
11 William Street
Hammondsport, NY 14840
(607) 569-3402 or 569-3483

Type of B&B: Inn.
Rooms: 4 with private bath.
Rates: 1/$65-75; 2/$75-95.

Rating: A- or 🐛🐛🐛 Excellent, far exceeds basic requirements.

Small Victorian-Italianate home built in 1835 is located at the southern tip of Keuka Lake in the Finger Lakes region, about twenty-five miles west of Corning. There are four guest rooms on the second floor. Each offers a private bath, air conditioning, and individual decor with special touches such as handmade quilts, stenciled walls, lace canopy beds, and white wicker furnishings. There is a beverage and snack center near the guest rooms with small refrigerator. Popular attractions in the area include Curtiss Museum, Corning Glass Museum, Watkins Glen auto racing as well as lake activities. Full breakfast specialties include baked French toast, lemon poppy seed waffles, and strawberry bread. No smoking. 1/$65-75; 2/$75-95. Senior, business, and auto club discounts. Travel agent.

Hamptons — also see the listing under Westhampton, NY.

Hamptons/Bellport

The Great South Bay Inn
160 South Country Road
Bellport, NY 11713
(516) 286-8588

Type of B&B: Inn.
Rooms: 6, 2 with private bath.
Rates: 1/$50; 2/$70-120.

Rating: B+ or ♛♛ Good, exceeds basic requirements.

Restored, late 19th-Century Cape Cod inn is located on Long Island's South Shore. It is in close proximity to the Hamptons and 8 miles southeast of exit 64 of the Long Island Expressway. Each of the six guest rooms are furnished in period antiques and feature the original wainscoting. Two offer a private bath. Stroll Bellport's historic shopping district and view the old historic homes or dine at a variety of fine restaurants. A town ferry is available to take you across to the village's private beach on Fire Island. Homemade scones, cereals, and breads are featured in the continental breakfast and lunch is available. The garden accommodates small weddings and gatherings. Families welcome. Restricted smoking. 1/$50; 2/$70-120. Senior discount. Travel agent.

Lake George/North Creek

The Copperfield Inn
224 Main Street, PO Box 28
North Creek, NY 12853
(800)424-9910 or (518)251-2500

Type of B&B: Country Inn with restaurant.
Rooms: 25 with private bath.
Rates: 1/$90-130; 2/$110-150.

Rating: AA or ♛♛♛♛ Outstanding.

Neo-classic European-style inn is within walking distance of the upper Hudson River and is located 75 miles from Albany and 20 miles northwest of Lake George. Twenty-five individually decorated guest rooms offer a private marble bath with Roman tub, sitting area, choice of king or queen bed, and color TV. Relax in the outdoor whirlpool or warm up in front of the fireplace. Work out in the gym, swimming pool, or tennis courts on the premises. Go skiing at Gore Mountain, white water rafting on the Hudson River, or visit the Adirondack Museum and the Garnet Hill Mines. A full breakfast features omelets made to order and dinners are available at the full service restaurant. Wedding and meeting facilities available. Families welcome. Wheelchair access. Restricted smoking. 1/$90-130; 2/$110-150. MC, V. 10% senior, corporate, and auto club discounts. Travel agent.

Lake George/Warrensburg

House on the Hill Bed & Breakfast
P.O. Box 248, Route 28
Warrensburg, NY 12885
(518) 623-9390 or (800) 221-9390

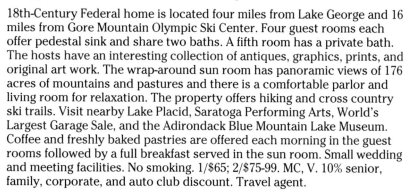

Type of B&B: Inn.
Rooms: 5, 1 with private bath.
Rates: 1/$65; 2/$75-99.

Rating: B+ or ♕♕ Good, exceeds basic requirements.

18th-Century Federal home is located four miles from Lake George and 16 miles from Gore Mountain Olympic Ski Center. Four guest rooms each offer pedestal sink and share two baths. A fifth room has a private bath. The hosts have an interesting collection of antiques, graphics, prints, and original art work. The wrap-around sun room has panoramic views of 176 acres of mountains and pastures and there is a comfortable parlor and living room for relaxation. The property offers hiking and cross country ski trails. Visit nearby Lake Placid, Saratoga Performing Arts, World's Largest Garage Sale, and the Adirondack Blue Mountain Lake Museum. Coffee and freshly baked pastries are offered each morning in the guest rooms followed by a full breakfast served in the sun room. Small wedding and meeting facilities. No smoking. 1/$65; 2/$75-99. MC, V. 10% senior, family, corporate, and auto club discount. Travel agent.

Guests write: *"Everything at the House on the Hill was great! Lovely rooms, delicious food, and warm and friendly hosts (Joe & Lynn Rubino).*

"We've been telling everyone that the best part of our vacation was definitely where we stayed — The House on the Hill. The kindness and more-than-friendly hospitality made us feel so comfortable. The advice on attractions to see was well appreciated. The breakfast was like no other and our morning conversations were interesting and enjoyable."
(Amy Berthiaume)

"Hospitality, great stories, and a great stay in Lake George!" (N. Schandler)

Lisle

Dorchester Farm
RD 1, Box 162, Keibel Road
Lisle, NY 13797
(607) 692-4511

Type of B&B: B&B home.
Rooms: 3 with private bath & cottage.
Rates: 1 or 2/$65-85.

Rating: A- or ♛ ♛ ♛ Excellent, far exceeds basic requirements.

Pre-Civil War Colonial home is located 20 miles north of Binghamton near exit 8 off Route 81. Three guest rooms with private bath are in the main house and there is also a separate cottage available. Enjoy the area's antique shops, swimming, sailing, windsurfing, or just relax on the Victorian porch overlooking the five-mile-long lake. Visit nearby Binghamton, Ithaca, and Cortland. Breakfast includes fresh fruit, omelets, Belgian waffles, sweet rolls, and blueberry muffins and is served in the antique-filled dining room with lake view. Restricted smoking. Resident dog and cats. 1 or 2/$65-85. MC, V.

Guests write: *"I have to say that this was one of the most unique and beautiful B&Bs I have been to. I could spend all day looking at her great antique collections of kitchenware, Teddy Bears, and furniture. The suite with its magnificent view of the lake was breathtaking and I felt very at home with my favorite Crabtree and Evelyn amenities which were so specially arranged in the bathroom."* (M. Vorhies)

"This was our first B&B experience. Any in the future will have a hard time measuring up to the charm and hospitality here." (L. Harwood)

"Everything was super. The house is beautiful, food delicious, gracious hosts. I was completely fascinated by the home." (E. Stiering)

"This is a 150 year old farmhouse that has been restored and is absolutely wonderful in every respect. But more important than the decor (which is extraordinary), the full delicious homemade breakfast and the lovely touches, is the warmth and entertaining side of the hosts." (J. Watson)

"We arrived at Dorchester at night greeted by a blazing fire. The next morning, we woke with a view of mist rising over the lake below our window. The feather-bed mattress and Laura Ashley quality linens almost made it impossible to get out of bed. Before exploring the gigantic turn-of-the-century barn and swinging in the chair above the lake, we feasted on a glorious breakfast of homemade muffins and breads, eggs, sausage, and a hot apple crisp to die for (I still dream about this apple crisp)." (H. Else)

New York City — See listings under Croton-on-Hudson and Staten Island.

Rochester

Dartmouth House B&B
215 Dartmouth Street
Rochester, NY 14607
(716) 271-7872 or 473-0778

Type of B&B: B&B home.
Rooms: 4, 2 with private bath.
Rates: 1/$45-70; 2/$55-80.

Rating: B+ or ♛♛ Good, exceeds basic requirements.

Spacious English Tudor built in 1905 is located in a quiet, city neighborhood near I-490. Choose from four guest rooms, two with private bath, and two offering semi-private bath. The decor is enhanced by the massive fireplace, family antiques, window seats, Oriental rugs, leaded glass windows, and beamed ceilings. Downtown Rochester is only one mile away. Walk to museums, antique shops, and restaurants or take an easy, three block walk to the George Eastman International Museum of Photography. The Strong Museum, Highland Park and several colleges are nearby. Full gourmet breakfast is served by candlelight and features several courses. No smoking. No pets. 1/$45-70; 2/$55-80. AE, MC, V. Travel agent.

Guests write: *"I feel like I'm coming home at Dartmouth House. Having to make a business trip to Rochester is now like having a home to go back to at the end of a long day. It beats cold, impersonal hotel rooms anytime. The bedrooms are spacious and comfortable. Each one has its own personality. I especially appreciate the large rooms so that I can spread out and work when I need to. Everything you could possibly need has been thought of from the hair dryers in each bathroom to the little baskets with shampoo, sewing kits, etc. Each room has a few snacks in a jar and cans of soda for each guest. I haven't had anyone make such a fuss of me since I left my parent's home over 30 years ago."* (C. Woodford)

Rochester/Fairport

Woods Edge Bed & Breakfast
151 Bluhm Road
Fairport, NY 14450
(716) 223-8877 or (716) 223-8510

Type of B&B: Private home.
Rooms: 2 with private baths & guest house.
Rates: 1/$50-90; 2/$60-90.

Rating: B or ♛♛ Good, exceeds basic requirements.

Woods Edge B&B is a contemporary home in a secluded setting located 20 minutes from downtown Rochester. Two antique-filled guest rooms with private bath are available. The private guest house features a living room with fireplace, dining area, fully equipped kitchen, bedroom with queen-size bed, and private bath with washer and dryer. Nearby museums, colleges, parks, the Erie Canal, and the Finger Lakes region offer many activities such as swimming, skiing, golfing, sailing, and sport fishing. Full breakfast is served with homemade specialties such as Dutch pancakes, fruit salad, or heart-shaped waffles. Families welcome. No smoking. Resident cat. 1/$50-90; 2/$60-90. Student discount. Travel agent.

Staten Island

Victorian Bed & Breakfast
92 Taylor Street
Staten Island, NY 10310
(718)273-9861

Type of B&B: Inn.
Rooms: 4 with 2 shared baths.
Rates: 1/$45; 2/$50-75.

Rating: B or ♛♛ Good, exceeds basic requirements.

Italianette Victorian built in the 1860s is just three miles west of the Staten Island Ferry to Manhattan and is located on the north shore of Staten Island in the town of West New Brighton. Four guest rooms share two baths. Many furnishings are original to the house and every room in the house has a marble fireplace and mantel. Afternoon tea with baked pastries is served in the dining room or on the verandah. Explore the nearby Early American village or Snug Harbor Cultural Center. New York City's famous attractions are just twelve minutes away by ferry. A full breakfast includes hearty entrees such as egg dishes, fruit pancakes, or blintzes. Families welcome. No smoking. 1/$45; 2/$50-75. AE. 10% senior and auto club discount. Travel agent.

Syracuse/Baldwinsville

Pandora's Getaway
83 Oswego Street
Baldwinsville, NY 13027
(315) 635-9571 or 638-8660

Type of B&B: Inn.
Rooms: 4, 1 with private bath.
Rates: 1/$45; 2/$75.

Rating: B- or ♥♥ Good, exceeds basic requirements.

Restored Greek Revival home set high on a hill with sloping lawns is listed on the National Historic Register and located twenty minutes from Syracuse. Choose from four guest rooms, one with private bath. Each room has individual decor and amenities such as a fireplace, color TV, or panoramic views. Relax on the front porch or in the large living room. Area attractions include nearby Finger Lakes, Lake Ontario, and nature center. Baked French toast is often on the full breakfast menu served in the formal dining room. Wedding and meeting facilities available. Families welcome. Restricted smoking. 1/$45; 2/$75. MC, V. Travel agent.

Guests write: *"Pandora's Getaway was our first encounter with a B&B. There were no hotels available so we thought we would give it a try. We stayed there out of necessity but it turned out to be a treat! Now our first preference would be a B&B. The food was homemade, delicious, and plentiful. The room was large with a fireplace all ready for us to use. The antiques added a quaint charm. The owners were very pleasant, gracious, and helpful."* (S. Amato)

"Pandora's Getaway is a delightful, cozy, warm, and friendly place. Quite different from a hotel room! After a very long, very stressful day, it was exactly what we needed and at a very reasonable price!" (L. Harrington)

Utica

The Iris Stonehouse
16 Derbyshire Place
Utica, NY 13501
(315) 732-6720 or (800) 446-1456

Type of B&B: B&B home.
Rooms: 3, 1 with private bath.
Rates: 1/$35-50; 2/$45-60.

Rating: A or ♛♛♛ Excellent, far exceeds basic requirements.

Set in the city close to area attractions, this 1932 stone Tudor home is on the local Register of Historic Homes and is 3 miles south of I-90 at exit 31. Leaded glass windows add charm to the eclectic decor of the three guest rooms with private or shared baths and central air. A guest-sitting room offers a comfortable area for relaxing, playing games, or watching TV. Area attractions include Munson-Williams-Proctor Art Institute, Children's Museum, Oneida County Historic Society, Utica Zoo, and F.X. Matt Brewery tour. In nearby Cooperstown and Rome, visitors can see the Baseball Hall of Fame, Farmer's Museum, Erie Canal Village and Fort Richey Game Farm. A full breakfast is served. No smoking. No pets. 1/$35-50; 2/$45-60. AE, MC, V. Travel agent.

Watkins Glen/Dundee

South Glenora Tree Farm Bed & Breakfast
546 South Glenora Road
Dundee, NY 14837
(607) 243-7414

Type of B&B: Inn.
Rooms: 4 with private bath.
Rates: 1/$55; 2/$65.

Rating: A- or ♛♛♛ Excellent, far exceeds basic requirements.

Gambrel roof barn is now an inn situated on an active tree farm of 140 acres that is located in the Finger Lakes region of New York near Seneca Lake. Four guest rooms feature a private bath, queen-sized bed, rocking chair, and handmade quilts and drapes. Relax in the common room reading or playing games. The surrounding wooded hills and fields offer acres to explore. Nearby attractions include wineries, wildlife reserves, Corning Glass factory, Grand Prix Raceway, and Watkins Glen. Outdoor recreation nearby includes fishing, swimming, and boating and the area is full of fine restaurants, gift stores, and antique shops. A continental plus breakfast is often served on the wrap-around porch and features home-baked goods and pastries. Families welcome. Wheelchair access. Restricted smoking. 1/$55; 2/$65. MC, V. Travel agent.

Westhampton Beach

Seafield House
2 Seafield Lane, P.O. Box 648
Westhampton Beach, NY 11978
(516) 288-1559

Type of B&B: Inn.
Rooms: 2 suites with private bath.
Rates: 2/$100-195.

Rating: B+ or ♛♛ Good, exceeds basic requirements.

Historic Victorian home built in 1880 is situated in town near shops and restaurants and located 3 miles south of Route 27, exit 63, or ninety minutes from Manhattan. There are two spacious guest suites with private bath, sitting room, antiques, and family treasures. Enjoy the warmth from the 1907 Modern Glenwood pot-belly stove or the fireplace in the parlor. An enclosed porch overlooks the tennis courts and swimming pool on the property. The beach as well as the shops on Main Street are just a short walk away as are local attractions such as historic homes, antique shops, golf, fishing, swimming, hiking, and bicycling. Full breakfast features home made goodies. No smoking. 2/$100-195.

Asheville

The Colby House
230 Pearson Drive
Asheville, NC 28801
(800) 982-2118 or (704)253-5644

Type of B&B: Inn.
Rooms: 4 with private bath.
Rates: 2/$75-95.

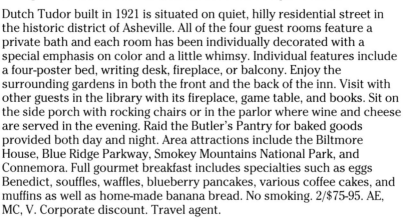

Rating: A+ or ♛ ♛ ♛ Excellent, far exceeds basic requirements.

Dutch Tudor built in 1921 is situated on quiet, hilly residential street in the historic district of Asheville. All of the four guest rooms feature a private bath and each room has been individually decorated with a special emphasis on color and a little whimsy. Individual features include a four-poster bed, writing desk, fireplace, or balcony. Enjoy the surrounding gardens in both the front and the back of the inn. Visit with other guests in the library with its fireplace, game table, and books. Sit on the side porch with rocking chairs or in the parlor where wine and cheese are served in the evening. Raid the Butler's Pantry for baked goods provided both day and night. Area attractions include the Biltmore House, Blue Ridge Parkway, Smokey Mountains National Park, and Connemora. Full gourmet breakfast includes specialties such as eggs Benedict, souffles, waffles, blueberry pancakes, various coffee cakes, and muffins as well as home-made banana bread. No smoking. 2/$75-95. AE, MC, V. Corporate discount. Travel agent.

Guests write: *"What makes the Colby House so special? The exceptional attractive exterior, the luxurious appointments in the library and dining room, the warmth and comfort of the beautiful bedroom, the delicious breakfast and perhaps most important, the Colby's personalities."*
(J. O'Connor)

"We enjoyed the Foxfire Room. The fireplace provided a warm and romantic setting which was just what we were looking for." (M. Plonk)
"All the special little touches, from the warm fire, to the sherry decanter, to the coffee in the morning. All contribute to making the Colby House a delightful place to stay." (J. G. Boozer)

"It was so wonderful to come home after a lot of sight-seeing and enjoy some delicious home-made cookies and a drink and then a nice glass of wine later in the day. We really appreciated the input on things to do in Asheville."
(L. Tarvin)

Asheville

Richmond Hill Inn
87 Richmond Hill Drive
Asheville, NC 28806
(704) 252-7313 or (800) 545-9238

Type of B&B: Country inn.
Rooms: 21 with private bath.
Rates: 2/$115-275.

Rating: AA or ♛♛♛♛ Outstanding.

Victorian country inn with restaurant was built in 1889 and sits majestically atop a hill overlooking the city which is three miles away. There are twelve guest rooms in the mansion and nine rooms in charming cottages situated around a croquet courtyard. Each of the 21 guest rooms feature private baths and many have fireplaces. Special appointments include Victorian furniture, Oriental rugs, and draped canopy beds. Savor American and nouvelle cuisine in the gourmet restaurant. Play croquet or visit the nearby Biltmore Estate, Blue Ridge Parkway, and downtown Asheville. Full breakfast may feature omelets or egg dishes, as well as fresh baked muffins and breads. Facilities are available for weddings, social events, and small business conferences. Restricted smoking. 2/$115-275. AE, MC, V. Travel agent.

Guests write: *"We spent two weeks in the mountains of Virginia, North Carolina, and Tennessee. We did not stay exclusively in B&B inns but Richmond Hill Inn was by far the nicest of the B&Bs we visited and superior to any motel or the condo we visited. They truly deserve 1st class status."* (F. Forehand)

"Richmond Hill Inn is a treasure and certainly worthy of comment. Clean and neat goes without saying, but how many forget the setting which is so essential to doing business. The art of their magirics was supreme and the staff congratulated. Only love can describe the way in which the finest cuisine here is served." (L. Brain)

"Everything is so well done. Our dinner was excellent and the gown I left behind was in the mail to me before I even called to inquire about it." (M. Rogers)

"The food was outstanding. This renovation of a Victorian mansion was remarkably well planned. The insulation in the walls provided great quiet" (R. Lee)

"This was our first stay in the new cottages. They are terrific! These folks do an absolutely first-rate job. Thanks to all the crew who keep the rooms and grounds so clean." (R. Spuller)

Asheville

The Wright Inn
235 Pearson Drive
Asheville, NC 28801
(704) 251-0789 or
(800) 552-5724 ext. 235

Type of B&B: Inn.
Rooms: 9 with private bath.
Rates: 2/$75-110; Carriage house/$175.

Rating: A- or ♛♛♛ Excellent, far exceeds basic requirements.

Historic Queen Anne home is situated in a neighborhood of stately Victorian homes in Asheville located seven blocks off I-240. There are nine guest rooms. Each has a private bath, turn-of-the-century decor, cable TV, and telephone; two have fireplaces. The Carriage House is a separate building on the grounds which is especially suited for families or small groups traveling together. It offers three bedrooms, full kitchen, two baths, living room, and dining room. Popular attractions in this area include Blue Ridge Parkway, Biltmore House and Gardens, Smokey Mountain National Park, Thomas Wolfe Home, and Cherokee Indian reservation. Full breakfast is served in a formal dining room and is not included in carriage house rates. No smoking. 1 or 2/$75-110; Carriage house/$175. MC, V. Travel agent.

Guests write: *"We were married at the Wright Inn in a simple and very elegant ceremony. It was exactly as we would have dreamed — only true to life. Betty, Gary and Sandra were all warm and very hospitable hosts who helped make this truly the happiest day of our lives."* (S. Talbot)

"The room was very nice and clean. The bed had a big soft down comforter. There was a little basket of candy kisses and bon-bons. The sheets and towels were trimmed in white lace. Breakfast was very good with a fruit cup, juice, coffee, hot tea, eggs, gravy, biscuits, link sausage, homemade preserves, and a friendship cake to top it off. Everything was delightful!" (C. Hayes)

"The breakfasts were wonderful! What did I like best? The attention to detail of Betty, the innkeeper." (K. Carpenter)

Beaufort

Captains' Quarters of Beaufort, Inc.
315 Ann Street
Beaufort, NC 28516
(919) 728-7711

Type of B&B: B&B home.
Rooms: 3 with private bath.
Rates: 1/$50-80; 2/$60-100.

Rating: A or ♛♛♛ Excellent, far exceeds basic requirements.

Historic turn-of-the-century Victorian home has been completely restored
and is situated one block from the waterfront in the heart of the Historic
District. There are three guest rooms on the second floor. Each has a
private bath, family heirlooms, and antique furnishings. Take part in the
inn's tradition to "toast the sunset" on the verandah or by the parlor
fireplace and celebrate the day with wines and fresh fruit juices. Explore
the nearby Outer Banks or walk to Maritime Museum, Old Burying
Grounds, shops, and restaurants. Airport transportation is available.
Continental plus breakfast includes fresh fruits and homemade breads
featuring Ms. Ruby's "Riz" biscuits. Restricted smoking. 1/$50-80; 2/$60-
100. MC, V. Travel agent.

Belhaven

River Forest Manor Inn and Marina
600 East Main Street
Belhaven, NC 27810
(919) 943-2151

Type of B&B: Country inn with restaurant.
Rooms: 9 with private bath.
Rates: 1 or 2/$48-75.

Rating: B or ♛♛ Good, exceeds basic requirements.

Historic riverfront mansion built in 1900 is located on the Pungo River
just east of Route 264. There are nine guest rooms throughout the inn and
each has a private bath and selection of Victorian antique furnishings.
The mansion has retained all of its original architectural treasures
including leaded glass doors, Ionic columns, elaborately carved oak
fireplaces, ornate plaster ceilings, leaded and stained-glass, and crystal
chandeliers. Tennis courts, swimming pool, hot tub, and boat marina are
on the premises as well as a restaurant and river room lounge. Guests
who arrive by boat can borrow golf carts equipped to run on regular city

streets. Continental breakfast. Dinner and smorgasbord available in the restaurant. Facilities available for meetings and social functions. 1 or 2/$48-75. MC, V.

Carthage

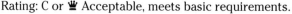

The Blacksmith Inn
703 McReynolds Street, PO Box 1480
Carthage, NC 28327
(800) 284-4515 or (919) 947-1692

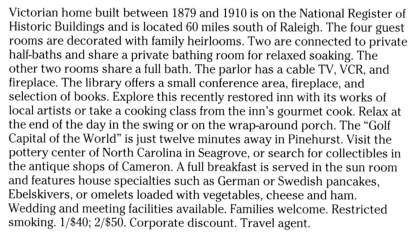

Type of B&B: Inn.
Rooms: 4 with shared baths.
Rates: 1/$40; 2/$50.

Rating: C or ♛ Acceptable, meets basic requirements.

Victorian home built between 1879 and 1910 is on the National Register of Historic Buildings and is located 60 miles south of Raleigh. The four guest rooms are decorated with family heirlooms. Two are connected to private half-baths and share a private bathing room for relaxed soaking. The other two rooms share a full bath. The parlor has a cable TV, VCR, and fireplace. The library offers a small conference area, fireplace, and selection of books. Explore this recently restored inn with its works of local artists or take a cooking class from the inn's gourmet cook. Relax at the end of the day in the swing or on the wrap-around porch. The "Golf Capital of the World" is just twelve minutes away in Pinehurst. Visit the pottery center of North Carolina in Seagrove, or search for collectibles in the antique shops of Cameron. A full breakfast is served in the sun room and features house specialties such as German or Swedish pancakes, Ebelskivers, or omelets loaded with vegetables, cheese and ham. Wedding and meeting facilities available. Families welcome. Restricted smoking. 1/$40; 2/$50. Corporate discount. Travel agent.

Clyde/Asheville

Windsong: A Mountain Inn
120 Ferguson Ridge
Clyde, NC 28721
(704) 627-6111

Type of B&B: Inn.
Rooms: 4 with private bath.
Rates: 1/$81-85; 2/$90-95.

Rating: A+ or ♛♛♛ Excellent, far exceeds basic requirements.

Contemporary log inn situated in a rural mountain setting is 4.5 miles off I-40 exit 24, and 36 miles west of Asheville. Choose from four spacious guest rooms, each with quality furnishings, private bath, Jacuzzi, high beamed ceiling, light pine log walls, Mexican tile floors, and a delightful decor scheme. There is an extensive videocassette library, piano, billiard table, swimming pool, and tennis court for guest's enjoyment. A new two-bedroom guest house built in 1992 offers complete privacy. Hosts raise llamas on the property and offer wilderness llama treks. Among area attractions are Great Smoky Mountain National Park, Appalachian Trail, Cherokee Indian Reservation, Biltmore House, Blue Ridge Parkway, hiking, skiing, and white-water rafting. Full breakfast. Facilities available for small group meetings. No smoking. 1/$81-85; 2/$90-95. MC, V. Travel agent.

Flat Rock

The Woodfield Inn
Box 98
Flat Rock, NC 28731
(704) 693-6016 or (800) 533-6016

Type of B&B: Inn.
Rooms: 20, 12 with private bath.
Rates: 1 or 2/$45-100.

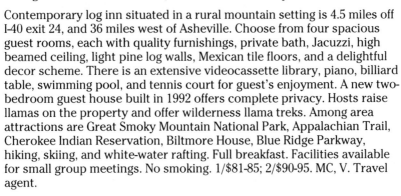

Rating: B- or ♛♛ Good, exceeds basic requirements.

Historic ante-bellum inn situated on twenty-five acres was built in 1850 and has been in continuous operation for 140 years. There are twenty guest rooms available. Each is decorated in the Victorian period with antique furnishings and hand-crafted coverlets. Most rooms offer a private bath and several have fireplaces. There are several common rooms on the property including a wine room, restaurant dining rooms, a parlor filled with antiques and collectibles, and a secret room where Confederate soldiers hid valuables during the Civil War. Area attractions include Flat Rock Playhouse, Carl Sandburg estate, Kenmure golf course, and Flat Rock historic sites. Continental breakfast. Function facilities include the gazebo and pavilion. Families welcome. 1 or 2/$45-100. MC, V. Senior, family, business, and auto club discounts. Travel agent.

Greensboro

Greenwood Bed & Breakfast
205 North Park Drive
Greensboro, NC 27401
(919) 274-6350 or (800) 535-9363

Type of B&B: Inn.
Rooms: 4, 2 with private bath.
Rates: 1/$60-65; 2/$75-90.

Rating: B or ♥♥ Good, exceeds basic requirements.

1911 Stick-style inn situated in the central Greensboro Historic District is surrounded by old oaks and a large park extending from the front yard. There are four guest rooms to choose from. Each has a sitting area and period furnishings and two offer a private bath. Enjoy the warmth from one of the working fireplaces in the foyer or parlor while being welcomed with a complimentary beverage and fresh fruit bowl upon arrival. There's a swimming pool on the grounds. A short drive away are fine restaurants, shopping areas, antique dealers, recreational areas, and historic sites. Visit nearby Revolutionary War Battleground, discount furniture shopping, and five area colleges. Continental plus breakfast features home-made muffins, breads, and fresh fruits. Small wedding facilities. 1/$60-65; 2/$75-90. AE, MC, V. Travel agent.

Guests write: *"This inn will always hold a special place in our hearts. The atmosphere here is warm and inviting. Our hostess made us feel right at home."* (M. Leffew)

"This home is a comfortable and relaxing place to relax when away from home on business. There is a warm setting and excellent service"
(R. Mixon)

Highlands

The Highlands Inn
4th & Main Street
Highlands, NC 28741
(794) 526-5036

Type of B&B: Country Inn with restaurant.
Rooms: 29 with private bath.
Rates: 1 or 2/$79-85.

Rating: A or ♥♥♥ Excellent, far exceeds basic requirements.

Three-story wooden Colonial building on the National Register of Historic Places is located in the heart of a small mountain town 60 miles southeast of Asheville. Choose from twenty-nine guest rooms decorated in either a country or traditional decor. Each has a private bath. Area attractions include auction galleries, antique shops, Highlands Playhouse, tennis courts, swimming pool, horseback riding, Dry Falls, Glenn Falls, and Bridal Veil. Extended continental breakfast features home-made sweet rolls, biscuits, and fresh fruit served in the dining room accented with Southern pottery. The Theater Room is perfect for meetings or special events. Wheelchair access. Restricted smoking. Families welcome. 1 or 2/$79-85. AE, MC, V.

Guests write: *"For the past eight to ten years, during the Spring, Summer, and Fall, we have on many occasions enjoyed the hospitality, accommodations, food, and people at the Highlands Inn and the Old Edwards Inn. Each time we leave, we look forward to our next trip and we have never been disappointed. The natural charm of the place, accented by the care and concern of owners, Rip and Pat Benton and their staff, makes every visit more enjoyable than the last visit."* (E. Baldwin)

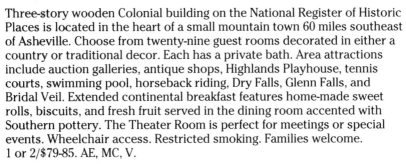

Highlands

The Old Edwards Inn
4th & Main Streets
Highlands, NC 28741
(704) 526-5036

Type of B&B: Country Inn with restaurant.
Rooms: 19 with private bath.
Rates: 1 or 2/$69-85.

Rating: B or ♥♥ Good, exceeds basic requirements.

The Old Edwards Inn, a sister inn to the Highlands Inn across the road, consists of the original 1878 building known as The Central House with a connecting brick building constructed in 1931. Reminiscent of a turn-of-the-century mountain town inn, it is surrounded by hemlocks and gardens and is 60 miles southeast of Asheville. The inn was added to the National Register of Historic Places in 1992 and offers nineteen refurbished rooms with paints, stencils, and wallpapers true to the Victorian/Country home period. Most rooms have a queen-size bed and all offer a private bath. The Moose Room, with its large moose head over the stone fireplace, invites guests to gather, converse, watch TV, or enjoy board games. An extended continental breakfast is served in the dining room of the Highlands Inn across the street and includes fresh fruit, cereal, biscuits, and home-made cinnamon buns. Restricted smoking. 1 or 2/$69-85. AE, MC, V.

Kill Devil Hills

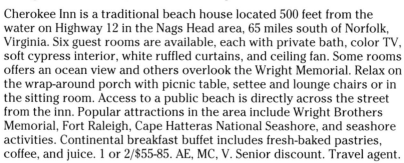

Cherokee Inn Bed & Breakfast
500 North Virginia Dare Trail
Kill Devil Hills, NC 27948
(919) 441-6127 or (800) 554-2764.

Type of B&B: Inn.
Rooms: 6 with private bath.
Rates: 1 or 2/$55-85.

Rating: B or ♛♛ Good, exceeds basic requirements.

Cherokee Inn is a traditional beach house located 500 feet from the water on Highway 12 in the Nags Head area, 65 miles south of Norfolk, Virginia. Six guest rooms are available, each with private bath, color TV, soft cypress interior, white ruffled curtains, and ceiling fan. Some rooms offers an ocean view and others overlook the Wright Memorial. Relax on the wrap-around porch with picnic table, settee and lounge chairs or in the sitting room. Access to a public beach is directly across the street from the inn. Popular attractions in the area include Wright Brothers Memorial, Fort Raleigh, Cape Hatteras National Seashore, and seashore activities. Continental breakfast buffet includes fresh-baked pastries, coffee, and juice. 1 or 2/$55-85. AE, MC, V. Senior discount. Travel agent.

Guests write: *"Lovely home! We've never had room service at a B&B before."* (S. Hallinan)

"This inn is neat, extremely clean and thoroughly enjoyable." (P. Elliott)

"My son felt it was just like Grandma's home." (W. Brooks)

"We had a very enjoyable stay as it was quite comfortable. It was pleasant to wake to the smell of delicious brewing coffee - like being at home."
(L. Kulick)

"The inn was rustic and one block from the ocean so you could smell the sea air. I loved my room - feminine with lots of pillows. The night I arrived there was a storm. The next day I wanted to go for a walk on the beach. They lent me a rain proof jacket and boots which I lived in. I was able to go out and have a great time." (J. Dail)

Nags Head

First Colony Inn
6720 South Virginia Dare Trail
Nags Head, NC 27959
(919) 441-2343 or (800) 368-9390

Type of B&B: Inn.
Rooms: 26 with private bath.
Rates: 1 or 2/$120-200.

Rating: A or ♛♛♛ Excellent, far exceeds basic requirements.

Located 80 miles southeast of Norfolk, Virginia, this shingle-style inn with two-story encircling verandahs is back in operation after an extensive, historic rehabilitation. Each of the twenty-six guest rooms is decorated with traditional furniture and English antiques and features a telephone, individual climate control, refrigerator, and a private bath with heated towel bars and imported toiletries. Some rooms offer Jacuzzis, VCRs, four-poster beds, bars with microwave or kitchenette, and balconies. There is an upstairs library with books, games, fireplace, and a pump organ. Explore the five acres of landscaped grounds, relax by the pool with sun deck, or walk along the boardwalk to the gazebo on the dune which overlooks the beach. Nearby is Cape Hatteras National Seashore, Wright Brothers Memorial, Fort Raleigh, The Lost Colony, and Elizabethan Gardens. Continental breakfast buffet includes specialties such as fruit breads and First Colony juice cordial. Wine, beer, and fruit & cheese baskets available. Small wedding and meeting facilities available. Families welcome. Wheelchair access. Restricted smoking. 1 or 2/$120-200. AE, MC, V. Travel agent.

Guests write: *"The delightfully pleasant library/game room reminded me of a favorite aunt's upstairs sitting room — a nice place to reminisce during the Christmas holidays and tastefully decorated for the occasion too."*
(S. Garner Rodgers)

— Comments continued on next page

"The owner and her staff were willing to go out of their way to make our stay comfortable as well as giving us a feeling of home. Even though we had reservations for one particular room, when possible, we were given a tour of all the other rooms. They are exquisitely decorated with antiques. We especially enjoyed tea and refreshments in the afternoon. The First Colony is located in a perfect setting, convenient to the ocean, to shopping, and yet is a private retreat. The breakfast was more than ample with lovely table settings, fresh fruit, pastries, and lots of coffee. A thoroughly wonderful experience." (M. Hoff)

"What a remarkable place this is! A real aura of history permeates the old building which is a truly superb blend of modern comfort with yesteryear. A rare and wonderful treat." (E. Gwynn)

"Our room was extremely comfortable, large, and airy. I was most grateful for the firm mattress on the bed. There were so many small things which were so pleasant it's hard to name them all. My husband and I would recommend it to the most experienced, worldly traveler without hesitation." (J. Van Egmond)

"The First Colony Inn is the most interesting accommodation I've stayed in from San Francisco to Moscow. My room (#26) was the cleanest I've ever seen. I will send everyone I know to First Colony Inn for 1st class service and comfort." (E. Woodall)

New Bern

Harmony House Inn
215 Pollock Street
New Bern, NC 28560
(919) 636-3810

Type of B&B: Large inn.
Rooms: 9 with private bath.
Rates: 1/$55; 2/$80.

Rating: A or ♛♛♛ Excellent, far exceeds basic requirements.

Historic Greek Revival inn built in 1850 is located two hours north of Wilmington in a town steeped in history. There are nine guest rooms with private bath. Each features antique furnishings and hand-crafted furniture by local artisans. Popular attractions in the area include Tryon Palace, Trent and Neuse Rivers, antique and specialty shops, and museums. Full breakfast includes a hot entree and homemade granola. Families welcome. No smoking. 1/$55; 2/$80. AE, MC, V. Travel agent.

Waynesville

Swag Country Inn
Route 2, Box 280-A
Waynesville, NC 28786
(704) 926-0430

Type of B&B: Country inn with restaurant.
Rooms: 12 with private bath.
Rates: 1/$108-188; 2/$118-198.

Rating: A or ♛♛♛ Excellent, far exceeds basic requirements.

Two-hundred year-old hand-hewn log lodge has a breathtaking setting at 5,000 feet in the mountains and is located 10 miles off I-40, exit 20. Choose from twelve guest rooms with unique decor, antique furnishings, patchwork quilts, local crafts, ceilings fans, and fireplaces. Several common rooms provide quiet havens for reading, conversing with other guests, or enjoying a blazing fire. Popular attractions here are hiking, fishing, bird watching, and games of croquet, badminton, horseshoes, and racquetball. Full breakfast, lunch and dinner are included in the rates. 1/$108-188; 2/$118-198. AE, MC, V. Open Memorial Day through October.

Guests write: *"I'm not sure I would have survived this year without my Swag Fix. As always my stay was absolutely delightful. Their ability to make everyone comfortable and feel completely at ease is to be commended."* (M. Barron)

"Ed and I enjoyed a wonderful long weekend at the Swag. The accommodations were grand and the site breathtaking. The food was delicious and their smiles wrapped it all beautifully." (L. James)

"The inn provided the perfect combination of rest and relaxation that we were both hoping for. They are to be commended for the accommodations, food, and hospitality. I would also like to commend them for the way the family has developed the Swag. As a native of North Carolina mountains and an architect, I have great admiration for someone who can fit a man-made structure into such a powerful landscape as this property." (C. Winstead)

"We were placed in the cabin and it was a delight to have the extra space. Erine had her first horseback ride, saw a deer, chased lots of butterflies and salamanders, walked in the river, and learned a little about birds and plants." (E. Smith)

Wilmington

Catherine's Inn on Orange
410 Orange Street
Wilmington, NC 28401
(800) 476-0723

Type of B&B: Small inn.
Rooms: 3 with private bath.
Rates: 1/$55; 2/$65.

Rating: A- or ♛♛♛ Excellent, far exceeds basic requirements.

Historic home built in 1875 is situated in a quiet residential area of the city. Three spacious guest rooms on the second floor offer a private bath, selected antiques, fireplace, telephone and central air-conditioning. Two common rooms on the main floor offer comfortable seating, antique furnishings, and pleasing decor. A landscaped garden and patio area in the back yard overlook a small water garden. Full breakfast. Function space for small weddings or meetings is available. 1/$55; 2/$65. V. Business travel discount.

Wilson

Miss Betty's Bed & Breakfast Inn
600 West Nash Street
Wilson, NC 27893-3045
(800)258-2069 or (919)243-4447

Type of B&B: Inn.
Rooms: 8 with private bath & suite.
Rates: 1/$50-60; 2/$60-70.

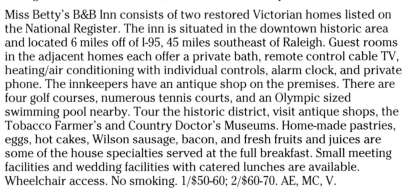

Rating: A- or ♛♛♛ Excellent, far exceeds basic requirements.

Miss Betty's B&B Inn consists of two restored Victorian homes listed on the National Register. The inn is situated in the downtown historic area and located 6 miles off of I-95, 45 miles southeast of Raleigh. Guest rooms in the adjacent homes each offer a private bath, remote control cable TV, heating/air conditioning with individual controls, alarm clock, and private phone. The innkeepers have an antique shop on the premises. There are four golf courses, numerous tennis courts, and an Olympic sized swimming pool nearby. Tour the historic district, visit antique shops, the Tobacco Farmer's and Country Doctor's Museums. Home-made pastries, eggs, hot cakes, Wilson sausage, bacon, and fresh fruits and juices are some of the house specialties served at the full breakfast. Small meeting facilities and wedding facilities with catered lunches are available. Wheelchair access. No smoking. 1/$50-60; 2/$60-70. AE, MC, V.

— *Comments continued on next page*

Guests write: *"I cannot praise Miss Betty's (Betty and Fred) highly enough. It's gorgeous, clean, homey...the hospitality is outstanding and we all (about 10 of us) had a marvelous stay while attending a family wedding."* (D. Tessitore)

NORTH DAKOTA

Luverne/Fargo

Volden Farm B&B
R.R. 2, Box 50
Luverne, ND 58056
(701) 769-2275

Type of B&B: B&B home.
Rooms: 2 rooms share one bath; also a private cottage.
Rate: 1/$40; 2/$50-75.

Rating: A- or ♛ ♛ ♛ Excellent, far exceeds basic requirements.

Wood farmhouse with a Scandinavian atmosphere is located 33 miles northwest of exit 71 off I-94. Choose from two guest rooms which share a private guest bath in the main house or the newly renovated "Law Office" which is a private cottage a few yards from the main house. The rooms have a comfortable country decor and feature a lace-canopy or metal bed. There are several common areas in the house which offer private areas for reading, sitting in front of a fireplace, playing a game of pool, or conversing with other guests. The farm has several acres inviting exploration and a small playhouse and swing set are available to delight children. Full breakfast specialties include Swedish pancakes or Danish Aebleskiver with fresh farm produce. Families welcome. No smoking. 1/$40; 2/$50-75.

Guests write: *"Joanne's attention to detail was great. She thought of everything (even a light over the bathtub to read by). I travel a great deal and this is one of the nicest places I have stayed in."* (M. Scholz)

OHIO

Additional information on B&Bs in this state is available from Private Lodgings (216) 321-3213.

OKLAHOMA

Additional information on B&Bs in this is available from Ozark Mountain Country B&B (800) 695-1546.

OREGON

Ashland

Mt. Ashland Inn
550 Mt. Ashland Road
Ashland, OR 97520
(503) 482-8707

Type of B&B: Inn.
Rooms: 5 with private bath.
Rate: 1/$75-120; 2/$80-125

Rating: A or ♥♥♥ Excellent, far exceeds basic requirements.

Hand-crafted of cedar logs cut on the surrounding property, the secluded Mt. Ashland Inn offers spectacular views of rock cliffs, forests, and mountain ranges. The inn is located 16 miles south of Ashland and six miles west of I-5, exit 6. Five guest rooms, each with private bath, take advantage of the views and feature individual temperature controls, hand-made quilts, and Northwest-style furniture. The living room on the main floor has a welcoming stone fireplace and over-stuffed furniture. Year-round recreation nearby includes hiking, skiing, white-water rafting, and biking. Area attractions include Oregon Shakespeare Festival, Britt Music Festival, and Rogue Valley sites. Hearty full breakfast includes home-baked breads and entrees. Complimentary beverages are served by the fire or on the deck each evening. No smoking. 1/$75-120; 2/$80-125. MC, V. Travel agent.

Guests write: *"What you can't imagine, you must see for yourself, are the special saddle-notchings in the corners, the chamfered beams that extend through the exterior wall, the log arches, magnificent stone fireplace. Impressive, too, are the handsome madrone and black oak headboards, the hand-carved mountain scenes on each guest room door, and decorative deck railing. Beautiful antiques and Oriental rugs add a richness to this quietly elegant inn. Each bedroom is a work of art with colorful handmade quilts and matching curtains."* (N. Bringhurst)

"We love the mountains around and all the beautiful hand-craftsmanship of Jerry and Elaine. The breakfasts are always wonderful and although we have stayed at the inn more than twenty times, they are always new! The location of the inn is spectacular - unbelievable views and crisp mountain air all around. A great place for meditation, reading, and getting away from the swarm of city life." (J. Bent)

Cloverdale

Sandlake Country Inn
8505 Galloway Road
Cloverdale, OR 97112
(503) 965-6745

Type of B&B: Inn.
Rooms: 3 with private bath & cottage.
Rates: 1/$60-95; 2/$65-100.

Rating: A- or ♛♛♛ Excellent, far exceeds basic requirements.

Two-story farmhouse built in 1894 is nestled on 2.5 acres just off the Three Capes Scenic Loop, 16 miles south of Tillamook. Three guest rooms in the main house offer fresh flowers, antique furnishings, and collectibles. A Honeymoon suite with four rooms on the second floor features a deck overlooking the garden, private dining room with refrigerator and claw-foot tub. The small, modest looking cottage is a treasure inside with a private bedroom, luxury bath with whirlpool tub for two, living room with black marble fireplace, and full kitchen. Popular attractions in the area include Netarts Bay, Cape Lookout State Park, Tillamook cheese factory, and beaches. Full breakfast with home-baked goods. Special gourmet picnic baskets are available at an additional cost for those arriving late at night, or for day trips in the area. No smoking. The Timbers cabin is wheelchair accessible. 1/$60-95; 2/$65-100. MC, V. Travel agent.

Guests write: *"The inn is nestled along the Oregon coast in a very secluded and wooded area. We could walk in the woods or traipse across an open meadow. We had the entire 2nd floor of this beautiful farmhouse to ourselves and enjoyed being pampered. Best of all were the breakfasts! There were so many things to do and see — all within 15-20 minutes from the inn."* (B. Earl)

"We were given a warm welcome and tour of the home... the Jacuzzi, outdoor lawns and swing, books, magazines, TV, VCR, radio, tape player,

and our living quarters. The tour was complete but short. Then we were promised privacy and we were given it!" Everything I ate intrigued my taste buds." (S. Fleischmann)

"We have stayed at the inn twice, each time in a different room. They were both exquisitely decorated in a very romantic style." (D. Pettijohn)

"Sandlake Country Inn is a peaceful retreat. My husband always said he would never set foot in a B&B but he took us back four times last year. The privacy, personal attention, and food have made it a place we will return to at least once a year." (E. Doyle)

"It's the last morning of our stay at Sandlake. I've lit a fire and am curled up on the sofa reflecting on the past few days. This has been a special time for us because it is the beginning time for dreaming, setting goals, and time for us alone. I don't think we could have found a more perfect place to do that and more." (J. Marcotte)

"From the moment we arrived and saw the heart cookie inscribed with our names and "eleven" for our 11th anniversary, we knew we chose the right place to celebrate. The beautiful room, the relaxing tub, the quilt, and luscious breakfasts all combined to create a perfect weekend." (J. Edbert)

"Last summer my husband and I made a tour of the B&Bs on the Oregon coast, only to discover that our initial judgment had been correct. The Sandlake Country Inn is by far the best. It is secluded, yet within easy driving distance of many points of interest and forms of entertainment. But the innkeeper, a superb hostess, and her gourmet breakfasts, are what keep us going back for more." (D. Grier)

"To be doted on and pampered like that yet still have privacy was wonderful! It was so quiet and restful there my husband and I could really focus on the specialness of our marriage relationship." (K. Hopfer)

Depoe Bay

Channel House Bed & Breakfast Inn
35 Ellingson Street, P.O. Box 56
Depoe Bay, OR 97341
(503) 765-2140 or (800) 447-2140

Type of B&B: Inn.
Rooms: 12 with private bath.
Rates: 1 or 2/$55-200.

Rating: A or ♛♛♛ Excellent, far exceeds basic requirements.

Oceanfront inn built high on the rocky shore of the rugged Oregon coastline is one block west of the south end of the Depoe Bay bridge. There are twelve guest rooms or suites, each with private bath. Special features of the deluxe rooms include private balcony, whirlpool baths, and ocean views. Walk to the town's center that has a good selection of seaside shops and restaurants. Area attractions include the beach, whale watching, and charter fishing. A full breakfast with pancakes, waffles, or omelets is served in the nautical dining room or in the guest room. No smoking. 1 or 2/$55-200. MC, V. Travel agent.

Guests write: *"There was genuinely warm and friendly hospitality here, lovely food presentation, comfortable beds, and clean accommodations. Loved the soothing sound of the surf and sea. Incomparable setting and the binoculars in the room was a nice touch."* (P. Lovell)

"The whirlpool was great and a unique experience for us to be right on the water." (K. Delich)

"When we take time to get-a-way we feel fortunate to know that we are treated so comfortably and welcome at Channel House. It is a good jumping-off place. Stay as long as you can!" (O. Wenzloff)

Seaside

Gilbert Inn Bed & Breakfast
341 Beach Drive
Seaside, OR 97138
(503) 738-9770

Type of B&B: Inn
Rooms: 10 with private bath.
Rates: 1or 2/$65-90

Rating: A- or ♥♥♥ Excellent, far exceeds basic requirements.

Gilbert Inn is an 1892 Victorian structure situated one block from the Oregon coast forty miles west of Portland. The inn offers ten guest rooms, each with private bath, queen-size bed, and a selection of wicker or antique furnishings. The main floor has a spacious fireplaced parlor and two pleasant breakfast rooms. The house features natural fir tongue and groove ceilings and walls and has been restored to look much like it did in 1892 except with modern comforts. The inn is within walking distance to the beach, promenade, shops, and restaurants in this small resort town. Full breakfast specialties of the house include French toast and home-made muffins. Families welcome. No smoking. Resident cat. 1or 2/$65-90. MC, V. Travel agent.

Additional information on B&Bs in this state is available from the following:
B&B Connections (800) 448-3619
B&B of Philadelphia (800) 220-1917
Hershey B&B Reservation Service (717) 533-2928
Rest & Repast B&B Reservation Service (814) 238-1484

Allentown

Coachaus
107-111 North Eighth Street
Allentown, PA 18101
(215) 821-4854 or (800) 762-8680.

Type of B&B: Large urban inn.
Rooms: 24 with private bath.
Rates: 1/$68-125; 2/$78-135.

Rating: A- or ♛ ♛ ♛ Excellent, far exceeds basic requirements.

Victorian European-style urban hotel has been restored and is located in downtown Allentown, 1.5 miles south of US-22 and 3.5 miles from I-78. There are twenty-four guest rooms that vary in size, decor, and amenities including rooms, apartments, and townhouses. Each has a private bath, cable TV, telephone, and air conditioning. Walk to fine dining, boutiques, antique shops, Old Allentown Historic District, and the Liberty Bell Shrine from the inn. Recreation nearby includes Dorney Amusement Park, skiing, hiking, white-water rafting, and biking. Full breakfast and evening refreshments offered daily. Families welcome. 1/$68-125; 2/$78-135. AE, Discover, MC, V. Family, weekly, and monthly rates available. Travel agent.

Allentown/Fogelsville

Glasbern
R.D. 1, Box 250
Fogelsville, PA 18051
(215) 285-4723

Type of B&B: Inn with restaurant.
Rooms: 23 with private bath.
Rates: 1/$80-100; 2/$95-225.

Rating: AA or ♛ ♛ ♛ ♛ Outstanding.

This original 1800's Pennsylvania barn has been refurbished into an inn with exposed timber, cathedral ceilings, and many windows. It is situated on one-hundred acres near Allentown, 2 miles northwest of the intersection of Routes I-78 and 100. Choose from twenty-three guest rooms with a mix of contemporary and antique furnishings, private bath, phone, TV, VCR and radio. Sixteen rooms have whirlpool baths, several also have a fireplace or wood-burning stove. Popular activities in the area include bicycling, parks, wildlife sanctuaries, wineries, antique markets, and covered bridge tours. Tennis, fishing, hiking, and skiing are nearby. Full breakfast. Country French dining is available in the restaurant Tuesday through Saturday. Facilities available for meetings and social functions. Wheelchair access. 1/$80-100; 2/$95-225. AE, MC, V.

Guests write: *"Glasbern has a very enjoyable and relaxed atmosphere, the food is excellent, and hospitality superb. We had our small wedding in front of the fireplace in November 1991 and dinner afterwards. The day could not have been more beautiful."* (A. Xander)

"We thoroughly enjoyed our stay at Glasbern. The service was excellent, atmosphere and decor of the rooms and lodge was outstanding. It was just what we needed after having a baby three months before." (D. Butler)

"They made our 34th Anniversary so special! Everything is already excellent and no improvement is necessary." (C. Kampmeyer)

Allentown/Emmaus

Leibert Gap Manor Bed & Breakfast
4502 South Mountain Drive
Emmaus, PA 18049-623
(800) 964-1242 or (215) 967-1242

Type of B&B: Inn.
Rooms: 4 with private bath.
Rates: 1/$75-115; 2/$85-125.

Rating: A+ or ♛♛♛ Excellent, far exceeds basic requirements.

Nestled on 15 acres in South Mountain near the cities of Allentown and Bethlehem, this 1980s Williamsburg-style manor is comprised of Mt. Vernon brick combined with a log cabin. It is hidden in the deep forest just minutes away from downtown Emmaus. Two upper level guest rooms decorated with canopy beds and antiques feature a widows walk with panoramic views of the Lehigh Valley. The two main level guest rooms are decorated with colonial furnishings. All rooms offer a private bath. Throughout the house, random width board floors and Oriental rugs are accented with antiques and collectibles. The solarium provides guests with space in which to read, have tea, and bird watch. Sit in front of the fireplace in the keeping room, play pool in the game room on the 19th Century pool table, explore the groomed hiking trails, or borrow a bike from the innkeepers. The inn is just minutes away from public swimming, tennis courts, and two golf courses. A wide variety of area attractions include the Allentown Fair, historic Bethlehem, cultural events, the Musicfest, Celtic Classic, art centers, museums, antique shopping, restaurants, and many sports activities. Full breakfast includes baked goods, fresh fruit plates, and a specialty entree. Small wedding and meeting facilities available. No smoking. 1/$75-115; 2/$85-125. MC, V. 10% senior, corporate, and auto club discounts. Travel agent.

Guests write: *"We celebrated our 10th Anniversary in the peaceful, secluded home of Pauline & Wayne Sheffer. We appreciated the care they took in preparing our breakfasts, including a special place setting on the morning of our Anniversary. The Early American beds and furniture added to the charm of our room."* (G. Farnham)

"We had a thoroughly enjoyable two night stay at Leibert Gap Inn. Our accommodations were beautiful and immaculate and our breakfasts were fantastic. We were happily impressed with the hospitality of our hosts and greatly appreciated their knowledge of the area." (B. Stellwagon)

"Our two night stay was delightful. We were treated like royalty in a spotless, comfortable and spacious inn. Our hosts were especially helpful in giving us directions and pointing out local events of special interest. Breakfasts were pleasurable experiences and not only delicious but attractive. Bird-watching and hiking were added attractions." (D. Dice)

"Great food - great place - great couple! They treated us like family — even better. Pressed and creased pillowcases were very impressive. Pauline even gave me her recipe for the apple butter she served." (B. Diana)

"Very clean, personable host and hostess. Outstanding breakfast and comfortable and attractive room." (R. Meyer)

Allentown/Bethlehem

Wydnor Hall
Old Philadelphia Pike
Bethlehem, PA 18015
(215) 867-6851

Type of B&B: Inn.
Rooms: 4, 2 with private bath.
Rates: 1/$85-95; 2/$95-105.

Rating: A or ♥♥♥ Excellent, far exceeds basic requirements.

Restored late-Georgian Manor house is located three miles south of Bethlehem on the historic Old Philadelphia Pike. Each of the four guest rooms has been furnished in the style of an English Country home with antiques and beautiful quilts. Two of the rooms offer a private bath.

Afternoon tea is served in an elegant and comfortable sitting room. Area attractions include historic sites in Bethlehem, Lehigh, Moravian, and Lafayette Colleges, Bach Festival Musikfest, and Celtic Classic. Full breakfast offers a choice from a varied menu. A morning coffee tray is delivered to guest rooms and afternoon tea is served daily. Restricted smoking. 1/$85-95; 2/$95-105. AE. Business travel discount. Travel agent.

Guests write: *"Our weekend stay at Wydnor Hall was similar to being the guest at a very grand and well-staffed home. The quality of the surroundings, the service, and the food was superb. From the coffee tray in the morning with newspaper, through the superb breakfast and afternoon tea (and wine), the comfort of the service and surroundings is on a par with a fine European hotel."* (P. Kuyper)

Bedford/Schellsburg

Bedford's Covered Bridge Inn
RD 1, Box 196
Schellsburg, PA 15559
(814) 733-4093

Type of B&B: Inn.
Rooms: 6 with private bath.
Rates: 1/$45-65; 2/$55-75.

Rating: B+ or ♥♥ Good, exceeds basic requirements.

Historic Victorian farmhouse near a trout stream and covered bridge is midway between Pittsburgh and Harrisburg near exit 11 off Route 76. Choose from six guest room with private bath, traditional as well as country decor, and views of the inn's grounds. Relax in the common room with fireplace and well-stocked library or explore the surrounding grounds with nearby streams. A restored smoke house next to the inn affords guests a place to warm up and chat by the fire after a day on the slopes at nearby Blue Knob Resort. Bike along scenic country roads, hike or cross country ski along miles of trails on the premises or the nearby 4,000 acre Shawnee State Park. It's a short walk to Schellsburg's antique shops and galleries. Discover the county's fourteen covered bridges and take a walking tour of Bedford's Historic District. A full breakfast might feature a garden frittata, eggs Benedict, or stuffed French toast. No smoking. 1/$45-65; 2/$55-75. AE, MC, V. Travel agent.

Guests write: *"The accommodations couldn't have been nicer."* (C. Beja)

"Bedford's Covered Bridge Inn is a home away from home." (C. Bradshaw)

Bethlehem/Easton

Lafayette Inn
525 West Monroe Street
Easton, PA 18042
(215) 253-4500

Type of B&B: Inn.
Rooms: 18 with private bath.
Rates: 1/$80-100; 2/$90-110.

Rating: A or ♛♛♛ Excellent, far exceeds basic requirements.

Historic Victorian inn nestled in the Lehigh Valley is situated two blocks from Lafayette College in a town that is located ninety minutes from New York City, Philadelphia, or the Pocono Mountains. There are eighteen guest rooms with private bath, custom decor, remote TV, and climate control system. Several rooms have kitchenettes. Nearby attractions include historic Easton, Bethlehem, New Hope, Bucks County, and Delaware River water sports such as canoeing and rafting. Continental breakfast includes homemade breads and muffins. Catered luncheons, dinner, and full breakfast are available at an additional cost. A catering service and function rooms are available for meetings, dinner parties, and social occasions. Families welcome. Restricted smoking. 1/$80-100; 2/$90-110. AE, MC, V. 10% senior and business discount.

Guests write: *"Upon entering, strong antiques and soft colors set the tone of the environment for total comfort and elegance. What a winning combination! Perhaps most importantly, I can honestly say that I've never slept better thanks to the quality of the mattresses. The rating I would give them is heavenly. The continental breakfast was most elaborate. We sampled an assortment of homemade breads, English muffins, and Chambard jellies."* (M. Rizzotto)

"We've stayed in cold, impersonal hotels, cutsie B&B's, and a lot in-between. May I tell you what they've done is a miracle. They've managed to blend efficiency, great taste, and fine manners in just the right amounts." (S. Miller)

"Having George Burns as a guest at this inn was the highlight of our stay. What a great flip-flop of clientele the Lafayette Inn boasts - all the celebrities at the State Theatre sharing the beautiful inn with all us stuffy corporate guys! They have the feel of a modern hotel - fax, copies, catering - yet such Old World charm." (R. Gilmore)

Bethlelem/Kintnersville

Lightfarm
2042 Berger Road
Kintnersville, PA 18930
(215) 847-3276 or (215) 847-2926

Type of B&B: Inn.
Rooms: 3 with private bath.
Rates: 1/$75-85; 2/$85-95.

Rating: A or ♛ ♛ ♛ Excellent, far exceeds basic requirements.

Georgian Federal with Greek Revival influences is fifty miles north of Philadelphia on a rural road between Bethlehem and New Hope. Choose from three guest rooms with private bath that have been decorated with period furnishings to honor the 18th-Century founding family of the Lightfarm. Explore the 92-acre working farm with sheep, flowers, and rich history. Enjoy afternoon tea, take a nature walk, or help with the farm chores. On-location archaeological site offers opportunities for learning about early days of American farm life. Visit Nockamixon State Park, Delaware River Country, and many antiques stores nearby. Pennsylvania Dutch full breakfast is served in the enclosed porch or formal dining room. Outdoor wedding facilities available. Families welcome. No smoking. 1/$75-85; 2/$85-95. MC, V. Extended stay, senior, and corporate discounts. Travel agent.

Guests write: *"We could not have had a more wonderful weekend. I think they've turned our city children into country kids!"* (M. Rosenthal)

"I will hold in my heart, a warm friendly home, a beautiful walk in the valley, and laying in bed watching the sheep." (A. Major)

"We so much enjoyed our stay and the warm hospitality shown to us and to the children. Lovely home!" (L. Sweeney)

Brackney

Indian Mountain Inn B&B
R.R. Box 68
Brackney, PA 18812
(800) 435-3362 or (717) 663-2844

Type of B&B: Country inn with restaurant
Rooms: 10, 8 with private bath.
Rates: 1/$65; 2/$75.

Rating: B- or ♛♛ Good, exceeds basic requirements.

Rustic lodge built in the late 1800s has been in operation for more than 75 years and is 12.5 miles south of Binghamton, New York. Eight of the ten guest rooms offer a private bath and several have queen-size beds. Sit in front of a wood stove in the dining or sitting room or relax in the whirlpool spa. The outdoor deck offers views of the surrounding countryside as well as deer and wild turkey. Five miles of groomed trails offer hiking, cross-country skiing, and mountain biking. Area attractions include several golf courses, fishing at the nearby trout-stocked Quaker Lake, and cultural sites in Binghamton. Quiche, crepes, and other gourmet items are some of the specialties offered at full breakfast. Wedding and meeting facilities are accommodated in the restaurant dining area. Families welcome. Wheelchair access. No smoking. 1/$65; 2/$75. MC, V. Travel agent.

Cook Forest

Clarion River Lodge
River Road
Cook Forest, PA 16217
(800) 648-6743
Fax: (814) 744-8553.

Type of B&B: Country inn.
Rooms: 20 with private bath.
Rates: 1 or 2/$72-109.

Rating: B+ or ♛♛ Good, exceeds basic requirements.

Contemporary inn constructed of stone and timber is a naturally secluded retreat 15 miles north of exit 13 off of I-80. Twenty guest rooms are available which offer private bath, TV, air-conditioning, and refrigerator. Relax in front of the massive eight-foot fireplace and take in the rustic beauty of the inn's cherry and butternut paneling, log beams, cathedral ceilings, and native stone architecture. Nearby recreational activities include snowmobiling, canoeing, horseback riding, hiking, and inner-tubing. Continental breakfast. Meeting and banquet facilities available. Full service restaurant on premises. No smoking. 1 or 2/$72-109. AE, MC, V. 10% senior and auto club discounts. Travel agent.

Eagles Mere

Eagles Mere Inn
Mary & Sullivan Avenues
Eagles Mere, PA 17731
(717) 525-3273

Type of B&B: Country inn with restaurant.
Rooms: 15 with private bath.
Rates: 1/$85-125; 2/$125-195.

Rating: B or ♛♛ Good, exceeds basic requirements.

Inn built high on Eagles Mere in the "Endless Mountains" of Northeastern Pennsylvania is 45 miles northwest of Wilkes Barre in a small, old-fashioned Victorian resort. Guests are accommodated in the 1878 Victorian inn and Garden House that offer a total of fifteen guest rooms with private bath. Stroll along the path of the mile-long Eagles Mere Lake, take a toboggan ride down the ice slide, explore the nearby forests, or go cross country skiing on the local trails. Four-season activities in the area include nature hikes on well marked trails, swimming and boating on private lake and beach, antiquing at shops and auction houses, and skiing, skating, and sleighing around the lake. Full breakfast specialties include French toast with raspberry brandy sauce or real maple syrup. Wedding and meeting facilities available. Families welcome. Restricted smoking. 1/$85-125; 2/$125-195. Rates include breakfast and gourmet dinner. MC, V. Travel agent.

Guests write: *"I commend them both on their hospitality. The food was impeccable and they were so friendly, charming, and helpful during our stay. We had not been recommended to them and just took a chance seeing there was an inn near the toboggan run. We truly had a much needed relaxing, yet elegant and casual weekend. It really met our needs."* (L. Mease)

"All the little things they did to help us with our daughter made it pleasant for us. It was such a nice feeling to come down and have the highchair and toys already set for us at the table. We enjoyed the warmth we felt there." (D. Shawson)

"We will always remember our 41st Anniversary as extra special. The warm hospitality, wonderful food, and the charming decor of our room and the entire inn more than lived up to our expectations." (M. Jereb)

— *Comments continued on next page*

"I'm not a great one for letter writing these days, but I had to let you know how much we enjoyed our stay. The town was charming, low-key, and relaxing in a way some of us really need! But to find the warm hospitality and creative dining makes the community perfectly complete. We hope to be back in winter for a sled run across the lake in winter." (E. Miller)

Eagles Mere

Shady Lane Bed & Breakfast
Allegheny Avenue, P.O. Box 314
Eagles Mere, PA 17731
(717) 525-3394

Type of B&B: Inn.
Rooms: 8 with private bath.
Rates: 1/$55; 2/$65.

Rating: B or ♛♛ Good, exceeds basic requirements.

Country-style rancher is now an inn with mountain-top views located in a quiet Victorian town forty miles northeast of Williamsport. Each of the eight guest rooms has its own temperature control and private bath. Share wine or tea in the afternoon with other guests or explore the Laurel Path which surrounds the nearby Eagles Mere Lake. The "Gas Light era" Eagles Mere Village offers quaint shopping. The inn is close to hiking, swimming, fishing, skiing, and tobogganing facilities. Special events abound such as Fine Art Exhibit and Sale, Flower Show, arts and crafts shows, Sullivan County Fair, PA Bowhunters Festival, and the Flaming Foliage Festival. Full country breakfast may include apple French toast or custard coffee cake. Wheelchair access. Restricted smoking. Murder Mystery Weekends. 1/$55; 2/$65. Senior and auto club discount. Travel agent.

Guests write: *" It's easy to see why Shady Lane B&B has been visited by so many people. Instantly Dennis and Pat are there to make you feel welcome. The view from the living/dining room areas is nothing short of breathtaking. As you look out over the Endless Mountains, you soon realize how tranquil Shady Lane is. It reminded us of a visit to a favorite relative or friend."* (S. Etchberger)

"My husband and I took our grown children and their mates to Shady Lane for the weekend. All ten of us thoroughly enjoyed the weekend and the hospitality of Dennis and Pat. Our room and bath were not only clean and attractive, but we had a wonderful view of the mountain ranges from our bedroom window." (J. Pownall)

"The facilities are excellent, clean, and well-maintained. Eagles Mere is a delightful, quiet resort. The lake is lovely. The people are friendly and just

plain nice. In the late afternoon, Dennis puts out wine and cheese. Fresh fruit is always available as are coffee, tea, and ice water. Breakfasts are great. Dennis is a good cook and is most agreeable to special needs and tastes. The best thing about Shady Lane is Pat and Dennis. They make you feel at home and are just perfect hosts." (S. Simpson)

Gettysburg

Baladerry Inn
40 Hospital Road
Gettysburg, PA 17325
(717) 337-1342

Type of B&B: Inn.
Rooms: 5 with private bath.
Rates: 1 or 2/$55-95.

Rating: A or ♛♛♛ Excellent, far exceeds basic requirements.

1812 Federal-style red brick home in a country setting once served as a hospital in the Civil War. The inn was renovated with an addition in 1977 and again in 1992, and is located 50 miles northwest of Baltimore, Maryland and 60 miles northwest of Washington, DC. Five guest rooms feature newly tiled private baths, queen or twin beds, and traditional furnishings. Read, chat, and relax in the great room with massive fireplace, sitting area, game/library area, and three sets of French doors that open onto a brick terrace. Relax on the terrace overlooking the surrounding four acres or escape to the calm of the gazebo. Play tennis on the inn's court or go biking. Visit nearby Gettysburg National Military Park, Eisenhower Farm, National Riding Stable, National Apple Museum and fruit orchards, and Ski Liberty. Enjoy the area's many restaurants, antique shops, wineries, colleges, and four golf courses. Full breakfast might include poached eggs or pancakes served with bacon or sausage and accented with a fresh fruit plate. Restricted smoking. 1 or 2/$55-95. MC, V. 10% senior, corporate, and auto club discount. Travel agent.

Gettysburg

Dobbin House Tavern Gettystown Inn
89 Steinwehr Avenue
Gettysburg, PA 17325
(717) 334-2100

Type of B&B: Country inn with restaurant.
Rooms: 5 with private bath.
Rates: 1 or 2/$75-95.

Rating: B or ♛♛ Good, exceeds basic requirements.

Civil War era home with restaurant is found on Business Route 15 south of
Gettysburg and overlooks the site where Lincoln recited the Gettysburg
Address. Each of the five guest rooms has individual decor, private bath,
period antiques, and refrigerator. The common room has a large videotape
collection of reenactments of the Battle of Gettysburg. Within walking
distance of the inn is the National Cemetery, National Park Service Visitor's
Center, Gettysburg Battlefield, tours of a secret "underground railroad,"
and museums. Full country breakfast includes home-baked breads.
Colonial American cuisine is available in the restaurant and tavern. Large
function rooms are available for meetings and weddings. 1 or 2/$75-95. AE,
MC, V. 10% senior or business travel discounts. Travel agent.

Guests write: *"The dining room was unique. It was filled with romantic
tables with a dinner-in-bed effect complete with the four-posters dressed with
hand-knitted canopies. After dinner, we returned to a room that was
romantic, warm, and full of old country charm. There were lace doilies,
silver brushes, an antique writing desk and bureau, and small, special soaps
and creams in the bathroom. Finally, breakfast was scrumptious! Fresh fruit
and juice, muffins and breads, bacon, homemade waffles and cheese-filled
omelets."* (K. De Lorenzo)

Gettysburg

The Tannery Bed & Breakfast
449 Baltimore Street
Gettysburg, PA 17325
(717) 334-2454

Type of B&B: Inn.
Rooms: 5 with private bath.
Rates: 1/$50; 2/$65-85.

Rating: B+ or ♛♛ Good, exceeds basic requirements.

Historic Gothic inn rich with Civil War history is located four blocks
south of the center of town. Five large guest rooms each feature a private
bath and traditional furnishings. A large activity room offers games and a

collection of books on the Civil War. Afternoon refreshments are often served on the spacious front porch. The Gettysburg tour buses are headquartered one block from the inn and well-known landmarks are within walking distance as well as shops and restaurants. Continental breakfast. Restricted smoking. 1/$50; 2/$65-85. MC, V.

Harrisburg/New Cumberland

Farm Fortune
204 Limekiln Road
New Cumberland, PA 17070
(717) 774-2683

Type of B&B: Inn.
Rooms: 4, 2 with private bath.
Rates: 1/$47-56; 2/$55-64.

Rating: A or ♛♛♛ Excellent, far exceeds basic requirements.

Limestone farmhouse built in the 1700's is situated on a hill overlooking the Yellow Breeches Creek just off Route 83 at exit 18-A. Each of the four guest rooms offer a double or twin beds, antique furnishings, and comfortable seating with good lighting. Two rooms offer a private bath and large porch area. Popular activities here are trout fishing on the property, sitting on the porch or terrace, and bird watching while enjoying the scenic view. An antique shop called the "Honeycomb Shop" is on the premises. Area attractions include historic homes, museums, antique shops, ski areas, and hiking. Hershey, York, and Lancaster County are a short drive away. Full breakfast. Function rooms are available for small meetings and weddings. Resident cat and dog. 1/$47-56; 2/$55-64. AE, Diners, Discover, MC, V. Travel agent.

Guests write: *"I discovered Farm Fortune B&B quite by accident while on a business trip. Since then I have become one of the many regulars who view the Farm Fortune and Chad and Phyllis Combs as extended family. I have had the pleasure of staying in every bedroom of the inn and each one is quite unique although the room with the private bath and balcony with rocking chairs and porch swing is my favorite. Phyllis prepares an excellent breakfast that is as pleasing to the eyes as it is to the taste buds and is always served on some of the Combs collectible dinnerware. While the house and the antiques are worth the trip, the best part of Farm Fortune is Chad and Phyllis and their hospitality. Farm Fortune has become a home away from home for me and many others."* (R. Rice)

"Our room was cheerful and pleasing to the eye. Very relaxing with a lovely view. Bathrooms was bright and clean! The food was luscious and presented

beautifully. Everything served looked like a picture. The family dog was as friendly and welcoming as the lambs. It was a fantastic weekend that we'll remember for many years to come." (C. Carson)

Harrisburg/Elizabethville

Inn at Elizabethville
30 West Main Street
Elizabethville, PA 17023
(717) 362-3476

Type of B&B: Inn.
Rooms: 7 with private bath.
Rates: 1/$55; 2/$60.

Rating: B or ♛♛ Good, exceeds basic requirements.

Small Victorian inn located in the heart of the state is one block west of the intersection of Routes 225 and 209. Built in 1883, the inn offers seven guest rooms with private bath and is decorated in Mission Oak and Arts & Crafts styles. Guests are welcome to use the dining, living, and conference rooms, as well as the kitchen, porch, and sun parlor. Area attractions include the Millersburg Ferry, an 18-hole golf course, Appalachian Trail hiking, hunting, fishing, and country auctions. Continental breakfast features cereals, juices, English muffins, coffee, and tea. Small meeting facilities available. Families welcome. No smoking. 1/$55; 2/$60. Business travel and long-term discounts available. MC, V. Travel agent.

Hershey

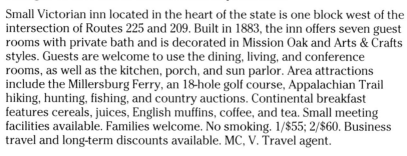

Pinehurst Inn B&B
50 Northeast Drive
Hershey, PA 17033
(717) 533-2603 or
(800) 743-9140

Type of B&B: Inn.
Rooms: 14, 1 with private bath.
Rates: 1 or 2/$45-54

Rating: C+ or ♛ Acceptable, meets basic requirements.

Historic brick inn on the north side of Hershey is located on Route 743, 6 miles south of I-81. There are fourteen air-conditioned guest rooms. The size, decor, and amenities of each room differs but one room offers a private bath. A nature and fitness trail is near the inn for workouts. Popular attractions in the area include nearby Hershey Park and

Museum, Rose Garden, Chocolate World, sports arena and stadium, theater, and outdoor recreation. Full breakfast features an egg dish or pancakes and hot, fresh muffins. Resident cat. Families welcome. Wheelchair access. No smoking. 1 or 2/$45-54. MC, V.

Kennett Square

Scarlett House
503 West State Street
Kennett Square, PA 19348
(215) 444-9592

Type of B&B: Small inn.
Rooms: 4, 2 with private bath.
Rates: 1 or 2/$65-75; Suite/$90.

Rating: A or ♛♛♛ Excellent, far exceeds basic requirements.

American Foursquare Victorian home has been completely restored and is located in the heart of Chester County off Route 1 South. There are four guest rooms with authentic period decor and furnishings; two offer a private bath. Two parlors on the main floor offer several comfortable nooks for fireside reading and conversing. Area attractions include Longwood Gardens, Brandywine River Museum, Chadds Ford Winery, Hagley Museum, Brandywine Battlefield, and Chadds Ford. The Brandywine River area offers canoeing, tubing, biking, hiking, and hot air ballooning. Shoppers come from all around to visit the antique and outlet shops in the area. Continental breakfast includes home-baked breads, scones, muffins, and fresh squeezed juice. Small function rooms available. No smoking. 1 or 2/$65-75; Suite/$90. Business travel discount.

Guests write: *"This was our 2nd visit to the Scarlett House. The room was very comfortable and nicely appointed and in keeping with the Victorian architecture. The breakfasts were plentiful, varied, and tasty. They've been successful at providing low fat, low cholesterol, high fiber food that is filling and enjoyable. The highlight of the visit was four hours of 'porching' — kicking back with a drink on the shaded front porch. Just relaxing, reading, and visiting with our friends."* (D. VanMetre)

"Breakfast was more than ample with some wonderful unique choices like a raisin bread pudding, a Waldorf salad, three or four different kinds of breads and muffins. If this wasn't enough, you had the old standby cereal only this time it was home-made granola along with fruit and yogurt. A wonderful get-away weekend." (F. Stern)

"This is a very comfortable B&B. The rooms are excellent with comfortable beds and modern baths. The hostess goes out of her way to be sure guests

needs are met and is helpful in recommendations and making reservations at local restaurants. Food is top rate. Breakfast offers refreshing varieties not the usual bacon and eggs and is prepared with health consciousness in mind. The location is very convenient to many local attractions." (R.T. Norman)

"Scarlett House was the perfect B&B to celebrate our 5th Anniversary. The room was beautifully done in Victorian elegance. After a great dinner we returned to find champagne in our room and flowers on the bed." (S. Ridyard)

"Immaculately clean. Stunningly decorated with antiques. Comfortable quilted and beautifully dressed beds. Good books to read. Thoughtful and caring hostess and host who had extensive information about the area in scrapbooks. Couldn't ask for more. This is from someone who has made visiting B&Bs a habit for ten years." (S. Hadley)

"The Scarlett House B&B was immaculate, tidy, in excellent condition, and we were greeted with a nice welcome. Tea was served as well as soft drinks in the evening. We then had a delightful full breakfast. It was a memorable good time." (E. Kennett)

Lancaster/Strasburg

Limestone Inn B&B
33 East Main Street
Strasburg, PA 17579
(717) 687-8392

Type of B&B: Inn.
Rooms: 5 with private bath.
Rates: 1 or 2/$75-95

Rating: A or ♕♕♕ Excellent, far exceeds basic requirements.

Historic Georgian-style home built circa 1786 is located 9 miles southeast of Lancaster, 3 miles south of Route 30 on 896. The home has been completely restored and is now listed on the National Register of Historic Places. There are five guest rooms with private bath. The master suite features a private bath, corner fireplace, queen-size spindle bed, original random plank floors, and antique furnishings. Area attractions include Amish country, buggy rides, Pennsylvania Railroad Museum, antique shops and outlets, miniature golf, fishing, hiking, and bicycling. Dinner with an Amish family can be arranged. Full breakfast. Resident dogs. Restricted smoking. 1 or 2/$75-95. AE.

Guests write: *"This is an excellent place. We have stayed in many hotels and inns in Europe and the U.S.A. and this was the best. Wonderful decor, excellent beds, great breakfast, good location (quiet and charming town), clean, neat, and best of all — Dick and Jan couldn't be more fun, cordial, or helpful. Our stay here was the highlight of our two and a half week trip."* (C. Carter)

Lancaster/Quarryville

Runnymede Farm Guest House B&B
1030 Robert Fulton Highway
Quarryville, PA 17566
(717) 786-3625

Type of B&B: B&B farm.
Rooms: 3 with shared baths.
Rates: 1/$40; 2/$43.

Rating: B or ♛♛ Good, exceeds basic requirements.

American Foursquare farmhouse built in 1923 is located 17 miles south of Lancaster. Choose from three guest rooms that share a bath. Each room is air-conditioned and offers a TV. Area attractions include quilt and antique shops, Amish farms, and historic sites. Recreation nearby includes tennis, bicycling, fishing, hiking, and golf. Full breakfast includes hot entree such as eggs or French toast, cereal, fruit, bacon, sweet rolls, coffee, and home-made jams and jellies. Families welcome. Restricted smoking. 1/$40; 2/$43.

Lancaster/Ephrata

The Smithton Inn
900 West Main Street
Ephrata, PA 17522
(717) 733-6094

Type of B&B: Inn.
Rooms: 7 rooms, 1 suite, all with private bath.
Rates: 1/$55-115; 2/$65-125; Suite/$140-170.

Rating: A+ or ♛♛♛ Excellent, far exceeds basic requirements.

Stone inn that first opened in 1763 stands in the historic part of the village on Highway 322, 2.5 miles west of access Highway 222. The inn's seven guest rooms and suite each offer a private bath, canopy and four-poster bed with Pennsylvania Dutch quilts, working fireplace, and comfortable sitting area. All rooms have a refrigerator, phone jack, chamber music, night shirts, fresh flowers, optional candle lighting, and several rooms have whirlpool tubs. Lancaster County's Old Order Amish and Mennonite people, still farming with horses and living the life of our ancestors, make this area a fascinating place. Attractions include farm tours, historic sites, handcrafts, daily auctions, farm markets, and the largest antique market in the East. Full breakfast with all-you-can-eat waffles, pastries, and fruit. Families welcome. Wheelchair access. No smoking. 1/$55-115; 2/$65-125; Suite/$140-170. AE, MC, V.

Lancaster/Bird In Hand

The Village Inn of Bird-in-Hand
Box 253
2695 Old Philadelphia Pike
Bird-in-Hand, PA 17505
(717) 293-8369

Type of B&B: Inn.
Rooms: 11 with private bath.
Rates: 1 or 2/$74-139.

Rating: A or ♛♛♛ Excellent, far exceeds basic requirements.

Mid-Nineteenth Century Victorian inn is 7 miles east of Lancaster on
Route 340. Each of the eleven guest rooms has its own private bath and
down-filled bedding. Four of the rooms are suites, some with king-sized
beds, whirlpool baths, and one with a working wood stove. Enjoy a
complimentary tour of the Dutch Country or visit the adjacent farmer's
market, country store, family restaurant, bakery, and number of quilt and
craft shops. Just a few minutes away are Lancaster County attractions
including museums, outlet shops, golf courses, and farmlands.
Continental breakfast and light evening snacks served daily. Restricted
smoking. 1 or 2/$74-139. AE, MC, V.

Lancaster/Elizabethtown

West Ridge Guest House
1285 West Ridge Road
Elizabethtown, PA 17022
(717) 367-7783

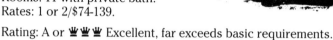

Type of B&B: Inn.
Rooms: 9 with private bath.
Rates: 2/$60-85

Rating: A+ or ♛♛♛ Excellent, far exceeds basic requirements.

Tucked midway between Harrisburg and Lancaster, this European Manor
can be found 4 miles off Route 283 at the Rheems-Elizabethtown exit. Nine
guest rooms with private bath are each decorated to reflect a different
historic period. An exercise room with hot tub and large social room are
in the adjacent guest house. Fish in one of two ponds or travel 20-40
minutes to local attractions such as Hershey Park, Lancaster County
Amish farms, outlet shopping malls, Masonic homes, and Harrisburg
State Capital. Full breakfast offers the choice of eggs, pancakes, or French
toast. Wheelchair access. No smoking. 2/$60-85. MC, V. Travel agent.

Guests write: *"Being a disabled veteran, I appreciated the ample access to the guest house and spacious parking. I had a large room, luxurious bathroom, all linens were changed every day, snacks and newspapers were available outside the bedroom door. The exercise room and hot tub were just across the hall and you can get full value in the breakfast alone. I stay in the Ritz Hotel in London, the George V Hotel in Paris, and the Waldorf in New York, but I always request accommodation at West Ridge Guest House in this area and I plan on accommodating and entertaining my guests here."* (R. Roberts)

Mercersburg

The Mercersburg Inn
405 South Main Street
Mercersburg, PA 17236
(717) 328-5231

Type of B&B: Country inn with restaurant.
Rooms: 15 with private bath.
Rates: 1 or 2/$110-180.

Rating: A+ or ♕ ♕ ♕ Excellent, far exceeds basic requirements.

Restored early 1900s Georgian Revival was originally a part of the six-acre estate of a prominent business man. The brick and slate mansion, listed on the National Resister of Historic Buildings, is 90 miles northwest of Washington, DC. Choose from fifteen rooms filled with either locally made furnishings or restored antiques. Each has a private bath and ten offer king-size four-poster beds with hand-knotted canopies. Enjoy panoramic views of the Tuscaroroa mountains of the Alleghenies and the rolling farmlands that surround the area. Visit Whitetail Ski Resort, Gettysburg, Harper's Ferry, or Antietam. Antique shops, hiking, and golfing are nearby. Home baked breakfast breads, sausage and egg casserole, and home-made sticky buns are often featured at a full breakfast. Six-course dinners are available. Wedding and meeting facilities available. Families welcome. Wheelchair access. Restricted smoking. 1 or 2/$110-180. Corporate rates. MC,V. Travel agent.

Milford

Black Walnut B&B Inn
R.D. 2, Box 9285
Milford, PA 18337
(717) 296-6322 or (800) 866-9870

Type of B&B: Inn.
Rooms: 12, 8 with private bath.
Rates: 1 or 2/$60-85.

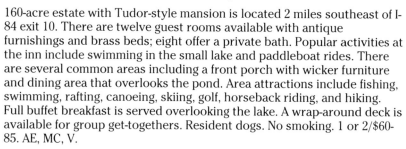

Rating: B- or ♛♛ Good, exceeds basic requirements.

160-acre estate with Tudor-style mansion is located 2 miles southeast of I-84 exit 10. There are twelve guest rooms available with antique furnishings and brass beds; eight offer a private bath. Popular activities at the inn include swimming in the small lake and paddleboat rides. There are several common areas including a front porch with wicker furniture and dining area that overlooks the pond. Area attractions include fishing, swimming, rafting, canoeing, skiing, golf, horseback riding, and hiking. Full buffet breakfast is served overlooking the lake. A wrap-around deck is available for group get-togethers. Resident dogs. No smoking. 1 or 2/$60-85. AE, MC, V.

Montgomeryville/North Wales

Joseph Ambler Inn
1005 Horsham Road
North Wales, PA 19454
(215) 362-7500

Type of B&B: Country inn.
Rooms: 28 with private bath.
Rates: 1/$85; 2/$140.

Rating: A- or ♛♛♛ Excellent, far exceeds basic requirements.

Colonial country inn situated on a twelve-acre estate of rolling countryside is 40 miles from Philadelphia near the intersection of Routes 202 and 309. Twenty-eight guest rooms are available in the main inn or the converted barn. Each room provides a private bath, antique furniture, four-poster bed, and Oriental rugs. Enjoy a stroll on the grounds or relax in three living rooms, one with massive, walk-in fireplace. Area attractions include Valley Forge, Peddler's Village, Skippack, picturesque New Hope, and historic sites of Philadelphia. Full breakfast. A restaurant on the premises offers dining. Families welcome. Facilities available for meetings and social functions. 1/$85; 2/$140. AE, MC, V. Auto club discount.

New Hope

Holly Hedge Estate B&B
6987 Upper York Road
New Hope, PA 18938
(215) 862-3136 or 862-2287

Type of B&B: Inn.
Rooms: 16 with private bath.
Rates: 1/$65-140; 2/$95-175.

Rating: B or ♛♛ Good, exceeds basic requirements.

Stone Colonial manor home set on 20 hillside acres is 3 miles north of
New Hope and 35 miles north of Philadelphia. The sixteen guest rooms
are furnished with French, American, and English antiques and
collectibles and each offers a private bath. Some feature fireplaces,
private entrances, or kitchen facilities. Explore the grounds with English
gardens, landscaped lawns, and a natural pool. Sit by the fireplace, relax
at pool side, or play cribbage in the parlor. Seasonal recreational
activities are abundant and the area offers shopping, antiquing, or touring
museums and galleries. Fresh fruit crepes, frittatas, home-made breads
and muffins, and special coffee blends are all a part of a full breakfast.
Wedding and meeting facilities available. Families welcome. Restricted
smoking. 1/$65-140; 2/$95-175. AE, MC, V. 10% Senior and corporate
discounts. Travel agent.

Oil City/Franklin

Quo Vadis Bed & Breakfast
"Whither Goest Thou?"
1501 Liberty Street
Franklin, PA 16323
(814) 432-4208

Type of B&B: Inn.
Rooms: 6 with private bath.
Rates: 1 or 2/$48-70 plus tax.

Rating: B+ or ♛♛ Good, exceeds basic requirements.

1867 Queen-Anne Victorian home accented with terra cotta is located
near the junction of Routes 8, 62, and 322, halfway between Pittsburgh
and Erie near the Ohio line. Six guest rooms each offer a private bath,
high ceilings, detailed woodwork, quilts, embroidery, and lacework, as
well as furniture that has been acquired by four generations of the same
family. Area attractions include the Historic District with Victorian
homes, DeBence Antique Museum, antique malls, Drake Well Museum

and Park with its 2.5 hour train trips, and outdoor recreation. Full breakfast includes fresh fruit, home-baked goods, croissants, and varied specialties on weekends. No smoking. 1 or 2/$48-70 plus tax. AE, MC, V. Travel agent.

Philadelphia/Lima

Hamanassett
P.O. Box 129
Lima, PA 19037
(215) 459-3000

Type of B&B: Inn
Rooms: 6 with private bath.
Rates: 1/$80-95; 2/$95-120.

Rating: A or ♛♛♛ Excellent, far exceeds basic requirements.

Federalist mansion tucked away near the heart of the Brandywine Valley is situated on 48 acres of gardens, paths, and trails and located 15 miles north of Wilmington, Delaware and 20 miles south of Philadelphia. Fresh flowers, fruit, and other amenities are offered in each of the seven guest rooms which have been decorated with antiques and Oriental rugs. Six rooms offer a private bath. A large, Federal-era fireplace is the focal point in the main living room/library where guests gather to converse and browse through the more than 2,000 volumes found on the bookshelves. Enjoy the views from the floor-to-ceiling dining room French doors overlooking gardens and 300-year-old trees. Explore the surrounding grounds with their four-season beauty. The nearby Brandywine Valley offers attractions such as Longwood Gardens, Hagley, Winterthur Museum and Gardens, Brandywine Battlefield, and Ridley Creek State Park. Famous Philadelphia sites are a short ride away. Full country breakfast consists of original recipe hot entrees as well as home-made breads, jams, and jellies. Catered dinners available. Large common rooms facilitate weddings and meetings and ample parking is available. 1/$80-95; 2/$95-120. MC, V.

"Not only was the hospitality warm, but Hamanassett was well kept, clean, and its antiques were in excellent condition. Plus, the generous assortment of snacks and chocolates strategically placed never left you hungry."
(B. Tinkelman)

"Besides a king-sized four-poster bed with a down comforter, we had a comfortable reading area, an abundance of books and up-to-date magazines, a television, fruit, candies, a stocked refrigerator, plenty of extra blankets and towels, a large bathroom with a stocked medicine cabinet and

a tub/shower. Without a doubt, breakfast with home-made breads and muffins, fresh fruit, and a table by a roaring fire in the dining room was one of the many highlights of our weekend." (D. Amadio)

Philadelphia

Thomas Bond House
129 South 2nd Street
Philadelphia, PA 19106
(215) 923-8523 or (800) 845-BOND

Type of B&B: Inn.
Rooms: 12 with private bath.
Rates: 1 or 2/$80-150.

Rating: A+ or ♛♛♛ Excellent, far exceeds basic requirements.

Brick Federal inn built in the 1700's is located one mile off I-95 in the Independence National Historic Park and was the former residence of an early Philadelphia physician. There are twelve distinctive guest rooms with private bath, period furnishings, TV, and telephone. Two rooms offer queen-size beds, sofa beds, working fireplaces, and whirlpool baths. Reproduction furniture, maps, and accessories are offered in the Key and Quill gift shop located in the inn. Continental breakfast is served weekdays and a full breakfast on weekends. Facilities are available for meetings and social functions. 1 or 2/$80-150. AE, MC, V. 10% business travel discount. Travel agent.

Pocono Mountains/Stroudsburg

Academy Hill House
707 Thomas Street
Stroudsburg, PA 18360
(717) 476-6575

Type of B&B: Private home.
Rooms: 3, 1 with private bath.
Rates: 1/$50-80; 2/$55-85.

Rating: A- or ♛♛♛ Excellent, far exceeds basic requirements.

Colonial Revival with Mission Arts & Crafts interior decor was originally the 1839 school building for which Stroudsburg's Academy Hill National Historic District is named. It is located in a quiet residential neighborhood 75 miles west of New York City and 85 miles north of Philadelphia in the Pocono Mountains. Three guest rooms, one with private bath and one with its own half bath, are decorated with wicker and lace, Morris wallpaper, Stickley furnishings, or Prairie-influenced designs. Sit by one of the fireplaces or explore the grounds. Walk one block to the Courthouse and three blocks to Main Street for business, cultural events, and shopping. The Poconos offer many activities as does the nearby Delaware Water Gap Recreational Area. Visit shopping outlets, antique stores, and historic sites. Weekends stays include a full breakfast that might include Lemon-ginger fruit in parchment or apple dumplings with maple cream. Weekday guests are treated to hearty continental breakfasts. Breakfasts are served on china, crystal, and silver before the fire or in the courtyard. Restricted smoking. 1/$50-80; 2/$55-85.

Pocono Mountains/Cresco

Crescent Lodge
Paradise Valley
Cresco, PA 18326
(800) 392-9400 or (717) 595-7486

Type of B&B: Country Inn with restaurant.
Rooms: 32 with private bath.
Rates: 1 or 2/$90-250.

Rating: A+ or ♛♛♛ Excellent, far exceeds basic requirements.

Built in 1920 and in continuous operation by the same family for 46 years, the Crescent Lodge is comprised of a main inn and private cottages and is located in the Pocono Mountains, 6 miles from Junction I-80 and I-380, and 35 miles north of Allentown. A total of thirty-two guest accommodations can be found in both the lodge and cottages. Each room offers a private bath, individual decor in pastels, lace, and florals, phone, and TV. Each of the cottages has a private wooden deck and several rooms offer a sitting room, fireplace, and sunken Jacuzzi. Browse in the on-site gift shop, relax at the heated pool, or enjoy the inn's outdoor activities on the tennis courts and hiking trails. This resort area offers golf, skiing, antiquing, outlet shopping, white water sports, and varied nightlife pastimes. Continental breakfast includes fresh fruit, pastries, and home-made jams. Dinner is available at additional cost in the restaurant on premises. Wedding and meeting facilities available. Families welcome. Restricted smoking. 1 or 2/$90-250. AE, MC, V. Travel agent.

Guests write: *"We are so grateful we stayed at Crescent Lodge. Starting with the warm and caring reception we received from Dorothy, to the delightful dinners and fun we had with Sharon and Holly, who gave us special service and got us fed and to our TV in time for 'Murphy Brown'. It is such a joyful opportunity to write and praise the employees and the beautiful lodge."*
(J. Pugh)

"Setting out to look for a place to stay the night we passed Crescent Lodge. What an inviting, pleasant atmosphere, even from the outside! Upon entering Crescent Lodge we felt so at home and everything was pretty and clean. We checked in immediately and had a wonderful dinner in the dining room and enjoyed the beautiful room in the lodge for the night. The next morning, breakfast was perfect in the lobby by the fire. The chef was so accommodating he made a special breakfast of eggs Benedict, which were the best I have ever had!" (J. Walters)

"I have traveled quite frequently throughout the United States and I have never experienced such superb surroundings and excellent food... I did not find one member of the staff that did not project a friendliness and consideration that could not help but make one's stay a pleasant one... My biggest complaint is that I was on assignment to write a book review but because of the staff and inn I never got to it. Everyone and everything was entirely too nice! Who could work under such conditions?" (J. Kurtz)

Slippery Rock

Applebutter Inn
152 Applewood Lane
Slippery Rock, PA 16057
(412) 794-1844

Type of B&B: Inn.
Rooms: 11 with private bath.
Rates: 1/$55-81; 2/$69-115.

Rating: A+ or ♛♛♛ Excellent, far exceeds basic requirements.

Federal Colonial inn built in 1844 is nestled in the rolling green meadows of rural Western Pennsylvania, 3 miles southeast of I-79 exit 30. Choose from eleven guest rooms, each with unique decor, antique furnishings, and private bath. Special features of the inn include 12-inch brick walls on a hand-cut stone foundation, exposed brick fireplaces, and original chestnut and poplar floors. The main floor offers a relaxing sitting room and parlor with fireplace. Area recreation includes golf, bicycling, jogging, and country walks. Full breakfast served daily. A cafe on the premises is open to guests and the public and serves lunch and dinner seven days a week. Full breakfast served daily to overnight guests. Families welcome. No smoking. 1/$55-81; 2/$69-115. MC, V. Travel agent.

Guests write: *"Applebutter Inn provided probably the most wonderful weekend that my husband and I have shared in our 22 years together. It was a journey into an era of simple, restful, quiet appreciation of grace and beauty. Our room was so beautiful with a cozy fire casting shadows on the carefully appointed pastel wall coverings. The four-poster net canopy bed, baskets of wild flowers, candles glowing in each window, wonderful goosedown comforters — each of these things added to such an unforgettable weekend. We came to the Applebutter to celebrate my birthday but in addition to that were able to renew our spirits and our love, and we'll be forever grateful for that."* (J. Raimondi)

"Applebutter Inn is charming! Each room has a name and that theme is carried out in the decor. There are beautiful antiques in each room, lovely quilts, and decorations. Each room has a guest book for comments. Breakfast is bountiful and delicious! It is served in an adjoining old school house where you can also get lunch or dinner if you don't want to stray far." (B. Rankin)

"The gracious hospitality and warmth of the inn staff and the inn itself was second to none. My room was a treasure of charm and comfort and the view spectacular of the rolling Pennsylvania farmland. I would enthusiastically welcome a chance to go back and recommend it to all looking for an inn filled with warm ambiance and gourmet, delectable fare." (C. Dayle)

"On a cold February night I've never felt such comfort and warmth. It's a true feeling of being brought back to the ambiance of the 1800's but with the 1990's standard of excellence." (C. Kohnfelder)

"All the kind people at Applebutter Inn and Schoolhouse cafe made our anniversary a very special one. Tell them to come out with their own cookbook and I will be the first to buy it even if it cost $50." (L. Herrod)

"The atmosphere was so elegant, but still cozy. The breakfast was delicious - there was no room for improvements. From the moment we arrived until departure we were thrilled." (E. Cratty)

Somerset

Glades Pike Inn
RD 6, Box 250
Somerset, PA 15501
(814) 443-4978

Type of B&B: Inn.
Rooms: 5, 3 with private bath.
Rates: 1/$40-70; 2/$50-80.

Rating: B- or ♛♛ Good, exceeds basic requirements.

Glades Pike Inn, a mid 19th-Century Colonial, once served as a stagecoach stop and is located 6 miles west of Somerset and 13 miles east of Donegal. The inn was remodeled in 1987 and features exposed wood floors, high ceilings, and brick construction. Each of the five guest rooms offers a double bed and three rooms have a private bath and woodburning fireplace. Relax in one of the large chairs in front of the fireplace in the living room or visit with other guests at the wine and cheese social offered on weekends. Area attractions include the Laurel Hill Hiking Trail, Hidden Valley and Seven Springs, resorts for skiing, Ohiopyle State Park for fishing and white water rafting, and many historic sites. Apple souffle pancakes are a house specialty often featured at the full breakfast. Families welcome. Restricted smoking. 1/$40-70; /$50-80. AE, M, V Travel agent.

State College/Pine Grove Mills

Split-Pine Farmhouse B&B
P.O. Box 326
Pine Grove Mills, PA 16868
(814) 238-2028

Type of B&B: Inn.
Rooms: 5, 1 with private bath.
Rates: 1/$50; 2/$65-100.

Rating: A- or ♛♛♛ Excellent, far exceeds basic requirements.

Simple Federal home built in the mid-19th Century is set in a rural area just minutes from Pennsylvania State University and State College, two hours west of Harrisburg and four hours outside of Philadelphia. Choose from five guest rooms with country views which feature an international collection of vintage and antique furnishings. One room offers a private bath. Relax in the formal sitting room with fireplace, baby grand piano, and French Liqueur Cabinet. Explore the surrounding acres of lawns and flowers with views of mountains and fields. Hiking, fishing, water sports, cross country skiing, and antiquing are all nearby. Area attractions include the Pennsylvania Arts Festival, Bellefonte Victorian Christmas, the Amish Market at Belleville, and the Dinner Train from Bellefonte to Tyrone. A full breakfast served at the dining room's mahogany table might feature mushroom ham crepes with spinach sauce, mushroom strudel, breakfast kabobs, nutty French toast or Santa Fe strata. Dinners, luncheons, teas, and receptions can be arranged. Restricted smoking. 1/$50; 2/$65-100. MC, V. Travel agent.

Guests write: *"Split Pine Farmhouse B&B has been our mainstay each football weekend for the past eight years. We have enjoyed warm hospitality and excellent food in uniquely original surroundings. Over the years we have stayed in all the bedrooms and find each one has individual charm while meeting high standards for comfort."* (M. Bieberbach)

— *Comments continued on next page*

"We loved our first visit for the setting, but especially because of Mae and her gracious manner. Mae truly puts herself out to please her guests. The breakfasts at Split Pine are what I call a 'happening'. Mae is a gourmet at cooking, presentation, and table setting. The anticipation of what our next breakfast will be is great fun!" (M. Mc Garvey)

"Elegant home is impeccably decorated. Such attention to details! Superb food was beautifully presented and served. Mae is a charming, warm, and cheerful hostess who knows how to pamper her guests." (S. Rosenberg)

"Breakfast is served in the beautiful dining room and is a special treat. The little extras provided and the friendly hospitality are just two reasons that we feel truly welcome and look forward to future visits." (M. Schmidt)

"Mae is very knowledgeable about antiques and a delight to sit and chat with. The inn is beautifully decorated. My nine-year-old son is especially fond of the cannonball bed. He also enjoys the beautiful sketches on the staircase wall." (B. Hiberman)

Wellsboro

Kaltenbach's Bed & Breakfast
RD #6 Box 106A
Wellsboro, PA 16901
(800) 722-4954 or (717) 724-4954

Type of B&B: Inn.
Rooms: 10, 6 with private bath.
Rates: 1/$35; 2/$60; Honeymoon suite/$125.

Rating: B- or ♛♛ Good, exceeds basic requirements.

Flagstone ranch house nestled on 72 acres of rolling hills is in northcentral Pennsylvania one hour north of Williamsport. Ten guest rooms with king or queen-size beds are available. Six rooms have a private bath and two rooms are honeymoon suites with oversized tubs-for-two. Explore this Tioga County farm with its sheep, pigs, rabbits, and beef cattle. Take a walk through meadows and the forest. Year-round recreation includes skiing at Denton Hill or Sawmill ski areas, cross country skiing and snowmobiling on trails at the farm, hiking, biking, fishing, and hunting. Visit the nearby Grand Canyon of Pennsylvania, Corning Glass Center, Coudersport Ice Mine, Watkins Glen Raceway, or the State Laurel Festival held annually. Full breakfast features eggs fixed five different ways, breakfast meats, and home-made jams, jellies, and baked goods. Wedding and meeting facilities available. Families welcome. Wheelchair access. No smoking. 1/$35; 2/$60; Honeymoon suite/$125. MC, V.

Guests write: *"The Kaltenbach Farm offers an appealing, rural family atmosphere in which anyone will feel welcome. The home offers large common areas and comfortable, private guest rooms and baths. A farm-style feast describes the usual breakfast, which features farm-raised meats and home-baked blue ribbon breads. Lee Kaltenbach, the owner, proved to be one of the most accommodating, friendly, receptive and interesting hosts that I have encountered during my extensive travels. "* (G. Gass)

Wilkes-Barre/Dallas

Ponda-Rowland Bed & Breakfast
R.R. 1, Box 349
Dallas, PA 18612-9604
(717) 639-3245

Type of B&B: Inn on a working farm.
Rooms: 3 with private bath.
Rates: 1 or 2/$55-85.

Rating: B+ or ♛♛ Good, exceeds basic requirements.

Mid-nineteenth-century plank frame home with beamed ceilings has a rural setting and is located 10 miles northwest of Wilkes-Barre off Route 309. Three guest rooms with private bath have been furnished with American Colonial antiques and country accents. Guests are invited to relax on the enclosed front porch or sit in front of the fire in the Great Room. Popular activities in the area include fishing at the family trout fishing park just up the road, local rail tours, Pocono Downs, canoeing, swimming, skiing, horseback riding, and tobogganing. Hay rides are offered on-site as well as visits with the farm's animals. A master timberframe craftsman has a shop on the premises. A hearty breakfast is served by the fire in the Great Room. Families welcome. Restricted smoking. 1 or 2/$55-85. MC, V. Travel agent.

Guests write: *"We were pleased with the accommodations, the area, touring the workshop, the genuine feeling of relaxation, and how much the Rowlands made us feel at home."* (E. Strollo)

"Mr. Rowland gave us all a ride up on top of the hill to see their geese, pigs, sheep, and rabbits. It was fall and being on top of a hill, the view was beautiful. It is fun staying here because we are treated like family, having the use of the property to swing, walk, play ball, swim, and watch TV." (M. Pilger)

"Any American antique furniture collector would be in awe of all the Rowland's furnishings, from the pewter to the antique tools in the converted

dairy barn which is now a wood-working shop. Everything was clean and the antique furnishings made one feel like you were stepping back in time visiting a country farm. " (V. Wright)

"Our room was clean and decorated in lovely antique fashion. The bed was especially comfortable and the sheets were the softest we have ever slept on. Our breakfast was delicious and plentiful consisting of fresh fruits, orange juice, blueberry and corn pancakes, and delicious fresh-brewed coffee. After breakfast we took a walk around the 130 acres and enjoyed ourselves as we encountered snow geese and numerous birds." (S. Buzzoro)

PUERTO RICO

Ceiba

Ceiba Country Inn
Carr # 977 KM 1.2
Ceiba, Puerto Rico 00735
(809) 885-0471
Fax: (809) 885-0471

Type of B&B: Large inn.
Rooms: 9 with private bath.
Rates: 1/$50; 2/$80.

Rating: B+ or ♕♕ Good, exceeds basic requirements.

Tropical architecture graces this fifteen-year-old countryside inn located on the east coast of Puerto Rico, thirty-five miles southwest of San Juan. There are nine guest rooms washed in white walls with colorful pillows, curtains, and bedspreads. Guests enjoy the palm trees and sea breezes as well as the surrounding ocean views and rolling hills. Visit nearby Luquino Beach, Seven Seas Beach, El Yunque Rain Forest, and the five marinas that are within twenty miles. Continental breakfast includes home-baked nut breads and a selection of tropical fruit. Function rooms available for small meetings. Families welcome. Wheelchair access. 1/$50; 2/$80. AE, MC, V. Travel agent.

Block Island

Blue Dory Inn
Dodge Street, Box 488
Block Island, RI 02807
(800) 992-7290 or (401) 466-5891

Type of B&B: Inn.
Rooms: 23, 15 with private bath.
Rates: 1/$65-95; 2/$65-170.

Rating: A- or ♛♛♛ Excellent, far exceeds basic requirements.

Victorian inn built at the turn-of-the-century is located at the head of
Crescent Beach, just a few feet from the sea and 12 miles from the
mainland. Comprised of four buildings, the inn offers twenty-three guest
rooms, fifteen with private bath. Each room offers an ocean or town view,
antique decor, and wall to wall carpeting. Some feature kitchen facilities
or a porch overlooking the sea. Take an early morning walk on the miles
of unspoiled beach just outside the door or walk to town to visit the
historic sites, restaurants, and shops. Continental breakfast is served in
the eat-in kitchen and includes fresh muffins, bagels, fruit, and flavored
coffees. Small wedding and meeting facilities available. Families welcome.
1/$65-95; 2/$65-170. AE, MC, V. 10% senior, corporate, and auto club
discounts. Travel agent.

Newport

Admiral Fitzroy Inn
398 Thames Street
Newport, RI 02840
(401) 848-8018, 848-8019 or
(800) 343-2863.

Type of B&B: Large inn.
Rooms: 18 with private bath.
Rates: 1 or 2/$65-150.

Rating: A- or ♛♛♛ Excellent, far exceeds basic requirements.

Admiral Fitzroy Inn is listed on the National Register of Historic Places
and located in the heart of Newport's waterfront district, 1.5 hours from
Boston. Choose from eighteen guest rooms with private bath and unique
hand-painted walls. The inn's roof-deck offers views of the harbor. The
narrow streets of this old seaport town boast examples of Victorian
architecture, Colonial houses, and summer cottage mansions along with
Fort Adams, restaurants, art galleries, and shops. A full breakfast includes
muffins, hot entrees, fresh fruit, croissants and is served in the breakfast

room or taken up to guest rooms. Complimentary beverages are served each evening. Meeting facilities available. Families welcome. Wheelchair access. 1 or 2/$65-150 with off-season discounts. AE, MC, V. Travel agent.

Newport

Cliffside Inn
2 Seaview Avenue
Newport, RI 02840
(800) 845-1811 or (401) 847-1811

Type of B&B: Inn.
Rooms: 12 with private bath.
Rates: 1 or 2/$125-205.

Rating: A+ or ♛♛♛ Excellent, far exceeds basic requirements.

Built in the late 1800s as a summer home for a Maryland governor, this seaside Victorian has been in operation for 22 years and is 35 miles east of Providence. The inn features period furnishings, floor to ceiling windows, and Laura Ashley fabrics. Each of the twelve guest rooms with private bath are decorated with antiques and decorator linens. Some rooms feature a fireplace or whirlpool bathtub. Sit by the fire in the parlor, relax on the porch, or explore Cliff Walk, the city's famous seaside walking trail, just one block away. Take an easy stroll to the beach or to the famous Newport mansions, go sailing, or tour the Old Colonial homes. Full breakfast specialties include walnut pancakes, eggs Benedict, or chambourd French toast. Afternoon appetizers are offered in the parlor. Restricted smoking. 1 or 2/$125-205. AE, MC, V. Extended stay discount. Travel agent.

Guests write: *"We give them high marks for the great muffins and coffee cakes they always hand make and serve along with their wonderful breakfast. I think each had their own special recipes. Our room was quiet, romantic and so very pretty. As if that wasn't enough, we had all of the beautiful Newport mansions to visit with Annette and Norbert giving us suggestions and also stories about some of the mansions or their owners."* (M. O'Brien)

"We stayed in the Attic Room in December. What a terrific hide-away the inn is. Everything was perfect!" (L. Ilberg)

" It's really a wonderful inn. Beautifully done. You have total privacy, it's near the water and the innkeepers, Annette and Norbert are especially sweet, kind, and extremely relaxing to be around. " (K. Pendleton)

" The 'Miss Beatrice Room' was perfect for us, and was outdone only by Annette's home-cooking at breakfast." (A. Boyle)

Newport

Melville House
39 Clarke Street
Newport, RI 02840
(401) 847-0640

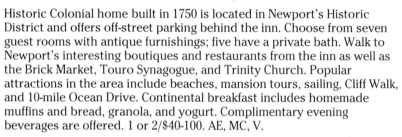

Type of B&B: Inn.
Rooms: 7, 5 with private bath.
Rates: 1 or 2/$40-100.

Rating: B+ or ♛♛ Good, exceeds basic requirements.

Historic Colonial home built in 1750 is located in Newport's Historic
District and offers off-street parking behind the inn. Choose from seven
guest rooms with antique furnishings; five have a private bath. Walk to
Newport's interesting boutiques and restaurants from the inn as well as
the Brick Market, Touro Synagogue, and Trinity Church. Popular
attractions in the area include beaches, mansion tours, sailing, Cliff Walk,
and 10-mile Ocean Drive. Continental breakfast includes homemade
muffins and bread, granola, and yogurt. Complimentary evening
beverages are offered. 1 or 2/$40-100. AE, MC, V.

Guests write: *"We continue to visit Newport several times a year. We
always stay at Melville House because the hospitality here adds as much as
any Newport sight or event to the pleasure of a weekend getaway. Friends
and relatives often join us and Rita and Sam, the innkeepers, make
newcomers feel as welcome as us old-timers. On learning that my husband
is a student of architecture and historic preservation, Sam had him climbing
up into the rafters and down into the original basement to see how his house
is put together. When we arrived for a weekend's anniversary celebration,
we discovered our lovely room decorated with balloons."* (B. Ismael)

*"The accommodations are comfortable with a quiet elegance. Much is done
to ensure a guest's comfort with excellent reading materials and extra
pillows and blankets. In addition, the house itself is like a mini-museum with
lots of beautiful paintings and antiques. Breakfast is a treat. Homemade
muffins and delicious coffee, granola, and yogurt. All this is served on
exquisite china."* (A. Calkins)

*"A group of us (seven couples) wanted a place to gather where we could
feel free to use the house during our reunion and not bother anyone. Rita
and Sam were the perfect hosts and Melville House the perfect place."*
(P. Willey)

Providence

The Old Court Bed & Breakfast
144 Benefit Street
Providence, RI 02903
(401) 751-2002 or 351-0747.

Type of B&B: Inn.
Rooms: 11 with private bath.
Rates: 1/$95-110; 2/$110-140.

Rating: B or ♛♛ Good, exceeds basic requirements.

Italianate brick home built in 1863 overlooks the Capitol and downtown Providence and is located on historic Benefit Street. Choose from eleven guest rooms with private bath and modified Victorian beds that are both unique and comfortable. Some rooms offer wet bars and all have been decorated to reflect the Victorian period. The common room features nineteenth-century decor with ornate Italian mantelpieces, plaster moldings, and twelve-foot ceilings. Walk to downtown in three minutes or to nearby Brown University, Rhode Island School of Design or the city's East Side with its interesting architecture and shops including Benefit Street's collection of Colonial and Victorian houses. Continental breakfast includes homemade breads. A fax machine and private telephones for guest rooms are available along with function rooms for weddings and meetings. 1/$95-110; 2/$110-140. AE, MC, V. 10% business discount. Travel agent.

Westerly

The Villa
190 Shore Road
Westerly, RI 02891
(800) 722-9240

Type of B&B: Inn.
Rooms: 7, 5 with private bath.
Rates: 1/$50-145; 2/$55-150.

Rating: B or ♛♛ Good, exceeds basic requirements.

The Villa was built in 1938 in the Dutch Colonial style with Mediterranean accents such as porticos, archways, and verandahs and is located 20 minutes east of Mystic, 50 minutes west of Newport. Choose from seven guest rooms, five with private bath. Two suites have a fireplace, sitting area, and private entrance. Each room offers color TV, refrigerators, and air conditioning. Explore the surrounding one and one half acres of landscaped grounds, gardens, and lawns which include a lovely in-ground swimming pool. Visit nearby Misquamicut Ocean beaches, Mystic Marine Life Aquarium, Foxwoods Casino, Mystic Seaport, and the Newport Mansions. An expanded continental breakfast buffet is served poolside and consists of assorted cereals, fresh fruit, home-made muffins, jellies and jams. In season, a complimentary Italian dinner is offered to Thursday evening guests. Families welcome. 1/$50-145; 2/$55-150. AE, MC, V. Senior, family, corporate, and auto club discounts available. Travel agent.

Guests write: *"The Villa is a very attractive, Mediterranean style house about a mile from the beach. It has a lovely in-ground pool for guest's use. Clean and well maintained. Innkeeper Jerry Maiorano is very friendly and makes delicious baked goods!"* (B. Alburger)

SOUTH CAROLINA

Additional information on B&Bs in this state is available from Historic Charleston B&B (803) 722-6606

Charleston

Thirty Six Meeting Street
36 Meeting Street
Charleston, SC 29401
(803) 722-1034 or 723-0949

Type of B&B: Private Home.
Rooms: 3 with private bath.
Rates: 1/$75; 2/$110.

Rating: B or ♛♛ Good, exceeds basic requirements.

Georgian home built in 1743 is situated in the heart of the Historic District a block and a half from the Battery. Each of the three guest suites features a private bath, rice bed, kitchenette, and period furnishings. Guests are invited to relax in the garden or to borrow bicycles to tour the Charleston area. Explore the interior of the residence with its examples of Georgian detailing or study the historic architecture of surrounding homes. Continental breakfast is provided in each of the rooms and includes freshly baked breads and pastries. Families welcome. Restricted smoking. 1/$75; 2/$110. MC, V. Travel agent.

Georgetown

1790 House
630 Highmarket Street
Georgetown, SC 29440
(803) 546-4821

Type of B&B: Inn.
Rooms: 6 with private bath.
Rates: 1 or 2/$65-115.

Rating: A or ♛♛♛ Excellent, far exceeds basic requirements.

Plantation-style 1790s inn is situated near the downtown business district of this historic port city and one hour away from Charleston. The home maintains many of its original features including a wrap-around verandah facing historic homes and its own gardens. Each of the air conditioned guest rooms, six in all, offer a private bath and Colonial furnishings. Some rooms have a separate sitting room with fireplace, a Jacuzzi tub, or an outside patio overlooking the gardens. Take a walking tour of the historic district, explore museums, shops, beaches, and nearby plantations. Borrow a bike from the inn to explore the downtown area. Recreation nearby includes boating, fishing, golf. Refreshments are served each afternoon. Full breakfast features gourmet specialties accented with home-made muffins and breads and is often served on the verandah. Wedding and meeting facilities available. Wheelchair access. Restricted smoking. 1 or 2/$65-115. MC, V. 10% senior and corporate discount. Travel agent.

Guests write: *"What a wonderful get-away! The hospitality was so gracious, the food delicious, and the special touches were icing on the cake"* (B. Burgess)

" I have enjoyed the fine accommodations at the 1790 House on two different occasions and John Wiley's friendly hospitality makes me feel like I'm spending the weekend with a good friend. He is sincerely interested in his guests, and in making them feel welcome. An overnight stay at the 1790 House is a special treat." (D. Huggins)

" The most pleasant B&B weekend yet." (S. May)

"They pampered us beyond our dreams. We had good conversation with guests and privacy with each other." (S. Erickson)

SOUTH DAKOTA

Additional information on B&Bs in this state is available from
B&B Western Adventure (406) 259-7993.

TENNESSEE

Ducktown

The White House Bed & Breakfast
Box 668, 104 Main Street
Ducktown, TN 37326
(800) 775-4166 or (615) 496-4166

Type of B&B: Inn.
Rooms: 3, 1 with private bath.
Rates: 1 or 2/$55-$60.

Rating: B- or ♛♛ Good, exceeds basic requirements.

Listed on the National Register Of Historic Places, this turn-of-the-century
Victorian home is 2 hours north of Atlanta, 90 minutes east of
Chattanooga, and 2.5 hours southwest of Asheville. Three air conditioned
guest rooms are available and one offers a private bath. Sit on the front
porch on the of the rocking chairs or go exploring in the small town of
Ducktown with its population of 535. The inn is convenient to antique
shops, flea markets, and golf courses. Three TVA lakes offer water skiing,
fishing, swimming, boating, and hiking. Go white water rafting or kayaking
on the Ocoee and Nantahala Rivers or visit the Cherokee Indian Heritage.
Baked grits souffle is sometimes featured at full breakfast and is accented
with home-made bread and rolls. Restricted smoking. 1 or 2/$55-$60.

Gatlinburg

7th Heaven Log Home Inn
3944 Castle Road
Gatlinburg, TN 37738
(800) 248-2923 or (615) 430-5000

Type of B&B: Inn.
Rooms: 4 with private bath.
Rates: 1 or 2/$59-99.

Rating: A or ♛ ♛ ♛ Excellent, far exceeds basic requirements.

7th Heaven Log Home Inn is located on the 7th green of Bent Creek Golf Resort with the Smoky Mountain National Park just across the road. Downtown Gatlinburg is a ten mile drive. Four log and knotty pine guest rooms with private bath open to a common recreation room with stone fireplace, professional billiard table, bumper pool table and fully equipped kitchen. Relax in the log gazebo hot tub that overlooks a creek, pond, and golf course with a view of the Smoky Mountains beyond. Three mountain swimming pools and tennis courts are within a few blocks. Nearby attractions include Dollywood Theme Park, craft and antique shops, indoor ice skating, white water rafting, and hiking trails. Enjoy the scenic aerial tram to Ober Gatlinburg for skiing, indoor ice skating or a ride on the 1800 foot Alpine Slide. "Eyeopener" coffee is set outside the guest room door each morning and a full "loosen your belt" breakfast follows. 1 or 2/$59-99. MC, V. Travel agent.

Guests write: *"This was a special Christmas in the Smokies. We thought we were homeless and we found a home here. Thanks to them for making Christmas a special day."* (M. Strangeways)

"Truly enjoyed our stay! The hospitality leaves no room for improvement and the food reminds me of a cruise. We'll be back, it was great!" (D Timmons)

"They made our New Years something to remember fondly. Our 1st B&B experience has been great. We loved how the towels smelled 'Downey-fresh'! Excellent breakfasts." (B. Baker)

" Next time we'll stay longer or maybe we just won't leave. Breakfast was really good and the pool table was really nice. Had lots of fun!" (S. Close)

"A trying afternoon spent trying to find somewhere to stay after a disappointment with our original reservations resulted in a 'heavenly' experience. The hosts offered a much appreciated reprieve from more frustration and a relaxing end to our ordeal." (N. Copeland)

"I can not recommend any improvements. Everything about 7th Heaven was great: the people, food, location, and accommodations! We miss the delicious breakfast and the warm, cozy atmosphere and everything about the 7th Heaven." (K. Murray)

"Ginger and Paul are extremely gracious hosts and really go over and above the call of duty. In our case, they baked us an Anniversary cake to celebrate our first week of marriage! (C. Peltier)

Greenville

Hilltop House Bed & Breakfast Inn
Route 7, Box 180
Greeneville, TN 37743
(615) 639-8202

Type of B&B: B&B inn.
Rooms: 3 with private bath.
Rates: 1/$55; 2/$70.

Rating: B+ or ♛♛ Good, exceeds basic requirements.

Victorian farmhouse built in 1924 is located 19 miles from I-81 exit 23 and sits on a bluff overlooking the Nolichucky River Valley which is surrounded by mountains. Choose from three guest rooms with private bath. One room offers a queen-size canopy bed and balcony overlooking the mountains. The parlor is furnished with English antiques and offers comfortable seating for viewing TV and VCR movies. Rocking chairs and a swing on the front porch are the best seats in the house from which to enjoy the view. Area attractions include Biltmore Estate, historic Jonesborough, antique shops, hiking trails, white-water rafting, mountain biking, and trout fishing. Full breakfast. 1/$55; 2/$70. AE, MC, V. 10% business travel discount. Travel agent.

Kodak

Grandma's House
734 Pollard Rd., PO Box 445
Kodak, TN 37764
(800) 676-3512 or (615) 933-3512

Type of B&B: Inn.
Rooms: 3 with private bath.
Rates: 1/$50; 2/$65-75.

Rating: A or ♛♛♛ Excellent, far exceeds basic requirements.

New Colonial home is located right in the center of East Tennessee, two miles off exit 407 of I-40, and is situated off a country lane leading to the French Broad River. Three guest rooms with private bath feature country decor with Hilda's home-made quilts, crafts, and paintings. One extra large room has a bay window and another features grandma's fancy iron bed. Relax in two common rooms with television, VCR, books, magazines, and games. Watch the sunset from the balcony or swing on the front porch. Minutes away are Knoxville, Oak Ridge, Norris, Pigeon Forge, Gatlinburg, and the Great Smoky Mountains. Visit historic sites, factory outlets, caverns, museums, and amusement parks. Full "farm-style" breakfast may include fruit soup, ham and egg puff, or buttermilk biscuits with gravy. No smoking. 1/$50; 2/$65-75. MC, V. Travel agent.

Guests write: *"The house was spotless on both of our stays. The food and company were fabulous!! I wouldn't stay in another hotel if I thought all B&Bs were as good as Grandma's House."* (T. McCall)

"Like good wine, this place gets better and better. Great cake! Great day! " (V. McGee)

"Great conversation and breakfast; lovely house and hostess. The only problem is that we live too far from Kodak to do this all the time!" (F. Lenzi)

"This was my first B&B experience and it was much enjoyed and appreciated. They made us feel at home. Don't change a thing!" (L. Emery)

Monteagle

Adams Edgeworth Inn
Monteagle Assembly
Monteagle, TN 37356
(615) 924-2669 or 924-2476

Type of B&B: Inn.
Rooms: 12 with private bath.
Rates: 1 or 2/$55-95; Suites/$125.

Rating: A or ♛♛♛ Excellent, far exceeds basic requirements.

Historic Victorian inn built in 1896 has been totally restored and is located on the grounds of famed Monteagle Assembly, a half mile from I-24, exit 134. There are twelve guest rooms with private bath. One large suite offers a king-size bed, living room with double sofa bed, and full kitchen. The Ambassador Room features a dramatic plantation bed which was original to the inn in 1896 and was recently found and repurchased. A large library on the main floor has a large collection of books and an inviting fireplace. A sauna and shower room are found on the lower floor of the inn with easy access to the gardens. A golf cart is available for touring the grounds of Monteagle Assembly. Area attractions include South Cumberland State Recreation Area with 120 miles of hiking trails, University of the South, (a Gothic replica of Oxford University), and spectacular scenery at Cathedral Falls and Fiery Gizard Trail. Continental breakfast may include the inn's prize-winning raspberry jam. A gourmet dinner is available at an additional charge upon advance reservation. 1 or 2/$55-95; Suite/$125. A fee is charged to enter Monteagle Assembly during several weeks in the summer. Travel agent.

Guests write: *"I particularly enjoyed the original art collection. Even in the bathroom, the walls were covered with lovely original etchings. The library was filled with shelves and shelves of diverse reading materials and the fireplace and cushy, comfortable chairs made this a delicious place to read away the evening. The porch has many wonderful rocking chairs for just sitting and visiting."* (B. McLure)

"The huge king-size beds are the most comfortable beds I have ever slept in. Wendy makes a wonderful sourdough bread and when I told her how much I like it, she gave me a loaf and some of her starter dough to take home so I could bake my own." (K. Hessinger)

Pikeville

Fall Creek Falls Bed & Breakfast
P.O. Box 309, Deweese Road, Route 3
Pikeville, TN 37367
(615) 881-5494

Type of B&B: Inn.
Rooms: 8, 6 with private bath.
Rates: 1/$ 45-65; 2/$60-75.

Rating: A or ♛♛♛ Excellent, far exceeds basic requirements.

Custom-built brick country manor home located on 40 acres of rolling hillside is just one mile from Fall Creek Falls State Resort Park and 50 miles north of Chattanooga. Guests are accommodated in one of eight, air conditioned guest rooms that have been decorated with a blend of Victorian and Country styles. Six have a private bath. A special "Sweetheart Room" features brass bed and a red, heart-shaped whirlpool. There are several sitting areas on the main floor where guests can visit, read, and relax. The nearby resort park offers tennis, fishing sports, hiking, horseback riding, swimming, and a championship golf course. Drive to nearby recreation areas that offer canoeing, and cave exploring. There are also a number of antique shops near the inn. A full breakfast is served in the country kitchen, dining room, or in the Florida room. Menus vary but might include house specialties such as pecan waffles or grilled muffins Benedict. Restricted smoking. 1/$ 45-65; 2/$60-75. Travel agent.

Guests write: *"This is the perfect place to get away, unwind and be pampered and still have your privacy. Doug & Rita are gracious hosts, full of warmth and humor, ready to go that extra mile to see that all your needs are met. Each room has its own special charm. From the pillows and towels to the candles, bubble bath, and mints — nothing has been left out or is not first rate. There is a welcoming 'homeyness' graced with elegance and charm here. I'm ready to go back for pecan waffles and maple butter and homemade muffins. It doesn't get any better than this."* (J. Upchurch)

"We were shown great hospitality and friendly service. They went out of their way to make us feel like we were at our own home. Wait until you try Doug and Rita's coffee and country breakfast. That's enough to make you come back again." (R. Layne)

"I enjoy getting away from a busy schedule to be pampered by Rita and Doug. The inn is very close to the beautiful, quiet Fall Creek Falls State Park. I would recommend it to anyone." (D. Volz)

TEXAS

Glen Rose

The Lodge at Fossil Rim
RT 1, Box 210
Glen Rose, TX 76043
(817) 897-7452

Type of B&B: Inn.
Rooms: 5, 3 with private bath.
Rates: 2/$125-185.

Rating: A or ♛♛♛ Excellent, far exceeds basic requirements.

Located on a 3,000 acre Wildlife Center which breeds exotic endangered species, this 3-level Ranch made of stone, cedar, and fir is located 75 miles southwest of Dallas. Choose from five guest rooms at the lodge. Three offer a private bath and fireplace. Other special amenities in some rooms include Jacuzzi, private patio, and king-sized beds. Unusual and antique furnishings accent the entire inn. Guests can relax in front of the large stone fireplace in the common room with cathedral ceiling, stained-glass window, large-screen TV, and beverage bar. The dining room and connecting deck features panoramic views of the countryside and surrounding wildlife. A lovely outdoor swimming pool with unusual natural environment and architecture is near the inn and reached by a short ride in the safari truck. The Center offers many activities to guests at an additional cost including safari rides and a behind the scenes look at the care and breeding of animals. Pecan waffles and smoked turkey quiche are just two of the entrees often offered at the full breakfast. The game room can be used for meeting facilities. Families welcome.

Restricted smoking. 2/$125-185. Special rates for booking entire lodge. AE, MC, V. Travel agent.

Guests write: *"The hospitality and the tranquillity of the Lodge (plus the wolves' greetings at eventide!) will be long remembered. I shall certainly spread the word back East to my friends."* (H. Hodge)

"This is the perfect place for nature lovers or anyone that just wants to relax." (D. Williams)

"I am so impressed with the facility and especially with Artie and Lisa, the managers. They make perfect hosts and take all measures to be sure that a stay is as near perfect as possible. The behind the scenes tour is a must during the stay and Artie provides the perfect guide. Feeding the rhinos and the giraffes was a highlight. Searching for arrowheads and fossils just added to the enjoyment." (J. Stratton)

"Truly peaceful places are a rare commodity" (G. Williams)

"I can better imagine what Karen Blixen and Denys Fenchhatton experienced on the African Plains...This gave me a glimpse into the beauty and passion of the wilds." (P. Grimes)

Jefferson

McKay House Bed & Breakfast Inn
306 East Delta Street
Jefferson, TX 75657
(903) 665-7322, or
from Dallas (214) 348-1929

Type of B&B: Inn and cottage.
Rooms: 7 rooms or suites
with private bath.
Rate: 1 or 2/$75-125.

Rating: A or ♛♛♛ Excellent, far exceeds basic requirements.

Historic Greek Revival inn with Victorian cottage was built in 1851 and is located 3 blocks east of Highway 59, 16 miles north of I-20. Each of the seven guest rooms or suites offers a private bath, antique furnishings, fresh flowers, and selection of Victorian night clothes guests can use. Area attractions and recreation include lakes, forests, Louisiana bayou, antique shops, boat tours, theaters, golf, and fishing. Full breakfast specialties include Chicken a la McKay, shirred eggs, and strawberry soup served in the garden conservatory. Families welcome. No smoking. 1 or 2/$75-125. MC, V. Travel agent.

— Comments continued on next page

Guests write: *"Furnished in antiques from the period of the house, guests may often sleep in the Victorian gowns and sleep shirts provided in each room. A full plantation breakfast is served in the conservatory with the ladies encouraged to choose a hat to wear to breakfast. The hosts are happy not only to recommend restaurants and things to see and do, but will also make reservations and purchase tickets for guests."* (N. Cox)

"Every corner of the inn is filled with interesting antiques and unique decorating touches that delight your senses and stir your memories. Breakfasts are satisfying presentations including homemade muffins, unique juices, local jams and jellies, and McKay House original main dishes, all blended with lively conversation among guests and hosts." (L. MacNeil-Watkins)

San Antonio

Bullis House Inn
621 Pierce Street
San Antonio, TX 78208
(512) 223-9426

Type of B&B: Small inn.
Rooms: 8, 2 with private bath.
Rates: 1/$41-65; 2/$45-69.

Rating: B or ♛♛ Good, exceeds basic requirements.

Neoclassical, white-columned mansion is located 2 miles northeast of downtown San Antonio off I-35. Choose from eight guest rooms which feature fourteen-foot ceilings, color TV, and air conditioning. Each room has been individually decorated in soft colors with antique reproductions and period pieces. Deluxe rooms offer a working fireplace and French windows. The inn's original architectural features have been preserved and include oak stairways, parquet floors, marble fireplaces, and crystal chandeliers. The inn has a swimming pool on the premises. Area attractions include Old Army Museum, Fort Sam Houston, Alamo, Sea World, Fiesta Texas, and missions. Continental breakfast. Function rooms are available for weddings and meetings. Families are welcome in special second floor rooms that can accommodate parties of six. 1/$41-65; 2$45-69. AE, MC, V. Travel agent.

San Antonio

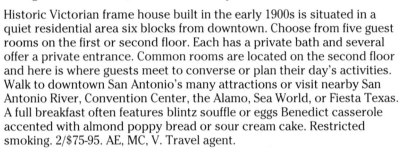

Norton Brackenridge House
230 Madison
San Antonio, TX 78204
(800) 221-1412 or (512) 271-3442

Type of B&B: Inn.
Rooms: 5 with private bath.
Rates: 2/$75-95.

Rating: B or ♛♛ Good, exceeds basic requirements.

Historic Victorian frame house built in the early 1900s is situated in a quiet residential area six blocks from downtown. Choose from five guest rooms on the first or second floor. Each has a private bath and several offer a private entrance. Common rooms are located on the second floor and here is where guests meet to converse or plan their day's activities. Walk to downtown San Antonio's many attractions or visit nearby San Antonio River, Convention Center, the Alamo, Sea World, or Fiesta Texas. A full breakfast often features blintz souffle or eggs Benedict casserole accented with almond poppy bread or sour cream cake. Restricted smoking. 2/$75-95. AE, MC, V. Travel agent.

Waxahachie

The Bonnynook Bed and Breakfast Inn
414 West Main Street
Waxahachie, TX 75165
(214) 937-7207 or
(800) 486-5936 (Outside TX)

Type of B&B: Inn.
Rooms: 4, with private bath.
Rate: 1 or 2/$70-100.

Rating: A or ♛♛♛ Excellent, far exceeds basic requirements.

Turn-of-the-century Victorian inn with wide porches and gingerbread accents is located 30 miles south of Dallas on I-35. Four antique furnished guest rooms offer a private bath and feature unique antiques such as a sleigh bed, Belgium antique bed, and 1920's Art Deco pieces. Several rooms have Jacuzzi tubs. Walk two blocks to the historic Town Square with its 1850 Courthouse. Nearby attractions include the largest concentration of Victorian gingerbread homes in the state as well as several antique shops, malls, and fine restaurants. Full breakfast. Function rooms are available for meetings and social occasions. Families welcome. Restricted smoking. 1 or 2/$70-100. AE, MC, V. Travel agent.

— *Comments continued on next page*

Guests write: *"The room made us feel the romance of the last century and the bubble bath was great. They've added so many unique touches. We'll never forget the delicious breakfasts."* (S. Peak)

"I can't think of a better way to spend a birthday than going away with the man you love and have been married to for almost fourteen years and coming to such a wonderful place as Bonneynook. We had a great time relaxing, taking a bubble-bath in the old claw-foot tub and just enjoying each other without the kids." (C. Parga)

"We ended our Christmas holiday with dinner at the Bonneynook. This stay was our first experience at B&Bs and it's just the prescription for two busy professionals from the big city. Bonneynook allowed us to imagine and experience what life was like when the world wasn't so busy faxing a report or E-mailing a memo. We'll carry the Bonnynook's grace and charm with us as we enter 1992." (P. Borchardt)

"We appreciated all the amenities, the sample menus from local restaurants, the fresh fruit tray, the tea and coffee service, the decanter of wine after our return from dinner, the three-course breakfast, the charming hospitality, and the Frank's Room with the beautiful Jacuzzi tub." (M. Matthews)

UTAH

Additional information on B&Bs in this state is available from Mi Casa Su Casa (800) 456-0682 or B&B Rocky Mountains (800) 733-8415

Park City

Washington School Inn
P.O. Box 536, 543 Park Avenue
Park City, UT 84060
(801) 649-3800

Type of B&B: Inn.
Rooms: 12 guest rooms and 3 suites, all with private bath.
Rate: 1 or 2/$75-225.

Rating: A+ or ♛♛♛ Excellent, far exceeds basic requirements.

Grand Victorian mansion built in 1889 has been completely restored and is now listed on the National Register of Historic Places. It's location is an urban residential area of Park City, 25 miles east of Salt Lake City. Each of the twelve guest rooms and three suites has a private bath and phone. A large suite on the third floor can easily accommodate families or couples traveling together. Popular attractions at the inn include the hot tub, sauna, and steam showers. This is a year-round recreation area with lit night skiing, hiking in the mountains, lakes, fly fishing, wind-surfing, golf, tennis, and mountain biking. Full breakfast. Facilities available for small weddings and meetings. Restricted smoking. 1 or 2/$75-225. AE, MC, V. Travel agent.

VERMONT

Alburg

Thomas Mott Bed & Breakfast
Blue Rock Road, Route 2, Box 149B
Alburg, VT 05440-9620
(802) 796-3736 or (800) 348-0843

Type of B&B: Inn.
Rooms: 5 with private bath.
Rates: 1 or 2/$55-70

Rating: A- or ♛ ♛ ♛ Excellent, far exceeds basic requirements.

Historic farmhouse built in 1838 is located near the junctions of Route 78 and 2 on northwestern Lake Champlain. There are five guest rooms with private bath, lake views, and homemade quilts. Popular attractions in the area include Missisquoi Wildlife Refuge, Auction House, Shrine of St. Anne, antique shops, and major ski areas of Montreal, Burlington, Stowe, Lake Placid, and Jay Peak. Year-round recreation includes ice-fishing, snowmobiling, ice boating, cross-country skiing, golf, swimming, hiking, canoeing, and bicycling. Full breakfast is individually prepared for each guest. Complimentary Ben & Jerry's ice cream served. Gourmet catered dinners are available on advance notice. No smoking. 1 or 2/$55-70. Discover, MC, V. Travel agent.

Guests write: *"I felt as though I was staying at my Grandfather's old log cabin. I found the house very cozy and comfortable and the host, Pat Schallert, was warm and friendly. The location is right on the lake and far from lots of traffic but close to the sights. Breakfasts were freshly prepared both mornings and Pat is a wonderful chef."* (W. Passman)

"The accommodation proved to be a tranquil haven where the surroundings were conducive to both relaxation and stimulation of mind, body, and soul. Beautiful scenery, appealing decor, and a host whose consideration for the comfort and needs of his guests seemed to know no bounds." (J. Griffith)

Arlington

Hill Farm Inn
R.R. 2, Box 2015
Arlington, VT 05250
(802) 375-2269 or (800) 882-2545

Type of B&B: Inn.
Rooms: 13, 8 with private bath.
Rates: 1/$40-90; 2/$60-110.

Rating: B or ♛♛ Good, exceeds basic requirements.

Hill Farm Inn has served as a farm vacation for guests for over eighty-five years and is located in the southwest corner of the state on land which was once part of a historic land grant. There are thirteen rooms in the main inn or guest house; eight offer a private bath. The decor of each room captures the simplicity and charm of a traditional New England farmhouse. A large living room offers comfortable chairs, sofas, and a fireplace. Battenkill River borders the farm and is fun for canoeing and fly-fishing. Other attractions in the area include Bennington Museum, Green Mountain National Forest, antique shops, hiking, bicycling, and skiing. Full country breakfast is included in the rates and a four-course dinner is available at an additional charge by advance reservation. Families welcome. 1/$40-90; 2/$60-110. AE, MC, V. Travel agent.

Guests write: *"I am a manufacturer's representative traveling through Vermont every two months and I stay at Hill Farm Inn. My room is always warm and comfortable. The living room is special in winter with a roaring fire where you can relax with cheese, crackers, and a beverage before dinner. The meals are wonderful and always presented in a very appealing manner. The savings over local hotels is very important to me."* (M. Kelsey)

"Going to Hill Farm Inn is like going to our second home. Several years ago my husband and I switched from our comfortable room in the main inn to a cozy cabin overlooking the Battenkill Valley and Mt. Equinox. Our porch, complete with two lounge chairs, allows us to relax in the clear Vermont air as we watch beefalo graze in the pasture and listen to the crickets and birds chirping around it. It is truly idyllic. Both the countryside and inn itself are unspoiled and possess a gentle spirit that quietly renews the soul." (D. Giaimo)

"As a skier and big eater, I find breakfast and dinner, with fresh baked muffins and bread, to be pleasingly diversified, very good and more than adequate for an active life. Discount tow tickets are available at the inn which saves money and standing in line at the slopes. We feel Hill Farm is more than a place to sleep because the spacious public areas provide opportunities for socializing, reading, watching TV, and playing games." (G. Noble)

"To have your children see a bird hatch its eggs in a tree outside their window and watch her feed the little birds, or have them chase little rabbits,

or walk down to see the cows nearby is what we love for our children to experience here. You can't get these experiences just anywhere." (L. Ryan)

Barre

Woodruff House
13 East Street
Barre, VT 05641
(802) 476-7745 or 479-9381

Type of B&B: B&B home.
Rooms: 2 with private bath.
Rates: 1/$50; 2/$65.

Rating: A or ♚ ♚ ♚ Excellent, far exceeds basic requirements.

Historic Queen Anne Victorian home is situated across from a quiet park near the village center and located halfway between Boston and Montreal at I-89, exit 7. There are two guest rooms available with private bath. Each is individually decorated with antiques, eclectic furnishings, and collectibles. There are two large common rooms which offer comfortable seating for viewing TV, quiet nooks for reading or conversing, and a large collection of interesting books. Area attractions include State Capitol, tour of the largest granite quarries in the world, and leaf peeping. Full breakfast is served with fine china, crystal, and silver in the formal dining room. No smoking. 1/$50; 2/$65.

Guests write: *"Robert and Terry prepared tea, crackers, cheese, and sliced fruits for us when we arrived very tired and hungry. They also prepared a late night snack for us before we went to bed. This was our first opportunity to stay at a B&B and we're now convinced if they're all like the Woodruff House we shall be customers for life."* (R. Sunday)

"We are the family of Dr. John H. Woodruff who brought his family back here to visit his brother and family. We were privileged to get to stay in his family home. It had been restored and was in great shape. The whole Woodruff family feels very fortunate to have our house in such beautiful shape and in such friendly hands." (J. Woodruff)

"Bob & Terry's sincere concern for our comfort and pleasure was unmatched by any other experience we've had in a B&B. The table was set with the finest details in this most authentic Victorian home. I stepped back in time." (B. Pivnick)

"After sleeping soundly under down comforters, we enjoyed warm conversation by candlelight over breakfast in an elegant dining room. We would choose this delightful bargain over a hotel or a condominium for any of our Vermont ski vacations." (G. Hills)

Chester

Henry Farm Inn
Green Mountain Turnpike
P.O. Box 646
Chester, VT 05143
(802) 875-2674

Type of B&B: Inn.
Rooms: 7 with private bath.
Rates: 1/$35-53; 2/$50-80.

Rating: B+ or ♛♛ Good, exceeds basic requirements.

Historic Colonial farmhouse situated on fifty forested acres of foothills was built in 1750 and is located ten miles from I-91 near Routes 103 and 11. There are seven guest rooms with private bath and several of the rooms feature working fireplaces. There are two fireplaced sitting rooms on the main floor for reading, conversing, and relaxation. Area recreation includes skiing, hiking, fishing, golf, and tennis. Full breakfast. Families welcome. No smoking. 1/$35-53; 2/$50-80. MC, V.

Fairlee

Silver Maple Lodge
R.R. 1, Box 8
South Main Street
Fairlee, VT 05045
(802) 333-4326 or (800) 666-1946

Type of B&B: Inn with cottages.
Rooms: 12, 10 with private bath.
Rates: 1/$38-58; 2/$46-64.

Rating: B or ♛♛ Good, exceeds basic requirements.

Historic country inn dating back to the late 1700s is on Route 5, half a mile south of I-91, exit 15. Choose from twelve antique-furnished guest rooms, ten with private bath. Private cottage accommodations offer knotty pine walls and wide board floors of lumber cut on the property. Relax on the wrap-around porch or play horseshoes, croquet, badminton, or shuffleboard on the lawn. Visit nearby Lake Morey, Lake Fairlee, Maple Grove Museum, St. Johnsbury, Quechee Gorge, and Saint Gaudens National Historic Site. Local recreation includes golf, tennis, fishing, boating, skiing, hiking, and hot air ballooning. Continental breakfast. Families welcome. 1/$38-58; 2/$46-64. AE, MC, V. Travel agent.

Guests write: *"We have stayed at the Silver Maple for several years and have never had a complaint except that the stay was always too short. The owners really care about their guests and always go out of their way to make us happy. We enjoyed everything immensely - the lovely room, good breakfasts, fabulous weather, interesting people, use of their video, comfortable lawn chairs, perfect location for everything we wanted to do and see."* (B. Solomon)

Jeffersonville

The Smuggler's Notch Inn
P.O. Box 280
Jeffersonville, VT 05464
(802) 644-2412

Type of B&B: Country inn.
Rooms: 11 with private bath.
Rates: 1/$40; 2/$60-75.

Rating: B or ♛♛ Good, meets basic requirements.

Historic country inn is located right in the village near Routes 108 and 15. Eleven guest rooms are available, each with private bath. Carefully restored, the inn boasts a brick fireplace, tin ceiling, hardwood floors, and an old-fashioned swing on the front porch. Stroll the wide streets in the village. Year-round activities include antique festivals, skiing, hiking, canoeing, swimming, and biking. Experience the New England fall foliage and watch a maple sugar house in production. Full breakfast frequently features pancakes, eggs, French toast, and muffins. Meeting and wedding facilities are available in the converted ballroom. Families welcome. 1/$40; 2/$60-75. AE, MC, V. 10% auto club, business travel, and senior discounts. Travel agent.

Guests write: *"The rooms at this inn are newly renovated with attractive decor and tiled bathrooms. The public rooms are old, as becomes an historic inn. The food is outstanding. We have never had such a choice of well-cooked breakfasts. The dinners are truly gourmet. There is a wonderful family atmosphere."* (J. Turnure)

Jericho

Homeplace Bed & Breakfast
RR 2, Box 367
Jericho, VT 05465
(802) 899-4694

Type of B&B: B&B home.
Rooms: 3 share 2 baths.
Rates: 1/$40; 2/$50.

Rating: A- or ♛♛♛ Excellent, far exceeds basic requirements.

Modern farmhouse is situated on one-hundred acres of woods and located 1.5 miles from Route 15 and 8 miles from I-89, exit 12. Choose from three guest rooms which share two baths and feature crewel-style spreads and embroidered pillowcases. The home is filled with European antiques, Vermont craftwork, and a large collection of books. Animals on the farm include horses, sheep, pigs, ducks, chickens, cats, dogs, and donkeys. Explore miles of cross-country or hiking trails. Area attractions include University of Vermont, Shelburne Museum, Stowe ski areas, and Lake Champlain. Full country breakfast may feature eggs, bacon or sausage, home-made rolls, and fruit. No smoking. 1/$40; 2/$50.

Killington

Inn at Long Trail
PO Box 267
Route 4
Killington, VT 05751
(802) 775-7181

Type of B&B: Country inn.
Rooms: 25 with private bath.
Rates: 1/$46-120; 2/$56-148;
Suite/$76-200.

Rating: C+ or ♛ Acceptable, meets basic requirements.

Traditional New England ski lodge situated in the Green Mountains is located east of Rutland and one mile west of Route 100 North. There are nineteen guest rooms or suites. Each offers a private bath and the suites feature working fireplaces. Popular activities here include relaxing in the living room, choosing a good book from the library, enjoying the hot tub, and watching TV. Area attractions include historic tours, antique shopping, skiing, hiking, horseback riding, and golf. Full breakfast. Function rooms are available for meetings, weddings, retreats, and family reunions. Families welcome. 1/$46-120; 2/$56-148; Suite/$76-200. MC, V. 10% senior, auto club, and family discounts. Travel agent. Open Summer, Fall, and Winter.

Londonderry

The Village Inn at Landgrove
RD 1, Box 215, Landgrove Rd.
Londonderry, VT 05148
(800) 669-8466 or (802) 824-6673

Type of B&B: Country inn with restaurant.
Rooms: 18, 16 with private bath.
Rates: 1/$50-90; 2/$55-105.

Rating: B- or ♛♛ Good, exceeds basic requirements.

Originally a farmstead built in the 1820s and added on to through the years, this "Vermont Continuous Architecture" inn is 80 miles northeast of Albany, New York, and 30 miles southeast of Rutland. Choose from eighteen guest rooms with Colonial decor and individual temperature control; sixteen offer a private bath. Dine by the fireplace in candlelit surroundings, relax in the Rafter Lounge or the whirlpool spa. Cross country ski from one of the marked trails leading from the inn into the national forest. Horse-drawn hay and sleigh rides are available and the stocked fishing pond becomes an ice skating rink during winter months. Play tennis, go golfing, hiking, or visit nearby antique and outlet shops. A full breakfast may feature blueberry pancakes or the "J-bar special-bit of everything". Wedding and meeting facilities available. Families welcome. Restricted smoking. 1/$50-90; 2/$55-105. AE, MC, V. Travel agent.

Guests write: *"Perhaps it's those blueberry pancakes, the delicious soup served as we sit around the wood-burner. It's a true feeling of welcome and being part of their magnificent family"* (B. Hill)

"I discovered the Village Inn as a biker's oasis while peddling along the back roads. The magnetic quaintness of the historic buildings and the genuine friendliness of the proprietor's mother as she presented each room of her 'home' were irresistible. Charm, warmth, home cooking and instant acceptance into a family atmosphere provide a country environment that relaxes and rejuvenates the body and soul." (P. Arnold)

"Charmingly nestled in the secluded, but accessible valley. Food is plentiful and tasty- just like Grandma's. It's like coming home." (N. Threlfall)

Ludlow

Andrie Rose Inn
13 Pleasant Street
Ludlow, VT 05149
(802) 228-4846 or (800) 223-4846

Type of B&B: Country inn and guest house.
Rooms: 10 with private bath.
Rates: 1/$85-100; 2/$100-115; Suites 2/$185.

Rating: A+ or ♕♕♕ Excellent, far exceeds basic requirements.

1829 country village inn is located at the base of Okemo Mountain Ski
Resort. Choose from ten uniquely decorated, antique-filled guest rooms
that offer designer linens, down comforters and pillows, and private baths.
Some rooms feature sloping ceilings and skylights, while others boast
whirlpool tubs. Luxury suites offer marble fireplaces, whirlpool baths, king
or queen-size canopy beds, stereo, and color cable TVs equipped with
VCR. Borrow bicycles to tour back roads and antique shops. Later, sip
fireside cocktails and enjoy complimentary hors d'oeuvres in the sitting
rooms. Area activities include downhill and cross-country skiing,
horseback riding, fishing, swimming, canoeing, tennis and golf. Full
breakfast often features blueberry pancakes, buttermilk waffles with Ben
and Jerry's Vermont ice cream, or a fresh broccoli and mushroom quiche.
Saturday night dinner available by advance reservation. Facilities available
for small weddings and meetings. No smoking. 1/$85-100; 2/$100-115;
Luxury Suites 2/$185. AE, MC, V. 10% senior discount.

Manchester Village

The Reluctant Panther Inn & Restaurant
PO Box 678, West Road
Manchester Village, VT 05254-0678
(802) 362-2568

Type of B&B: Country inn with restaurant
Rooms: 16 with private bath.
Rates: 1/$135-255; 2/$175-295.

Rating: A or ♕♕♕ Excellent, far exceeds basic requirements.

1850 Colonial building surrounded by tall trees has views of Mount
Equinox and is located 90 minutes northeast of Albany, New York. Sixteen
guest rooms have been individually decorated and offer a private bath,
air conditioning, and color TV. Four of the guest rooms have a king-size
bed, Jacuzzi, and fireplace or wood-burning stove. Enjoy the "welcoming"
bottle of red wine in each room, relax in the sitting room, or sit at the

fireplaced bar. Walk to a nearby bookstore, antique shops, the Equinox Hotel, or the Battenkill River. Just minutes away is Manchester Village with shops, a general store, and factory outlets. Visit the Hildene Southern Vermont Art Center or the Fly Fishing Museum, as well as concerts, playhouses, and auctions. Cinnamon amaretto French toast is one of the specialties offered at a full breakfast. A la Carte dinner at the on-site restaurant is available. Restricted smoking. Conference facility. 1/$135-255; 2/$175-295. AE, MC, V. Travel agent.

Proctorsville

Okemo Lantern Lodge
Main Street, P.O. 247
Proctorsville, VT 05153
(802) 226-7770 or (802) 226-7495

Type of B&B: Country inn with restaurant.
Rooms: 10 with private bath.
Rates: 1/$45; 2/$90.

Rating: B or ♛♛ Good, exceeds basic requirements.

Okemo Lantern Lodge was built in the early 1800s and is nestled in a classic New England village three hours north of Boston. The inn has been restored as a traditional Victorian home accented with natural butternut woodwork and original stained-glass windows. Ten guest rooms with private bath are furnished with wicker, antiques, and in some cases, canopy beds. Warm weather guests favor the heated pool, front porch, and perennial gardens. Curl up by the fire in a big arm chair, explore the house with its winding staircase and other Victorian features, or take in the Vermont countryside which offers four-season activities such as biking, skiing, snowmobiling, hunting, antiquing, and leaf-watching. Full breakfast features eggs any style, fresh fruit, freshly-made sausage and smoked ham. Dinner plan is available as are small wedding and meeting facilities. Families welcome. Restricted smoking. 1/$45; 2/$90. AE, MC, V.

Guests write: *"Wonderful hospitality! We'll be back."* (R. Mango)

Stowe

Inn at the Brass Lantern
717 Maple Street
Stowe, VT 05672
(802) 253-2229 or (800) 729-2980

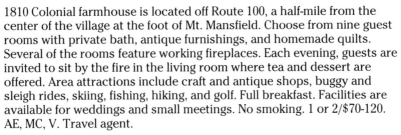

Type of B&B: Inn.
Rooms: 9 with private bath.
Rates: 1 or 2/$70-120.

Rating: A or ♛♛♛ Excellent, far exceeds basic requirements.

1810 Colonial farmhouse is located off Route 100, a half-mile from the center of the village at the foot of Mt. Mansfield. Choose from nine guest rooms with private bath, antique furnishings, and homemade quilts. Several of the rooms feature working fireplaces. Each evening, guests are invited to sit by the fire in the living room where tea and dessert are offered. Area attractions include craft and antique shops, buggy and sleigh rides, skiing, fishing, hiking, and golf. Full breakfast. Facilities are available for weddings and small meetings. No smoking. 1 or 2/$70-120. AE, MC, V. Travel agent.

Stowe

Spruce Pond Inn
1250 Waterbury Road
Stowe, VT 05672
(802) 253-4236 or (800) 283-1853.

Type of B&B: Country inn with restaurant.
Rooms: 7 with private bath.
Rates: 1/$40-50; 2/$45-120.

Rating: B+ or ♛♛ Good, exceeds basic requirements.

Spruce Pond Inn is an historic Colonial home built in 1820. There are seven guest rooms with private bath and cable TV, and one room features a fireplace. Popular activities here include skating on the pond near the inn and sitting in front of the fireplace after a full day of skiing. Nearby attractions include Ben & Jerry's Ice Cream Factory, hiking, biking, and cross-country skiing. A full breakfast features homemade pastries and granola and is served in front of the bay windows in the dining room. The dinner menu includes heart-healthy entrees. Function rooms are available for large meetings and weddings. No smoking. 1/$40-50; 2/$45-120. MC, V. 10% senior discount. Travel agent.

Vergennes

Emerson's Guesthouse B&B
82 Main Street
Vergennes, VT 05491
(802) 877-3293

Type of B&B: Guesthouse.
Rooms: 5, 1 with private bath.
Rates: 1 or 2/$35-65.

Rating: B+ or ♛♛ Good, exceeds basic requirements.

Historic guesthouse built in 1850 is located a half-mile from the junctions of Route 7 and 22A, and is surrounded by landscaped lawns and gardens. There are five spacious guest rooms and one offers a private bath. Guests enjoy strolling the garden areas, relaxing on the porch or in the common rooms. Area attractions include Shelburne Museum, Morgan Horse Farm, and Kennedy Brothers Marketplace, golf, tennis, swimming and bicycling. Full breakfast includes homemade jams, jellies and breads. 1 or 2/$35-65.

Waitsfield

Mad River Inn
P.O. Box 75
Tremblay Road off Route 100
Waitsfield, VT 05673
(802) 496-7900 or (802) 496-6892

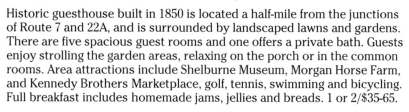

Type of B&B: Inn.
Rooms: 9 with private bath.
Rates:1/$49-95; 2/$59-125.

Rating: A or ♛♛♛ Excellent, far exceeds basic requirements.

Surrounded by the Green Mountains and in the heart of the Mad River Valley, this Victorian is situated one mile north of Waitsfield off of Route 100. Period fabrics, furnishings, and finishes as well as feather beds are featured in each of the nine guest rooms with private bath. Relax in the Victorian parlor with fireplace. The living room has large picture windows and authentic antiques. The Queen Anne dining room reflects the decor of an English tea room where a complimentary afternoon tea is offered daily. The area is perfect for four- season sports such as golfing, skiing, hiking, and swimming. Ben & Jerry's Ice Cream factory is nearby as are Cold Hollow Cider Mill, Warren Store, Green Mountain Chocolate Factory, and the picturesque Green Mountains. Gourmet breakfast starts with fresh juice and includes harvests from the inn's organic garden. Special dishes include oven baked French toast, Southwestern strata, and fresh fruit crepes. Saturday ski season dinners and group gourmet dinners available as well as wedding and meeting facilities. Families welcome. Restricted smoking. 1/$49-95; 2/$59-125. AE, MC, V. Travel agent.

Warren

The Sugartree, A Country Inn
RR 1, Box 38, Sugarbush Access Rd.
Warren, VT 05674
(800) 666-8907 or (802) 583-3211

Type of B&B: Inn.
Rooms: 10 with private bath.
Rates: 1/$55-66; 2/$80-124.

Rating: B or ♛♛ Good, exceeds basic requirements.

Saltbox-style inn has an exterior reminiscent of a European hotel and is located thirty miles southwest of Montpelier, 1/4 mile west of the Sugarbush Ski area. Waverly wallpaper, custom-designed stained-glass, ruffled country curtains, and handmade quilts are featured in the ten guest rooms with private bath. Enjoy biking, golfing, tennis, hiking, swimming, and antiquing as well as leaf watching or exploring covered bridges and white steepled churches. Both alpine and cross country skiing are available in the area. A full breakfast might offer egg and three cheese casserole, waffles, French toast, or pancakes with home-made syrups and butters. Wedding and meeting facilities available. Wheelchair access. No smoking. 1/$55-66; 2/$80-124. AE, MC, V. Extended or midweek stay discounts. Travel agent.

Guests write: *"This little inn reminds me of someplace in the Swiss Alps. It's tucked into a mountainside and is really cozy. It has window boxes brimming with flowers, the rooms are furnished with antiques and canopy beds, and the breakfasts are tasty. You won't go hungry there. There is no traffic, the roads are fun to drive on, and the scenery is right off a calendar."* (Mrs. Hughes)

"Two thumbs up! In an era when one is often treated as merely another paying customer, Frank and Kathy have succeeded in creating a mountain retreat where every guest is treated as a treasured visitor. Kathy spoils you with good food and lively conversation on a chilly evening and Frank pampers you with roaring fires in the living rooms. There might be a deadly game of Trivial Pursuit in progress one evening and 15 guests laughing crazily over a game of dictionary the next. This is Vermont as I always hoped it would be." (S. Beck)

"A very clean, charming and warm B&B with charming and accommodating hosts. Great breakfasts!" (B. Mower)

Vermont

Waterbury/Stowe

Black Locust Inn
R.R. 1, Box 715
Waterbury Center, VT 05677
(802) 244-7490 and (800) 366-5592

Type of B&B: Inn.
Rooms: 6 with private bath.
Rates: 1/$55-79; 2/$65-95.

Rating: A or ♛♛♛ Excellent, far exceeds basic requirements.

Historic farmhouse built in 1832 is situated in the hills near Stowe and located five miles north of I-89, exit 10. There are six guest rooms which feature a brass bed, private bath, antique furnishings, and polished wood floors. A common room on the main floor offers a cozy corner with a wood stove. A game table is situated by a large bay window. Area attractions include major ski areas, Cold Hollow Cider Mill, Ben & Jerry's Ice Cream Factory, and outdoor recreation. Full breakfast is served on linen and snacks are offered each afternoon. No smoking. 1/$55-79; 2/$65-95. Discover, MC, V. 10% senior discount. Travel agent. Open year-round except for two weeks in April and November.

Weathersfield

Inn at Weathersfield
P.O. Box 165, Route 106
Weathersfield, VT 05151
(802) 263-9217 or (800) 477-4828
Fax: (802) 263-9219

Type of B&B: Country inn.
Rooms: 12 with private bath.
Rates: 1/$117.50-120; 2/$175-205.

Rating: A+ or ♛♛♛ Excellent, far exceeds basic requirements.

Large country inn located 5 miles north of Springfield was built in 1795 and is rich in history. Each of the twelve guest rooms offers a private bath, period antiques, working fireplace, and views of the surrounding countryside. There are five common rooms at the inn including the library with a collection of 4,000 books and a game and exercise room on the lower level. The restaurant and lounge on the premises serves a five-course dinner and offers live piano music nightly. A full breakfast and afternoon tea are served in the library or on the pleasant sunporch. Recreation in the area includes tennis, fishing, hiking, and skiing. A pond on the premises offers ice-skating in winter. Several function rooms are available for meetings and weddings. Rates include breakfast, tea, and dinner. 1/$117.50-120; 2/$175-205. AE, Carte Blanche, Diners, Discover, MC, V. Business travel and package discounts. Travel agent.

West Dover

Austin Hill Inn
Route 100
West Dover, VT 05356
(800) 332-RELAX or
(802) 464-5281
Fax: (802) 464-1229

Type of B&B: Large inn.
Rooms: 12 with private bath.
Rates: 1/$55-115; 2/$65-125.

Rating: A- or ♛♛♛ Excellent, far exceeds basic requirements.

Newly renovated Country Colonial inn is located outside the village of West Dover just off Route 100. Choose from twelve guest rooms, each with private bath and individual decor; several offer a private balcony. For moments of relaxation there are several common rooms with a fireplace as well as a swimming pool. Area attractions include fishing, boating on Lake Whitingham, Mt. Snow Ski Resort, golf at Haystack or Mt. Snow championship courses, designer outlet stores, antique malls, and the Marlboro Music Festival. Full New England country breakfast, afternoon tea, and complimentary wine and cheese served daily. Candlelit dinners are available for private parties. The inn specializes in "Murder Mystery" weekends throughout the year. There are several function rooms on-site for meetings and social occasions. No smoking. 1/$55-115; 2/$65-125. AE, MC, V.

Guests write: *"You dream of the perfect New England inn and you come to Austin Hill, and there it is! Roaring fires in cozy, beautifully appointed sitting rooms, country-style bedrooms complete with rocking chairs, afghans, candlelight, and chocolates at bedtime, and a friendly, courteous and eager staff. It all sounds like a movie set and it's like a movie set come to life."* (R. Seider)

"I have grown accustomed to the efficiency of modern hotels but Austin Hill Inn has spoiled me. Their friendly dogs, charming and comfortable appointments, and most of all the gracious warmth of the staff have set better standards." (H. Levy)

"Although our stay at the inn was very brief, for two weary travelers, it brought needed relief. Their cheery warm welcome as we entered the door was like that of a good neighbor. Who could ask for anything more? With

four married children and seven grandchildren, we on occasion look for a hideaway. We'll be back." (B. Ford)

"Another bright star has been added to the twinkling Vermont sky, the Austin Hill Inn. Walk through the door and step into a world of warmth and charm from days gone by. Once you arrive you're treated like a special guest but feel like part of the family." (P. Kerantzas)

Wilmington

Nutmeg Inn
West Molly Stark Trail
Route 9
Wilmington, VT 05363
(802) 464-3351

Type of B&B: Large inn.
Rooms: 13 with private bath.
Rates: 1 or 2/$70-190.

Rating: A or ♛♛♛ Excellent, far exceeds basic requirements.

Early-American farmhouse built in 1777 stands near a mountain brook near the junctions of Routes 9 and 100 in the village center. There are thirteen guest rooms or suites and each offers a private bath, brass or iron bed, quilts, and antique dressers. Many of the rooms offer cable TV, nine feature a working fireplace, and one suite has a VCR and private balcony overlooking Haystack Mountain and the surrounding meadows. Several of the older rooms feature exposed beams and slanted ceilings which reflect the rich history of the inn. The original carriage house offers a living room with fireplace, TV, and piano, and there is a small library with a collection of books. There is an extensive plate collection on display throughout the inn. Recreation nearby includes skiing, leaf peeping, scenic drives, hiking, antiquing, fishing, boating, and golfing. Full breakfast and afternoon or evening beverages served daily. Families welcome. Wheelchair access. Restricted smoking. 1 or 2/$70-190. AE, MC, V.

Guests write: *"This is the most beautiful and gracious inn we've ever stayed in. Excellent French toast! The inn had all of the luxury of being away, yet the comfort of being home."* (P. Quasius)

"I am the mother of three children. My husband attends school and works so our lives are very busy. We try to get away as often as possible. But no place ever made us feel more rested and relaxed as the Nutmeg Inn." (S. McHugh)

Wilmington

Trail's End, A Country Inn
Smith Road
Wilmington, VT 05363
(802) 464-2727

Type of B&B: Inn.
Rooms: 15 with private bath.
Rates: 1/$90-120; 2/$90-160.

Rating: A+ or ♛ ♛ ♛ Excellent, far exceeds basic requirements.

Rustic country inn in a tranquil setting is located in the heart of Deerfield Valley, a half mile east of Route 100 North. Choose from fifteen guest rooms or suites, each with private bath, individual decor, and family heirlooms. Available to guests are an outdoor swimming pool, clay tennis court, stocked trout pond, and English flower gardens. Four-season recreation includes canoeing, horseback riding, hiking, golfing, sleigh rides, and downhill or cross-country skiing. Full breakfast includes homemade granola and a varied choice of entrees such as pancakes, waffles, egg dishes and breakfast meats. Afternoon refreshments are served daily. Families welcome. Facilities available for meetings and social functions. 1/$90-120; 2/$90-160. MC, V.

Guests write: *"My husband and I went to Trail's End on our Honeymoon. We were very impressed with the atmosphere and hospitality. Bill and Mary Kilburne make you feel more like a family than a guest."* (K. Bird)

"Friendly smiles, warm hospitality, and a make-yourself-at-home feeling, are always present. My wife and I have returned every year since our first visit." (P. Diana)

"Mary and Bill treat us like family. Their warmth permeates the inn in the rooms, the food, and the total ambiance of Trail's End. This is our fifth year at the inn and the only check that I look forward to writing all year." (P. Marier)

"My wife and I return with friends each year to this comfortable refuge. Mary and Bill preside with gracious concern for our comfort and subtle attention to detail while including us in the extended family that shares this happy hearth." (J. Batson)

"There are always cookies and lemonade in the summer and hot cider in the winter plus bowls of nuts and apples for nibbles. The rooms are charming and each one furnished differently." (W. Gross)

"We have visited Trail's End for four years in a row and it is always a treat. Bill and Mary are terrific hosts and they are enormously proud of their inn. They continue to improve the rooms. The Saturday night dinner is always fun and Bill's poached eggs are famous." (D. Celani)

Woodstock

Deer Brook Inn
HCR 68, Box 443
Woodstock, VT 05091
(802) 672-3713

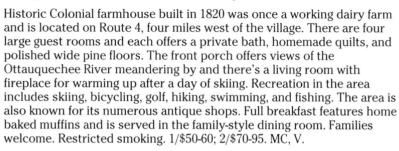

Type of B&B: Inn.
Rooms: 4 with private bath.
Rates: 1/$50-60; 2/$70-95.

Rating: B+ or ♕♕ Good, exceeds basic requirements.

Historic Colonial farmhouse built in 1820 was once a working dairy farm and is located on Route 4, four miles west of the village. There are four large guest rooms and each offers a private bath, homemade quilts, and polished wide pine floors. The front porch offers views of the Ottauquechee River meandering by and there's a living room with fireplace for warming up after a day of skiing. Recreation in the area includes skiing, bicycling, golf, hiking, swimming, and fishing. The area is also known for its numerous antique shops. Full breakfast features home baked muffins and is served in the family-style dining room. Families welcome. Restricted smoking. 1/$50-60; 2/$70-95. MC, V.

Guests write: *"This was a warm and welcoming place to return to after some rather cold and un-welcoming ski slopes. We've been having breakfast withdrawal since we left! Cereal and grapefruit aren't making it and Gary (my husband) is after me to make quiche."* (J. Moffie)

"We had a wonderful stay and the breakfast was wonderful. There was only one other inn we stayed at during our month of traveling that could match the feeling of welcome and the sense of home that Deer Brook Inn offers." (A. Muratet)

Woodstock

Woodstocker B&B
Route 4, 61 River Street
Woodstock, VT 05091
(802) 457-3896

Type of B&B: Inn.
Rooms: 9 with private bath.
Rates: 1/$60-110; 2/$65-115.

Rating: B+ or ♕♕ Good, exceeds basic requirements.

Historic Cape Cod home built in 1830 is located ten miles from I-89 and I-91 on Route 4. There are nine guest rooms or suites and each offers a private bath. A comfortable living room on the main floor has a mix of Scandinavian-style and contemporary furnishings and provides a quiet place for reading or playing board games. The inn offers a spa on the premises and is within walking distance of village shops, galleries, restaurants, theater, and the village green park. Area attractions include factory outlets, bicycling, tennis, skiing, hiking, and golf. Full buffet breakfast. Families welcome. 1/$60-110; 2/$65-115. MC, V. Travel agent.

Guests write: *"I have stayed in numerous B&B establishments and have found this one to be unique. Perhaps it is the sincere friendliness of the charming host and hostess, Liza and Romano. This couple is professional and at the same time presents a family-like environment. The accommodations are comfortable, clean, and homey - like a visit to Grandmother's house."* (D. Lepore)

VIRGINIA

Additional information on B&Bs in this state is available from Guesthouses Bed & Breakfast (804) 979-7264.

Blacksburg

Sycamore Tree Bed & Breakfast
P.O. Box 10937
Blacksburg, VA 24062
(703) 381-1597

Type of B&B: Inn.
Rooms: 6 with private bath.
Rates: 1 or 2/$65-110.

Rating: A or ♛♛♛ Excellent, far exceeds basic requirements.

Circa 1990 farmhouse nestled at the foot of Hightop Mountain is located four miles east of Blacksburg's city limits. Six guest rooms with private bath are furnished with antiques and country accessories. Common rooms on the main floor include a living room and family room with fireplace and the porch offers views of the mountain meadow and wildlife. Area attractions include golf, hiking, antique stores, fine restaurants, museums, historic buildings, and nightly entertainment in the neighboring towns and universities. Full Southern-style breakfast. No smoking. 1 or 2/$65-110.

Bumpass/Lake Anna

Rockland Farm Retreat
Lake Anna
3609 Lewiston Road
Bumpass, VA 23024
(703) 895-5098 or (301) 384-4583

Type of B&B: Country inn.
Rooms: 6 with shared baths.
Rates: 1 or 2/$50-60.

Rating: C- or ♛ Acceptable, meets basic requirements.

Victorian plantation situated on seventy-five acres was built in 1820 and is located 15 miles south of Fredericksburg off I-95. There are six guest rooms with shared bath. Relax on the large front porch and in the living room, or explore the 75 acres of farmland with its wildlife, farm buildings, livestock, and vineyard. The inn is near Lake Anna water sports, horseback riding, hunting, golf, hiking, and bicycling. Host speaks French and Spanish. Full breakfast. Facilities are available for weddings, family reunions, retreats, and meetings. Families and pets welcome. Restricted smoking. 1 or 2/$50-60. AE. 10% family discount. Travel agent.

Champlain

Linden House Bed & Breakfast
P.O. Box 23
Champlain, VA 22438
(804) 443-1170 or (804) 443-5474

Millikan

Type of B&B: Inn.
Rooms: 6, 3 with private bath.
Rates: 1/$45; 2/$85.

Rating: A or ♛♛♛ Excellent, far exceeds basic requirements.

Colonial inn located minutes away from historic Tappahanock and 35 miles south of Fredericksburg was established in 1750 and is on the National Register of Historic Buildings. The six guest rooms, three with private bath, are furnished with antiques and some have sitting areas, fireplaces, Jacuzzi with steam bath, or views of the English Garden and landscaped yard. Relax on the porch or patio with a glass of lemonade, explore the two hundred acres of historic surroundings, or take a cruise on the Rappahanock River. Stratford Hall, Wakefield and Westmoreland State Park are nearby and the area's antique shops offer hours of exploring. Full breakfast with a Plantation menu vary with the seasons and might include omelets presented with fresh fruit in Pina Colada dip. The English Basement provides space for weddings and meetings. 1/$45; 2/$85. MC, V. Family discount.

Guests write: *"They sent us home with wonderful goodies. We got engaged on Friday night after our delicious dinner. The Linden House will always be very meaningful to us."* (C.Smith)

"The Linden House is a lovely place. Ken and Sandy are wonderful hosts. The food is great. The service good. The staff puts you at ease and make you feel comfortable. They go the extra mile for their guests." (P. Briggs)

Charles City

North Bend Plantation B&B
12200 Weyanoke Road
Charles City, VA 23030
(804) 829-5176 or (800) 841-1479

Type of B&B: Inn.
Rooms: 4 with private bath.
Rates: 1 or 2/$95-110.

Rating: A or ♛♛♛ Excellent, far exceeds basic requirements.

General Sheridan used this historic plantation home on 250 acres as his headquarters during the Civil War. The home, built in 1819, is a historic landmark, and is located halfway between Williamsburg and Richmond in Virginia Plantation country, off Route 5. There are four guest rooms on the second floor and each has a private bath, family antiques, color TV, and lovely period decor. One suite offers two connecting bedrooms, one with queen-bed and the other with single bed. There's a modern bath between the bedrooms and this suite offers ideal privacy for three people. Several common rooms at the inn include summer porches with wicker furnishings, a billiard room, and parlor which boasts a collection of rare books and antique furnishings. Popular activities here include walks on the property, a refreshing swim in the pool, bike riding on country roads, plantation home tours, antique shops, a public golf course, and Colonial Williamsburg attractions. Full country breakfast. 1 or 2/$95-110.

Guests write: *"Our stay was delightful! They walked us through history and served a delicious breakfast and we enjoyed the breakfast chats with George."* (A. Southworth)

"The setting, the books, the room, the breakfast, and especially the Coplands was delightful." (W. Canup)

"It's wonderfully peaceful here. We really enjoyed traversing the field with Ridgely and looking at the Civil War trenches. The fox hunt was splendid!" (A. Bedwell)

"Our accommodations were historic and comfortable and the girls were right at home playing around the farm. Ridgley gave us a wonderful trip down to the river during which we met a herd of llamas. Both hosts are tireless in sharing their knowledge of the area and their enthusiasm for the history of their property and families. The hospitality of the Coplands is exceptional and privacy is a much appreciated option after a day of sightseeing." (N. Engeman)

Charlottesville/Scottsville

Chester Bed & Breakfast
Route 4, Box 57
Scottsville, VA 24590
(804) 286-3960

Type of B&B: Inn.
Rooms: 5, 1 with private bath.
Rates: 1 or 2/$65-100.

Rating: A- or ♛♛♛ Excellent, far exceeds basic requirements.

Historic Greek Revival home built in 1847 is located 17 miles south of Charlottesville near Routes 726, 20, and 6. There are four second-floor guest rooms with shared baths or a downstairs guest room with four-poster bed and private bath. The entire inn is air-conditioned and each guest room features a woodburning fireplace. The first floor living room has a fireplace and fine art collection and the second-floor library offers informal seating and an interesting selection of books. The extensive grounds include an unusually large number of tree specimens. Bicycles and a kennel for pets are available. Area attractions include Monticello, Ashlawn, University of Virginia, winery tours, canoeing and tubing on the James River, skiing, and golf. Full breakfast. 1 or 2/$65-100. AE. Travel agent.

Guests write: *"The Chester B&B feels like a home away from home. The owners are engaging hosts and made us feel comfortable the minute we walked in the door. Breakfast was decadent with fresh bread, grapefruit, Swedish pancakes, bacon, sausage, and good strong coffee. The bedroom had a comfortable king-size bed, woodburning fireplace — a bargain at $75.*

"We have enjoyed staying at Chester twice. It is a beautiful drive from Charlottesville and our daughter is at University of Virginia. The downstairs room with the private bath is particularly comfortable. Love the conversation and great full-size breakfasts!" (T Ingram)

— *Comments continued on next page*

"Wonderful place! Large rooms are nicely furnished. Well-planned and beautifully prepared breakfasts. It's located in a lovely quiet Virginian countryside. The owners breed dogs but they are quiet and well-mannered (and outside). Smoking is permitted. Recommended for anyone who finds other B&Bs a bit dull!" (W. Piez)

"The best B&B we stayed at due to the hospitality of Dick and Gordon. The beautiful and immaculate house, the fine cuisine, and the roaring cheery fireplaces. They create a warm and lively social environment for a group of people who arrive, but don't remain, strangers. " (J. Marx)

"Beautiful surroundings, warm and hospitable hosts — this is an extremely relaxing ambiance and ideal place for a weekend getaway. " (D. Schwartz)

"What a unique experience. Breakfast is a gourmet treat. Don't be in a hurry but enjoy the atmosphere and conversation. We were treated more like friends than customers." (E. Pryor)

"Chester B&B is excellent! It fulfills all your expectations of what a B&B should be. " (F. Snell)

Charlottesville/North Garden

Inn at the Crossroads
Route 2, Box 6
North Garden, VA 22959
(804) 979-6452

Type of B & B: Inn.
Rooms: 5 with in-room sinks
and shared baths.
Rates: 1 or 2/$59-69

Rating: A- or ♛♛♛ Excellent, far exceeds basic requirements.

Historic landmark tavern built in 1820 is located 9 miles south of Charlottesville off Route 29 at Route 692. Named for different facets of art and literature, each of the five guest rooms are designed to be as close to what they might have been in the original days of the tavern. Take time to unwind with a book and explore the grounds which open to the foothills of the Blue Ridge. The inn is ideally located near Monticello, Ash Lawn, Michie Tavern, and Montpelier. Full breakfast. Small meeting facilities available. Restricted smoking. 1 or 2/$59-69. MC, V. Travel agent.

Guests write: *"The hot breakfasts were excellent, imaginative, delicious, and beautifully presented. The rooms were cozy, cheerful, and tastefully appointed. The proprietor was friendly, gracious and helpful."* (W. Shen)

"If you are looking for a friendly host, wonderful food, comfortable rooms, and a relaxed countryside location all wrapped up in an historic building, this is the place to go! I've never had such a wonderful time, nor felt so driven to return again and again. Don't miss this stop if you're in Charlottesville." (E. Gerller)

"Since it was Valentine's Day, we were treated with heart-shaped cookies waiting for us in our room and fresh flowers for breakfast. Lyn, who is also the sous chef at a popular restaurant in Charlottesville, served cinnamon pears and baked herb eggs one morning, and French toast with blueberry sauce the second morning. The inn is in the country with wonderful country roads all around. We enjoyed the king-size bed, electric blanket, and terrycloth robes. " (M. Alexander)

"Our weekend Anniversary celebration began with the warmest of hospitality and a return in time to this circa 1820 inn's atmosphere. We discovered complimentary champagne in our room upon arrival, enjoyed the surrounding views of the Blue Ridge foothills and distant farms, and a stroll in the countryside." (B. Simon)

"If you are interested in history, antiques, fabulous scenery, and undoubtedly the greatest innkeepers, this place is for you! The food is outstanding and served with such grace and friendliness that all their guests become friends on the first meeting." (S. Terry)

"Each room has an information packet detailing the history of the inn, what your room originally was, and background on the furnishings of each room. In the public room is an album with fascinating photographs for the restoration. The breakfast was pancakes, cider syrup, carrot cake, orange juice, fruit, and sausage." (M. Bentson)

"Even six months pregnant, we still felt as pampered as newlyweds. We appreciated their helpfulness and hospitality and the breakfast - wow!" (R. Plant)

"The house has a great feeling of being at home. I thank them for allowing me to bang on their piano and for those tasty blueberry pancakes." (A. Morris)

Christiansburg

The Oaks B&B Country Inn
311 East Main Street
Christiansburg, VA 24073
(703) 381-1500

Type of B&B: Inn.
Rooms: 5 with private bath.
Rates: 1 or 2/$75-120.

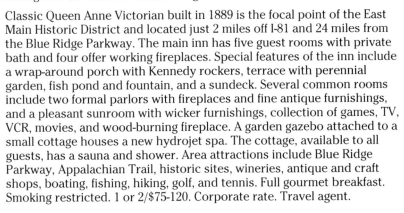

Rating: AA- or ♛♛♛♛ Outstanding.

Classic Queen Anne Victorian built in 1889 is the focal point of the East
Main Historic District and located just 2 miles off I-81 and 24 miles from
the Blue Ridge Parkway. The main inn has five guest rooms with private
bath and four offer working fireplaces. Special features of the inn include
a wrap-around porch with Kennedy rockers, terrace with perennial
garden, fish pond and fountain, and a sundeck. Several common rooms
include two formal parlors with fireplaces and fine antique furnishings,
and a pleasant sunroom with wicker furnishings, collection of games, TV,
VCR, movies, and wood-burning fireplace. A garden gazebo attached to a
small cottage houses a new hydrojet spa. The cottage, available to all
guests, has a sauna and shower. Area attractions include Blue Ridge
Parkway, Appalachian Trail, historic sites, wineries, antique and craft
shops, boating, fishing, hiking, golf, and tennis. Full gourmet breakfast.
Smoking restricted. 1 or 2/$75-120. Corporate rate. Travel agent.

Gordonsville

Sleepy Hollow Farm B&B
16280 Blue Ridge Turnpike
Gordonsville, VA 22942
(703) 832-5555

Type of B&B: Inn.
Rooms: 4 rooms and 2 suites
with private bath.
Rates: 1/$50-75; 2/$60-95.

Rating: A or ♛♛♛ Excellent, far exceeds basic requirements.

Historic Colonial farmhouse is located 25 miles northeast of
Charlottesville and 3 miles north of Gordonsville on Route 231. There are
six guest rooms available with private bath in the main house or in a
separate cottage. One room in the main inn offers a whirlpool and
working fireplace. The cottage rooms are all two-room suites which
feature either a working fireplace or wood-burning stove. Area attractions

include Montpelier, Monticello, museums, national park, historic areas, antique and craft shops, wineries, tennis, fishing, swimming, canoeing, bicycling, and horseback riding. Full breakfast. Facilities available for meetings and weddings. Families welcome. 1/$50-75; 2/$60-95. MC, V. Travel agent.

Guests write: *"I want to thank them for their warm hospitality. They were so gracious not to mind the midnight vigils in the TV room and to share their movie watching time with us. Everything was lovely and the food delicious, but most appreciated - the hugs!"* (E. Arsic)

"We had a lovely visit and were thrilled with the surprise birthday party they provided." (S. Miller)

Leesburg

Fleetwood Farm B&B
Route 1, Box 306-A
Leesburg, VA 22075
(703) 327-4325

Type of B&B: B&B home.
Rooms: 2 with private bath.
Rates: 1 or 2/$95-120.

Rating: A or ♛♛♛ Excellent, far exceeds basic requirements.

Plantation Manor home built in 1745 is a Virginia Historic Landmark on the National Registry of Historic Places and is located in Loudoun Hunt Country. Choose from two unique guest rooms, each with private bath (one with large Jacuzzi), fireplace, and air-conditioning. Enjoy the use of the living room with TV, games, books, and fireplace as well as cook-out facilities, horseshoes, croquet, and gardens. A canoe and fishing equipment are also available. Explore this working sheep farm and grounds with its Colonial herb garden, apiary, and several spoiled cats which live on the property. Area attractions include Manassas Battlefield, Harper's Ferry, festivals, vineyards, antique shops, and horseback riding. Full breakfast includes homemade jams, jellies, and honey. Restricted smoking. 1 or 2/$95-120.

Luray — See Stanley

Reedville

Cedar Grove Bed & Breakfast Inn
Route 1, Box 2535, Fleeton Road
Reedville, VA 22539
(804) 453-3915

Type of B&B: Inn.
Rooms: 3, 1 with private bath.
Rates: 1 or 2/$50-80.

Rating: A- or ♛♛♛ Excellent, far exceeds basic requirements.

Colonial Revival inn built in 1913 is situated on Virginia's Northern Neck right on the Chesapeake Bay at Fleeton Point, and located on Route 657, three miles from Reedville. Three antique-filled guest rooms are available. The suite offers a private bath and balcony with water views. Guests are invited to relax in the Victorian parlor or in the casual sunroom where books and TV are available. Borrow bicycles for a countryside ride, play tennis on the property, stroll the beach, or just relax watching the fishing boats going by on the Bay. Nearby are the Tangier and Smith Island cruises, charter fishing excursions, and historical attractions. Full breakfast is served on fine china in the formal dining room. Restricted smoking. 1 or 2/$50-80. Travel agent.

Guests write: *"The hosts are gracious, the food is excellent, and one feels as though they have gone back in time to a more relaxed and elegant way of living, yet with all the conveniences of today. I loved the porch and the room made me feel I was a special guest. It is lovely, so clean, and beautifully decorated."* (S. Ramos)

"My husband and I appreciated the well-kept rooms, tidy and thoroughly clean with added touches such as a fresh flower, an interesting book or magazine, cookies or refreshments to enjoy - all giving the impression that we were not just a paying guest but they wanted our stay to be special." (D. Amsl)

"Cedar Grove was so relaxing; from the first moment we arrived and spent some time sipping wine on the sunporch to the walk where I became engaged. The food was outstanding and the hospitality exceptional." (S. Snader)

"What a pleasurable experience that was. The host and hostess were most gracious and we so thoroughly enjoyed spending time with them learning about the inn and about how they came to own Cedar Grove." (D. Kreling)

Stanley

Jordan Hollow Farm Inn
Route 2, Box 375
Stanley, VA 22851
(703) 778-2285 or 778-2209

Type of B&B: Country inn with restaurant.
Rooms: 21 with private bath.
Rates: 1 or 2/$140-180.

Rating: A- or Excellent, far exceeds basic requirements.

Restored Colonial horse farm nestled on 145 acres of rolling hills and meadows and surrounded by the Shenandoah National Park is located six miles south of Luray. Two separate lodges on the property offer twenty-one guest rooms with private bath, handmade furniture, and family heirlooms. The top priced rooms are spacious with lovely furnishings, whirlpool tubs, and working fireplaces. There is a mini-barnyard with farm animals, and pony rides for children are available by appointment as well as horseback rides into the mountains. Popular activities here include swimming, hiking mountain trails, relaxing on the porch, and nearby fishing, skiing, and golfing. Area attractions include Luray Caverns, Skyline Drive, and the New Market Battlefield Museum. The rates include breakfast and dinner for two. Function rooms for weddings and meetings are offered. Families welcome. 1 or 2/$140-180. Discover, MC, V. Travel agent.

Staunton

The Sampson Eagon Inn
238 East Beverley Street
Staunton, VA 24401
(800) 597-9722 or (703) 886-8200

Type of B&B: Inn.
Rooms: 4 with private bath.
Rates: 1/$65-80; 2/$75-90.

Rating: A or ♛♛♛ Excellent, far exceeds basic requirements.

Circa 1840 Greek Revival mansion with some Italianate and Victorian touches has been restored and is located in Staunton's Historic Landmark District of Gospel Hill which is 150 miles southwest of Washington DC and 120 miles west of Richmond. Four guest rooms have been furnished with period antiques and feature a private bath, air conditioning, queen-size canopy bed, sitting area, and TV equipped with VCR. Relax in the living room or out on the porch overlooking a side garden. Stroll through the neighborhood with its historic architecture or walk one block to downtown for specialty and antique shops. Nearby attractions include the Woodrow Wilson Birthplace and Museum, Museum of American Frontier Culture, Mary Baldwin College, Skyline Drive and the Blue Ridge Mountains. Grand Marnier souffle pancakes, pecan Belgium waffles, or eggs Benedict are full breakfast specialties. Restricted smoking. 1/$65-80; 2/$75-90. Senior and corporate weekday, and auto club discount. Travel agent.

Strasburg

Hotel Strasburg
201 South Holliday Street
Strasburg, VA 22657
(703) 465-9191

Type of B & B: Hotel and
inn with restaurant.
Rooms: 25 with private bath.
Rates: 1 or 2/$69-149.

Rating: B or ♛♛ Good, exceeds basic requirements.

Victorian hotel and adjacent inn built in 1895 are located 2 miles off of I-81 in downtown Strasburg. The entire hotel has been renovated and features a collection of art and antique period pieces throughout the restaurant and parlor as well as in the guest rooms themselves. Each room offers a private bath, telephone, and TV. Special suites in the small inn next door offer lots of privacy, unusual decor and architectural features, and whirlpool baths. There is a restaurant and intimate pub on premises. Area attractions include Skyline Drive, Strasburg Emporium antique market, Wayside Theaters, Belle Grove Plantation, caverns, and Wayside Wonderland's beach. Continental breakfast. Facilities are available for small meetings and social functions. 1 or 2/$69-149. AE, MC, V. 10% auto club and senior discounts; 25% business travel discount. Travel agent.

Virginia Beach

Barclay Cottage
400 16th Street
Virginia Beach, VA 23451
(804) 422-1956

Type of B&B: Inn.
Rooms: 6, 3 with private bath.
Rates: 1 or 2/$65-80.

Rating: B or ♛ ♛ Good, exceeds basic requirements.

Southern Colonial beach cottage was built in the late 19th-Century and is located two blocks from the beach and 18 miles east of Norfolk. Six guest rooms are available, three with private bath, and each features antiques dating from the early 1900s including stage coach trunks and Victorian lamps. The verandahs have wicker chairs and rockers on which to sit and sip lemonade on hot summer days. Watch television or play backgammon in the living room. There's a regulation horseshoe court and golf putting green in the yard. The cottage is located in the heart of the Virginia Beach recreation area and Williamsburg is a short drive away. Fresh home baked breads and muffins accent a full breakfast. Restricted smoking. 1 or 2/$65-80. MC, V. 10% senior, corporate, and auto club discounts. Travel agent.

Williamsburg

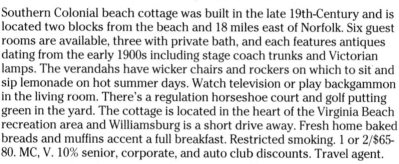

Indian Springs Bed & Breakfast
330 Indian Springs Road
Williamsburg, VA 23185
(800)262- 9165 or (804)220- 0726

Type of B&B: Inn.
Rooms: 4 with private bath.
Rates: 1 or 2/$74-105.

Rating: B or ♛ ♛ Good, exceeds basic requirements.

Situated in a neighborhood adjacent to the College of William and Mary, this 1976 Dutch Colonial is a short walk to Colonial Williamsburg and located fifty miles east of Richmond. Private baths are offered in all of the four guest rooms which have a country decor and overlook a deeply wooded ravine. Three are suites with king-size feather-beds and private sitting rooms. Take afternoon tea in the formal living room, relax on the large deck with its expansive view, or walk to nearby Colonial Williamsburg. Area attractions include Busch Gardens, Jamestown/ Yorktown, Williamsburg Pottery, and varied outlet shops. Full breakfast is accented with home-made muffins and fresh ground coffee. Families welcome. No smoking. 1 or 2/$74-105. Travel agent.

Guests write: *"Kelly and Paul are great hosts. We enjoyed every minute of our stay. The rooms are furnished thoughtfully for our comfort. Breakfasts were great, providing a good base for our day."* (D. Brown)

Williamsburg

Newport House
710 South Henry Street
Williamsburg, VA 23185-4113
(804) 229-1775

Type of B&B: B&B home.
Rooms: 2 with private bath.
Rates: 1 or 2/$90-120.

Rating: A- or ♕♕♕ Excellent, far exceeds basic requirements.

Newport House is a careful reproduction of an original 1756 house and it is located within a five minute walk of Colonial Williamsburg. There are two spacious guest rooms with private bath, four-poster bed, period American antiques and reproduction furnishings. There is a large parlor on the main floor with fireplace and a collection of books. Guests are invited to stroll through the flower, herb, and vegetable gardens or join in a Colonial dance in the upstairs ballroom on Tuesday evenings. Hostess is a registered nurse who enjoys making eighteenth-century clothing. Host is former captain of an historic full-rigged ship and is now an author and publisher of history books. Area attractions include historic sites in Jamestown and Yorktown, the James River Plantations, and Busch Gardens. Full breakfast specialties often include apple-cinnamon waffles, specialty breads, baked apples, and authentic Colonial recipes. Families welcome. 1 or 2/$90-120. Travel agent.

Guests write: *"John and Cathy Millar have created an establishment which truly enhances a visit to Williamsburg. The house and the beautiful furnishings perfectly combine 20th-Century comfort with 18th-Century elegance and taste. The facilities are superb, the breakfasts delightful, and the conversation uncommonly pleasant."* (B. Smith)

"The two rooms that are set aside for guests, the Philadelphia Room, and the Newport Room, make other accommodations in Williamsburg look shabby. Each morning, breakfast is enlivened by delightful conversation and the antics of Sassafras, the rabbit, and Ian, the Millar's little boy. For those visitors who wish to be close to the center of the restored area, but far from the maddening crowd, Newport House is perfectly located. It is but a short walk from Duke of Gloucester Street, but the quiet that surrounds it is always welcomed." (C. Potter)

Woolwine

Mountain Rose Bed & Breakfast
Rt. 1, Box 280
Woolwine, VA 24185
(703) 930-1057

Type of B&B: Inn.
Rooms: 5 with private bath.
Rates: 1/$60-70; 2/$60-85.

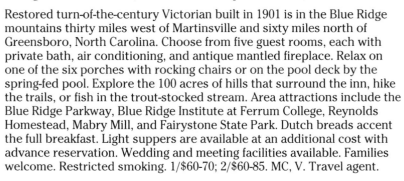

Rating: B+ or ♛♛ Good, exceeds basic requirements.

Restored turn-of-the-century Victorian built in 1901 is in the Blue Ridge mountains thirty miles west of Martinsville and sixty miles north of Greensboro, North Carolina. Choose from five guest rooms, each with private bath, air conditioning, and antique mantled fireplace. Relax on one of the six porches with rocking chairs or on the pool deck by the spring-fed pool. Explore the 100 acres of hills that surround the inn, hike the trails, or fish in the trout-stocked stream. Area attractions include the Blue Ridge Parkway, Blue Ridge Institute at Ferrum College, Reynolds Homestead, Mabry Mill, and Fairystone State Park. Dutch breads accent the full breakfast. Light suppers are available at an additional cost with advance reservation. Wedding and meeting facilities available. Families welcome. Restricted smoking. 1/$60-70; 2/$60-85. MC, V. Travel agent.

WASHINGTON

Eastsound — See Orcas Island.

Leavenworth

Haus Rohrbach Pension
12882 Ranger Road
Leavenworth, WA 98826
(509) 548-7024 or 548-5038

Type of B&B: Inn.
Rooms: 12, 8 with private bath.
Rates: 1/$55-135; 2/$65-160.

Rating: A- or ♛♛♛ Excellent, far exceeds basic requirements.

European-style Alpine inn is at the foothills of the Washington Cascades, 25 miles from Wenatchee and 100 miles east of Seattle. Choose from

twelve guest rooms, eight with private bath. Three modern suites offer
spacious accommodations, fireplace, and whirlpool tub overlooking the
valley below. The main inn has a large gathering room with wood-stove
and deck with comfortable chairs to enjoy the mountain and valley views.
The property maintains an in-ground swimming pool. Go hiking, rafting,
fishing, windsurfing, biking, or skiing. Visit the Bavarian village of
Leavenworth, just two minutes away, with its many shops and
restaurants. The full breakfast is served out on the deck in warmer
weather and may include sourdough pancakes, "Dutch Babies", and
home-made cinnamon rolls. Meeting facilities available. Families
welcome. Wheelchair access. No smoking. 1/$55-135; 2/$65-160. AE, MC,
V. 10% senior discount. Travel agent.

Orcas Island/Eastsound

Outlook Inn on Orcas Island
Box 210, Main Street
Eastsound, WA 98245
(206) 376-2200

Type of B&B: Country inn with restaurant
Rooms: 33, 15 with private bath.
Rates: 1/$44.50-89; 2/$47-94.

Rating: B- or ♥♥ Good, exceeds basic requirements.

Victorian inn built in 1888 is located on Orcas Island at Eastsound Village
80 miles northwest of Seattle. The inn is situated on the bay with its own
private beach, pond, and flower gardens. The main structure has
nineteen rooms, one with private bath, and features hand-carved beds,
marble topped dressers, and period pieces. A newly constructed building
houses ten guest rooms which have a more typical motel layout with
private bath, some selected antique furnishings, TV, and phone. Sit at the
turn-of-the-century brass bar, relax on the beach, or go hiking, sailing, or
fishing. Home-made cinnamon rolls accent a continental breakfast.
Additional meals are available in the restaurant. Spacious wedding and
meeting facilities available. Families welcome. Wheelchair access.
1/$44.50-89; 2/$47-94. AE, MC, V. Off season corporate, and auto club
discounts. Travel agent.

Guests write: *"The morning of the wedding, parents, wedding guests, bride
and groom enjoyed a lovely champagne brunch in a quaint, European
atmosphere, complete with chamber music. The food was attractively
presented and very good. Everyone at the Outlook Inn went just one step
further to make our stay very special and memorable."* (Mrs. Kallos)

"It wasn't until I moved into my beautiful room at the Outlook, with its perfect view of the church and the water that I really felt like a pampered bride!" (S. Kallos)

"We particularly enjoyed our two meals. They were as promised. The staff was pleasant and efficient. This is a special place." (S. Pochop)

Port Angeles

Domaine Madeleine
146 Wildflower Lane
Port Angeles, WA 98326
(206) 457-4174

Type of B&B: B&B home.
Rooms: 2 with private bath.
Rates: 1/$69-99; 2/$89-135.

Rating: A+ or ♕♕♕ Excellent, far exceeds basic requirements.

This waterfront contemporary home overlooking the Strait of Juan de Fuca is located just outside Port Angeles on Washington's Olympic Peninsula. There are two guest rooms with private bath, king-size bed, water view, TV/VCRs, complimentary movies, designer robes, French perfumes, and fresh fruit basket. The deluxe second-floor room offers a private 30-foot balcony, fireplace, Jacuzzi tub, and stereo system. The first floor Impressionist room overlooks both the water and a replica of Monet's garden. An elegant living room on the main floor features a 14-foot high basalt fireplace, antique furnishings, and a hand-built harpsichord. Guests are welcome to take a nature tour of the surrounding five acres, or walk on the beach at nearby Dungeness Spit. Lawn games are available. Area attractions include Olympic National Park, Hoh Rain Forest, Lake Crescent, Wild Game farm, Sol Duc Hot Springs, and recreation such as skiing, fishing, horseback riding, and hiking. A full breakfast includes fresh fruit, daily baked bread served with local cheeses, gourmet entrees, dessert, and hazelnut-flavored French roast coffee. Facilities are available for small weddings and meetings. 1/$69-99; 2/$89-135. MC, V. 10% senior discount. Travel agent.

Guests write: *"Words of praise seem inadequate to describe Madeleine and John - they are perfect hosts. It is obvious that they take great pride in every aspect of their home. Breakfasts are absolutely the best we've ever had at a B&B. The first morning's fresh fruit, fresh muffins, salmon and scallop Newberg, and chocolate mousse rivaled many dinners we have eaten in terms of quality, quantity, and presentation."* (J. Rachap)

"The center piece of the Domaine is the view. It fills every room, especially the master bedroom where the view is enjoyed from a king-size featherbed

or gracious private balcony. The waves send up their greeting from the shoreline a hundred feet below. The beds are without exception the finest experience possible in the art of goose down comfort. (L. Ferris)

"The wonderful house with its sweeping view is full of treasures and classic and contemporary reading materials. Every need in our sleeping and bathing quarters was anticipated: robes, toiletries, French perfume, books, VCR, stereo, TV, fruit basket and more! As with the rest of our experience, attention to detail while meeting every guest's need were the hallmark of John and Madeleine's service." (J. Dillon)

"Nowhere have I found lodgings that compared to Domaine Madeleine. I consider four criteria in determining where to stay when I travel: accommodations, food, uniqueness, and hospitality. Domaine Madeleine excels in all these categories. The care and attention to detail in the appointments of Domaine Madeleine stand without rival. The culinary expertise of both John and Madeleine translate into feasts of seven or more courses at the breakfast table. The distinctive nature of the art work and furnishings at Domaine Madeleine impress professional collectors and amateurs alike. Finally, the genuine warmth and friendliness impressed me most of all." (M. Mann)

"The waterfront location and setting are extraordinarily beautiful with views of Victoria on Vancouver Island, the San Juan Islands, and Mt. Baker. The home is beautifully appointed and warm. Every possible comfort has been seen to including down covers on the mattresses, fruit baskets, bathrobes, TVs and videos in each room, interesting books, cassette player with tapes. But best of all are the hosts!" (D. Brown)

Port Townsend

Bishop Victorian Guest Suites
714 Washington Street
Port Townsend, WA 98368
(206) 385-6122 or (800) 824-4738

Type of B&B: Inn.
Rooms: 13 with private bath.
Rates: 1/$54-79; 2/$68-98.

Rating: B- or ♛♛ Good, exceeds basic requirements.

Victorian hotel built in 1890 has been completely restored and is located right in the heart of downtown Port Townsend near the ferry terminal. The lower floor of the building is used as a storefront and a flight of steps leads to the inn's lobby. Thirteen guest suites are furnished with some period pieces and offer private bath, sitting area, full kitchen, and one or two bedrooms. Walk to area shops, restaurants, and the ferry terminal.

Area attractions include Olympic National Park (40 minutes by car), Mt. Baker, the Cascades, Admiralty Bay, and Fort Worden State Park, known for its use in the movie, "An Officer and A Gentleman". Continental breakfast. Families welcome. Restricted smoking. 1/$54-79; 2/$68-98. AE, MC, V. Senior discount.

Seattle

Capital Hill House
2215 East Prospect
Seattle, WA 98112
(206) 322-1752

Type of B&B: B&B home.
Rooms: 3, 1 with private bath.
Rates: 1/$45-55; 2/$45-65.

Rating: C+ or ♛ Acceptable, meets basic requirements.

Traditional brick home built in 1932 has been a B&B for nine years and is situated in a quiet urban residential neighborhood 2 miles from the University of Washington and 15 minutes from downtown Seattle. There are three second-floor guest rooms, one with private bath. The downstairs offers a spacious parlor where guests gather for relaxation and conversation. This is a convenient location for seeing all of Seattle's cultural and tourist sights. Full breakfast. Families welcome. Restricted smoking. Resident dog. 1/$45-55; 2/$45-65. Cash, personal checks or traveler's checks only.

Seattle

Continental Inn
955 10th Avenue East
Seattle, WA 98102
(206) 324-9511 or 323-4141

Type of B&B: Inn.
Rooms: 4 , 1 with private bath.
Rates: 1/$62-87; 2/$72-97.

Rating: B or ♛♛ Good, exceeds basic requirements.

Georgian Brick Colonial is in a designated historic area two blocks north of the Broadway District on Capitol Hill, 1.4 miles from the downtown city center. Each of the four guest rooms has been decorated to reflect the spirit of four different cities: Kobenhavn, Paris, Madrid, and Casablanca. All rooms have color TV and private telephone; two have refrigerators;

one private bath features a Jacuzzi. Sit by the fire in the thirty-two foot living room with its art collection (a hobby of the owners) or out in the private yard with tables and chaise lounges. Visit nearby University of Washington, Seattle University, Volunteer Park, Seattle Asian Art museum, or the downtown Pike Street Market. Omelets, waffles, or pancakes are offered at a full breakfast. Wedding and meeting facilities available. Restricted smoking. 1/$62-87; 2$72-97. MC. Senior discount. Travel agent.

Sequim

Greywolf Inn
177 Keeler Road
Sequim, WA 98382
(206) 683-5889 or 683-1487

Type of B&B: Inn.
Rooms: 6 with private bath.
Rates: 2/$62-110

Rating: B or ♛♛ Good, exceeds basic requirements.

Northwest contemporary inn is nestled atop a five wooded acre country estate on the Olympic Peninsula, a scenic two hour drive from Seattle via Highway 101. Choose from six guest rooms with private bath, each decorated in a special theme with king, queen, or twin beds. Guests are welcome to enjoy the broad decks, gardens, and meandering walk in the woods or relax by the fire with a good book from the inn's library. Area attractions include Olympic National Park, Hurricane Ridge, Hoh Rain Forest, Dungeness Spit, and the Juan de Fuca Straits. The Victoria ferry at Port Angeles is less than thirty minutes by car. Full breakfast is served in a cheerful French Country dining room overlooking Sequim and the Dungeness Valley and includes a hot entree accompanied by fresh fruits, breads, and pastries. Restricted smoking. 2/$62-110. AE, MC, V. Travel agent.

Guests write: *"Greywolf Inn was a delightful discovery. All linens, furniture, and appointments are top-of-the-line. Rooms have the warmth of home by displaying family mementos. This warmth and attention to detail was extended to breakfast that was served on the glass-walled porch overlooking fields and woods. The meal was so attractively presented my husband took a photo of our plates!"* (D. Clarke)

"Staying at the Greywolf was like a touch of home with their full library of books and a roaring fireplace. You really felt like more than a guest, almost like a member of the family. They personally took us and our daughter to an unusual outdoor zoo that was the highlight of our visit." (J. Miller)

"Our stay at Greywolf Inn has been a thoroughly delightful and refreshing experience. The comfortable bed in our room provided us with the best sleep we have had in years. We are very impressed with the quiet beauty of this place, its immaculate cleanliness, and the impeccable good taste and graciousness of our hosts." (E. Nordstrom)

"Since spending three nights at Greywolf Inn in August, we have sent three other parties there to enjoy the gourmet breakfasts and country atmosphere with wonderful hospitality. Each group found Greywolf far exceeded their expectations." (J. Dunham)

"Peggy's tasty orange muffins and fresh brewed coffee kept us longer than necessary at the table all the while gazing through the windows across meadows full of wildflowers that crept toward wooded vistas in the distance. Walking paths are everywhere. Travelers looking for comfort, beauty, restful ease far from the maddening crowd, will find Greywolf Inn the place to seek out and enjoy." (V. Caisse)

Yakima

37 House
4002 Englewood Avenue
Yakima, WA 98908
(509) 965-5537 or 965-4705

Type of B&B: Inn.
Rooms: 6 with private bath.
Rates: 1 or 2/$65-120.

Rating: A or ♛♛♛ Excellent, far exceeds basic requirements.

37 House is a lovely 7,500 square-foot mansion built in the 1930s that has been completely restored and is situated in a quiet residential area overlooking the city located 140 miles east of Seattle. There are six guest rooms with shuttered window panes, custom Waverly curtains and bedspreads, window seats under the eaves, and fully tiled private baths. One suite on the second floor offers two bedrooms, a sitting room, and full bath. The main floor offers a knotty-wood pine-paneled library with fireplace and TV, a fireplaced living room, and elegant dining room. A lower level recreation room is more informal and offers TV and fireplace with comfortable chairs and a sofa. The grounds of the estate include a tennis court and English garden. Area attractions include Yakima Valley wineries and the Sun dome. Full breakfast includes fresh-baked muffins, fresh fruits, and a special hot entree. Function rooms for meetings and weddings are available. Families welcome. No smoking. 1 or 2/$65-120. AE, MC, V. Business travel discount. Travel agent.

— Comments continued on next page

Washington

Guests write: *"The breakfast of eggs Benedict was cooked to order and we've never tasted better. I can't say enough about the 37 House. It is what I always thought B&Bs should be like but never experienced."* (D. Williamson)

"This was my husband's first experience at a B&B and he was surprised he liked it so well. I have stayed in B&Bs before but this one is first rate. We thoroughly enjoyed ourselves. I think perhaps we shall make it an annual Anniversary event and I'm so glad they saved this wonderful house from the wrecker's ball." (F. Webb)

"This was a home I had often admired during my growing-up years in Yakima and it was fun staying there as a guest. The manager graciously moved us to another room when we expressed a concern about noise from the traffic during the night. We were given the master suite at no added expense and appreciated this courtesy very much. Our breakfast was delicious and attractively presented." (S. Parkhill)

"The accommodations were wonderful. The hospitality was especially warm and the house was very beautiful. It was like being at home because we could use the kitchen and there was fresh fruit and homemade cookies for us to enjoy." (S. Albers)

Yakima

Tudor Guest House Bed & Breakfast
3111 Tieton Drive
Yakima, WA 98902
(509) 452-8112

Type of B&B: Inn.
Rooms: 6, 3 with private bath.
Rates: 1/$55-65; 2/$65-85; Bridal suite:$150.

Rating: B or ♛♛ Good, exceeds basic requirements.

English Tudor mansion surrounded by formal hedges, variety of trees, flowers, and garden pool, is 150 miles east of Seattle. The six guest rooms reflect the European flavor found throughout the house. Each room has been decorated with 19th-Century antiques and three have a private bath. The all-white Bridal suite has a bar, claw foot tub, and satin with lace decor. Sit by one of the leaded glass windows or explore this historic home with its archways, marble-faced entry, and ribbon mahogany wood-work. Relax in the living room with its tile fireplace and oak floor, or in the sun room with hand-made tile flooring laid in patterns. The Washington Wine Country is twenty minutes away and five golf courses, two public swimming pools and tennis courts are nearby. Enjoy horseback riding, hiking, camping, fishing, hunting, boating, and skiing in the Cascade

Mountains or a picnic on the grounds for a quiet retreat. Three walls of lead glass windows highlight the dining room where a full breakfast is offered with such specialties as filled crepes, croissants with smoked cheddar cheese, eggs, and a three-cheese breakfast quiche. No smoking. 1/$55-65; 2/$65-85; Bridal suite: $150. MC, V. Senior discount.

WEST VIRGINIA

Petersburg

Smoke Hole Lodge
P.O. Box 953
Petersburg, WV 26847
(304) 242-8377
(winter phone only,
no phone in summer)

Type of B&B: Mountain lodge.
Rooms: 7 with private bath.
Rates: 1/$90; 2/$165.

Rating: A or ♛ ♛ ♛ Excellent, far exceeds basic requirements.

Spacious newly-rebuilt mountain lodge and ranch on 1,600 remote wilderness acres is 12 miles south of Petersburg, close to Monongahela National Forest. Choose from five comfortable and pleasant guest rooms with pine furnishings on the second floor. There are also two dormitory rooms on this level that together can sleep nine. Each room offers a private, modern bath with shower. The ranch runs on kerosene, wood, and bottled gas as it has neither electricity nor phone. This makes for a fascinating turn-of-the-century experience. The ranch is an angus cattle operation, and many other animals live there as well. The property abounds with deer and on occasion a bear is sighted. This is a relaxing, get-away-from-it-all spot for the whole family. Enjoy bass fishing on the pond, swimming, inner-tubing, and hiking on the property. Hearty full breakfast, lunch, and dinner are included in the rates, as is round-trip transportation from Petersburg where hosts will meet you for the hour-and-a-half trip up the mountain by four-wheel drive. Families and pets welcome. 1/$90; 2/$165. Travel agent or write above address. Open May through October.

Romney

Hampshire House 1884
165 North Grafton Street
Romney, WV 26757
(304) 822-7171

Type of B&B: Inn.
Rooms: 5 with private bath.
Rates: 1/$50; 2/$80.

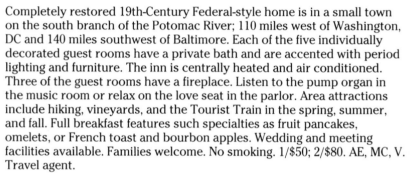

Rating: B+ or ♛♛ Good, exceeds basic requirements.

Completely restored 19th-Century Federal-style home is in a small town
on the south branch of the Potomac River; 110 miles west of Washington,
DC and 140 miles southwest of Baltimore. Each of the five individually
decorated guest rooms have a private bath and are accented with period
lighting and furniture. The inn is centrally heated and air conditioned.
Three of the guest rooms have a fireplace. Listen to the pump organ in
the music room or relax on the love seat in the parlor. Area attractions
include hiking, vineyards, and the Tourist Train in the spring, summer,
and fall. Full breakfast features such specialties as fruit pancakes,
omelets, or French toast and bourbon apples. Wedding and meeting
facilities available. Families welcome. No smoking. 1/$50; 2/$80. AE, MC, V.
Travel agent.

Valley Chapel/Weston

Ingeberg Acres
Millstone Run Road
P.O. Box 199
Valley Chapel, WV 26446
(304) 269-2834

Type of B&B: Farm B&B.
Rooms: 3 with shared bath.
Rates: 1/$39; 2/$59.

Rating: B or ♛♛ Good, exceeds basic requirements.

Ingeberg Acres is a 450-acre horse and cattle breeding farm located in the
heart of West Virginia. There are three second-floor guest rooms which
share a bath and offer air conditioning. Popular activities here are
watching and helping with the farm chores, hiking on marked trails,
birdwatching, swimming in the pool, and relaxing on the patio and deck.
Hunting is allowed on the property with special permission. Full breakfast
is served family style. Families welcome. No smoking. 1/$39; 2/$59. 10%
auto club, business travel, family, and senior discounts.

Baraboo

Pinehaven Bed & Breakfast
E13083 Highway 33
Baraboo, WI 53913
(608) 356-3489

Type of B&B: Inn.
Rooms: 4 with private bath.
Rates: 1/$50-60; 2/$55-65.

Rating: B+ or ♛♛ Good, exceeds basic requirements.

Chalet-style contemporary inn surrounded by pines and overlooking a small private lake is located three miles east of Baraboo on Highway 33. Each of the four guest rooms offer a private bath and distinctive decor with features such as homemade quilts, crocheted coverlets, or matching comforters and shams. The view of the lake and Baraboo Bluffs is outstanding from the inn's upper verandah and lower decks. Guest enjoy strolling the grounds, crossing the river on the 1890s bridge, and seeing the host's Belgian horses. Area attractions include Circus Museum, Devil's Lake State Park, Wisconsin Dells, and International Crane Foundation. A full breakfast includes specialties such as broccoli-rice quiche, morning glorious muffins, raspberry cream-cheese coffee cake, and peach French toast. No smoking. 1/$50-60; 2/$55-65. MC, V.

Burlington

Hillcrest Bed & Breakfast
540 Storle Avenue
Burlington, WI 53105
(414) 763-4706

Type of B&B: Small inn.
Rooms: 6, 4 with private bath.
Rates: 1 or 2/$60-140

Rating: A- or ♛♛♛ Excellent, far exceeds basic requirements.

Edwardian home built in 1908 is situated on the crest of a hill with panoramic view of the valley and waterways below and is located off Highway 11 West. There are three guest rooms with individual decor and one offers a private bath. Special features of the rooms include queen-size carved oak or walnut beds, river views, period antique furnishings, lace curtains, and Oriental rugs. A converted carriage house offers three new deluxe guest accommodations. Two offer a fireplace and Jacuzzi and one is a large suite that runs the length of the second-floor with two bedrooms and Jacuzzi tub. The lower porch on the main house offers antique wicker furniture and views of the surrounding lakes and rivers. Guest enjoy exploring the landscaped grounds and restored gardens. Area attractions include antique shopping, golfing, skiing, swimming, and boating. Full breakfast. No smoking. 1 or 2/$60-140.

Cedarburg

Washington House Inn
W62N573 Washington Avenue
Cedarburg, WI 53012
(414) 375-3550 or (800) 554-4717

Type of B&B: Inn.
Rooms: 29 with private bath.
Rates: 1 or 2/$59-139.

Rating: A or ♛♛♛ Excellent, far exceeds basic requirements.

Historic Victorian urban inn is centrally located in the town's Historic District, 3 miles west of I-43, exit 17. There are twenty-nine guest rooms throughout the complex and each features a private bath, antiques, cozy down quilts, fireplaces, and fresh flowers. Deluxe suites offer Jacuzzi tubs and unique architectural features. Area attractions include historic Cedar Creek Settlement, antique shops, and Pioneer Village. Continental breakfast includes fresh-baked muffins and fresh-squeezed juices. Function rooms are available for weddings and meetings. Families welcome. Wheelchair access. 1 or 2/$59-139. AE, Diners, Discover, En Route, MC, V. 10% senior and auto club discounts. Travel agent.

Guests write: *"It was the most wonderful romantic place we've ever been. The interior was beautiful, the atmosphere was perfect. It was truly everything I thought it would be and more."* (C. Urbanek)

Chetek

The Lodge at Canoe Bay
W16065 Hogback Road
Chetek, WI 54728
(800) 568-1995

Type of B&B: Inn.
Rooms: 7, 4 with private bath.
Rates: 1 or 2/$89-159.

Rating: B+ or ♛♛ Good, exceeds basic requirements.

A-Frame lodge is situated on 280-acres of wooded land surrounding a 50-acre lake in northern Wisconsin, 90 miles east of the Twin Cities. Four deluxe guest rooms feature a two-person whirlpool tub, separate shower, and sitting area. Three additional rooms are available that share a spacious and modern hall bath. Gather with other guests around the massive fieldstone fireplace in the great room with soaring cathedral ceiling. A TV room offers comfortable furnishings and cable stations. Relax in the private whirlpools, or go cross country skiing, ice-skating, boating, swimming, fishing, and bicycling on the grounds. This area offers a very private and quiet retreat with nature, a spring fed lake, and oak and aspen forest. Specialty teas and coffees are offered with a variety of pastries in a continental breakfast basket brought to your room or enjoyed on the deck overlooking the lake. Dinner is available by advance reservation and features northern Wisconsin cuisine with fresh ingredients, wild rice, fresh-baked breads, and fruit pies. Wheelchair access. No smoking. 1 or 2/$89-159. MC, V. Senior and auto club member discounts. Travel agent.

Kenosha

The Manor House
6536 3rd Avenue
Kenosha, WI 53143
(414) 658-0014

Type of B&B: Inn.
Rooms: 4 with private bath.
Rates: 1 or 2/$100-140.

Rating: A- or ♛ ♛ ♛ Excellent, far exceeds basic requirements.

Historic Georgian manor house built in the 1920's is in the heart of the Lakeshore Historical District of Kenosha and overlooks Lake Michigan, yet is only four miles from I-94. There are four second-floor guest rooms with private bath, cable TV, rich fabrics, Oriental carpets, and 18th-Century antiques. A small sitting area found between two bedroom wings offers a private corner for relishing breakfast or viewing the lake. The first floor common rooms are spacious and opulent with unusually fine antiques and appointments. A lower level offers special conference facilities. The grounds include a fountain, rose garden, gazebo, and many varieties of trees. Area attractions include the nearby Historic District, museums, beaches, golf courses, and county parks. Continental breakfast includes seasonal fruits. Restricted smoking. 1 or 2/$100-140. AE, MC, V. Business discount available.

Guests write: *"This was the best place to enjoy our 11th Anniversary. It was truly relaxing with super, gracious hosts."* (B. Mooney)

— *Comments continued on next page*

"The Manor House is very pretty and comfortable, elegant, and cozy - a relaxing weekend get-away and wonderful one-year wedding anniversary." (A. Kelman)

Lake Delton

The Swallow's Nest B&B
141 Sarrington, P.O. Box 418
Lake Delton, WI 53940
(608) 254-6900

Type of B&B: B&B home.
Rooms: 4 with private bath.
Rates: 1/$50-60; 2/$55-65.

Rating: B+ or ♛♛ Good, exceeds basic requirements.

Contemporary home in a wooded setting is located just off I-90 and I-94. There are four second-floor guest rooms with private bath and air conditioning. Several common areas on the first floor feature monastery windows, a two-story atrium with skylights, library with fireplace, decks overlooking the lake, wildflowers, and a gazebo by a waterfall. The host's photography studio and gallery are on the premises. Area attractions include Wisconsin Dells, Lake Delton, Devil's Lake State Park, downhill skiing, Circus World Museum, antique shops, and restaurants. Full breakfast. No smoking. 1/$50-60; 2/$55-65. MC, V.

WYOMING

Additional information on B&Bs in this state is available from B&B Western Adventure (406) 259-7993.

BRITISH COLUMBIA, CANADA

Additional information on B&Bs in this province is available from
City & Sea B&B Registry (604) 853-1962 or Town & Country B&B in British
Columbia (604) 731-5942

Victoria

Prior House B&B Inn
620 St. Charles Street
Victoria, BC, Canada V8S 3N7
(604) 592-8847

Type of B&B: Inn.
Rooms: 5 with private bath.
Rates: 1 or 2/$65-160.

Rating: A+ or ♛♛♛ Excellent, far exceeds basic requirements..

Historic Edwardian mansion built in 1912 is located in a quiet
neighborhood near downtown Victoria. There are five guest rooms
located throughout the inn. The ballroom on the lower level and the 3rd
floor suite have been converted into accommodations especially suited
for families. A large master bedroom on the second floor boasts a
bathroom almost as large as the bedroom and features wrap-around
mirror walls and ceiling, three marble sinks and vanities, Jacuzzi tub, and
separate shower. Originally built for the King's representative in British
Columbia, no expense was spared in the quality of materials used in
building the inn whose special features include rich oak paneling, stained-
glass windows, antique furnishings, and carved stone terraces
overlooking a large garden. Area attractions include Government House,
Empress Hotel, Parliament Buildings, and Royal British Columbus
Museum. Full gourmet breakfast and evening refreshments are served
daily. Families welcome. Function rooms are available for meetings and
social functions. No smoking. 1 or 2/$65-160. MC, V. 10% auto club,
business travel, and senior discounts. Travel agent.

NEW BRUNSWICK, CANADA

Fredericton

Happy Apple Acres
R.R. 4
Fredericton, NB, Canada E3B 4X5
(506) 458-1819

Type of B&B: Inn.
Rooms: 3 with private bath plus
separate guesthouse.
Rates: 1/$45; 2/$60.

Rating: B+ or ♛♛ Good, exceeds basic requirements.

Happy Apple Acres is situated in a rural area atop a hill with water views
and it's located about ten minutes from downtown Fredericton which is
the capital of New Brunswick province. The main inn offers a two-room
suite with private bath and sauna. A separate guesthouse offers two guest
rooms. The special Honeymoon Room is popular for its heart-shaped
whirlpool bath and when the Honeymoon package is requested, this
room is outfitted with fresh flowers, chocolates, fruit basket, and terry
robes. Area attractions include parks, beaches, skating ponds, skiing,
camping, and hiking. The property includes an orchard of apples from
which guests are welcome to pick in season. The breakfast menu features
fresh fruit, apple pancakes with apple syrup, chunky apple muffins, or
fruited French toast with maple syrup. Resident dog. 1/$45; 2/$60
(Canadian). Honeymoon packages and business travel discounts
available.

Guests write: *"The sweetheart tub is a unique experience and the
accommodations and hospitality excellent. We still have very pleasant
memories of our stay with the Hamilton's."* (S. Eiseman)

*"We loved the dogs, the fireplace, the sauna, blueberry pancakes, and the
warm hospitality."* (S. Munger)

ONTARIO, CANADA

Additional information on B&B in this province is available from
Metropolitan B&B Registry of Toronto (416) 964-2566 or Toronto Bed &
Breakfast (416) 588-8800

Toronto/Mississauga

By the Creek Bed & Breakfast
1716 Lincolnshire Blvd.
Mississauga, Ontario, Canada L5E2S7
(416) 891-0337 or (416) 278-5937

Type of B&B: Private home.
Rooms: 3, 2 with private bath.
Rates: 1/$35-40; 2/$55-60.

Rating: B or ♛♛ Good, exceeds basic requirements.

Built in 1958, this split-level home overlooks the Etobicoke Creek on the
border of Metropolitan Toronto. Each of the three guest rooms have been
individually decorated and are air conditioned; two offer a private bath.
One of the rooms is a large suite which encompasses the entire lower
level of the home and is perfect for families. A large living room is a
favorite gathering place for guests and it showcases the host's paintings
and art collection. A large sunroom with comfortable furnishings
overlooks the spacious backyard. Relax in front of one of the two
fireplaces or the two patio decks overlooking the creek. Walk to public
golf course and the shopping mall. Visit the nearby Canadian National
Exhibit, International Centre, and Stage West or take the QEW to Niagara
Falls. A full breakfast consists of fresh fruit, cereal, and a hot dish.
Families welcome. Wheelchair access. No smoking. 1/$35-40; 2/$55-60.
MC. Senior and corporate discounts. Travel agent.

Guests write: *"As a regular guest for the past few months due to a new
teaching contract, I can highly recommend this B&B. Surroundings are
warm, comfortable, very clean, and tastefully decorated with many artifacts
and antiques. I particularly enjoyed the relaxing evenings and great fruit
salads for breakfast. The hosts have extensive knowledge of the area's
history and are most helpful in suggesting the best travel routes and methods
to get there."* (D. Gidley)

*"Such a fine alternative to staying at motels! Here is a quiet setting with a
nice garden overlook at breakfast time. I spent a cozy comfortable night in
spacious decorative surroundings. Helpful advice and a car lift to the station
made for a good day as a tourist in Toronto."* (K. Busch)

— *Comments continued on next page*

"The home is tastefully decorated with a warm ambiance. Gardens are extremely well maintained to an English look and standard. One would never realize that you are minutes away from a bustling metropolitan city." (C. Nunn)

"The hosts are very hospitable and will go out of their way to accommodate their guests with varying schedules." (J. Patrie)

QUEBEC, CANADA

Montreal

Manoir Ambrose
3422 Stanley
Montreal, QC, Canada H3A 1R8
(514) 288-6922
Fax: (514) 288-5757

Type of B&B: Urban inn.
Rooms: 22, 15 with private bath.
Rates: 1/$30-60; 2/$55-75.

Rating: C or ♛ Acceptable, meets basic requirements.

Turn-of-the-century Victorian brownstone is located in the heart of the city. There are twenty-two guest rooms between the two buildings that are joined in the center. While there is a wide variety in the size, decor, and quality of the guest rooms, each offers a TV, radio, and phone and fifteen have a private bath. A breakfast room on the lower level is a pleasant area where guests help themselves to a continental breakfast and beverages. From the inn, it's a short walk to restaurants, theaters, shopping, and convenient public transportation. There's limited off-street parking behind the inn. Continental breakfast. 1/$30-60; 2/$55-75. MC, V. Travel agent.

Midwestern United States

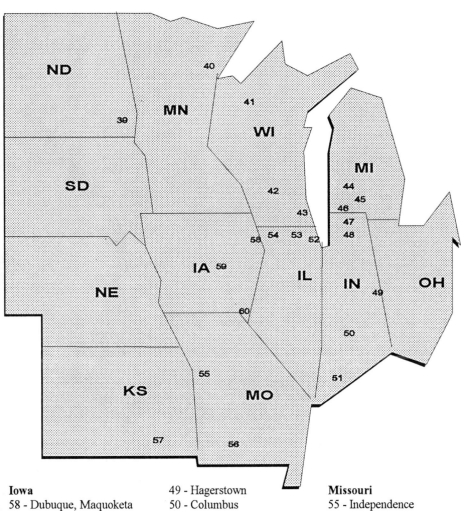

Iowa
58 - Dubuque, Maquoketa
59 - Homestead
60 - Fort Madison

Illinois
52 - Evanston, Wheaton
53 - Rockford
54 - Galena

Indiana
47 - Middleburg
48 - Warsaw

49 - Hagerstown
50 - Columbus
51 - Newburgh

Kansas
57 - Wichita

Michigan
44 - Fennville, Saugatuck
45 - Augusta, Battle Creek
46 - Union Pier

Minnesota
40 - Duluth

Missouri
55 - Independence
56 - Springfield

North Dakota
39 - Luverne

Wisconsin
41 - Chetek
42 - Baraboo, Lake Delton
43 - Cedarburg, Burlington,
     Kenosha

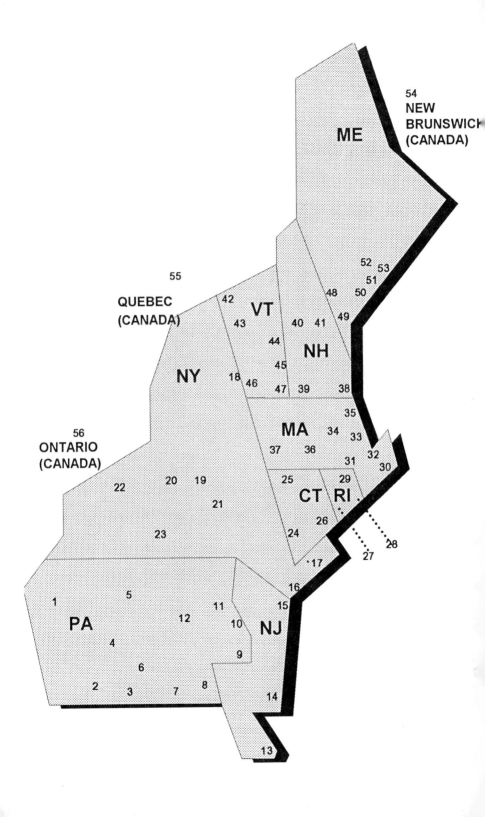

Northeastern U.S. & Canada

Pennsylvania
1 - Franklin, Slippery Rock
2 - Somerset
3 - Mercersburg, Gettysburg
4 - Pine Grove Mills
5 - Wellsboro
6 - Harrisburg area: Elizabethtown,
Elizabethville, Hershey, New Cumberland
7 - Lancaster Area: Ephrate, Quarryville,
Paradise, Strasburg, Bird-In-Hand
8 - Philadelphia Area: Kennett Square, Lima
9 - New Hope, North Wales
10 -Allentown, Bethlehem, Emmaus, Easton,
Fogelsville
11 -Stroudsburg, Milford
12 -Dallas

New Jersey
13 - Cape May
14 - Bay Head, Spring Lake
15 - Chatham

New York
16 - New York City area: Croton-on-Hudson,
Staten Island
17 - Bellport, West Hampton
18 - Elizabethville, North Creek, Warrensburg
19 - Barneveld, Dolgeville, Utica
20 - Baldwinsville, Casenovia
21 - Cooperstown, Lisle
22 - Canandaigua, Fairport, Rochester
23 - Corning, Dundee, Elmira, Hammondsport

Conneticut
24 - New Milford, Ridgefield
25 - Norfolk
26 - Mystic, New London

Rhode Island
27 - Westerly, Block Island
28 - Newport
29 - Providence

Massachusetts
30 - Cape Cod area: Chatham, Dennis, Dennis
port, East Orleans, East Sandwich, Eatham,
Edgartown, Falmouth, Harwichport, Hyannis,
Martha's Vineyard, Nantucket, Oak Bluffs,
Sandwich, VIneyard Haven, West Yarmouth,
Yarmouth, Yarmouthport
31 - Attleboro
32 - Boston's South Shore:Cohassett
33 - Boston, Cambridge
34 - Concord
35 - Essex, Rockport
36 - Amerst, Barre, Princetown, Sturbridge
37- South Lee, Great Barrington
38 - Hampton, Hampstead
39 - Jaffrey, Wilton

New Hampshire
40 - Franconia, North Woodstock, Wentworth
41 - Bartlett, Gorham, Jackson, North Conway

Vermont
42 - Alburg
43 - Barre, Jeffersonville, Jericho, Stowe,
Vergennes, Waitsfield, Warren, Waterbury
44 - Fairlee, Killington, Woodstock
45 - Chester, Ludlow, Londonderry,
Proctorsville, Weathersfield, Woodstock
46 - Arlington, Manchester
47 - West Dover, Wilmington

Maine
48 - Fryeburg
49 - Kennebunk, Portland
50 - Bath, Boothbay Hbr, Freeport, Wiscasset
51 - Camden, Spruce Head, Tenants Harbor
52 - Belfast, Searsport
53 - Sullivan Harbor, Bar Harbor

Canada
54 - Fredrickton, New Brunswick
55 - Montreal, Quebec
56 - Mississauga/Toronto, Ontario

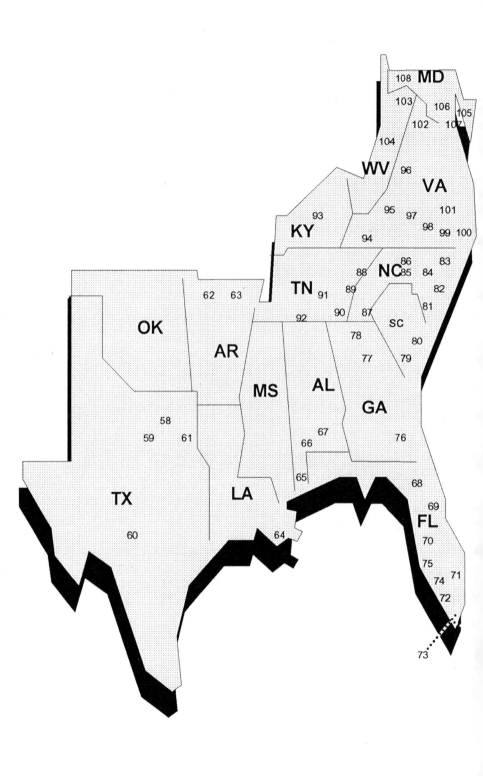

Southeastern United States

Alabama
65 - Orange Beach
66 - Forest Home
67 - Montgomery

Arkansas
62 - Eureka Springs
63 - Hardy

Florida
68 - Amelia Island, Orange Park
69 - Daytona Beach
70 - Orlando, Maitland, Lake Wales
71 - Palm Beach
72 - Miami
73 - Key West
74 - Sanibel
75 - Holmes Beach, St. Petersburg

Georgia
76 - Savannah
77 - Atlanta
78 - Blairsville, Dahlonega

Kentucky
93 - Lexington

Louisiana
84 - New Orleans

Maryland
105 - Berlin, Oxford, Salisbury, Snow Hill, St.
    Michaels
106 - Annapolis, Burtonsville, Olney, Silver
    Spring
107 - Solomons
108 - Hagerstown

North Carolina
1 - Wilmington
2 - Beaufort, New Bern, Belhaven

83 - Kill Devil Hills, Nags Head
84 - Wilson
85 - Carthage
86 - Greensboro
87 - Asheville, Clyde, Highlands, Flat Rock,
    Waynesboro

South Carolina
79 - Charleston
80 - Georgetown

Tennessee
88 - Greeneville, Kodak
89 - Gatlinburg
90 - Ducktown
91 - Pikeville
92 - Monteagle

Texas
58 - Waxahachie
59 - Glen Rose
60 - San Antonio
61 - Jefferson

Virginia
94 - Blacksburg, Christiansburg
95 - Staunton
96 - Luray, Strasburg
97 - Charlottesville, Gordonsville, North
    Garden, Scottsville
98 - Bumpass
99 - Charles City, Williamsburg
100 - Virginia Beach
101 - Champlain, Reedville
102 - Leesburg, Middleburg

West Virginia
103 - Romney, Petersburg
104 - Valley Chapel

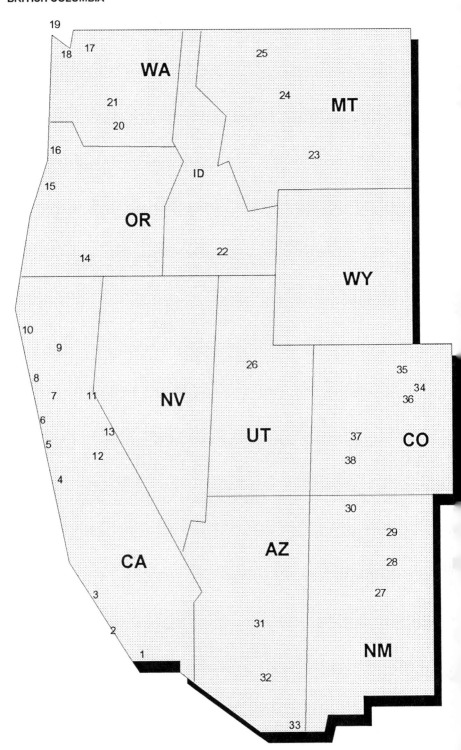

BRITISH COLUMBIA

Western United States & Canada

Arizona
1 - Sedona
2 - Phoenix
3 - Bisbee

California
- San Diego
- Laguna Beach, Seal Beach, Newport Beach, Santa Monica
- Santa Barbara, San Luis Obispo, Baywood Park
- Cambria, Pacific Grove
- Aptos, Davenport, Palo Alto, San Gregorio, San Jose, Santa Cruz
- Alameda, Berkeley, San Francisco
- Geyersville, Napa, Sonoma
- Fort Bragg
- Red Bluff, Redding
0 - Eureka, Ferndale
1 - Lotus, Tahoe City
2 - Arnold, Groveland, Murphys
3 - Bridgeport

Colorado
4 - Arvada, Denver
5 - Steamboat Springs
6 - Breckenridge, Leadville
7 - Crested Butte, Redstone
8 - Telluride

Idaho
- Sun Valley

Montana
23 - Three Forks
24 - Helena
25 - Columbia Falls

New Mexico
27 - Albuquerque
28 - Santa Fe
29 - Taos
30 - Los Ojos

Oregon
14 - Ashland
15 - Depoe Bay, Cloverdale
16 - Seaside

Washington
17 - Seattle, Eastsound
18 - Sequim, Port Angeles, Port Townsend
20 - Yakima
21 - Leavenworth

Utah
26 - Park City

British Columbia, Canada
19 - Victoria

Alaska

1

2

3

1-Fairbanks
2-Anchorage, Chugiak, Matanuska
3-Juneau

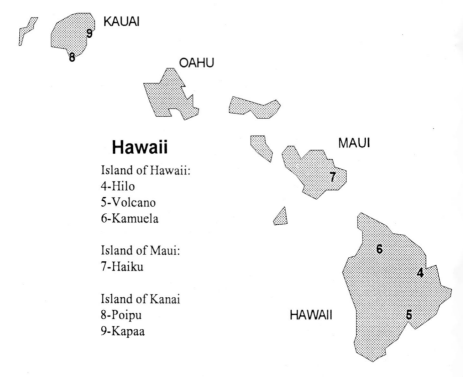

KAUAI

9

8

OAHU

Hawaii

Island of Hawaii:
4-Hilo
5-Volcano
6-Kamuela

Island of Maui:
7-Haiku

Island of Kanai
8-Poipu
9-Kapaa

MAUI

7

6

4

HAWAII

5